Kosovo

Kosovo
Perceptions of War and
its Aftermath

Edited by

Mary Buckley and Sally N. Cummings

continuum
LONDON • NEW YORK

Continuum
The Tower Building, 11 York Road, London SE1 7NX
370 Lexington Avenue, New York, NY 10017 6503

First published 2001

British Library Cataloguing-in-Publication Data
A catalogue record for this book is available from the British Library.
ISBN 0-8264-5669-3 (hardback)
    0-8264-5670-7 (paperback)

Library of Congress Cataloging-in-Publication Data
Kosovo: perceptions of war and its aftermath / edited by Mary Buckley
and Sally N. Cummings.
      p. cm.
    Includes index.
    ISBN 0-8264-5669-3 (cloth)–ISBN 0-8264-5670-7 (pbk.)
    1. Kosovo (Serbia–History–Civil War, 1998–Foreign public opinion. 2.
    Geopolitics–Balkan Peninsula. 3. National security–Europe. I. Buckley,
    Mary (Mary E.A.) II. Cummings, Sally N.

DR2087.6.F67 K67 2001
949.7103–dc21   2001037096

Typeset by BookEns Ltd, Royston, Herts.
Printed and bound in Great Britain by
The Cromwell Press, Trowbridge, Wiltshire

Contents

CONTENTS

List of Contributors

Mary Buckley is Professor of Politics at Royal Holloway, University of London. Her books include *Women and Ideology in the Soviet Union* (1989) and *Redefining Russian Society and Polity* (1993). In 1999/2000 she was recipient of a Leverhulme Research Fellowship to look at political debates in post-Soviet Russia.

Martin Clark is Reader in Politics at the University of Edinburgh. He is the author of *Modern Italy 1871–1995* (1996, 2nd edn) and of *The Italian Risorgimento* (1998).

Michael Clarke was Professor of Defence Studies at King's College, University of London, and Director of the Centre for Defence Studies. He has been a specialist adviser to the House of Commons Foreign Affairs Committee, having been involved in the Defence Committee's investigation into the Kosovo campaign. He has previously held posts at the Universities of Wales at Aberystwyth, Manchester and Newcastle upon Tyne, and been a researcher at The Brookings Institution, Washington DC and at the Royal Institute of International Affairs in London.

Sally N. Cummings is Lecturer in Politics at the University of Edinburgh. Recent publications include *Kazakhstan: Centre–Periphery Relations* (2000) and (ed.) *Power and Change in Central Asia* (2001).

Roland Dannreuther is Director of New Issues in Security at the Geneva Centre for Security Policy and a senior Lecturer in Politics at the University of Edinburgh. Recent publications include *Cosmopolitan Citizenship*, co-edited with Kimberly Hutchings (1999), *The Soviet Union and the PLO* (1998) and *Creating States in Central Asia* (1994).

John Erickson FBA, FRSE is Professor Emeritus, Honorary Fellow in Defence Studies at the University of Edinburgh. He specializes in Soviet and Russian military policy, military organization and geopolitics. His publications include *The Soviet High Command* (1962, 1984, reprinting); *Stalin's War with Germany: The Road to Stalingrad* , vols 1 and 2 (1975, 1984); *The Road to Berlin* (1983) and with David Dilks (ed.), *Barbarossa: the Axis and the Allies* (1994).

Rick Fawn is Lecturer in International Relations and Director of the Centre for Russian, Soviet and Central and East European Studies at the University of St Andrews, Scotland. His recent publications include *The Czech Republic: A Nation of Velvet* (2000) and (co-ed.) *The Changing Geopolitics of Eastern Europe* (2001).

Adrian Hyde-Price is Professor of Politics and International Relations at the University of Leicester. He has lectured at the Universities of Birmingham, Manchester and Southampton and was Research Fellow at the Royal Institute of International Affairs. His publications include *Germany and European Order: Enlarging NATO and the EU* (2000); *The International Politics of East Central Europe* (1996); and *European Security Beyond the Cold War* (1991).

Richard McAllister is Senior Lecturer in Politics at the University of Edinburgh. He is author of *From the EC to EU* (1997) and has contributed to many other books including J. E. Fowler (ed.) *France Today* (1997) and to such journals as *Journal of Common Market Studies* and *Common Market Law Review.*

James Mayall is Sir Patrick Sheehy Professor of International Relations and Director of the Centre of International Studies at the University of Cambridge. He has written widely on nationalism and international relations, international society and problems of ethnic and religious conflict since the end of the Cold War. His most recent publications include his edited volume *The New Interventionism: UN Experience in Cambodia, former Yugoslavia and Somalia* (1996) and *World Politics, the Limits of Progress* (2000).

Gabriel Partos is a writer and broadcaster on central European and Balkan affairs, working as the South-East Europe Analyst of the BBC World Service. Some of his reports and articles are available on the news.bbc.uk Web site. He is the author of an interview-based history of the Cold War entitled *The World that Came in from the Cold* (1993).

Sabrina P. Ramet is a Professor of International Studies at the Norwegian University of Science and Technology. She is the author of seven books, among them *Balkan Babel: The Disintegration of Yugoslavia from the Death of Tito to the War for Kosovo* (3rd edn) (1999).

Robert Singh is Lecturer in Politics at Birkbeck College, University of London. His books include *The Farrakhan Phenomenon: Race, Reaction and the Paranoid Style in American Politics* (1997) and *The Congressional Black Caucus* (1998).

Joanne van Selm is Lecturer and Researcher in International Relations at the University of Amsterdam in the Institute for Migration and Ethnic Studies and Visiting Scholar at the Institute for the Study of Social Migration (ISIM), Georgetown University. She is co-editor of the *Journal of Refugee Studies* and edited *Kosovo's Refugees in the European Union* (2000).

Joanne Wright is Director of European Studies at Royal Holloway, University of London, where she holds a Jean Monnet Chair in European Security Integration. As well as numerous articles on aspects of European security, she published *Northern Ireland: Policing Divided Societies* (2000). She is currently working on a Jean Monnet funded project on the 'internationalization' of policing agencies.

Michael Yahuda is Professor of International Relations at the London School of Economics and Political Science and head of department. He has a special interest in the foreign relations of China and in the international relations of East Asia. He has written more than 100 articles in scholarly journals and has written five books, including *The International Politics of the Asia Pacific, 1945–1995* (1996) and *Hong Kong: China's Challenge* (1996).

Acknowledgements

We are most grateful to the British Academy for funding a conference around the chapters of this book at Royal Holloway, University of London on 15–16 September 2000. Without this generosity the conference would not have been organized. Gratitude is also due to the Foreign and Commonwealth Office for its contribution. At Royal Holloway, Stuart Kerr and Richard Jordison were most helpful in matters of bookings and organization.

It has been a pleasure to work with Caroline Wintersgill, our editor at Continuum, who has been supportive throughout the process. For help with the selection of maps we should like to thank Sue Crisp in the geographic support main building of the Ministry of Defence and Rona Morrison in the map room of the main library of the University of Edinburgh.

Mary Buckley
Sally N. Cummings

Note

This book uses the Library of Congress transliteration system of Russian with the exception of names and words whose more customary English forms are now widely adopted. Thus El'tsin and Astaf'ev become Yeltsin and Astafev. Soft signs have also been taken out.

The Balkans before the Congress of Berlin in 1878

Ottoman Lands in 1830

1830 Date of Independence

1817 Date of Autonomy

AUSTRO-HUNGARIAN EMPIRE

RUSSIAN EMPIRE

Moldavia 1829

Transylvania

Banat

Slavonia

Sava

BOSNIA

Dalmatia

Herzegovina

SERBIA 1817

Wallachia 1829

Danube

Morava

BULGARIA

BLACK SEA

ADRIATIC SEA

OTTOMAN EMPIRE

Maritsa

Montenegro
1852 Principality

Vardar

RUMELIA

ITALY

Albania

MACEDONIA

IONIAN SEA

Epirus

Thessaly

AEGEAN SEA

Kingdom of GREECE 1830

MEDITERRANEAN SEA

Dnestr

General Staff Map Section, GSGS 11858(CAD), Edition 2-GSGS, March 1993 354/93

Produced under the direction of Director General of Military Survey, Ministry of Defence, United Kingdom 1993

Users should note that this map has been designed for briefing purposes only and it should not be used for determining the precise location of places or features. This map should not be considered an authority on the delimitation of international boundaries nor on the spelling of place and feature names. Maps produced by the Defence Geographic and Imagery Intelligence Agency (DGIA) are not to be taken as necessarily representing the views of the UK government on boundaries or political status.
© Crown copyright 2000

EUROPE IN 1912

General Staff Map Section, GSGS 11971(CAD), Edition 1-GSGS (CAD), May 1993 602/93

Produced under the direction of Director General of Military Survey, Ministry of Defence, United Kingdom 1993

Users should note that this map has been designed for briefing purposes only and it should not be used for determining the precise location of places or features. This map should not be considered an authority on the delimitation of international boundaries nor on the spelling of place and feature names. Maps produced by the Defence Geographic and Imagery Intelligence Agency (DGIA) are not to be taken as necessarily representing the views of the UK government on boundaries or political status.
© Crown copyright 2000

EUROPE IN 1946

Western limit of Soviet influence

Area of Allied Control

Kilometres
0   200   400   600   800   1000

ATLANTIC OCEAN

SWEDEN

FINLAND

NORWAY

DENMARK

IRISH FREE STATE

UNITED KINGDOM

NETHER-LANDS

BELGIUM

LUX.

GERMANY

POLAND

USSR

CZECHOSLOVAKIA

FRANCE

SWITZ.

AUSTRIA

HUNGARY

ROMANIA

ITALY

YUGOSLAVIA

BLACK SEA

BULGARIA

CORSICA

ALBANIA

PORTUGAL

SPAIN

BALEARIC IS.

SARDINIA

GREECE

TURKEY

SICILY

Malta

SP. MOROCCO

ALGERIA (France)

TUNISIA

CRETE

CYPRUS

SYRIA

MOROCCO

LEBANON

General Staff Map Section, GSGS 11971(CAD), Edition 3-GSGS (CAD), May 1993 602/93

Produced under the direction of Director General of Military Survey, Ministry of Defence, United Kingdom 1993

General Staff Map Section GSGS 11863(CAD), Edition 5-GSGS, July 1993 1122/93   Produced under the direction of Director General of Military Survey, Ministry of Defence, United Kingdom 1993

Users should note that this map has been designed for briefing purposes only and it should not be used for determining the precise location of places or features. This map should not be considered an authority on the delimitation of international boundaries nor on the spelling of place and feature names. Maps produced by the Defence Geographic and Imagery Intelligence Agency (DGIA) are not to be taken as necessarily representing the views of the UK government on boundaries or political status. © Crown copyright 2000

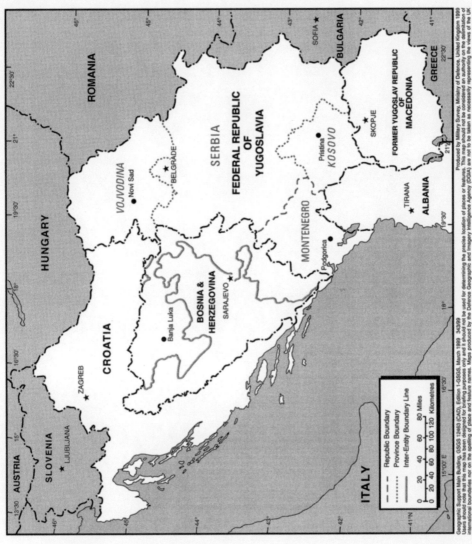

AUSTRIA
SLOVENIA
LJUBLJANA ★
ZAGREB ★
CROATIA
ITALY
HUNGARY
ROMANIA
VOJVODINA
Novi Sad ●
BELGRADE ★
SERBIA
FEDERAL REPUBLIC
OF
YUGOSLAVIA
Banja Luka ●
BOSNIA &
HERZEGOVINA
SARAJEVO ★
MONTENEGRO
Podgorica ●
KOSOVO
Pristina ●
SOFIA ★
BULGARIA
SKOPJE ★
FORMER YUGOSLAV REPUBLIC
OF
MACEDONIA
GREECE
TIRANA ★
ALBANIA

Republic Boundary
Province Boundary
Inter-Entity Boundary Line

0   20   40   60   80 Miles
0 20 40 60 80 100 120 Kilometres

Introduction

MARY BUCKLEY AND SALLY N. CUMMINGS

Assumptions and objectives

The intervention by NATO in Kosovo was arguably the most important development in international relations at the close of the twentieth century and had a huge impact on the states immediately affected. Ten years after the fall of communism in Eastern Europe, hostilities between NATO and Serbia immediately led to further questioning of the nature of the so-called 'new world order', which, for optimists, was meant to be one of greater co-operation rather than conflict. More sober realists were less surprised that the euphoria accompanying the fall of the Berlin Wall had evaporated, perhaps foreseeing that the historic end to the painful division of Europe would be followed by tensions, conflicts and war based on ethnicity and nationalism. For the first time, NATO deployed its armed forces in war and placed the controversial doctrine of humanitarian intervention firmly on the international agenda; the war thus conceived represents a turning point.

Appalled by ethnic cleansing in Bosnia and then Kosovo, Western politicians may have felt committed to a moral crusade and a so-called 'just war' against Slobodan Milošević as tyrant, but nonetheless their bombing campaigns contributed to a refugee crisis, already triggered by ethnic cleansing and deportations. Critics in the West dubbed the result a 'humanitarian disaster'.[1] Over 800,000 ethnic Albanians left Kosovo, hundreds of thousands were internally displaced and estimates suggested that 7,000 Kosovar Albanians were killed during the hostilities, which included blundered bombings of refugee convoys and also a direct hit on the Chinese embassy in Belgrade.[2] Criticisms of NATO's handling of the bombing gained further momentum in August 2000 upon the publication of a secret document that revealed the failures in precision bombing. When, two months later, an all-party Commons Select Committee on Defence reported on their eight-month investigation of the war, newspaper headlines blazoned charges of poor planning, weapons failures and of a worsening of the disaster of fleeing refugees.[3] Against the critics, defenders of NATO's actions argued that globalization made possible the enforcement of moral standards worldwide and that in certain conditions humanitarian interventionism was justified.

How the intervention was perceived in the run up to and during the campaign indeed varied greatly across and within states. Leaders in Britain and in the US portrayed their actions as 'just' and morally upright, whereas 98 per cent of the Russian population decried them as inappropriately aggressive. The US, in particular, was accused by Russian and Chinese leaders of wanting to become the world's police force, even gearing up for the Third World War. Various interpretations within the Western alliances also complicated the campaign. Clinton and Blair could not rely upon the unqualified support of leaders in Italy or Greece; nor did they always agree with each other about the scale, nature or timing of the campaign. New members of NATO in Eastern and Central Europe had to confront uneasy issues of identity and security. Poland, Hungary and the Czech Republic, now keen to prove their loyalty as new members of NATO, found themselves at war with a state once an ideological ally, much to the chagrin of Russian leaders. Differing views about the significance of NATO's bombing campaign carried serious implications for domestic politics within states, contributing to tensions between the executive and legislature in the US and in Russia, and having an impact on broader social movements such as the German Greens.

The purpose of this book is to bring together area specialists who have detailed knowledge of their respective systems with those who work on more general questions of international relations, thus combining the strengths of the fields of comparative politics and international relations. The volume includes states that were directly involved in the formulation of an international response as well as those on the periphery of the conflict. The inclusion of both highlights the considerable variation of key states' perceptions of national interest and what constitutes legality and legitimacy, and how individual actors' domestic constraints and forces, as well as differing perspectives of political and military leadership, fed into the crisis.

There are four main objectives: firstly, to discuss how perceptions of NATO intervention in Kosovo and reactions to it varied across states and within states; secondly, to examine how different understandings among leaders, opposition parties, political commentators and public opinion in turn fed back into domestic politics in different states (into government, political parties and movements); thirdly, to explore the broader implications of the war and its aftermath for European security, alliances and geopolitics; and fourthly, to consider the perceptions of those most affected – the refugees – and to assess the relevance of humanitarian interventionism in the post-Cold War world.

This book sets out to highlight the role of perception in international politics. The conceptual lens, paradigms or frameworks through which political actors view reality in turn affects their understanding of the behaviour of others and their reactions to it. Actions do not always appear logical or rationally tailored to what leaders say and the gap between word and deed in politics can be huge. Nonetheless, leaders' statements and reactions are what others, in turn, respond to, react against, ignore or champion as well. Whether or not leaders always believe what they or others say varies according to circumstance and this can be elusive for the student of politics. Data gathering on stated views of war, of both leaders and citizens, however, can result in useful portraits of changing claims, perceptions, threats and outcomes. Opinion polls also illustrate similarities and differences across states.

The book is predicated upon two central assumptions. The first is that grasping the perceptions of political actors is a crucial subjective dimension to the understanding of politics and political behaviour, whatever the nature of the domestic political system. Political statements, actions, threats and non-decisions are partly shaped by assessments of situations and also constrained by context, circumstance and possibility. The second is that domestic and foreign policies dynamically interlink, in particular the latter having its roots in the former and also feeding back into it.

Our aims are relatively modest. We do not set out to test any particular cognitive or theoretical claim by matching it with observations from the Kosovo crisis, at least not in any scientific sense. Rather, contributors were asked to classify the range of reactions to NATO bombing within states, looking at executive, legislature, opposition parties, public opinion and media. In so doing, authors identify the major individuals and groups who expressed views, indicate the degree of their unity or disunity and discuss the significance of the span of assessments in given states for domestic, foreign and defence policy. The book assumes that both elite and non-elite perceptions matter because leaders and parliaments, albeit to varying degrees, take public opinion into account and react to it, even if more in their rhetoric than in final decisions about how to act.

The chapters consider the relevance of history, tradition, beliefs, myths, images, perceptions, misperceptions and attitudes. Within the field of international relations, since the 1950s, scholars who focus on decision-making have paid special attention to the distinction between psychological and operational environments, stressing the importance of taking into account image, perception, misperception, and groupthink. Facts do not speak for themselves but have to be selected, ordered and given meaning. What decision-makers consider to be the case must be assessed along with prevailing conditions and how events unfold. Key names in the literature include Harold Sprout and Margaret Sprout, Robert Jervis,

Kenneth Boulding, Ole R. Holsti, K. J. Holsti, Irving Janis, Leon Mann, Alexander George, Robert Axelrod and Stephen van Evern.[4] Policy makers as individuals and in organizations have cognitive, affective and evaluative structures that feed into their decisions about how to act and respond. Political actors develop an image of others and of their intentions and misperception results when the image is inaccurate or distorted through the prism of crisis and war. Actors, however, may tend to perceive what they expect, fitting data into existing expectations and images. They thus act according to how the world appears to them, which may not be how it 'is'. Foreign policy can be especially prone to divergence between image and reality because leaders operate in an environment that can be unstable and complex and in which linguistic and cultural barriers need to be overcome.

Isolating the influence of cognitive factors from those of history, mythology, the nature of the international system, balance of power, geopolitics, ideology, bureaucracy, political infighting, ambition, defence priorities or budgetary constraints is hazardous. These and other factors interact in complex ways. Hence this book is not about decision making *per se,* as process, but about the outcomes of a particular policy pursued by NATO and about how NATO bombing was received, interpreted and discussed, and why. We focus in particular on perceptions as expressed in member states and in states that are important actors in world politics and whose views the Western alliance cannot afford to overlook. Evidence suggests serious diversity and divergence across states as well as shared assessments, characteristic of a heterogenous world, notwithstanding alleged processes of globalization.

Chapter breakdown

Four wars have shaken the Balkans since 1991: over Slovenia, Croatia, Bosnia and Herzogovina, and now Kosovo. Roland Dannreuther sets the scene in Chapter 1, explaining the origins of the clash of 'incommensurable nationalisms' between the Serbian and Albanian nations, both of whom claim Kosovo as part of their homeland and draw on competing interpretations of history to justify their claims. Dannreuther argues that the situation is highly complex and that there are serious legal, moral and practical difficulties for external powers in adjudicating the conflict. Sabrina Ramet elaborates further upon Serbian perceptions, highlighting the tenacious role played by mythology, dating back to the Battle of Kosovo in 1389. In Serbian memory, Serbs were in Kosovo before Albanians, and that matters hugely. Moreover, Serbs remember communist rule as a time when Kosovo benefited disproportionately from Yugoslav federal funds, yet Albanians nonetheless rioted, raped Serbian women and terrorized Serbian men. Ramet underscores the fact that Serbian memory can indeed be selective, yet indicates that beliefs about local Albanians harassing Serbs ran deep, even if fuelled by rumour. Although a repetitive spiral of harm, resentment and reprisals has characterized the last century, this is more complex than the acting out of 'ancient hatreds'. The context of state collapse, failure to build legitimate state institutions with a rule of law and local factors need to be taken into account.

Gabriel Partos assesses the consequences of NATO intervention with respect to the former Yugoslav republics of Bosnia and Herzegovina, Croatia, Macedonia and Slovenia. He highlights how these countries were faced with immediate threats and long-term opportunities. The threats arose from the possibility of spill over of popular opposition leading to renewed domestic tensions and of negative economic repercussions. It was hoped that NATO's intervention would put an end to a decade of inter-ethnic violence in the former Yugoslavia that regional leaders had largely attributed to President Slobodan Milošević's regime in Belgrade. The subsequent settlement could then provide the stability that was essential for economic reconstruction across the Balkans, possibly even accelerating the integration of these republics into Euro-Atlantic security, political and economic structures.

The intervention by NATO could not have taken place without the leadership of the US and its superior military infrastructure. Robert Singh notes that two-thirds of the strike missions were flown by US aircraft and Michael Clarke draws attention to the fact that Europeans found it difficult to interface with US forces due to a huge technological gap. Singh discusses how the decision to bomb was taken at a time of 'visceral distrust and enmity' between White House and Congress in the aftermath of disclosures of the relationship between President Clinton and Monica Lewinsky. Bitter partisanship was one of its consequences. While public opinion supported intervention on humanitarian grounds, albeit without American bloodshed, leaders again felt themselves pressured to sort out a distant conflict and in a way that implied acting with questionable legality because the UN Security Council had not sanctioned action. Finally, after hesitation, Clinton invoked the dangers of appeasement and pledged to ensure through intervention that the conflict did not spread. The lesson of the Vietnam War was that to deploy ground troops meant that large-scale losses might occur, which argued for the use of bombardment instead. Bosnia and Iraq had also taught that bombs can get results.

British Prime Minister Tony Blair was highly committed to military action for a humanitarian end, even acquiescing in the closing down of diplomatic options, and was more willing than Clinton to send in ground troops in order to see victory. Michael Clarke shows that the British stated aim was not to change Milošević's mind, as the Americans declared to be their goal, but instrumentally to reduce his military capability. Throughout the bombing, Britain was a loyal ally of the US and staunch upholder of NATO, contributing to every level of the operation. But as Michael Clarke argues, a gap became evident between British ambitions for a new European political and military order and the ability to realize it without the further development of military capabilities to lessen dependence on the US. He holds that Britain's role as bridge between the US and Europe in security matters may be much harder to play in future.

Despite unanimity in the Labour leadership about military action, Clarke illustrates concerns within the Ministry of Defence and Foreign Office about mixed political signals, stretched resources, a likely long haul and the range of targets. Alex Salmond of the Scottish National Party was the only party leader against the operation, although others criticized mistakes in bombing, human suffering and the use of cluster bombs. Clarke sums up British public opinion as exhibiting 'weary realism'.

With Britain, France had been co-chair in the Rambouillet negotiations. Richard McAllister points out that, due to cohabitation between a Gaullist President and a Socialist Prime Minister, just as the 'majority' would support the government headed by Prime Minister Lionel Jospin, so too the potential 'opposition' were loyal to their man, President Jacques Chirac. Critics on the margins were the communists and far-left groups and on the right the 'eurosceptics' and 'sovereignists'. A distinct issue for France, however, was its precise military role because it was not a full member of NATO's Integrated Military Command. The question was how to participate and maintain national control. Morover, traditional hostility to the US made it awkward to accept American leadership; but to do otherwise would have required a European defence system, higher defence spending and surrendering more sovereignty.

Like France, Germany had to grapple with its identity, but for very differerent reasons: with a dubious basis in international law, the 'Red–Green' coalition swiftly approved combat against a sovereign state for the first time since 1945. Adrian Hyde-Price notes that the 'defining moment' was 'remarkable for its lack of controversy' in parliament. He shows how German leaders were motivated by a perception of their responsibility towards NATO, a sense of moral and political responsibility for suffering in Kosovo and also anxiety about another potential wave of asylum seekers. All opposition parties, except the Party of Democratic Socialism (PDS) gave their backing. German leaders, however, were reluctant to label the action as 'war.' Their foreign policy, a 'peace policy', had awkwardly come to include bombing in German leaders' attempts to become a 'normal' great power.

Italy has had very close links to the Balkans. After being an Italian protectorate, in 1939 Albania was formally annexed and briefly became part of the Italian Empire. Since 1991, Albanian migrants have been welcomed in Italy as cheap labour, but 'blamed' for robberies, drugs and prostitution. Martin Clark argues that many in the south were reluctant to go to war to help Albanians; and many in the north remembered with gratitude Serbian assistance to Italian partisan units. Despite hostile public opinion, economic and security benefits deriving from NATO membership meant that the makers of foreign policy had, in Clark's view, 'no choice' but to be loyal to the Alliance. In addition, the war enabled Italy to show its European credentials, which it felt were questioned by the Germans. Instigation of a 'Rainbow' humanitarian mission was designed to conciliate Catholics and other critics, making the war more palatable. Participation in the bombing was lukewarm.

Like the German and Italian governments, but for different reasons, leaders in the states of central and south-eastern Europe wanted to demonstrate their loyalty to NATO, as either new or aspiring members. Rick Fawn traces how governments in Poland and Hungary were keen to show how NATO could rely on them, whereas leaders in the third new member, the Czech Republic, with the exception of President Vaclav Havel, were ambivalent or opposed to the action, indifferent to their military obligations, thus representing the weakest central European link for NATO. The official response in the Czech Republic contrasted with reactions in Slovakia, Bulgaria and Romania, where leaders supported NATO, in part because they hoped to be included in the process of European integration. Opposition to the bombing was generally stronger among publics than among the elites, but even in the case of Bulgaria, despite its cultural ties to Serbia and the economic costs of the crisis for trade, and notwithstanding its suffering of accidental bombing, the centre-right government remained loyal to NATO. Leaders expected an offer of accession to the EU in return. So far, as Fawn illustrates, they have been given thanks and rhetoric, but not the desired offer. Also highly significant is the fact that Hungary, Bulgaria and Romania denied their airspace to Russian forces, happily standing up to the state whose 'threat' made them turn westwards for support.

Reactions in Russia, among elites and in the public, were quite distinct from those in all the above states. None the less, despite the 98 per cent of the population who were opposed, there were different emphases in the arguments made. From a content analysis across the ideological spectrum of the Russian press, Mary Buckley illustrates the different nuances across responses of political leaders and commentators and the various recommendations made. Controversies resulted over diplomacy, military preparedness, mercenaries, the Union of Belarus, Russia and Yugoslavia, the impeachment of Yeltsin and Chernomyrdin's role as peace envoy. There was unanimity, however, about the US 'double standard' and its hypocrisy in lecturing Russia on its campaign in Chechnia within the Russian Federation, after having itself caused loss of life in Kosovo miles away from the US. Predictably, the terms 'humanitarian interventionism' and 'limited sovereignty' were opposed in the new Russian foreign policy concept, adopted in 2000.

Leaders in the other eleven members of the Commonwealth of Independent States (CIS), argues Sally N. Cummings, were engaged in a 'delicate balancing act' beween the US and Russia, showing varying responses that defy simple categorization. Most hostile to NATO were Belarus and Tajikistan, but for different reasons. Leaders in Moldova and Turkmenistan declared neutrality. In Ukraine, President Kuchma condemned the bombing, but divorced Kosovo from his general foreign policy priorities, maintaining friendship with the US. Keener to show support for NATO, President Heydar Aliev of Azerbaijan offered troops to be part of the Turkish contingent and President Eduard Shevardnadze of Georgia announced that NATO had no choice. Reactions in Kyrgyzstan included backing for Russia from the Defence Ministry and support for NATO by President Askar Akaev. Uzbekistan also sought close relations with the US. More complicated responses in Armenia compared Kosovo to Nagorno-Karabakh. Cummings explains the diversity of reactions in terms of geopolitics, flux in alignments, local conflicts and different views of humanitarian issues and self-determination.

Like Russians and Belorussians, Chinese leaders and the public reacted intensely against NATO's campaign and students, in particular, were incensed by NATO's bombing of the Chinese embassy in Belgrade. Michael Yahuda argues that deeply xenophobic nationalist sentiments were released at a time when Chinese leaders felt slighted anyway by US leaders and viewed NATO's actions as a US 'strategy for global intervention'. The Kosovo crisis, however, ultimately had minimal impact on domestic and foreign policy. Leftist hardliners were unable to use it to alter the path of domestic reform and the general priorities of Chinese foreign policy remained. Chinese leaders, like the Russians, did clarify their opposition to humanitarian interventionism. Their dilemma, suggests Yahuda, is that economic reform entails necessary relations with an outside world whose norms could undermine the basis for Communist Party rule.

Although Middle Eastern states were divided in their reactions, Dannreuther argues that the picture of Muslims fleeing Christian invaders evoked resilient perceptions of Christian hostility to the Muslim world and a nostagia for the inter-enthnic toleration of the Ottoman Empire. Turkish leaders actively supported NATO, providing planes, bases and a peacekeeping force. Saudi Arabia, the United Arab Emirates, Egypt and Jordan gave verbal support and humanitarian aid, with the latter two withdrawing ambassadors from Belgrade. The Palestine Authority also backed the US. By contrast, Syria, Iraq, Libya and Algeria, like Russia and China, condemned NATO, while Iran and Israel remained ambivalent.

Dannreuther explores the complexities of these reactions and explains why there was greater Arab consensus over Bosnia than Kosovo.

Conflicts in the world and military interventions can have serious implications not just for relations within regions but also for security arrangements and trust in alliances. Joanne Wright argues that the case of Kosovo confirmed existing trends in European security, namely European expansion and a broadening of activity rather than initiating new activity. It highlighted, however, some of the problematic aspects of these trends, in particular changing norms and the readiness to defend human rights as well as to promote them, which caused leaders to re-examine practices and values with some urgency. Wright explores relations with Russia, the sequencing of new memberships, security guarantees, flexibility, norms, relations between the European Union, West European Union and NATO and burden sharing. She concludes that neither institutional design nor security capabilities match the current rhetoric of commitment to a security agenda that includes human rights. This seriously affects credibility.

Looking globally, John Erickson contends that geopolitics is now resurgent, even rampant. NATO's eastwards enlargement was a 'geopolitical detonator,' followed by the 'explosion' of NATO's Operation Allied Force, prompting genuine concern in Russia that NATO was now a 'self-mandating organization' and in China that NATO could globalize with more 'out-of-area' activities. This occurred in a wider context of a shifting geostrategic centre of gravity towards the Caspian, the Caucasus, the eastern Mediterranean and the Balkans. Geopolitical and geostrategic imperatives are also complicated by the geoeconomics of oil exploitation. Russia has gone from 'geopolitical extrovert' to 'geopolitical introvert,' anxious for 'control of space'. Erickson notes the difficulties for Russia of either cooperating with the US or confronting it, traces Russian-Chinese relations, and discusses the significance of the new Russian military doctrine, which reinstated nuclear 'first use'. He concludes pessimistically that Kosovo generated the dangerous and bizarre oxymoron of 'humanitarian warfare'.

It was the plight of the people of Kosovo fleeing ethnic cleansing and enduring deportation and bombing raids that deeply moved citizens across states, albeit more in some countries than in others. Joanne van Selm clarifies the legal distinctions between an 'internally displaced person', 'refugee' and 'asylum seeker'. She then discusses the mixed reactions of the refugees to NATO, which included distrust, gratitude, horror, anger, a feeling of loss of control over their lives and a desire to return home. She poses the important question of whether NATO intervened to protect those who might become refugees or rather to shield their own populations from potential asylum seekers and illegal immigrants.

James Mayall stresses that NATO consistently emphasized the human-itarian justification for its action. He discusses the political and intellectual background to the debate on 'humanitarian interventionism', arguing that this concept has an ambiguous place in the theory and practice of international society. This is because the principle of sovereignty remains the foundation of both international law and the diplomatic system, despite globalizing trends. He draws comparisons across the cases of UN intervention in Somalia, Rwanda, Iraq, Bosnia and Herzegovina, Albania, Cambodia, Namibia, East Timor, Sierra Leone and the Democratic Republic of the Congo. Mayall also highlights the extent of peace enforcement, from immediate to ultimate responsibility, and its difficul-ties. Questions of how best to reconstruct society afterwards and thereby to prevent a recurrence of the intitial crisis can be hard to answer in situations where the state itself has failed or where a dismantling of previous authority is required.

The collection aims to bring greater scholarly depth to our under-standing of the Kosovo crisis and some appreciation of the reasons underpinning varying reactions to it in different states and among the people most affected. Governments and policymakers at national and international levels need to confront more squarely the long- and short-term implications of humanitarian interventionism, its various dimensions under different conditions of geopolitics, state collapse and ethnic mix and what it means for state sovereignty. Further debate is needed on for what and how much the UN and NATO are responsible, with what legality, and on whether 'humanitarian warfare' is a genuine threat.

The first major international attempt to address the aftermath of Kosovo was concluded with the publication in October 2000 of a report by the Independent Commission on Kosovo, which had been set up in August 1999 upon the initiative of Swedish Prime Minister Goeran Persson. Chaired by Justice Richard Goldstone of South Africa, its eleven members gave a 'central recommendation' that the best option for Kosovo's future is 'conditional independence' within the famework of a Balkan Stability Pact.[5] This means expanding the autonomy and self-government promised by Resolution 1244 (a 'unique hybrid' designed to prepare the province for autonomy and self-government) through negotiation between Kosovo, its neighbours and the international community.

The commission further recommends the presentation of a principled framework for humanitarian intervention, which could be used to guide future responses to imminent humanitarian catastrophes. This framework includes three threshold principles that must be met before intervention is legitimate. These are: the suffering of civilians due to severe patterns of human rights violations or the breakdown of government; the commit-ment to protect the civilian population; and a reasonable chance of ending the humanitarian catastrophe. How individual states perceive these recommendations forms another chapter in the complex and enduring story of the international community's response to humanitarian catastrophes.

Notes

1. Christopher Layne, 'Collateral damage in Yugoslavia', in Ted Galen Carpenter (ed.), *NATO's Empty Victory* (Washington, DC: Cato Institute, 2000), p. 52.
2. *Ibid.*
3. *Independent,* 25 October 2000, p. 1.
4. Harold and Margaret Sprout, *Man–Milieu Relationship Hypotheses in the Context of International Politics* (Princeton, New Jersey: Centre of International Studies, 1956); Robert Jervis, *The Logic of Images in International Relations* (Princeton, New Jersey: Princeton University Press, 1970) and *Perception and Misperception in International Politics* (Princeton, New Jersey: Princeton University Press, 1976); Kenneth E. Boulding, *The Image* (Ann Arbor: Michigan University Press, 1956); Ole R. Holsti, 'The Belief System and National Images', *Journal of Conflict Resolution,* vol. 6 (September 1962), pp. 608–17; K. J. Holsti, *International Politics: A Framework for Analysis* (New York: Prentice Hall, 1995), pp. 270–8; Irving L. Janis and Leon Mann, *Decisionmaking* (New York: Free Press, 1977); Alexander L. George, 'The "Operational Code": A Neglected Approach to the Study of Political Leaders and Decision-Making', *International Studies Quarterly,* vol. 13 (1969), pp. 190–222; Robert Axelrod (ed.) *Structure of Decision: The Cognitive Maps of Elites* (Princeton, New Jersey: Princeton University Press, 1976); Robert Axelrod, *Framework for a General Theory of Cognition and Choice* (Berkeley, California: Institute for International Studies, 1972); Stephen van Evera, *Causes of War: Power and the Roots of Conflict* (Ithaca, New York: Cornell University Press, 1999).
5. http://www.kosovocommission.org

CHAPTER ONE

War in Kosovo: History, Development and Aftermath

ROLAND DANNREUTHER

It is one of the paradoxes of modern international politics that an economically impoverished territory in a little-known part of Europe with a population of only two million should become the focus of the most serious international conflict of the last years of the twentieth century. The 'problem' of Kosovo, which has its origins in the late nineteenth century, assumed an international significance with the dissolution of communist Yugoslavia. The initial suppression of Kosovo's autonomy by Slobodan Milošević in 1989–90 significantly contributed to the subsequent wars of violent secession in Slovenia, Croatia and Bosnia and Herzegovina. Similar acts of Serbian suppression in Kosovo in late 1997 and during 1998 provided the context for direct intervention by external powers, which resulted in the NATO-led war and occupation of Kosovo in 1999. This intervention also contributed to the most serious international conflict of the post-Cold War period, threatening to undermine the grounds for consensus and cooperation between the great powers, most notably between the West and China and Russia.

One major reason why Kosovo has exerted such a disproportionate influence on international politics is that the 'problem' of Kosovo exemplifies some of the most divisive dilemmas and contradictions in contemporary international relations. At its core, the conflict in Kosovo involves a clash of incommensurable nationalisms – between the nationalist self-expressions of the Serbian and Albanian nations which both claim Kosovo as an integral part of their national homelands. For external powers, the issue of how to adjudicate between these competing claims, particularly in the context of disintegrating multinational states or empires, represents a highly complex and essentially unresolved dilemma. There remains no real consensus on the legal, moral and practical criteria for granting the right of secession or, perhaps more accurately, even if there is a fragile consensus, it is essentially arbitrary in its nature. Thus, Slovenia is granted the right to independence whereas Kosovo is formally denied such a right even though there is little difference in the popular will and support for such independence between the two peoples.

The conflict between the Serbian/Yugoslav authorities and the Kosovar Albanians also brought out into the open another highly divisive issue concerning the right of sovereignty. The issue here is the degree to which the right of sovereignty should be treated as sacrosanct, effectively excluding the right of outside powers to intervene in the internal affairs of other states, or whether external intervention can be deemed legitimate when a state engages in the mass abuse of the human rights of its own population. The NATO coalition that waged the war against Yugoslavia essentially decided that the Yugoslav authorities had forfeited, at least temporarily if not permanently, the right to political and territorial control over Kosovo due to the systematic abuse of the human rights of the Kosovar Albanian population. This decision in favour of humanitarian intervention has perhaps been the most controversial of the post-Cold War period and has raised fundamental and divisive questions about the nature and form of the emerging international order.[1]

Kosovo's significance lies primarily, therefore, in how the continuing conflict has become a prism through which some of the most contentious and unresolved questions of contemporary international politics have been debated. It is for this reason that the perceptions of external powers and countries of the developments within Kosovo are of such critical importance. The purpose of this chapter, though, is to provide the essential background and context to the conflict in Kosovo and the subsequent events and developments that culminated in the war of 1999 and the assumption of Kosovo as a *de facto* international protectorate under joint NATO and UN control.

The historical legacy

As with all competing national movements, Serbs and Albanians present their own contrasting versions of past historical events and developments to justify and legitimate their respective national claims. For the Kosovar Albanians, the historiographical assumption is that they are the true descendants of the Illyrians, the original ancient indigenous people of the territory. For the Serbs, Kosovo has a particularly emotional resonance as the site of the battle in 1389 of *Kosovo Polje* which is depicted, with only partial historical veracity, as where the Serbian army, under Tsar Lazar, was heroically defeated by the Ottoman forces.

Although much ink has been spilt debating the differing interpretations

13

of these ancient events, this has not helped to explain the principal causes or origins of the national conflict between the Serbs and the Kosovar Albanians.[2] In essence, the conflict is not driven by tribalism and ancient history, which actually offers many examples of Serb-Albanian co-operation. Rather, the roots of the conflict lie in the modern development of nationalist self-definition, which was imported into the region from Western Europe in the nineteenth century and was used as an ideological tool for securing greater autonomy within, or independence from, the Ottoman Empire. Unfortunately, for both Serbs and Albanians, Kosovo assumed a central and critical expression of their respective claims for national self-identity. For the Albanians, it was in the Kosovar town of Prizren that a great 'league' of notables, religious leaders and clan chiefs was established in 1878 and which has subsequently been assumed as the historical turning-point of the Albanian national movement. The Serbs, for their part, projected Kosovo as the 'cradle' of the Serbian people and as the national and religious heart of their nation.[3]

From the latter part of the nineteenth century, therefore, there has been an inevitable clash between the competing Serb and Albanian claims for the territorial and national status of Kosovo. The 'facts' of history cannot help to resolve this conflict since the competing claims are, in reality, based on a fabrication or, in Benedict Anderson's terms, an 'imagining' of history to promote very modern forms of communal and national self-identity.[4] In practice, the decision to determine which of these two claimants should have territorial sovereignty over Kosovo has consistently been at the power and discretion of the major external powers. In this regard, the Great Power settlement of 1912, in the ✳ aftermath of the Balkan War which saw the Ottoman Empire lose large tracts of its European possessions, was to be the key critical development. In this dispensation, the state of Albania was created, which undermined Serbia's ambition of gaining access to the Adriatic Sea. In compensation, however, Kosovo was incorporated into Serbia.

This decision of 1912 to include Kosovo within Serbia, however arbitrary the basis of that decision might have been, has been consistently confirmed by the international community subsequently. After the First World War, Kosovo was incorporated into the Kingdom of the Serbs, Croats and Slovenes; likewise after the Second World War, Kosovo remained within the Socialist Federal Republic of Yugoslavia; and in 1996, the Federal Republic of Yugoslavia was belatedly recognized with Kosovo as an integral part of the Serbian Republic. Despite the consistency with which the integrity of Yugoslavia has been recognized, the Albanian population within Kosovo has just as consistently welcomed external actors who might secure their independence from Serbia and Yugoslavia. Thus, there was generally support for the brief Austro-Hungarian occupation during the First World War and for the Italian annexation during the Second World War. There was also considerable Kosovar Albanian disappointment in relation to Tito's decision not to permit the incorporation of Kosovo into Albania after the war, which it was believed had been implicitly agreed in 1943 by the respective communist parties.[5] Following these earlier examples, the Kosovar Albanians supported the NATO intervention on their behalf in 1999, even though the NATO allies have continued to assert the territorial integrity of Yugoslavia.

The failure of the Serbs and the Albanians in Kosovo to accommodate their respective national claims has contributed to a history of mutual intolerance and periods of extreme repression. The initial conquest of Kosovo by the Serbian forces in 1912 was accompanied by a level of brutality that shocked liberal opinion of that time. In 1914, an international commission of enquiry set up by the Carnegie Endowment concluded that the Serbian campaign had a systematic and planned nature: 'Houses and whole villages reduced to ashes ... such were the means which were employed and are still being employed by the Serb-Montenegrin soldiery, with a view to the entire transformation of the ethnic character of regions inhabited exclusively by Albanians.'[6] In the interwar period, there was likewise a policy of Serb colonization of Kosovo, not unlike the French colonization of Algeria, and an agreement was actually reached with Ankara for transferring hundreds of thousands of Albanians to Turkey, which was only not implemented due to the onset of the Second World War.[7] There are, therefore, clear historical parallels with the Serb plans in 1999, as defined in Operation Horseshoe, which promoted the mass expulsion of Kosovo Albanians to provide the conditions for Serb ethnic domination of the territory.[8]

In response to this consistent pattern of Serb repression, the indigenous Albanian population of Kosovo has demonstrated a similar lack of toleration for the ethnically Serb population. At times when the Albanians have been in a position to assume political ascendance, such as during the Italian occupation from 1941-3, there have been similar acts of revenge and ethnic expulsion as those perpetrated by the Serbs. In general, the historical record provides little evidence of significant pluralist inter-ethnic accommodation within Kosovo. Where there has been a regime of toleration, it has been essentially enforced under conditions of authoritarian and repressive rule. Throughout the Yugoslav period, the two ethnic groups lived separate communal existences and there was almost no intermarriage or other significant intercommunal integration. It is, therefore, not surprising that the expressed ambition of the intervening Western powers in 1999 to preserve the inter-ethnic disposition of Kosovo has been so difficult to secure. On his arrival into Kosovo in July 1999, Bernard Kouchner, the leader of the UN Mission in Kosovo (UNMIK), declared his resolve to 'build an inter-ethnic Kosovo ... The Balkans should be synonymous with freedom, open society, and brotherhood.' It was only rather belatedly at the end of the year that he acknowledged that 'we found out and it's a lesson, that one oppression [can] conceal another.'[9]

In retrospect, it was the period from 1974 to 1989 that instituted the regime that most successfully managed inter-ethnic relations between the majority Albanian population and the Serb minority. In response to the increasing nationalist tensions within Yugoslavia in the late 1960s and early 1970s, Tito instituted a policy of ethno-national devolution that permitted a high level of Albanization of the province. In the 1974 constitution, the autonomous Kosovo province, along with Vojvodina, was elevated to a status equivalent to that of the six full republics, which included full representation on the main federal Yugoslav bodies. Kosovo effectively became a 'virtual republic', with its own parliament, constitution, police force, university and central bank. As Veton Surroi, the editor of the Kosovar daily *Koha Ditore*, has argued, this experience was perceived to be of 'the existence of Kosovo as a state ... and created the identity of Kosovars (mainly Albanians) as citizens of that state.'[10]

The problem was that this experience of statehood was still constrained by the constitutional absence of a right of secession, which was formally permitted within the constitutions of the six full republics but not in Kosovo. This led, particularly after Tito's death, to Albanian agitation for greater autonomy and independence. At the same time, Serb disaffection with the constitutional innovation of 1974 became more pronounced and led to the conviction that the arrangements were designed to emasculate Serbia's rightful influence and power as the largest constituent nation within the Federation. The fact that Kosovo and Vojvodina could join together to outvote Serbia on federal bodies was a particular source of contention. In addition, the significant demographic changes within Kosovo, which saw the Serb minority being reduced from 27 per cent of the population in 1953 to about 10 per cent in the mid-1980s, intensified Serb fears and concerns.[11]

The situation in Kosovo was, therefore, a critical element in the post-Tito evolution of a hardline Serbian nationalist movement. The Serbian Academy of Sciences set out an influential Memorandum (leaked to the press in 1989) that denounced the 1974 constitution, described the Serbs in Kosovo as undergoing a 'physical, political, juridical and cultural genocide', and recommended a policy that promoted the 'integrity of Serbia' as the overriding foreign policy objective. Within the ruling communist establishment, it was Slobodan Milošević who capitalized on this growing Serbian nationalist self-assertion so as to ensure his own political ascendance. In a carefully stage-managed visit to Kosovo in 1987, Milošević gave his full support to the local Serb Kosovars and, in a widely publicized speech, stated that 'you shouldn't abandon your land just because it is difficult to live, because you are pressured by injustice and degradation ... No one should dare to beat you.'[12] In the ensuing nationalist fervour that swept the Serbian population, Milošević replaced his old mentor, Ivan Stambolić, as President of the Serbian League of Communists and then brutally dissolved the autonomy of Kosovo (along with Vojvodina) in 1989–90.

More than anything else, it was this demonstration of Serb domination and bullying towards Kosovo that accentuated the anxieties of the other republics within Yugoslavia and contributed to the emergence of competing nationalisms in opposition to Serbia. In 1991, this culminated in the declarations of independence of Slovenia and Croatia which initiated the first wars of secession. In 1992, the declaration of independence of Bosnia and Herzegovina provoked an even bloodier and more protracted conflict, which was only pacified in November 1995 through the agreement reached in Dayton, Ohio. Even though each of these wars developed their own dynamic and had their specific causes and origins, the earlier developments in Kosovo had provided the initial catalyst for the subsequent descent into violence.

No peace and no war

Surprisingly, however, Kosovo remained subdued and peaceful, although under conditions of martial law, during the early 1990s, while war waged in other parts of the former Yugoslavia. The leaders of the other besieged republics – Slovenia, Croatia and Bosnia and Herzegovina – constantly requested the Kosovar Albanians to initiate hostilities so as to open a new front against the now Serb-dominated Yugoslav National Army. In September 1991, following the examples of Slovenia and Croatia, the outlawed Kosovo Assembly undertook a referendum that resulted in an overwhelming majority in favour of independence. In May 1992, elections were also held for the republican assembly. These were comprehensively won by the Democratic League of Kosovo (LDK). The LDK leader, Ibrahim Rugova, was at the same time elected President of the Republic of Kosovo.

Despite the popular support for separation from Serbia and Yugoslavia, Rugova refused steadfastly to escalate Kosovar Albanian resistance to the level of armed confrontation. In part, this was driven by his personal commitment to a Gandhian form of non-violent resistance but there were also less idealistic reasons for adopting this stance. Rugova was well aware that the Serbs were looking for a justification to engage in a mass expulsion or extermination of the Kosovar Albanian population and the developments in Bosnia and Herzegovina, where the Serb forces engaged in just such acts of extreme brutality, only confirmed this assessment. The Kosovar Albanians also had no access to significant sources of arms or trained military personnel to offer effective resistance to a determined Serb military campaign. In addition, Rugova calculated that a policy of non-violent resistance would be the most effective in securing the support of the international community who, he believed, would ultimately have to recognize the legitimacy of the Kosovar right to self-determination, as so clearly articulated in the September 1991 referendum.[13]

With the main formal institutions in Kosovo now controlled by the Serbs, and with most Kosovar Albanians having been sacked or having resigned their posts, Rugova set out to establish a formidable array of parallel institutions, which would provide a concrete expression of *de facto* Kosovar independence. The exiled Kosovar government, under the leadership of Prime Minister Bujar Bukoshi, ensured that the extensive Kosovar diaspora communities contributed a recommended 3 per cent of their income to the work of the government. These funds, along with the contributions made by Albanian families and businesses within Kosovo, were distributed to the municipal councils where they were spent on education, health care, culture, science, sports, agriculture and social assistance. By 1997, roughly 25,000 individuals were working in these sectors and were directly on the payroll of the LDK.[14]

In many ways, this exercise in developing a coherent set of parallel institutions, which sustained an autonomous Kosovar existence in a period of Serb repression, can be considered a remarkable achievement. It is perhaps the closest that this region has come to developing a vibrant civil society, but, in the final analysis, the exercise was to prove a failure. The most critical problem was that the international community failed to respond in the expected manner to the evidence of the 'good behaviour' of the Kosovar Albanians. Indeed, the Dayton Agreement, which was signed in November 1995 and brought peace to Bosnia and Herzegovina, deliberately excluded any consideration of the status or situation in Kosovo.[15] The recognition of the Republika Srpska within the Federation of Bosnia and Herzegovina also appeared, for many Kosovar Albanians, to be a recognition that violence does pay territorial dividends. Moreover, the deal made at Dayton elevated Milošević as the key interlocutor and mediator for the international community.[16] One consequent result was the international recognition in 1996 of the Federal Republic of Yugoslavia without any substantive provisions for the respect of minority rights or any precondition for the restoration of the autonomy of Kosovo.

All of these developments suggested to many Kosovar Albanians, particularly amongst the elites, that Rugova's strategy of non-violence was bankrupt. The international community, far from respecting and recognizing Kosovar good behaviour, actually took the relative calm in Kosovo as a justification for ignoring Kosovo's claim for special treatment. Moreover, by 1997 the conditions were emerging for the Kosovar

Albanians to assume a more violent campaign to promote their national claims. During 1997, the Albanian state effectively disintegrated, after the Sali Berisha government became ensnared in the collapse of pyramid-selling schemes, and vast amounts of arms, raided from military stores, flowed across the mountains into Kosovo. At the same time, the shadowy Kosovo Liberation Army (KLA, or UCK in the Albanian acronym) emerged as an independent fighting force in Kosovo and initiated small-scale guerrilla attacks on Serb police and presumed Albanian collaborators.[17]

A failed exercise in coercive diplomacy

By the beginning of 1998, the rising level of violence in Kosovo finally forced the external powers to consider the situation within the province. The US took the lead and Robert S. Gelbard, the special representative for the implementation of the Dayton Agreement, went to Belgrade on 23 February. The position adopted by Gelbard was favourable to the Serbian position. Although it was still asserted that the overarching sanctions regime on Yugoslavia would not be lifted until Kosovar autonomy had been restored, he did offer some concessions, in recognition of Milošević's tacit co-operation with the Dayton agreement, which included the easing of some sanctions and permission to establish a Yugoslav consulate in New York. More significantly, he asserted that the KLA was 'without any question a terrorist group', which effectively gave the green light to the Yugoslav authorities to manage the problem in Kosovo at its discretion, if within the limits of prudence and restraint.[18]

The ensuing Serbian offensive, which was launched a week after Gelbard's visit, involved the customary Serb brutality with the destruction of villages, summary executions and the systematic use of terror. On 5 March, the Yugoslav police attacked the family compound of a well-known KLA leader, Adem Jashari, killing 58 members of his extended family. This event, more than any other, galvanized the Kosovar Albanian resistance and thousands flocked to join the KLA. By late spring, a major insurrectionary war had emerged within Kosovo with increasing numbers of casualties and large-scale displacement of population. By the end of June, an estimated 350 people had been killed in Kosovo with about 60,000 becoming refugees within Kosovo and 11,000 fleeing into Albania and Montenegro. It was also estimated that Belgrade had deployed up to 25,000 special police in the area.[19]

In the face of this clear evidence of the excessive Serb response, the US quietly dropped the 'terrorist' association with the KLA, though without condoning the maximalist objectives of the group, and reasserted its traditional view that the Serb/Yugoslav authorities were the principal instigators of the violence. In the following few months, a panoply of international bodies and institutions weighed in to condemn the violence. On 9 March, the international 'Contact Group' (consisting of six members; the US, UK, France, Germany, Italy and Russia) condemned the 'use of excessive force by Serbian police against civilians' as well as 'terrorist actions by the Kosovo Liberation Army'.[20] Three weeks later, UN Security Council Resolution 1160 was passed and imposed an arms embargo on the region and, at the end of May, NATO issued a strong statement defining the situation in Kosovo as 'unacceptable'. In June, the EU agreed, with the US, to impose a new ban on investments in Serbia and to freeze Serbia's foreign assets.

In all these diplomatic endeavours, the spectre of Bosnia haunted the decision-making of the major external players. For the key Western actors, the two lessons of Bosnia were: first, Serbia/Yugoslavia must be treated as the principal aggressor; and, second, that any diplomatic pressure must be allied with a credible military threat, which could only be provided by NATO. There were, though, complications with the Bosnia–Kosovo analogy. Unlike Bosnia, any NATO threats of air strikes would represent a direct and indisputable intervention into the territorial integrity and political sovereignty of Yugoslavia, of which Kosovo was internationally recognized as a constituent element. Moreover, Russia's forceful opposition to any expeditionary role for NATO effectively precluded gaining UN Security Council authorization for NATO's declared objectives. Amongst the NATO allies, most notably for the incoming SPD–Green German government but also for the Italian and French governments, it was politically extremely sensitive to authorize such a role for NATO given these circumstances.

In addition, the presumption of a clear-cut division between 'good Kosovars' and 'bad Serbians' was problematic. In reality, there was considerable convergence of interests between the major external actors and Serbia/Yugoslavia in ensuring that the maximalist objectives of the KLA were not secured. Given the enormous efforts being made to promote a multi-ethnic Bosnia, the West was not willing to support the KLA's project of an ethnically pure Albanian Kosovo within a 'Greater Albania'. The broader regional consequences of such a development, with its threat of destabilizing all the neighbouring countries, meant that Western interests remained, in opposition to those of the KLA, committed to preserving the territorial integrity of Yugoslavia, although with a new autonomous disposition for Kosovo.

The US, therefore, faced considerable difficulties in gaining the support of its allies for a forceful NATO stance. In June, the most that could be contemplated was some NATO admonitory exercises over Albania and Macedonia. On 23 September, however, the UN Security Council finally issued a more strongly-worded resolution (Resolution 1199), which demanded 'immediate action' to bring peace to Kosovo. On

20

1998

13 October, the North Atlantic Council authorized General Wesley Clark to issue an Activation Order (ACTORD) for air strikes on Yugoslavia. With the pressure now ratcheting up, Richard Holbrooke, who had been brought back to seek a negotiated settlement, was finally able to convince Milošević to reach an agreement that would satisfy the demands of the United Nations and the international community. After eight months of the Serbian offensive, which had caused 750 deaths and had created 250,000 embittered refugees, a degree of peace was re-established in Kosovo.[21]

This peace was not to last long. In reality, the Holbrooke–Milošević accord was fatally flawed on a number of counts. In the first instance, given all the coercive pressure placed on the Serbian authorities, it was remarkably generous towards Belgrade. It permitted the Serbs to maintain the police and military levels that had been in place prior to February 1998 when the province had been effectively under martial law. The implementation of the agreement was also to be policed by 2000 unarmed members of the OSCE who would have no mandate or capability to enforce the settlement. But, most critically, the agreement was only made with one side of the conflict and did not gain the support of the KLA. Indeed, the KLA, which had been almost totally crushed by the Serbian offensive, capitalized on the Serb withdrawal to regroup their forces and to regain control of territory that had been vacated by the withdrawing Serb forces. Quite naturally, the Serbian police and military leaders bitterly complained to the OSCE about these developments over which the OSCE, given its mandate and capabilities, was quite powerless to act.[22]

When, in retaliation to the KLA provocations, Serbian hostilities were resumed in December 1998, the West was again confronted by the same dilemmas and divisions over what action should be taken. However, now, after almost a year of prevarications and the issuing of empty military threats, Western resolve and the credibility of NATO were being increasingly questioned. A decisive catalyst for more forceful action occurred with the evidence of a Serbian massacre of 45 Kosovars in Račak on 15 January 1999, which was immediately broadcast to the world by the OSCE head of mission, William Walker. In the aftermath of this event, US Secretary of State, Madeleine Albright, convened her European allies and demanded that the time for vacillation and talk had ended and that any further diplomatic *démarches* must be backed by the explicit and credible threat of force against Belgrade. This time, the reluctant European allies concurred and the French and the British, who were enjoying a new *entente cordiale* after the St Malo agreement in October to strengthen the EU's defence capabilities, agreed to host a conference at Rambouillet where the Yugoslav and Kosovar delegation would be required to sign a preprepared peace settlement. In the background, NATO's ACTORD for air strikes on Yugoslavia was reactivated.

1999

Rambouillet was an unusual conference because the terms of settlement were essentially dictated by the convening states and the local parties to the dispute were given the option either to sign or to face military retaliation.[23] In practice, there was room for negotiation but there has been a vigorous debate about whether the conference was deliberately designed to secure a Serbian/Yugoslav rejection. In this context, much attention has been given to Appendix B of the proposed interim agreement, which permitted NATO forces 'free and unrestricted passage and unimpeded access throughout the FRY', which would presumably have been completely unacceptable to the Yugoslav authorities.[24] While it does seem that the British and French negotiators did genuinely seek to conclude a settlement that would be acceptable to both sides, the US was rather more ambivalent. While not excluding an agreement signed by both parties, the US negotiators also thought that an acceptable alternative would be a settlement which the Serbs rejected and the Kosovars accepted. This second scenario had the benefit, according to Jamie Rubin, US Assistant Secretary of State, 'of creating clarity where previously there had been ambiguity. And clarity as to which side was the cause of the problem and clarity about which side NATO should defend and which side NATO should oppose.'[25]

Whatever the intentions of the convening parties, the Serb/Yugoslav delegation failed to assent to the proposed settlement. It does not appear that Appendix B was a significant sticking point: rather, the delegation, or more importantly President Milošević, consistently rejected the agreement as a whole and refused to countenance any prospect of NATO forces being permitted to enter into Kosovo and thereby onto Yugoslav territory. In their revision of the draft agreement, which the Yugoslav delegation presented on 15 March, there were comprehensive deletions and additions to the text, even deleting the term 'peace' in the title.[26] With the Serbian side recalcitrant, the problem then came that the Kosovar delegation also refused to sign up to the agreement with their main concern being that, at the end of the three-year interim period, there was no explicit provision for the people of Kosovo to determine the final status of the territory.

Thus, after three frustrating weeks, neither of the two delegations was ready to sign the proposed agreement and the conference was concluded, but there was an agreement to meet in Paris on 15 March and, at this meeting, the Kosovar delegation finally signed the peace plan but only after the US had given a unilateral declaration that a referendum would be held at the end of the three-year interim period. With this Kosovar signature, the path was now finally cleared for the initiation of the NATO air campaign onto Yugoslav territory.

War and peace

1999

On 24 March, the implementation of Operation Allied Force was authorized, which envisioned a phased application of NATO air forces, with each phase being introduced after a political decision made by the North Atlantic Council.[27] This limited and phased application of air power, with its demand for regular political authorization for any escalation of the campaign and its exclusion of the option of a ground offensive, was driven by a number of factors. There was the objective requirement to maintain Alliance unity in the absence of a strong consensus for a large-scale military offensive against Yugoslavia. Among Western capitals, there existed considerable political sensitivity to civilian casualties, which meant that collateral damage was to be avoided as far as possible. There was also a resolve not to grant the military a *carte blanche* to execute the military campaign. The limited nature of the initial hostilities was also driven by a political presumption that a short air campaign was all that was required to bring Milošević to the bargaining table. As in Bosnia, so it was thought that in Kosovo, Milošević would quickly buckle once NATO demonstrated that it was serious in its application of military force. Madeleine Albright betrayed just such thinking when she declared on the first day of the campaign that 'I don't see this as a long-term operation. I think it is something that ... is achievable within a relatively short period of time.'[28]

Milošević refused, though, to play his alloted role. Instead, with the withdrawal of the OSCE verifiers and with Yugoslavia under NATO bombardment, he authorized the preprepared plan for a comprehensive ethnic cleansing of the Kosovar Albanian population, which resulted by the end of the war in about 850,000 refugees being forced out of the province and 300,000–400,000 being internally displaced within Kosovo.[29] Through this escalation of the conflict, Milošević demonstrated that he had no intention of allowing NATO to secure a rapid victory.

The brutality of the Serbian offensive and the enormity of the refugee crisis created a condition of near panic in the capitals of the Atlantic Alliance. There was no avoiding the fact that the allies had failed to achieve two of the three objectives that President Clinton had set the day that the bombing started: 'to deter an even bloodier offensive against innocent civilians in Kosovo and, if necessary, to seriously damage the Serbian military's capacity to harm the people of Kosovo.'[30] In response to this, the second phase of the campaign, which extended air strikes to attacking the Serbian forces directly involved in the offensive, was authorized three days after the start of the campaign on 27 March. However, with the Yugoslav air-defence system still offering resistance, the NATO airplanes were limited to flying at 5000 metres, which greatly constrained their ability successfully to attack and destroy the well-

23

disguised and mobile Serb military and paramilitary targets. This phase of the campaign did little to prevent the mass movement of the Kosovar Albanian population or even, as with the rocket attack on two refugee convoys on 14 April, to ensure that those fleeing did not themselves become the targets of military attack.

With the air command, in particular, becoming increasingly restive with the political constraints imposed on their activities, the pressure was exerted to escalate the campaign to a third phase, involving air strikes on militarily significant targets within Serbia itself. On the eleventh day of the campaign, on 3 February, the war was taken into the heart of Belgrade with an attack on the Yugoslav Interior ministry. However, this time the escalation was not authorized by the North Atlantic Council and France, in particular, claimed that it had not been consulted. At the NATO Summit on 23 April, the US finally obtained support for a substantial expansion of the campaign, with the target list increasingly focused on so-called sustainment targets – petroleum, lines of communication, electrical grids, and command-and-control centres. But, this ever-increasing list of strategic targets only accentuated the anxiety of many of the NATO allies, who feared that further accidental civilian casualties could erode public support for the operation. In this regard, the attack on the Chinese Embassy in Belgrade on 8 May created a major public relations crisis for NATO. Among the NATO allies there was also intense debate over the appropriate targets to be struck, with the US military in particular feeling itself unnecessarily constrained by political interference, most notably by France.[31] Despite the seeming failure of the air campaign to achieve its political objectives, it was only ten weeks into the campaign when the US leadership finally indicated that 'other military options' were not ruled out, and that there was clear evidence that the logistics for a ground offensive were being prepared. A week after this decision, Milošević finally agreed, on 3 June, to a peace plan that would lead to the ending of hostilities.

There were clearly a number of strategic miscalculations in the NATO military campaign. There was the mistake of allowing the Bosnian precedent dictate strategic thinking towards Kosovo. On any objective assessment, the situation prevailing in Kosovo in 1999 was markedly different from that of Bosnia in 1995, not least that Serbian national interests were more engaged in Kosovo and that the Serbian forces were not, as in Bosnia in late 1995, under threat of military defeat. In addition, the limited nature of the initial air attacks, and the explicit exclusion of the option of a ground offensive, meant that NATO's intervention lacked both the critical elements of surprise and credibility. The failure to predict or prepare for the subsequent refugee crisis was also reprehensible. It was not as though such a Serbian response was unprecedented – just such a strategy had been implemented in Bosnia five years earlier and had been carefully documented and analysed.[32]

Milošević's gamble in escalating the crisis through the creation of a refugee crisis did certainly have its initial intended effect of causing a real crisis for the Western leadership and for NATO military planners. But, in the longer term, it was to prove a strategic error. As the streams of Kosovars fled into neighbouring countries, under the intense and watchful glare of the international media, the solidarity of the NATO allies was strengthened. With large numbers of Albanians also being given asylum in Western countries, the need to ensure the defeat of the Serbian forces became a critical domestic issue so as to expedite the return of these refugees to their country of origin. Without the refugee crisis, it is difficult imagining the Alliance holding together for two weeks, let alone the eleven weeks that it eventually took to secure the Serb withdrawal. The initial failure of the air campaign also threatened the very credibility of NATO, which meant that previously excluded options, such as a ground offensive, were more seriously considered.

In the end, Milošević's gamble resulted in a confrontation with NATO that the West could not afford to lose. It was when Milošević finally realized this that he consented to the demands made for a cessation of hostilities. The escalation of the military campaign certainly contributed to this decision, most notably when Milošević realized that NATO was seriously considering a ground offensive. The impact of the air campaign was more problematic, because it appears that very little damage was actually inflicted on the Yugoslav/Serbian forces within Kosovo.[33] However, the increasing damage being caused to Serbia's infrastructure, such as bridges, electricity installations and military-industrial plants, did probably undermine Serbian resistance to a climbdown. On the political front, Russia's decision to recommend that Belgrade cuts its losses was a significant contribution to the final decision. By the middle of the campaign, the Yeltsin leadership, which had felt greatly constrained and even threatened by the unprecedented tide of popular anti-NATO and anti-Western sentiment, was desperate for a resolution of the conflict so as to avoid a fatal breakdown of Russian relations with the West. Yeltsin selected his faithful ally, Victor Chernomyrdin, to act as the messenger for this decision, which he loyally did at the expense of any remaining political ambitions.

1999

The UN Security Council Resolution 1244, which was adopted on 10 June and provided the basis of the final agreement, also offered Belgrade a number of face-saving concessions. First, the UN was given a central role in the administration of Kosovo. Second, there was no specific mention of NATO's role in the Kosovo Force (KFOR) and there were none of the controversial status-of-forces provisions, such as the infamous Appendix B, which had appeared so unpalatable in the initial Rambouillet agreement. In addition, Russia was granted a definite role as a participant in the military implementation of the agreement. The future status of Kosovo was also kept deliberately vague with the UN Resolution making repeated references to the Rambouillet Accords and the fact that the people of Kosovo can enjoy 'substantial autonomy within the Federal Republic of Yugoslavia'.

The aftermath of the war

With the Yugoslav acceptance of the peace agreement and the consequent suspension of NATO air strikes on 10 June, the Yugoslav forces withdrew from Kosovo on schedule and, apart from a potentially serious Russian–NATO dispute over Priština airport, NATO and the UN Mission for Kosovo (UNMIK) came in to fill the vacuum. The record of the *de facto* NATO and UN protectorate since June 1999 is mixed. On the positive side of the ledger, there has been the considerable success of securing the return of the vast majority of the refugees who had streamed out of the province during the period of the war. The economic reconstruction of the province has also gained a significant momentum and the Kosovars have demonstrated considerable resolve and ingenuity in revitalizing the local economy. The UNMIK administration, despite a very shaky start and with the continuing problem of often failing to secure the promised support of international donors, has had some successes in building up an administrative framework for Kosovo. In December, the Interim Administrative Council of Kosovo was set up with representatives from the three Albanian main political formations and, in June 2000, managed to secure the presence of Serbian representatives.[34]

However, the failure of NATO and UNMIK to provide a stable security environment and to prevent the returning Kosovar Albanians from engaging in acts of vengeance on the remaining Serb population has been the major disappointment. As could have been predicted by even a superficial reading of history, the Kosovar Albanians were in no mood to forgive their Serb neighbours, many of whom were directly complicit in the acts of brutality and expulsions during the war. It is estimated that as many as 125,000 of the roughly 200,000 Serbs who lived in Kosovo before the NATO bombing have fled or been driven out.[35] Roma, Turks and Muslim Slavs have also been the subject of intimidation and attacks. Although the numbers of Serbs killed in revenge are far fewer than the Albanians killed during the war (general estimates are now about 7000 Kosovar Albanians killed during the war and 400–500 Serbs killed in revenge), it is not a good record, particularly as there have been 44,000 NATO troops providing protection.[36] These developments have clearly greatly complicated NATO's declared intention of preserving a multi-ethnic Kosovo. Moreover, the remaining Serbs in the province have consolidated in the northern part of the province, around the town of Mitrovica, which has led to a *de facto* partition of Kosovo.

The continuing problem of the ambiguity of the future status of Kosovo accentuates the problems and divisions within Kosovo and with the region more generally. It is now generally, if reluctantly, recognized that there is almost no circumstance in which the Kosovar Albanians would be willing to submit themselves to Yugoslav or Serb sovereignty. Some have suggested that, given this reality, recognition should be given to Kosovo independence. It is almost impossible, however, to obtain an international consensus behind such a proposal. The alternative, though, of continued ambiguity and uncertainty over the future disposition of the territory breeds its own pathologies.[37] Within Kosovo, it is extremely difficult to construct viable and lasting civil and political institutions when the underlying legal and political framework is undetermined. More broadly in the region, the sense of uncertainty, and the fear that a mono-ethnic Kosovo might gain independence, creates great insecurities amongst neighbouring countries, most notably Macedonia but also Montenegro, who themselves have substantial Albanian minorities.

With all these post-conflict developments, the 'problem' of Kosovo continues to present major challenges for all external powers seeking to provide a lasting and durable settlement for the territory and for the region more generally. How to manage the dilemmas that the problem of Kosovo presents, such as how to determine the status of the entity and how to satisfy the competing Serb and Albanian national and sovereign claims, continues to be highly divisive and essentially unresolved. As such, Kosovo remains a prism through which some of the most divisive issues of post-Cold War international politics continue to be debated and determined. It is for this reason that the perceptions of outside powers towards Kosovo, both in terms of what has happened and what will happen in the future, remains of such critical importance.

Notes

1. For a discussion of some of these legal and moral questions, see Adam Roberts, 'NATO's "Humanitarian War" over Kosovo', *Survival*, vol. 41, no. 3 (Autumn 1999), pp. 102-23; Marc Weller, *The Crisis in Kosovo 1989-1999: International Documents Volume 1* (Cambridge: Documents and Analysis Publishing, 1999), pp. 24-33; and Catherine Guichard, 'International Law and the War in Kosovo', *Survival*, vol. 41, no. 2 (Summer 1999), pp. 19-34.

2. For the best account of the history of Kosovo, see Noel Malcolm, *Kosovo: A Short History* (Basingstoke: Macmillan, 1998). See also Miranda Vickers, *Between Serb and Albanian: A History of Kosovo* (New York: Columbia University Press, 1998); and Barbara Jelavich, *History of the Balkans: Vols 1 and 2* (Cambridge: Cambridge University Press, 1989 and 1993).

3. John M. Fraser, 'The Kosovo Quagmire: What are the Issues? Should we Care?' *International Journal*, vol. 53, no. 4 (Autumn 1998), pp. 601-8.

4. Benedict Anderson, *Imagined Communities: Reflections on the Origins and Spread of Nationalism* (London: Verso, 1983).
5. Malcolm, *op. cit.*, pp. 307–8.
6. Carnegie Endowment for International Peace, *Report of the International Commission to Inquire into the Causes and Conduct of the Balkan Wars* (Washington DC: 1914), p. 95; reproduced as *The Other Balkan Wars: A 1913 Carnegie Endowment Inquiry in Retrospect, with a New Introduction and Reflections on the Present Conflict by George F. Kennan* (Washington DC: Carnegie Endowment for International Peace/Brookings Institution Publications, 1993).
7. Tim Judah, *The Serbs: History, Myth, and the Destruction of Yugoslavia* (New Haven and London: Yale University Press, 1997), pp. 149–50.
8. For the Horseshoe Plan, see R. Jeffrey Smith and William Drozdiak, 'A Blueprint for War: The Serbs' Military Campaign was Meticulously Planned for Months', *Washington Post National Weekly Edition*, 19 April 1999.
9. Quoted in Lenard J Cohen, 'Kosovo: "Nobody's Country"', *Current History* (March 2000), pp. 119–20.
10. Veton Surroi, 'Kosovo Political Life: Past as Prologue', *The International Spectator,* vol. 35, no. 1 (January–March 2000), p. 27.
11. See the population statistics from 1948–91 in Tim Judah, *Kosovo: War and Revenge* (New Haven and London: Yale University Press, 2000), p. 313.
12. Quoted in Allan Little and Laura Silber, *The Death of Yugoslavia* (London: Penguin, 1995), p. 37.
13. For a good acount of Rugova's strategy, see Richard Caplan, 'International Diplomacy and the Crisis in Kosovo', *International Affairs*, vol. 74, no. 4 (October 1998), pp. 751–2.
14. Andrew March and Rudra Sil, 'The Republic of Kosova (1989–1998) and the Resolution of Ethno-Separatist Conflict: Rethinking "Sovereignty" in the Post-Cold War Era', *Working Paper for Browne Center for International Politics, University of Pennsylvania*, 1999, p. 10.
15. For the reasons for this as argued by one of the key mediators, see Pauline Neville-Jones, 'Dayton, IFOR, and Alliance Relations in Bosnia', *Survival*, vol. 38, no. 4 (Winter 1996–7), pp. 58–9.
16. For considering Milošević as the lynchpin for Dayton, see Richard Holbrooke, 'The Road to Sarajevo', *New Yorker*, 21 and 28 October 1996, pp. 88–104.
17. For the background to the KLA, see 'The Kosovo Liberation Army: A Struggle for Power', *Strategic Comments*, vol. 5, no. 4 (May 1999), pp. 1–2.
18. Quoted in R. Craig Nation, 'US Policy and the Kosovo Crisis', *International Spectator*, vol. 33, no. 4 (October-November 1998), p. 3. The remarks can also be found in the text of Special Representative Robert S. Gelbard, Press Conference, Belgrade, Serbia and Montenegro, 23 February 1998 at http://www.state.gov/www/policy_remarks/1998.
19. These figures are taken from Tim Youngs and Tom Dodd, *Kosovo*, Research paper 98/73 for the House of Commons, 7 July 1998, p. 18.
20. 'Statement on Kosovo', London Contact Group Meeting, 9 March 1998, cited at http://secretary.state.gov/www/travels/980309_kosovo.html.
21. The figures are from the UNHCR as quoted in Ministry of Defence of the

United Kingdom, *Kosovo: Lessons from the Crisis*, June 2000, at http://
www.mod.uk/news/kosovo/lessons/chapter2.html, pp. 2-3.

22. See comments made by Major General John Drewienkiewicz of the Kosovo
Verification Mission in Allan Little, *Moral Combat: NATO at War*, BBC2
television, 12 March 2000. The transcript for this is at http://news.bbc.co.uk/hi/
english/static/events/panorama/trans.../transcript_12_03_00.

23. For the most extensive analysis of the Rambouillet negotations, see Marc
Weller, 'The Rambouillet Conference on Kosovo', *International Affairs*, vol.
75, no. 2 (April 1999), pp. 211-51.

24. For the text of Appendix B, see Weller, *The Crisis in Kosovo 1989-1999*, p.
469. For examples of those who saw this as a deliberate provocation, see
Christopher Layne and Banjamin Schwarz, 'Kosovo II: For the Record', *The
National Interest*, (Fall 1999), pp. 9-15; and Noam Chomsky, 'Lessons of War:
Another Way for Kosovo?' *Le Monde Diplomatique*, (March 2000).

25. Quoted in Little, *op. cit.*

26. Weller, *The Crisis in Kosovo 1989-1999*, pp. 480-90.

27. Details of the phased approach can be found in Federation of American
Scientists, 'Operation Allied Force: Operation Noble Anvil', *Military Analysis
Network*, at http://www.fas.org/man/dod-101/ops/allied_force.htm.

28. 'Interview with Secretary of State Madeleine Albright', *Online Newshour*, 24
March 1999.

29. The UNHCR commissioned an independent evaluation of the Kosovo refugee
crisis, which made serious criticisms of the organization's preparedness for
the crisis. It also provides a detailed breakdown of the numbers and evolution
of the crisis. See UNHCR, *Kosovo Refugee Crisis: An Independent Evaluation
of UNHCR's Emergency Preparedness and Response*, February 2000, at
http:unhcr.ch/evaluate/kosovo/toc.htm.

30. Quoted in Ivo H. Daalder and Michael E. O'Hanlon, 'Unlearning the Lessons of
Kosovo', *Foreign Policy*, (Fall 1999), p. 130.

31. See comments by Lt General Mike Short, Commander, Allied Air Forces in
Little, *op. cit.*

32. Mark Danner, 'Endgame in Kosovo', *New York Review of Books*, (6 May 1999),
p. 9.

33. John Barry and Evan Thomas, 'The Kosovo Cover-Up', *Newsweek*, (15 May
2000).

34. Leonard J Cohen, 'Kosovo: "Nobody's Country"', *Current History*, (March
2000).

35. David Rohde, 'Kosovo Seething', *Foreign Affairs*, vol. 79, no. 3 (May/June
2000), pp. 70, 117-23.

36. Ibid. See also Esdpen Barth Eide, 'The Internal Security Challenge in Kosovo',
The International Spectator, vol. 35, no. 1 (January-March 2000), pp. 49-63.

37. For an excellent analysis of these issues, see Susan L. Woodward, 'Kosovo and
the Region: Consequences of the Waiting Game', *The International Spectator*,
vol. 35, no. 1 (January-March 2000), pp. 35-47.

CHAPTER TWO

The Kingdom of God or the Kingdom of Ends: Kosovo in Serbian Perception

SABRINA P. RAMET

Serbian perceptions of Kosovo have been filtered through a thick layer of mythology built around the history of the province, and most especially around the Battle of Kosovo on 28 June 1389. Central to this mythology is the legendary figure of King Lazar, who fell on the field of battle. According to legend, Lazar was visited by an angel on the eve of battle. The angel offered him a choice between an earthly kingdom and a heavenly kingdom. If you choose the earthly kingdom, the angel explained, you will sweep the enemy from the field of battle, win a great victory, and secure your earthly kingdom for your lifetime. But if you choose a heavenly kingdom, the angel continued, your army will be crushed, you yourself will suffer a martyr's death, and your earthly kingdom will be set on a path to eventual extinction, but you will have a special place in the Kingdom of God. Lazar, as is well known, chose the Kingdom of God.

As Serbs understand this legend, Lazar's choice of the 'eternal kingdom' secured for Serbs an eternal claim to Kosovo, by sacralizing Kosovo. As sacred Serbian soil, Kosovo has been, for Serb nationalists at least, if not for other Serbs as well, beyond rival claims, whether based on demographic changes, political shifts, or democratic referenda. Kosovo *is* the Serbian heavenly kingdom.[1]

There is, however, a third choice – the Kingdom of Ends, the discussion of which I shall defer until the conclusion.

As Serbs remember it*

For Serbs, Kosovo is the cradle of the medieval kingdom, the Serbian 'Jerusalem', the final resting place (in a monastery near Prizren) of Tsar Dušan the Mighty, and, of course, the site of that famous battle. As Serbs remember it, they were there first and the Albanians were latecomers to the area, benefiting from Ottoman rule and from the flight of Serbs under Ottoman pressure. Albanians, for their part, dispute this chronicle, but my concern here is with describing specifically *Serbian* memories and perceptions of Kosovo's history.

Serbs remember that it was the defeat of the Turkish army at the gates of Vienna in 1683 and the military and demographic repercussions of that defeat, which opened the doors to Albanian migratory movement into Kosovo from areas southwest of the region. At the height of Habsburg military success, Austrian forces conquered Belgrade. Encouraged by this development, Serbs in Kosovo rose up against their Ottoman overlords. But then the Ottomans revived and swept the Austrians out of Serbia. Fearing for their lives, some 200,000 Serbian families followed the Serbian Orthodox Patriarch of Peć, Arsenije III Crnojević, on a long trek from Kosovo to Habsburg-held Vojvodina in 1690. This migration became paired, in Serbs' minds, with Lazar's defeat and was identified as a second great 'defeat'; it was also seen as confirming the sacralization of the Serbian title to Kosovo.

Some Serbs remained in Kosovo, of course. As the number of Albanians in Kosovo increased, so too did contacts between local Serbs and Albanians. In villages where Albanian Muslims were in the majority, those Serbs who remained often converted to Islam and, through continued contact with their Albanophone co-religionists, gradually became Albanianized. Moreover, as the result of the common religion shared with the ruling Ottomans,[2] the Albanians became the most loyal guardians of a decadent empire. The League of Prizren, which Albanians recall as a defence measure, is given an aggressive cast by at least some Serbian historians. Milja Šćepanović, for example, claims that, between 1878 and 1912, some 150,000 Serbs were driven out of Kosovo by Albanian nationalists committed to the programme of the 1878 League.[3]

Serbs and Albanians recall the interwar kingdom (1918–41) differently. According to Branko Petranović, considered in his lifetime the dean of Serbian historians, the secessionist Kosovë Committee (established in Albania in 1919) was a 'terrorist' organization. Indeed, the Kosovë Committee signed an agreement on co-operation with the Bulgarian terrorist organization IMRO in 1920, on joint actions against the young

---

* This section is adapted from a part of my 'Kosovo: A Liberal Approach', *Society*, vol. 36, no. 6 (1999), pp. 62–9, with permission of Transaction Publishers.

South Slav state.[4] The Serbs have traditionally thought of themselves as the statebuilders and guardians of Yugoslavia, but have never considered Albanians suitable material for Yugoslav citizenship. In the interwar years, Belgrade negotiated with Ankara in order to arrange for the forced emigration of Kosovo's Albanians to Turkey. In 1935, Turkey agreed to accept some 200,000 Albanians; in 1938, the Turkish government agreed to accept another 40,000 Albanian families from Yugoslavia.[5] The outbreak of World War Two cut short the completion of the Yugoslav plan.

As for World War Two, Serb historians have damned the wartime Balli Kombëtar movement as 'counter-revolutionary' or 'anti-Yugoslav' (the term of choice depending on the year in which the particular historian is writing) and portray the Bujan Conference of 1943, at which the Albanian *communists* insisted on the postwar assignment of Kosovo to Albania as, at best, a breach of the discipline necessitated by the requirements of a common anti-fascist struggle.[6] Petranović writes that during the years 1941–4, Albanians set fire to Serbian homes, plundered Serbian property, and murdered local Serbs, creating an atmosphere of terror.[7] Serbs remember the years of communist rule as years in which Kosovo was the beneficiary of a disproportionately large portion of special federal funds to stimulate the province's economy, in which the near-total illiteracy in the region was almost entirely overcome, and in which the Albanian provincial leadership increasingly obtained for itself, after 1968, the de facto powers of a republic leadership.[8] Serbs forget, or downplay, the fact, for example, that whereas Serbs and Montenegrins accounted for only 27 per cent of Kosovo's population in 1953, they accounted for 50 per cent of the membership of the Communist Party in Kosovo and held 68 per cent of positions of authority in the province.[9]

Yet, as the Serbian version of history continues, in spite of all of the advantages and benefits enjoyed by Kosovo's Albanians, the Albanians repeatedly rioted (most notably in 1968 and 1981), began to exert pressure on local Serbs after 1966, and, in the course of the 1980s, escalated tensions by resorting to the rape of Serbian women, terror against Serbian men, and arson directed against Serbian religious facilities in Peć. Even today, Serbs remember the 'Martinović affair' of more than fifteen years ago, in which a 56-year-old Serb peasant named Djordje Martinović, with a glass bottle inserted in his anus, blamed local Albanians for his situation.[10]

According to the Belgrade weekly magazine *NIN*, some 24,209 Serbs and Montenegrins emigrated from Kosovo between April 1981 and December 1987; many of these moved to Serbia proper, bearing tales of harassment and violence at the hands of local Albanians.[11] An opinion poll conducted among Serb households in Kosovo between 1985 and 1986 found that some 46.4 per cent of Serbs complained of verbal harassment by Albanians, with 35.2 per cent citing material damage caused by Albanians and 10.4 per cent citing Albanian aggression against Serb women and children.[12] The veracity of such reports has been disputed by Viktor Meier, however, who alleges that the genuinely felt fears of Serbs were built on a foundation of rumours and innuendoes, in which few Serbs could actually cite real victims by name.[13] Be that as it may, the assertive, even repressive policies undertaken by Serbian President Slobodan Milošević against Kosovar Albanians in the late 1980s[14] were welcomed both by Serbs in Kosovo and Serbia proper and by Serbs in emigration.

Violence begets violence

The history of Serb-Albanian relations over the past hundred years documents the way inflicted harm begets resentment which, in turn, begets reprisals, which, in turn, inflict new harm. Serbian and/or Yugoslav authorities had the upper hand in the interwar era, in the postwar period until 1968, and again from 1987 to 1999. The Albanians had the upper hand during World War Two (under Italian occupation), during the years 1969–87, and, arguably, have it once more since June 1999. As each side has gained the upper hand it has exacted revenge for past wrongs, forgetting that, in choosing innocent members of the 'enemy nation' for punishment, it creates new wrongs to be avenged and thereby perpetuates the cycle.

When the Milošević regime, enjoying, as of July 1992, the trust and support of a mere 23.7 per cent of Serbs,[15] and having abolished the autonomy of both provinces (Kosovo and Vojvodina) in early 1989, intensified the repression of Kosovar Albanians in the early 1990s, Ibrahim Rugova, president of the Democratic League of Kosovë, responded by calling on Albanians to desist from violence, to foreswear a recourse to arms, and to practise passive resistance. Even as Albanians were sacked from their jobs and evicted from their flats – only because they were Albanians – Rugova held fast to this course, offering the Belgrade regime a unique opportunity to change course and institute the rule of law in Kosovo. But the Serbs themselves did not enjoy the rule of law, as was demonstrated in the periodic attacks on and subversions of the independent media in Serbia, for example.[16]

The Belgrade news agency Tanjug, the daily newspaper *Politika,* and Radio-Television Belgrade were key resources in the Milošević regime's efforts to convey its interpretation of events to both a domestic and an international audience. Hence, for example, at the end of December 1995, after the signing of the Dayton Peace Accords, from which any serious discussion of Kosovo had been excluded in advance,[17] Tanjug carried a brief story in which Vojislav Živković, the president of the Kosovo and Metohija provincial committee of the ruling Socialist Party of Serbia, was reported to have declared that the rights enjoyed by Albanians, Turks, and other 'minorities' in Kosovo 'exceeded European and world standards on minority rights.'[18] In fact, however, there was no relaxation in Belgrade's harsh policies vis-à-vis the Albanians of Kosovo.

But the Serbian views of the situation in Kosovo were far from monolithic, much as the Belgrade regime tried to pretend otherwise. In September 1996, for example, local Kosovar Serbs affiliated with the Serbian Resistance Movement joined the Paris-based World Serb Congress in issuing a statement repudiating in advance any agreements which might be concluded by Milošević and castigating his regime for 'a catastrophically-conducted national policy.'[19]

Even as the situation spiralled out of control in the early months of 1998, Serbs remained divided. According to an opinion poll published in the opposition newspaper *Naša borba* on 6 April 1998, 42 per cent of Serbs surveyed wanted to see the Albanians expelled from Kosovo, whether forcibly or peacefully, whereas 27 per cent of Serbs polled thought that the best solution was to extend cultural autonomy to the Albanians of Kosovo. Some 6 per cent preferred to partition the province between Serbs and Albanians, with 3.3 per cent favouring the upgrading of Kosovo to 'republic status' on a par with Serbia and Montenegro. A mere 1.8 per cent of Serbs favoured granting Kosovo the independence sought by the majority of local Albanians.[20] (Such a division of opinion was nothing new. In an interview conducted on the territory of Serbia excluding Kosovo by the Partner Agency, 25–28 July 1995, some 37.1 per cent of Serbs polled had expressed opposition to the Federal Republic's engaging in a war with NATO over Bosnia, whereas 24.4 per cent had endorsed the concept of fighting NATO.[21])

By this point, Miroslav Šolević, once a collaborator of Milošević's but, by now, one of the leaders of the opposition Serbian Resistance Movement, was talking about his fears of 'a possible betrayal of Kosovo by the Šešelj-Milošević red axis', and suggesting that the SRM might preemptively declare a Serbian Republic of Kosovo-Metohija to be headed by Bishop Artemije (Radosavljević) of Raška-Prizren, himself closely associated with the SRM.[22] About the same time, a two-day convention in Belgrade sponsored by the Serbian Orthodox Church closed with the adoption of a declaration holding 'the fanaticism of the ethnic Albanian community' and 'the totalitarian regime imposed by the Serbian authorities' equally responsible for the deepening crisis in Kosovo,[23] while Bishop Artemije mused, 'Had Belgrade acted by offering the Albanians serious talks, even five years ago, we would not [be] in the position [in which] we find ourselves today.'[24]

Be that as it may, Šolević, Artemije, and other prominent Kosovar Serbs, for all of their criticism of the Milošević regime, remained deeply Serbocentric, as confirmed by SRM figure Kosta Bulatović's assertion in 1996 that Radovan Karadžić was the greatest of all Serbs. Moreover, as Thomas Schmid has emphasized, what was especially striking was the deafening silence among Serbian intellectuals and opposition figures concerning the sufferings being inflicted on Kosovo's Albanians.[25]

In any event, Milošević was deaf to all calls for conciliation and even after his October 1998 agreement with US special envoy Richard Holbrooke, in which he promised to pull back his forces from Kosovo and de-escalate, the Yugoslav president continued to escalate. Albeit in the face of repeated provocations by the KLA, the Yugoslav Army high command drew up plans for 'Operation Horseshoe', which it launched on 24 December, with the objective of 'cleansing' the province of most of its Albanians.[26] But even as Belgrade authorities prepared this deadly campaign, which would drive some 20,000 Albanians from their homes in the course of January 1999,[27] the daily newspaper *Politika,* mouthpiece of the Belgrade regime, reminded its readers of the American film, *Wag the Dog,* in which a film director, working on contract with the White House, concocted a fake documentary about an imaginary war in Albania, in order to distract the American public from the sexual escapades of the president.[28]

One of those who dissented from the regime's strategy vis-à-vis Kosovo was General Momčilo Perišić, then Chief-of-Staff of the Yugoslav Army. In October 1998, as Milošević was finalizing plans for 'Operation Horse-shoe', General Perišić delivered a bold speech to a group of political leaders in Gornji Milanovac, warning them that the regime's policies were pushing the country toward war with NATO and that such a war would have serious consequences for the people of the FRY.[29]

Neither Yugoslav President Milošević nor Serbian President Milan Milutinović was impressed by this warning. On the contrary, the speech cost Perišić his job. Then came the massacre of 45 Albanian civilians in the town of Račak on 15 January – a massacre which shocked the world and contributed to the Western resolve to enforce international norms in Kosovo. Under the sponsorship of the Balkan 'contact group', a peace conference was convened at Rambouillet, France, on 6 February. When the conference adjourned for three weeks on 22 February, the FRY representatives returned home swearing that they would never sign any 'ultimatum' drawn up at Rambouillet. Oddly, as AIM correspondent Philip Schwarm reported at the time, although the Serbs were now facing a ticking clock, 'ordinary people in Serbia acted as if they had just won a lottery prize.'[30] A month later, after the Albanians but not the Serbs accepted the compromise formula approved by the mediators at Rambouillet, Serbia found itself at war with NATO.

... Until Great Birnam Wood to High Dunsinane Hill Shall Come...[31]

After the seemingly endless threats issued by NATO's foreign ministers against Milošević during 1998, the aerial campaign launched by NATO on 24

March 1999 seemed almost surprising. For a few weeks the Serbian response was almost unanimous: Serbs donned anti-NATO T-shirts, flocked to anti-NATO rock concerts, and generally rallied to the Belgrade regime. The faculty of the University of Belgrade issued an appeal on 1 April, calling on fellow academics and sympathetic publics around the world 'to raise their voice[s] against [the] criminal NATO aggression on Yugoslavia in their crazy idea to create a new totalitarian order in the world.'[32] Serbs became agitated at reports that NATO air strikes had damaged an Orthodox monastery in Zemun.[33] At the same time, Serbs rejected most Western news reports about Serb violations of the human rights of Albanians and, according to *Washington Post* reporter Michael Dobbs, to the extent that Serbs believed at least some of the reports, they simply did not care.[34] There was a basic consensus among Serbs generally, indeed among both regime supporters and opposition, that Kosovo is Serbian and must remain part of Serbia – a sentiment that is still a factor in post-Milošević Serbia – and that the NATO aerial campaign against the FRY constituted 'criminal aggression'.[35] And throughout all of this, Serbian television blasted NATO as a neo-Nazi alliance, regularly comparing US President Clinton to Hitler.

As the war entered its second month, however, Serbian spirits began to crack. Attendance at the anti-NATO rock concerts shrivelled. State television stopped claiming that NATO aircraft were being shot down one after another. The devastation of oil refineries, bridges, and civilian objects began to drive Serbs to distraction. In the latter half of May, anti-war (anti-regime) protesters took to the streets in Kruševac and Aleksandrovac, defying charges by Serbian Deputy Prime Minister Vojislav Šešelj that their protests were being coordinated with NATO councils. Mass desertions and unrest among garrison forces near the capital prompted authorities to demand that soldiers surrender most of their ammunition; in Kosovo, the breakdown of discipline among Yugoslav Army recruits became so serious that special forces were dispatched to enforce discipline and restore order; and in Pančevo, several hundred people, women being prominently represented among them, demonstrated against the mobilization of reservists.[36] Anti-regime demonstrations spread to Čačak and to towns across southern Serbia, in spite of the best efforts by Yugoslav security forces. In essence, the war allowed the widespread hostility toward the illegitimate regime to percolate to the surface. It was thus a direct line from the anti-regime protests *during* the war to the anti-regime protests and demands for Milošević's resignation (including on the part of Patriarch Pavle of the Serbian Orthodox Church) *after* the war.

On 10 July 1999, after seventy-eight days of bombardment and the firing of 23,000 bombs and missiles against Serbia, and after Yugoslav troops had begun their withdrawal from Kosovo, NATO suspended its bombing campaign. Milošević went on Serbian television that same evening to boast: 'We have shown that we have an invincible army, and I am sure that we have the best army in the world.'[37]

Serbian perceptions of post-campaign Kosovo

A year later, by which time Kosovo seemed, to some observers, to be well on the way to being administratively separated from the rest of Serbia, Milošević was still singing the praises of his military forces which, he said, had proven during the campaign with NATO (in spite of desertions, unrest, and near mutiny)[38] 'that they were invincible'.[39] Characterizing the situation of non-Albanians in Kosovo as 'tragic'[40] while denying that there were *any* mass graves in Kosovo,[41] Belgrade spokespersons continued to hammer at the theme that Kosovo was an inalienable part of Serbia and that the Serbian/Yugoslav army would eventually return to the province to restore Belgrade's sovereignty there.[42]

In spite of all of this bravado on the part of the political establishment, public trust in Milošević plummeted to an all-time low in mid-June 1999, when an opinion poll conducted by the prestigious Institute for Public Opinion Research (in Belgrade) found that only 15 per cent of Yugoslavs (Serbs and Montenegrins) trusted Milošević most – down from 30 per cent before the inception of NATO's aerial campaign in March.[43] More telling was a July 1999 poll conducted among 200 telephone subscribers in Serbia-proper (without Vojvodina or Kosovo), which recorded that 71.5 per cent of respondents said they were 'not satisfied' with the results of Milošević's domestic and foreign policies over the previous decade, with another 5.5 per cent indicating that they were only 'partially satisfied' with Milošević's policies; only 20 per cent claimed to be satisfied with what Milošević had accomplished, and 3 per cent said that they had no opinion.[44] The same survey found that 29 per cent felt that Milošević should resign his office, with 54.6 per cent expressing the conviction that Milošević would not leave office peacefully.[45] In keeping with these results, an August 1999 opinion poll found that only 24 per cent of the electorate favoured the ruling coalition (Milošević and Šešelj), with 33 per cent preferring the opposition Serb Renewal Movement and Alliance for Change. By February 2000, support for the ruling coalition had dwindled to 14.3 per cent, with 55.2 per cent declaring their intention to vote for the opposition; by that point, only 11.8 per cent of Serbs said that Milošević was the politician they trusted most.[46]

In an effort to divert the Serbian public's anger away from Milošević, *Politika* – still Serbia's most influential newspaper[47] – hammered away at themes of injustice against Serbs and Albanian 'terrorism'. A December 1999 article in *Politika* claimed that only Serbs were being arrested and tried for disturbances in Kosovska Mitrovica.[48] Articles published in November 1999 declared that the general situation in Kosovo was worse than it had been before the arrival of UN forces, blamed KFOR and UNMIK for the flight of Serbs from Kosovo, claimed that Serbs sitting in prisons in Kosovo had been falsely accused, and reported that the kidnapping and killing of Serbs were continuing.[49] There was some basis for such reports, to be sure. The New York-based Human Rights Watch reported in August 1999, for example, that more than 164,000 non-Albanians (mostly Serbs) had already fled Kosovo, that Albanian civilians had been burning and looting Serb and Roma property, and that Serb and Roma men had been abducted and beaten, some of them remaining missing at the time the report was filed.[50] *Politika* continued to report that 'Albanian bandits' or 'Šiptar terrorists' were attacking, raping, and killing local Serbs.[51] Individual cases of Serbs being attacked were reported in detail, though no attention was paid to Serb atrocities against Albanians either past or present, while the health of Serbian women and children was said to be seriously threatened.[52] Nor did *Politika* shy from spreading the blame for the plight of Serbs. The policies of the Milošević regime were not to blame for the Serbs' predicament, of course, but exclusively Albanian 'extremists' and their Western benefactors – above all 'the mendacious, corrupt super-dictator Clinton'[53] and the NATO alliance, said by *Politika* to be usurping the UN's authority.[54] Whitehall and Washington were both accused of hiding information about the aerial campaign of spring 1999,[55] even as *Politika* accused the late Croatian President Tudjman of having authorized a transfusion of Croatian arms to the KLA.[56] Montenegro, which had declared itself 'neutral' during NATO's aerial campaign, also increasingly came under attack in the regime's press.

Addressing a congress of the ruling Socialist Party in February 2000, Milošević demanded that the NATO-led peace mission in Kosovo be ended and KFOR troops withdrawn, while denouncing his opposition critics as pro-Western 'colonizers, toadies, and cowards.'[57] Života Cosić, co-chair of the Yugoslav Committee for Cooperation with the UN mission, in a speech delivered on the 185th anniversary of the second Serbian uprising, told his audience that 'the people in Serbia are still fighting for the preservation of the sovereignty and integrity of their state.'[58] Amidst all of this bravado, a group of parliamentary deputies in Belgrade nominated Milošević for the Nobel Peace Prize for 2000.

Solely suffering saves the Serbs?

'Solely solidarity saves the Serbs' – thus, the traditional rallying cry of Serbdom, the quadruple 'S' scrawled on buildings and walls. But such solidarity as the Milošević regime was able to manufacture in the dozen years leading up to the NATO aerial campaign did not save the Serbs from poverty, loss of loved ones, loss of homes, loss of hope, flight from ancestral hearths in Croatia, Bosnia and Herzegovina, Kosovo. Milošević, unlike Lazar, chose an earthly kingdom but went down to defeat, thus sharing Lazar's fate anyway. The suffering which Milošević and his coterie have inflicted on the Serbs and their neighbours cannot save them physically, any more than Lazar's choice of the heavenly kingdom could give him an earthly one. But perhaps Serb sufferings might 'redeem' the Serb side 'in history' as it were, justifying them as the 'real victims'. Some (including Serb nationalists) would argue this position.

Accordingly, the 1999/2000 school year in Serbia began with the reading of a prepared letter from Minister of Education Jovo Todorović in all schools, damning NATO's 'aggression'. Still endeavouring to present themselves as blameless, righteous victims of NATO's warmongering and American hegemonism, Serbian authorities ordered the opening (in December 1999) of a special 'NATO bombing exhibition' at the Yugoslav Aviation Museum. Among the items on display were the wreckage of the F-117A Stealth fighter aircraft brought down by a Yugoslav SAM missile on 27 March and a piece of the bomb which demolished the Chinese embassy in Belgrade.[59]

Among those who rejected the regime's endeavour to capitalize on Serb suffering was Miloš Minić, once SFRY Foreign Minister. For Minić, the route to the rehabilitation of the Serbs lay not through self-righteous posturing, not through blaming everything on 'Albanian bandits', 'super-dictator Clinton', and American hegemonism, not through lamentations about Serb misfortunes, but through a resolute effort to bring guilty parties to justice. 'In the eyes of Kosovo Albanians and the world and European public,' Minić warned in an open letter to Milošević, 'the whole Serb people will be guilty until those who ordered and excecuted war crimes are discovered and tried.'[60] Demanding the immediate resignations of Milošević and other leading figures in the Belgrade regime, Minić demanded to know, who gave the orders to cleanse Kosovo of its Albanian population, calling for respect for the notion of accountability.

What Minić was prescribing was, of course, no less than a restoration of the rule of law and respect for human rights, elements of the liberal project excluded *a priori* from Milošević's formula for arbitrary rule. But Minić's solution is, in fact, the key to Serbia's escaping from the seemingly endless cycle of repression, poverty, media censorship, warfare, and violations of the rights of Serbs and non-Serbs alike, all in the name of The Nation. Properly understood, liberal idealism provides a schematic for moral life, a life based on respect for the humanity of others, on the acknowledgement of others as ends in themselves. In place of dreams of national conquest (the earthly kingdom) or pretensions to divine validation (the heavenly kingdom conjured by the legend of Lazar's choice), liberal idealism offers a programme for the ever closer approximation to the Kingdom of Ends, a state of being defined by Kant as 'a systematic union of rational beings under common objective [moral] laws … to which we can belong as members only if we are scrupulous to live in accordance with maxims of freedom as if they were laws of nature.'[61]

But until October 2000, the Federal Republic of Yugoslavia appeared to be drifting further away from any notion of the rule of law. With the constitutional amendments adopted on 6 July, Milošević, whose term of office was to have expired before the end of 2000, endeavoured to give himself a new lease on presidential life. The Montenegrin government of President Milo Djukanović immediately rejected the amendment and drifted closer toward declaring independence, in spite of the closure of border traffic between Bosnia and Herzegovina and Montenegro, by the Yugoslav Army, in mid-month.[62] As of mid-July, a mere 9 per cent of Montenegrins were said to still trust the Belgrade government.[63] In Kosovo, where mutual resentment between Serbs and Albanians remained at a high fever, Serbian police came under mortar attack in mid-July, in spite of the international presence.[64] The Serbian south was also spinning out of control, with Serbs and Albanians claiming to have been victimized by each other, and with sporadic fighting and casualties.[65]

Through all of this, allegations were hurled back and forth about Serb civilians who were thought to have been kidnapped and either killed or incarcerated in camps run by Kosovar Albanians, or Albanian civilians who were still being held in Serbian prisons.[66] In the context of the deteriorating situation in the country and the general sense that Milošević and his family were losing all touch with reality,[67] the regime's claim that internationally sought Islamic terrorist Osama bin Laden had taken up residence in Kosovo[68] was scarcely believable.

That the nature of people's perceptions of reality (in this case, especially of Kosovo) may contribute to a political culture which is more or, alternatively, less supportive of democratic values is well known. As Francis Fukuyama has noted, '[D]emocratic institutions rest on a healthy society, [and] civil society in turn has precursors and preconditions at the level of culture.'[69] This suggests, further, that democracy, true democracy, must be understood as involving far more than merely holding elections, as various scholars have appropriately emphasized.[70] Leaving aside the problem of illiberal democracies,[71] *liberal democracy* may be understood, as John Rawls has suggested, in terms of 'the idea of a well-ordered society … effectively regulated by a political conception of justice'[72] – a formulation which, on the face of it, would seem to have much in common with Pope Leo XIII's vision, as outlined in *Rerum novarum* (1891). To begin (or continue) the ascent to such a concept, the starting point, as Vernon Bogdanor has noted, is to recognize the ineluctable necessity of transcending national chauvinism[73] – an undertaking for

CHAPTER FOUR

American Perceptions

ROBERT SINGH

Kosovo was essentially an American war. There was relatively little argument within America – either during or after the war – that the US and its NATO allies fought and won a 'just war'. That they did so solely from the air without a single combat casualty assisted this interpretation, marking another watershed in modern warfare and, despite the embarrassing technical errors, confirming the supreme technological and military status of America's armed forces. That achievement, however, failed to resolve long-standing questions about America's international interests, responsibilities and capacities. Like the Gulf War of 1991, Kosovo represented a qualified military success whose political triumph was markedly less clear.

Kosovo was a province that few Americans could place on a map unassisted and it was clearly within the European sphere of influence. Europe, however, again proved itself incapable of resolving its problems. Lacking the military infrastructure necessary to mount a decisive bombing campaign, the war was instead run and largely conducted by Americans: US aircraft flew two-thirds of the strike missions. Virtually all the targets were identified using US intelligence and nearly every precision-guided weapon was launched from American aircraft. When discussions commenced about a land invasion, few critics contested the declaration of US Secretary of State, Madeleine Albright, that America was 'the indispensable nation'. As the new NATO secretary general, George Robertson, observed in August 1999, NATO's European members collectively spent on arms the equivalent of two-thirds of the annual US defence budget but – through duplication and uncoordinated planning – possessed nothing like two-thirds of America's defence capability.

American perceptions of Kosovo were shaped by three factors: a post-Cold War era of unprecedented peace and prosperity; an American public committed to bloodless military victories; and an elite political dissensus of unusual magnitude and intensity. Rarely have such visceral distrust and enmity between the White House and Congress accompanied an American military operation. While opinion polls showed most Americans supporting the war's humanitarian impulses, and the US Senate quickly voted its endorsement of the air war, the more partisan House of Representatives made no official comment on the war until one month after it had begun. Even then, the House failed to endorse, condemn, or stop the war.

Kosovo was thus the subject of the most polarized elite political divisions in America of any post-Vietnam conflict. The reasons for this had as much to do with domestic politics as matters of national security interests. Most significant was the recently concluded and unsuccessful impeachment of President Bill Clinton. The bitter partisanship that had informed events from the disclosure of Clinton's 'inappropriate beha- viour' with Monica Lewinsky in January 1998 to his acquittal by the Senate in February 1999 delayed decisive action by America and fuelled a protracted battle between the president and the Republican 106th Congress over Kosovo. However, these conflicts ultimately had relatively little substantive effect on US involvement in the war. Divisions within the Republican Party left Congress taking up a negative but ineffective role. Fortuitously for NATO, the absence of a clear opposition and compelling alternative narrative helped to consolidate American public opinion behind the war – provided that US ground troops were not employed.

Ultimately, Kosovo's main legacy for America was a revitalized defence establishment able to enforce international police actions subject to sufficient political will. In the latter regard, however, Kosovo reflected and reinforced, rather than resolved, domestic divisions over the shape of America's post-Cold War foreign policy, participation in multilateral organizations, and military preparedness. Whilst confirming American willingness to participate in limited 'humanitarian' interventions, Kosovo highlighted the essentially unilateral nature of American decisions to intervene.

The strategic context

Kosovo marked a watershed in international relations as the US-led NATO military strikes on a sovereign nation state to protect human rights. But for many in America, the 'American century' ended in disturbingly familiar fashion: with US forces deployed in distant countries sorting out the consequences of the genocidal tendencies of undemocratic regimes. Although Theodore Roosevelt had articulated a duty to intervene in a sovereign state's internal affairs to stop 'systematic and long-extended cruelty and oppression' at the beginning of the twentieth century (ostensibly to justify a war curtailing Spanish barbarities in Panama and Cuba but also to secure US interests in those dominions), only a war in which both national security and democratic values are at stake produces a united domestic American response for military intervention.[1] Kosovo was similar to every twentieth-century military conflict in which the US was directly involved, bar the Second World War. Whilst many opinion-formers supported intervention on humanitarian grounds, a significant minority from across the political spectrum saw no security interests at stake in the Balkans.

From the *realpolitik* right, James Baker observed that '[w]e have no dog in this fight' whilst Henry Kissinger argued in February 1999 that:

> The proposed deployment in Kosovo does not deal with any threat to American security as traditionally conceived ... We must take care not to treat a humanitarian foreign policy as a magic recipe for the basic problem of establishing priorities in foreign policy ... I see no need for US ground forces.[2]

Among less conservative figures, Noam Chomsky advised that 'If you can't do no harm, then do nothing' whilst Lee Hamilton, former Democratic chairman of the House International Relations Committee, argued that:

> there are greater threats to our national interests than those posed by the problems of the former Yugoslavia. If we don't put the perpetual crisis there into proper perspective, we will be less able to respond to the real threats to our security and national interests.[3]

In a rare moment of decisiveness, President Clinton rejected such caution. Deliberately echoing critics of 1930s appeasement, he stated on 26 February 1999 that:

> we have a clear national interest in ensuring that Kosovo is where the trouble ends ... and if we don't stop the conflict now, it clearly will spread. And then we will not be able to stop it, except at far greater cost and risk.[4]

However ironic it was that the president who had campaigned for re-election in 1996 by promising to 'build a bridge to the twenty-first century' now proposed doing so by destroying bridges in Europe, Clinton emerged from the war confident that Kosovo had set a new precedent – a 'Clinton Doctrine' – for humanitarian intervention to halt genocide and ethnic cleansing. Yet almost immediately, in July 1999, Secretary Albright qualified the new doctrine by observing that every circumstance was unique and presidential decisions on the use of force must occur on a case-by-case basis. National Security Advisor Sandy Berger added that in cases of genocide the US needed to weigh its national interest in a nation before deciding to employ military power. Even as it was announced, the Clinton Doctrine remained an aspiration, not reality.

That the US eventually took the lead in Kosovo owed much to the post-Cold War environment. With the Cold War's end, no ideological enemy emerged for the US to replace Soviet communism. Islamic fundamental-ism failed to materialize as the global threat that some predicted and the emergence of regional trading blocs did not occasion serious protec-tionist measures.

Moreover, the question of whether, when and how to intervene arose at a time of unprecedented postwar economic buoyancy. The US had not only triumphed over the USSR in the Cold War but had also overcome the challenge to its economic ascendancy recently posed by Japan. In 1989, eight of the ten largest multinationals in the world were Japanese; by 1999, all ten were American. The Dow Jones index leaped from 2000 at the start of the 1990s to 11,000 by 1999. Against routine expectations that the economic bubble was about to burst, Alan Greenspan's shrewd stewardship of the Federal Reserve Board combined high growth, low inflation and falling unemployment. Financially, America could 'afford' a potentially messy foreign entanglement.

The political costs of endangering peace and prosperity were markedly more complex. Although every post-World War Two administration engaged in U-turns on foreign policy of greater or lesser magnitude, most had chartered a course during the Cold War that possessed some coherence and clarity. By contrast, the Clinton foreign policy's guiding principles – beyond homilies to 'enlargement and engagement' – remained obscure. Kosovo witnessed the worst European atrocities since the Second World War; hence it was no surprise that Clinton was asked publicly whether a fundamental principle informed the decision to go to war. His answer was equally predictable: 'If somebody comes after innocent civilians and tries to kill them *en masse* because of their ethnic background or their religion, and it is within our power to stop it, we will stop it.'

Such idealistic rhetoric, in the spirit of Woodrow Wilson and John F. Kennedy, was rather late in arriving in the penultimate year of a two-term presidency mired by a succession of scandals. It also ignored the reality that, besides an idealistic justification, the US must also have clear strategic interests involved and a reasonable assumption that military operations would not yield excessive American casualties. Such pragmatism had seen the US withdraw from a humanitarian mission in Somalia after 18 military deaths in 1994 and the dispatch of only 2100 troops and 57 air transports to help with refugee relief in Rwanda – despite mass genocide – in 1994–6. As one assessment noted: 'Absent a strategic guidepost, Clinton's foreign policy has been broad but shallow; many international initiatives underway but few resources and little time devoted to any because of a lack of priorities.'[5]

No foreign policy issue demonstrated this better than what Warren Christopher, Clinton's first Secretary of State, described as the 'problem from hell': Bosnia. As a candidate, Clinton had criticized President Bush for standing by while human rights were violated in Bosnia. That stance helped to sharpen the partisan differences and marked 1992 as the first presidential election since 1960 when the Democratic candidate adopted a more hawkish foreign policy than his Republican opponent. Once in office, however, and despite periodically tough talk, Congress, the Pentagon, and America's allies opposed strong action and Clinton appeared vacillating, 'like a cork bobbing about on the waves'.[6]

The same two strategic questions again vexed the administration in 1998-9: whether to intervene and how. The 'Vietnam syndrome' continued to condition administration thinking on both. Whether to intervene was problematic not only in terms of legality but also strategically. The US had at least given formal acceptance of international law and conventions in prior conflicts, not least in gaining UN approval for the Gulf War in 1991. In Kosovo, the impossibility of Security Council approval for intervention notwithstanding, the assertion of US power appeared flagrant and disturbing. NATO intervention in the sovereign affairs of another state set a troubling precedent and led to the expression of a virulent anti-American nationalism in Russia, China and Iran not witnessed since the early 1980s. The bombing of the Chinese embassy in Belgrade caused particularly deep diplomatic disquiet.

Although the case to intervene was powerfully advanced by the Department of State and Albright, whose personal history abetted her moral arguments, the question of how to assure an effective resolution of the Serb conflict dominated the Pentagon and National Security Council (NSC). The implementation issue was complicated by questions of whether a war could be won by air power alone or whether a limited ground campaign was necessary. The dangers of intervention turning into a prolonged stalemate were familiar post-Vietnam considerations. What rendered the comparison especially powerful, however, was the notion that NATO forces could vanquish Serb forces by air power alone – a disturbing echo of General Curtis LeMay's advocacy of 'bombing North Vietnam back to the Stone Age'. As Colin Powell observed during the Kosovo campaign, 'the challenge of just using air power is that you leave it in the hands of your adversary to decide when he's been punished enough. So the initiative will remain with President Milošević.'[7]

For the administration, a prospective ground war involved not only the consideration of 'tolerable' military personnel losses and public support for another distant multilateral mission but also strategic considerations – primarily, whether the Pentagon could conduct a war against Serbia without undermining its responsibilities elsewhere and, secondarily, whether NATO aggrandisement would provoke Russia and China. Critics of military involvement were especially concerned by the latter possibility, the military by the former. Under the Pentagon's 1997 Quadrennial Defence Review, the US was supposed to have the capacity to fight two regional wars beginning nearly simultaneously and then overlapping chronologically. War against Serbia could theoretically count as one of these, but the strategy was directed at Iraq and North Korea, based on a fear that both 'rogue states' could cause trouble simultaneously (as occurred in 1994).

Such concerns were compounded by the size of US armed forces, which was one-third smaller than in the 1980s and almost 15 per cent smaller than the Bush administration had envisaged when drawing up its blueprints for the post-Cold War military. As Table 4.1 reveals, the military underwent a massive downsizing after 1991. Simultaneously, however, US forces were severely stretched in their commitments, being deployed from the Persian Gulf through the Western Pacific to the Balkans. As a result of 'doing more with less,' the *leitmotif* of Bush-era planning and Clinton-Gore 'reinventing government' dictats, military readiness (indicated by metrics such as spare parts inventories, condition of major weapons, and personnel shortfalls) was in decline. As one critic noted: 'If readiness deserved a grade of C during the 1970s, an A- in the 1980s, and an A in the early 1990s, it has now declined to perhaps a B/B+.'[8]

Against these cautionary concerns, proponents of intervention argued that the military costs of a limited ground invasion would be politically bearable and would be more so than the costs to NATO credibility – and

Table 4.1 America's downsized defences: 1989 vs. 1999

	1989	1999
Active-duty military personnel	2.2 million	1.4 million
Military bases	495	398
Strategic nuclear warheads	10,563*	7,958
Army		
Main battle tanks	15,600	7,836
Armoured personnel carriers	27,400	17,800
Navy		
Strategic submarines	36	18
Tactical submarines	99	66
Air Force		
Tactical fighter squadrons**	41	52
Long-range combat aircraft	393	206

Notes: *September 1990; **Squadrons contain 12–24 aircraft
Source: International Institute for Strategic Studies (*The Military Balance* 1988/89 and 1998/99)

ethnic Albanians – that might result if the air war was lost. The expansion of NATO had been a cornerstone of Clinton administration strategic thinking that could not easily be abandoned. The admission of Hungary, Poland and the Czech Republic to NATO as it celebrated its fiftieth anniversary – in late April in Washington DC – could not therefore have been more apt or disastrous (depending on the viewpoint). For the American command (as Milošević ultimately recognized), the diplomatic and political stakes were too high to accept anything other than clear military victory. The failure to topple Saddam Hussein in 1991 had loomed over successive administrations and partially eroded the public legitimacy of the Desert Storm operation in America. A repetition was intolerable.

Public opinion

Successive American administrations since Gerald Ford have consistently applied the central 'lesson' of Vietnam: not to deploy ground troops in a conflict where large-scale losses might occur. The exception – the Gulf War of 1991 – was hailed by Bush as ending the 'Vietnam syndrome'. Total US losses were about 400 dead (nearly half from direct enemy action and the remainder from accidents, mines, and 'friendly fire'). The Clinton administration nonetheless continued to operate on the basis that American casualties would not publicly be tolerated.

Part of the explanation for the administration's indecisiveness on the Balkans during 1998 derived from this assumption as much as from Clinton's preoccupation with 'Monicagate'. The picture of the American public's attitudes to international affairs is somewhat more complicated than stereotypes of isolationism suggest, however.

Diplomatic historians have traditionally seen most Americans as lacking interest in or knowledge of foreign affairs, responding emotionally to foreign events, and deferring to elites (especially presidents) in determining foreign policies. Current research challenges this notion, arguing that public opinion is mostly sensible and stable, if not expert. For the most part, the public responds rationally to the information that it receives. From the mid-1970s, most Americans acknowledged the existence of global commitments and the interdependence of America and the rest of the world. Support for military intervention, however, was less reliable post-Vietnam. The public rallies behind a president who monopolizes the dissemination of information in a crisis but may turn against the White House when alternative information sources become available. On this view, the public seldom has a direct impact on specific decisions, but can and does establish a climate of opinion that policy-makers must take into account. According to Shapiro and Page:

A strong aversion to using US troops and a preference for negotiated settlements, arms control, and cooperative relations run through decades of public opinion data. The American public is willing to fight when it perceives a clear threat to US interests but is very reluctant to do so unless there is no alternative.[9]

One of the hallmarks of Clinton's approach to governing was his attentiveness to public opinion. During his first two years as President, however, Clinton was unmotivated by foreign policy. He had promised in 1992 to focus 'like a laser beam' on domestic issues. That his predecessor's enthusiasm for foreign policy had contributed to his defeat had become folklore in the Clinton camp. Moreover, like Carter and Reagan, the former Governor of Arkansas had only limited experience in international affairs. His approach was freewheeling and discursive, not visionary or decisive. The only thing that Clinton would not do in foreign policy was allow somebody else to make the decision. Proponents of intervention within the administration – most notably Albright – acknowledged the lack of public enthusiasm for deploying troops but asserted that it was imperative to assume a leadership role in maintaining a tolerable world order. Opponents, emphasizing that American interests rather than values should govern decisions, derided Clinton for viewing foreign policy as 'social work'.

Clinton's close attention to public opinion posed particular dilemmas on Kosovo. On the one hand, as the Gulf had shown in 1991, once American troops were in action, the public historically closed ranks behind them. On the other, until they were deployed, that endorsement was either absent, uncertain or opposed by – at minimum – a substantial minority of Americans.

The American public's attitudes on Kosovo were sophisticated, complex and divided. Most Americans did not believe that any vital American interests were at stake but also held that US involvement in Kosovo was appropriate. Polls for ABC News in April, May and June 1999 found that narrow majorities (56, 54, and 55 per cent, respectively) believed the US had been right to become militarily involved (with 41, 42, and 41 per cent, respectively, holding intervention to be mistaken). Other surveys found that most Americans supported air strikes against Serbia and US ground involvement in an agreed NATO peacekeeping force.

As Table 4.2 notes, although a majority even supported the use of American ground troops to force a resolution, this disappeared if casualties occurred (and, throughout the conflict, most Americans believed a ground war was inevitable). Nonetheless, in response to a poll for ABC News/Washington Post on 28 April 1999, 65 per cent of those surveyed believed the US would avoid another Vietnam whilst 31 per cent believed it would not.

Table 4.2 American support for US ground forces in Kosovo (April 1999)

Category	Support	Opposition	No opinion
Send in ground troops	57	39	4
• if some casualties	44	50	5
• if 100 casualties	37	57	6
• if 500 casualties	31	62	7
• if 1000 casualties	26	66	7

Question: 'Suppose the bombing does NOT stop Serbia's military action in Kosovo. Would you support or oppose the US and its European allies sending in ground troops to try to end the conflict in Kosovo?'
N = 506.
Source: 8 April 1999, ABC News.

Polls showed throughout the conflict that a narrow majority approved of Clinton's handling of the intervention whereas a sizeable minority (between 30 and 40 per cent) disapproved. A solid majority, however, did not believe the President had said enough to explain America's involvement in Kosovo. Most Americans also doubted that the final peace agreement would bring lasting peace to the region and distrusted Serbia to implement its terms.

The surveys revealed a public that endorsed a limited American military action for humanitarian reasons. That response was a function partly of familiar doubts about the merits of intervention where national interests are not clearly at stake and partly of concerns about the efficacy of ground deployments since Vietnam. Such mixed public reactions strongly contributed to the decision to wage the 15,000-foot bombing campaign to minimize casualties that, together with the initial ruling out of a ground war, arguably prolonged the conflict substantially. These decisions were also, however, a result of discordant political reactions in Washington.

Starr Wars and Kosovo

Politically, Kosovo became a proxy for the conflicts between Clinton and Capitol Hill that increased exponentially with the Republican takeover of Congress in 1995. Displaying the type of disloyalty to the commander-in-chief that they had decried of Democrats during the 1980s, Republican leaders labelled the conflict the 'Clinton–Gore war' (disregarding the participation of eighteen other nations in the air campaign). Some lawmakers even conducted freelance diplomatic missions to Moscow and Belgrade. Political tensions peaked in late April and early May 1999 when a seemingly schizophrenic House voted to require congressional approval for the use of ground troops, deadlocked on a vote authorizing US involvement in the air war despite ongoing missions, yet doubled the emergency supplemental appropriation that Clinton had requested to conduct the war.

During 1998, Clinton had won fifteen of twenty foreign policy and defence votes in the Senate, but only four of thirteen in the House. Nonetheless, Norman Ornstein described the Kosovo vote as 'the most embarrassing moment on the House floor I've witnessed in thirty years of watching Congress, because it came closer to lawmakers undermining the troops in the field than anything I've ever seen.' He argued that 'a lot of actions taken by Congress collectively during the conflict were based less on an assessment of our national security interests, and more on an animosity towards Bill Clinton.'[10] Anthony Cordesman agreed that:

> the US government effectively blundered into (Kosovo), and in the process, it became obvious that the executive branch and the Congress have no clear way to decide whether to go to war, to provide legislative approval of the conflict, or to reach any formal consensus on the scale of military action. It may be that one of the lessons of modern war is that the United States must muddle into war, muddle through it, and muddle out.[11]

Conflict between the two ends of Pennsylvania Avenue was neither new nor surprising. There was never genuine bipartisan support for containment during the Cold War. Rather, presidents from Truman to Johnson enjoyed majority support in Congress, comprising the President's party and a significant bloc of the other party. With the breakdown of support for Johnson in foreign policy in 1966, successive administrations faced hostile sniping of varying degrees of consequence from Capitol Hill. Although he faced a Democratic Congress, Jimmy Carter had confronted fierce Republican attacks over Panama and SALT II. Similarly, both Reagan and Bush encountered attempts by successive Democratic Congresses to enlarge their foreign policy influence, such that accusations of an 'imperial Congress' seeking to 'micromanage' foreign policy became routine. Congressional action on foreign policy, however, typically addressed strategic and structural concerns. Not only did executive–legislative conflict reach unprecedented levels in 1999 but it also encompassed crisis level policy. Both long- and short-term factors account for the intensity.

In the longer term, the two main political parties had become increasingly polarized by the time of Clinton's election victory in 1992. The Republican Party had emerged as a genuinely conservative party. A rump of moderates remained in governors' mansions, the Senate and, to a lesser extent, the House, but the Rockefeller type of Republican familiar to Americans from the 1930s to the 1970s had effectively disappeared from the congressional party. Simultaneously, the erosion of the southern Democrats had left the Democratic Party in Congress more homogeneous than at any point since 1932. The parties remained coalitions, but the result of their diminished intra-party divisions was that inter-party conflict was more frequent, wide-ranging and intense.

For example, under Clinton, Republicans refused to approve the payment of back dues to the UN whilst leaving the US essentially leaderless in the assembly by holding up the nomination of UN Permanent Representative Richard Holbrooke for almost one year. Arms control agreements, such as the Comprehensive Test Ban Treaty, were stalled (and in this case rejected by the Senate in October 1999). Pentagon officials were alarmed at Republican efforts to kill the air force's next generation fighter, the F-22, pass a massive tax cut that analysts held could reduce spending on armed forces by nearly $600 billion over ten years, and close the US Army School of the Americas. Republican leaders also repeatedly blocked Pentagon efforts to close unneeded bases to save money.

Such divisions reflected generational changes as well as battles between defence hawks and budget hawks. With the end of the Cold War and the communist threat, many 'Reagan Republicans' lost their ideological verve. Bush's defeat by Clinton, whose message was directed to domestic affairs, was also a lesson to many. The 'Contract with America', the Grand Old Party (GOP) platform for the 1994 congressional elections, hardly mentioned foreign policy or national security, beyond supporting a national missile defence system. Moreover, those elections heralded a new generation of Republican lawmakers markedly less inclined to an assertive international role. With Newt Gingrich's resignation in 1998 after the disappointing midterm congressional elections, the House leadership was captured by Republicans with a less internationalist bent. Queried about his opposition to funding the IMF, for example, Majority Leader Dick Armey of Texas observed, 'I've been to Europe once – I don't need to go again.'

A second long-term factor was the replacement of the New Deal era by the era of divided government. Clinton's re-election in 1996 made him the first Democratic president to win a second term of office since Franklin D. Roosevelt in 1936. But with the exception of Truman in 1946, Clinton's Democratic predecessors faced Democratic Congresses on entering office and, despite midterm losses, retained undivided party control of the White House and Capitol Hill. However notable Clinton's re-election, arguably of greater significance was the Republicans regaining control of both houses of Congress – the first time that this had occurred since 1928. With marked partisan divisions overlaying the institutional divisions established by the US Constitution, the 'invitation to struggle' for control of foreign policy became virtually an open-ended one inhibiting presidential dominance.

Finally, there was Clinton himself. On the one hand, many Republicans and some within the military continued to harbour grave reservations about the commander-in-chief, personally and politically (ironically, given his role in consolidating the 'Reagan revolution'). Allegations of draft-dodging, Vietnam protest, and drug taking had surrounded Clinton before he entered the White House. The 'gays in the military' debacle of early 1993 confirmed to many sceptics his unfitness to be commander-in-chief. Republican hawks also exploited a public scepticism towards multilateral action under UN auspices, employing the name of Secretary-General Boutros Boutros-Ghali to personify all that was 'un-American' about the UN. Despite his unique constitutional position, Clinton's claim to loyalty was thus more tenuous than that of any post-Second World War president.

On the other side of the equation, however, Clinton pursued the familiar pattern of second-term presidents – either denied or guarding first term victories – in seeking an historic legacy based primarily on foreign policy. Frustrated by his first-term failures (health care, job stimulus, and tax cut packages) and faced by a Republican Congress, Kosovo offered Clinton a relatively rare opportunity for an historic triumph.

Reinforcing (and reflecting) these longer term considerations, the most important short-term factor shaping the Kosovo conflict was the president's impeachment. The Lewinsky affair and the Independent Counsel investigation by Kenneth Starr had dominated 1998. Allegations that Clinton's foreign policy was an imitation of the film *Wag the Dog* plagued the president throughout the year, undermining the political credibility of US military strikes on Afghanistan, Sudan and Iraq. However much these charges lacked evidential support, Clinton's preoccupation with the scandal contributed to the sense of stasis that surrounded administration policy on Kosovo during 1998 and assisted Albright's leading role in intra-administration discussions.

It would be misleading to attribute the intense partisan and institutional skirmishing simply to the impeachment saga. The Cold War's end had prompted some remarkable reversals in political positions on Capitol Hill. Liberal Democrats, for example, who had traditionally been a reliably pacifist and anti-interventionist force in Congress, became among the most forceful proponents of US intervention in Haiti, Somalia and Rwanda. Conversely, Republicans who had defended the Reagan/Bush excursions into Grenada, Libya, Panama and the Gulf now exhibited a marked reluctance to support military intervention abroad (whether under UN guise or not).

Impeachment nonetheless aggravated the partisan and institutional wrangling to levels unseen even during the Iran-Contra scandal of 1986–7, although the consequences were more of delaying rather than determining administration action on Kosovo. The war offered Clinton a chance to put impeachment behind him and regain some of the leadership authority he had forfeited. Democrats were naturally reluctant to dissent from administration policy, whereas Republican Party divisions – ideological, strategic, tactical, and bicameral – were equally significant in tempering concerted resistance and precluding a coherent Republican position. Few in the (predominantly southern) Republican congressional leadership had extensive experience of international affairs. More respected voices, such as Senator Richard Lugar (Republican – Indiana), lacked the institutional influence of others, such as Senator Jesse Helms (Republican – North Carolina), chair of the Senate Foreign Relations Committee, whose approach was driven as much by ideological as diplomatic imperatives. Although Majority Leader Trent Lott had spent three years in the position in the Senate, Dennis Hastert had only become Speaker of the House at the end of 1998. The Republicans therefore possessed no clear or authoritative voice of opposition, much less one commanding widespread public support.

Political outspokenness on Kosovo was tempered further by the forthcoming presidential election. Most aspirant Republican candidates for 2000, including Governor George W. Bush, Elizabeth Dole, John Kasich, Lamar Alexander and Steve Forbes, maintained a studious silence or Clintonian ambiguity over ground forces. The only clear criticisms of intervention came from the doomed candidacies of Pat Buchanan and Dan Quayle, reflecting the isolationist and aggressively unilateralist elements within the Republican coalition, respectively. The only senior Republican to come out unequivocally in favour of ground forces was Senator John McCain of Arizona. A former prisoner of war in Vietnam and independent-minded legislator, McCain's position was consistent and respected within and outside Washington. He was, however, an isolated figure among Republicans.

The legacy of such partisan bitterness continued after the war ended. For example, House Armed Services Committee Chairman Floyd Spence (Republican – South Carolina) sparked uproar on 1 July 1999, when he made a routine motion on the House floor to send the defence authorization bill to a House-Senate conference committee. In doing so, Spence backed an effort by committee Democrats to 'recognize the achievement of goals' by US forces and the Clinton administration in Kosovo. Republican hardliners seized the opportunity to launch another attack on Clinton's handling of the war. Representative Randy 'Duke' Cunningham (Republican – California), for example, termed the legislative commendations of the administration 'sickening'. Although the

House eventually voted for the language, 261–162, most Republicans were opposed.

Legacies

The 'indispensable nation' continues to maintain its global commitments in the face of a populace whose relative insularity is impressive. But America's world role post-Kosovo remains unresolved. Whatever the political, diplomatic and military calculus of decision-makers, America invariably occupies a 'catch-22' position in post-Cold War conflicts. American political and military dominance invariably reinforces the 'CNN effect': international calls for US intervention when 'something needs to be done'. Yet where American reluctance to intervene is frequently condemned around the world as vacillation, US intervention invariably elicits charges of Yankee imperialism. Wanted yet unwanted, America frequently remains damned whether it does or does not intervene militarily.

In this regard, the nascent doctrinal transition from a Cold War deterrence-based use of force to prevent governments from doing bad things outside their borders to a new doctrine of force as a police function compelling governments to do good things within their borders is a highly problematic one. In ruling out the sending of US troops to Indonesia in a peacekeeping effort in September 1999, Defence Secretary Cohen stated that America 'cannot be, and should not be viewed as, the policeman of the world'.[12] Once again, allegations of double standards inevitably arose, but the difficulty of maintaining America's domestic imperative for bloodless victories and its need to maintain UN or NATO coalition unity (dictating restraint on the application of force) with the brutality of civil wars and genocide (demanding rapid resolution) is a constant one resistant to universal prescriptions.

Whether or not the US represents the world's *de facto* police officers, Kosovo revived debates over whether America's armed forces are sufficiently large or properly structured for this role – in addition to being able to wage two major regional wars simultaneously. Kosovo's demands on the US air force were enormous, with that branch committing a greater percentage of its fleet than during either Desert Storm or Vietnam. The overall evaluation of America's state of preparedness for war was nonetheless positive. The technological advantage of American forces was overwhelming over both the Serbs and its NATO allies: US forces supplied 70 per cent of the air assets for the war and possessed the necessary electronic jamming aircraft, precision-guided weapons, stealth technology, and advanced command-and-control systems that the Europeans lacked.

The use by NATO of limited means to seek decisive ends prematurely led senior administration officials to pronounce the end of the 'Powell doctrine' – the notion that the US should use military force only after exhausting all other alternatives and then only decisively and over-whelmingly to achieve clearly defined political objectives. The Serbian military was relatively poorly armed and small – depending on the unit of measure, about one-third to one-tenth the size of the pre-Desert Storm Iraqi forces (and comparable in terms of equipment quality). Moreover, not only was the KLA ground force crucial to eventual Serbian withdrawal, but NATO did not prevail until it tripled its air armada, bombed for many more weeks than originally planned, and talked convincingly about deploying ground forces. That is, the military strategy became increasingly successful as it became increasingly muscular – precisely Powell's point. Hardly surprising, then, that the budget appropriations for defence increased substantially in 2000.

Finally, Kosovo's impact on American domestic politics – and hence its future foreign policy – was marginal. The 2000 election assisted the war's conclusion. It would have been politically suicidal for vice-president Gore to seek the presidency with US ground forces at war in the Balkans. Kosovo reinforced the lesson of 1992, when George Bush won in excess of 80 per cent support from those Americans who placed foreign policy as a priority issue – but only 8 per cent of Americans placed international issues as such. Despite Governor George W. Bush's attempts to make foreign policy a key issue in the presidential election of 2000, most Americans' attentions remained resolutely domestic: jobs, health care, and the merits of tax cuts versus increased social spending.

Kosovo thus confirmed Clinton's historic legacy as the first in a succession of post-1991 domestic policy presidents rather than the author of a new humanitarian militarism in US foreign policy. In fuelling American concern over a potential European decoupling from a US-led NATO (albeit one married to severe doubts over European political will and financial capacities to forge a common foreign and defence policy of consequence), however, the conflict exacerbated tensions within the Western alliance. More importantly, by reviving Russian and Chinese fears of an aggressive American hegemon, the Kosovo war left Clinton's successor confronting an international system – and a divisive domestic and international debate over national missile defence – at least as problematic as the one the former Arkansas governor had inherited.

Conclusion

The obvious contrast with the war which America ended the 1990s was the one that had begun the decade. In the Gulf, a Second World War veteran, former diplomat, and Republican occupied the White House. Bush skilfully constructed and managed a broad international coalition under the UN flag to repel Iraqi forces from Kuwait. Operational control was ceded to generals Powell and Schwarzkopf. Political and military figures conducted a skilled public relations campaign and exuded an air of calm, clear and focused purpose. As a result, Bush's approval ratings in March 1991 reached 91 per cent, but could not secure him a second term. Kosovo, by contrast, was a NATO action led by only the second American president to be impeached, a second-term Democratic baby-boomer who had not only avoided serving in Vietnam but protested against the intervention whilst in England. An avowed domestic policy president 'won' a war but failed to achieve his historic legacy thereby.

Kosovo marked not the beginning of American allegiance to interventionism but the outermost limit, less heralding a new era of US humanitarian intervention than highlighting the profound difficulties of such a course. The domestic political support that intervention won – like that of the president – was broad but shallow. Attempts to demonize Milošević as a Hitler figure foundered, partly through the troubling precedent of Hussain, partly owing to Clinton's inability to sell the rather laboured appeasement analogy and partly through the absence of a domestic American constituency for Kosovo. Just as Cuba had revealed Kennedy's commitment to 'pay any price' and 'bear any burden' in defence of liberty to be rhetorical, so the Kosovo-inspired 'Clinton doctrine' of humanitarian intervention was dead on arrival. For the US, global indispensability remains invariably subject to stringent domestic political limits.

Notes

1. Samuel Huntington, *American Politics: The Promise of Disharmony* (Cambridge MA.: Belknap Press, 1981).
2. Henry Kissinger, 'No US Ground Forces in Kosovo', *Washington Post*, 22 February 1999, p. A15.
3. Lee Hamilton, 'Too Involved in Kosovo', *New York Times*, 1 February 1999, p. A27.
4. White House press release, 26 February 1999.
5. Emily O. Goldman and Larry Berman, 'Engaging the World: First Impressions of the Clinton Foreign Policy Legacy', in Colin Campbell and Bert Rockman (eds), *The Clinton Legacy* (New York: Chatham House Publishers, 2000), p. 252.
6. Elizabeth Drew, *On The Edge: The Clinton Presidency* (New York: Simon & Schuster, 1994), p. 283.
7. Eric Schmitt, 'The Powell Doctrine is Looking Pretty Good Again', *New York Times*, 4 April 1999, p. A5.

8. Michael O'Hanlon, 'Military Dimensions of a Ground War in Kosovo', unpublished paper (1999), p. 5. See also: Ivo H. Daalder and Michael E. O'Hanlon, 'Unlearning the Lessons of Kosovo', *Foreign Policy*, no. 116 (Fall 1999), pp. 128–40.
9. Robert Shapiro and Benjamin Page, 'Foreign Policy and Public Opinion', in David A. Deese (ed.), *The New Politics of American Foreign Policy* (New York: St. Martin's Press, 1994), p. 220.
10. Cited in James Kitfield, 'Kosovo, Lessons Learned', *National Journal*, 24 July 1999, p. 2156.
11. Cited in Kitfield, *ibid.*
12. Cited in Ben MacIntyre, 'Clinton Rules Out Troops for East Timor', *The Times*, 10 September 1999, p. 18.

CHAPTER FIVE

British Perceptions

MICHAEL CLARKE

The Kosovo crisis appears, in retrospect, to mark the critical turning point in post-Cold War European security. It was, in effect, NATO's first meaningful war and an offensive military operation against another European country. The crisis to which it was responding was unambiguously domestic within former Yugoslavia. The action was undertaken without an explicit mandate from the UN, and although NATO maintained its unity throughout the bombing campaign, the whole operation was surrounded by international and domestic controversy. It had the effect of drawing NATO, and the EU, into the security and development of south-eastern Europe and seemed to have created a sea change in European relations between Russia and the NATO powers.[1]

For Britain, as one of the key allies in the political and military coalition against Serbia, the Kosovo crisis also seems to have marked a number of turning points. In one sense, Britain's action was traditional and typical: backing its American ally to the hilt, playing as great a role as it could in the military operation, being quite comfortable in promoting a belligerent strategy to further a humanitarian end; indeed, arguing privately with the US that once begun, such military action must be seen through to its logical conclusion, up to and including an invasion of Kosovo. All of this was within the mainstream of British security thinking both during and after the Cold War. On the other hand, the Kosovo crisis also dramatized a series of structural changes in European defence with which Britain would be less comfortable and which would play to some notable British weaknesses more than its strengths. More immediately, the Kosovo crisis emphasized a certain gap between British ambitions for a new political and military order in European security and its own abilities to live up to them. In the short term, the Kosovo crisis appears to have bolstered a traditional British approach to the future of European security: in the longer term, however, it is likely to emphasize change.

This general ambiguity in the orientation of Britain towards European security and in the effect the Kosovo crisis can be seen to have had on

British security thinking, runs all the way through the analysis. For the sake of clarity, the analysis will be divided into four sections: Britain's national role, the political leadership, domestic politics and public attitudes. In all cases, the apparent clarity of the British position is underscored by some significant ambiguities.

Britain's national role and the Kosovo crisis

As a state actor – one of the diplomatic players in the crisis – Britain's attitude to Kosovo was highly conditioned by the experience of the previous seven years. Britain was fulfiling a traditional role in the Kosovo crisis. Its military intervention in former Yugoslavia began in 1992 with its support for UNPROFOR in the protection of humanitarian aid deliveries. Its role had quickly expanded, however, as also had its frustration at all of the warring parties to the conflict. British forces were probably the most subject to 'mission creep' on the ground throughout the whole UNPROFOR deployment.[2] Although Britain always pursued a 'muscular' form of peace support operation, Britain and France had long opposed the 'lift and strike' policy favoured by the US in Bosnia – since British and French troops were on the ground and hence vulnerable to the backlash of such a policy – but as the crisis finally tipped towards all out war in 1995 Britain threw its weight behind a shift from peace support, to involvement in outright coercion in engineering a military outcome. It took a large part in 'Operation Deliberate Force' and in the formation of a European Rapid Reaction Force to operate on the ground in Bosnia, pushing the Serbian leadership into an accomodation.[3] After the Dayton Agreement of 1995 Britain played a prominent part in the deployments of both IFOR and SFOR, providing the command and framework nation for one of the three multi-national divisions in Bosnia, MND (SW). Britain, therefore, had as big a historical stake as anyone in the stability of Bosnia and an awareness that further crises in former Yugoslavia could destabilize the fragile peace which Dayton had created but which was difficult to maintain in the face of all the inconsistencies of that agreement. British policy-makers also saw President Milošević as both the key to success in the wars of Yugoslav dissolution, as well as the principal problem.

In a secondary sense, too, Britain had a major stake in the politics of the Kosovo crisis. As the security situation in Kosovo deteriorated so NATO's credibility was clearly on the line. The IFOR and SFOR deployments in Bosnia were explicitly not UN forces but were undertaken by NATO on behalf on the UN. The Alliance itself, and the US in particular, had assumed responsibility at least for the security situation in the southern part of former Yugoslavia. In many ways, British policy-makers were uneasy at the prospects of intervention in a province of an independent

European country – the former Yugoslavia. But the Alliance was already implicated in the problem by its presence in Bosnia, through the danger of spill-over from a Kosovo crisis that would unravel the Dayton Agreement, by a general consensus in the Alliance that it could not stand by whilst ethnic cleansing or physical atrocities continued in other parts of former Yugoslavia. Not least, British policy-makers were aware that Western military intervention, although it had been under the auspices of the UN rather than NATO, had a tarnished reputation from the embarrassments of the Bosnian safe areas – in particular Srebrenica and Gorazda – where allied forces had been unable to prevent war crimes being committed almost within their sight. By the time it came to action in Kosovo in March 1999, there was no doubt in official minds that the 'credibility' of the NATO powers was one of the key motivations.[4]

Britain's commitment to NATO is very deep seated and instinctive. Britain was instrumental in its foundation and the alliance had always represented a very cost-effective vehicle for British diplomacy, which proved its worth during the Cold War. In the post–Cold War era Britain was more anxious than anyone else in Europe to demonstrate the continued relevance of the alliance to European security. This was also a very delicate time for the alliance because its first round of enlargement was to be celebrated at the April 1999 Washington Summit with the addition of Poland, Hungary and the Czech Republic. The unity of the alliance (at a time of anniversary and enlargement) and its credibility were therefore regarded as major secondary objectives by British decision-makers in this crisis. Indeed, some critics have argued that these were primary objectives and, in themselves, sufficient to account for the willingness of Britain and the US to use force against Belgrade.[5] This argument, however, overstates the degree of calculation with which British and American policy-makers entered the crisis.

The key to understanding Britain's attitude in the development of the crisis lies in the duality between Britain's new commitments to stability in former Yugoslavia, and in the preservation of the Dayton peace implementation process, and the old commitments Britain was busy redefining in relation to NATO and the alliance's role in Europe. This duality created a powerful pragmatic instinct among key British policy-makers to accept the momentum of events during 1998–9 and follow staunchly the lead of the United States.

What is interesting about Britain's attitude in the development of the crisis is how willingly it acquiesced in the closing down of diplomatic options to the point where NATO had boxed itself into the use of force. For a country that prides itself on its ability to keep all diplomatic options open, and deal in 'a businesslike way' with adversaries the US finds repulsive, Britains seems to have attempted to exert little influence on Washington in the earlier stages of the crisis to avoid self-fulfilling prophecies of enforcement action. In December 1997 NATO foreign ministers had expressed concern about Serbian army and irregular forces operating in Kosovo. This was the first official intervention by the Alliance and expressed appropriate concern. It is now clear that there was evidence of informal British military contingency planning prior to the initiation of NATO contingency planning on 6 May 1998. This was never intended as a prelude to any unilateral military or diplomatic intervention by Britain, however, and was merely to inform and influence the planning process in NATO.[6] A British committee met at the end of 1997 to consider Kosovo and the permanent joint headquarters first considered national contingency planning on 7 April 1998.[7] All planning until summer 1998 was, in any case, concerned with the containment of the Kosovo crisis rather than dealing with it directly. British and NATO planners were particularly concerned about the stability of Macedonia and Albania. In June 1998 Britain had tried to promote a toughly worded resolution in the UN, which would have authorized the use of 'all necessary measures' to enforce its terms under Chapter VII of the UN charter. This resolution was, in the event, never put because of anticipated vetoes from Russia or China, but by the end of June 1998 there was a clear shift, at least in London, to accept the prospect of direct military involvement in the growing Kosovo crisis.[8] The Rubicon was not crossed, however, until the crisis of September/October 1998 with the issuance by the North Atlantic Council of an ACTWARN followed on 1 October by an ACTREQ. On 8 October the North Atlantic Council approved the Operational Plan for air strikes against Serbia and on 13 October approved two ACTORDS for air operations approximately 96 hours afterwards. Having gone to the brink of military action against Milošević, US envoy Richard Holbrooke managed, at the eleventh hour, to secure a diplomatic agreement on 16 October in which Milošević appeared to have backed down and agreed to reduce Serbian military and police forces in Kosovo to 'pre-crisis' levels, agreeing with the OSCE to establish a Kosovo Verification Mission. Though this appeared to be a diplomatic victory, it had the effect of putting NATO's credibility at stake and created in London an expectation that Milošević would not honour the agreement and would continue to defy both the alliance and world opinion. It is now clear that Britain's willingness to take the leading role in the formation of an extraction force in Macedonia was also part of an instinctive understanding that it was necessary to deploy some forces into the theatre of operations in anticipation of the failure of diplomatic efforts.[9] The expectation of conflict brings forward the reality of it and when the Račak massacre occurred on 15 January 1999 the alliance began to gear up for the inevitability of a military response. In truth, there should still have been a good deal of room for diplomatic manoeuvring at this stage, particularly in light of the work of the Kosovo Verification Mission. But American exasperation with Milošević, the problem of NATO credibility, the approach of the Washington summit in April and the knowledge that Milošević was looking to play on NATO disunity, all convinced British policy-makers that the momentum of events was probably now unstoppable.

When the action was finally initiated on 24 March 1999 the British Defence Secretary was clear and robust in its defence. On the day the air campaign was initiated he told MPs 'that action is taken on behalf of all NATO allies with the aim – the clear and, I believe, justified aim – of averting a humanitarian disaster.'[10] Although American statements made it clear that the air operation was in pursuit of a coercive strategy to change the mind of President Milošević, the British view was that the bombing was strictly instrumental – a policy of denial rather than coercion. The military action, said George Robertson, was

> not to bomb common sense or even self-interest into the mind of President Milošević but to reduce the military capability that is being used against a civil population … Our objective here is not to get into his mind. It is to use strategic precision bombing on military targets to reduce his ability to order the kind of ethnic cleansing that we have seen up to now.[11]

Having initiated the operation, Britain maintained its traditional role as a staunch ally of the US, and upholder of NATO action. At a military level, it contributed to every aspect of the operation. The total number of air sorties by NATO during the war was 38,004. Britain contributed 1618 to this total, of which 1008 were strike sorties. This was achieved with a contribution of 48 aircraft by the end of the operation, out of a NATO total of 829. The UK released 1011 weapons, around half of them cluster bombs – generally over Kosovo itself – the remaining split more or less equally between precision guided munitions and gravity bombs.[12] Britain's contribution in some of the air infrastructure tasks was also important, particularly in air-to-air refuelling where its facilities were vital to other nations – no less than 85 per cent of the fuel dispensed by the British tankers went to non-British allied aircraft. Britain was the only one of America's allies that could contribute Cruise missiles to the air operation, and *HMS Splendid* launched 20 Tomahawk Land Attack Missiles (TLAMs) against the total of 218 American TLAMs launched. The British aircraft carrier, *HMS Invincible*, was diverted to the Adriatic for 39 days on its passage through the Mediterranean returning from operations in the Gulf, and contributed combat air patrols to the allied operation. Not least, UK commanders and units formed the core of the KFOR and AFOR troop contributions in Macedonia and Albania respectively, contributing over 10,500 troops and most of their head-quarters.[13] Originally intended as an extraction force to back up the Kosovo Verification Mission, KFOR in Macedonia became the framework for the eventual force that moved into Kosovo in June 1999 while AFOR in Albania dealt primarily with humanitarian problems and played some considerable role in stabilizing Albania during the crisis. At least at the level of military operations, therefore, Britain could be seen to make positive and significant contributions to all aspects of the NATO operation.

Whilst all this represents aspects of continuity in British security thinking, however, it is also clear that this crisis was the precursor to some important changes in Britain's attitude towards its future role and in particular in the transatlantic relationship. Firstly, the involvement in Kosovo was sufficiently different in kind from previous operations in former Yugoslavia to make unavoidable the need to deal with security in the region as a whole. The conclusion of the Stability Pact was recognition of this and emphasizes a politico/economic commitment across the whole region. Secondly, the Kosovo crisis dramatized the ambiguities of US commitments in European security, emphasizing the reluctance of Washington to be drawn further into military deployments in Europe, and its inclination to resort to aerial coercion to achieve its objectives. This poses dilemmas for Britain, as a loyal ally of the US, in those cases where it leaves the US/British position exposed in the eyes of other European allies. In the 'lift and strike' controversy in Bosnia, Britain and France were united in their opposition to the US, although they expressed it in different ways. In the air operations over Iraq in enforcement of the No-Fly Zones, France ostentatiously withdrew from the operation, leaving Britain and the US to maintain an increasingly unpopular military action. Britain has always tried to play a bridging role between the US and Europe in military security matters and the Kosovo crisis – despite its military success – indicates that this will be a much harder role to play in the future.

Thirdly, and partly as a response to this dilemma, Britain has realized the pressing need now for the Europeans to develop some critical military capabilities to lessen the reliance on the US. The ability of all the European allies, including Britain, to interface with US forces in the Kosovo operation was severely questioned as the seventy-eight day bombing campaign continued. The difficulties for the Europeans, particularly in activating rapid ground force deployments in Macedonia and Albania, was both embar-rassing and dangerous to the whole operation. It was no coincidence that the experience of the Kosovo crisis was followed by a strong British commitment to the European Security and Defence Policy (ESDP) project that had been initiated in the Franco-British St Malo Summit at the end of 1998. In particular, Britian committed itself strongly to the 'headline force goals' agreed at the Helsinki European Council in December 1999, to provide the Europeans with a division-sized ground force capable of short-term deployment and sustainable for up to a year, with the associated air and maritime assets.[14] The Kosovo crisis had exposed cruelly for the British the military gap between European allies who were frankly lacklustre in their ability to deploy real assets and their American ally who was becoming increasingly volatile, risk averse and frustrated with the Europeans. For Britain, the old problem of trans-Atlantic burden sharing has revisited them in its starkest form yet: to maintain NATO's political cohesion, the Europeans must be seen tangibly to do more, even at the risk of changing the basis of the alliance; NATO must change to stay the same, and it is in Britain's clear interest to try to engineer the process on this side of the Atlantic.

Given the delicacy and importance of these nuances in the British position it is hardly suprising that there were many ambiguous under-currents in the spectrum of British political opinion, which during the crisis appeared fairly consensual.

The political leadership

On the whole, the political leadership in Britain accepted what it regarded as the inevitable course of action in supporting the bombing campaign against Serbia. In this, there was a general acceptance that two major prerequisites had to be met: the maintenance of allied unity, and the conduct of operations in such a way that allied losses were minimized or eliminated altogether. NATO was going out of area, in a situation of extreme political delicacy, operating, in the words of the NATO Air Commander, 'with the omnipresent mandate of no collateral and no allied loss of life.'[15] The second prerequisite was a key to the first, because it was perceived that any allied losses would severely affect public support for the operation throughout the alliance. It was accepted, from the beginning, that collateral damage would be done on the ground and that there would be civilian casualties of this campaign, no matter how carefully it was prosecuted. But the effect of this on public opinion could not be anticipated.

Within this general acceptance of the inevitable, however, British policy-makers expressed a number of nuances. Whilst the political leadership proclaimed itself to be clear about the objectives – the Prime Minister, Foreign Secretary and the Minister of Defence, were all extremely robust in their defence of the action in support of the humanitarian principles – it is also the case that many officials within the MOD and Foreign Office seemed to have been troubled by the mixed political objectives that were being pursued in the campaign. The military were frankly exasperated and in some cases highly critical of the difficulty of translating mixed political signals into clear military requirements. Certainly, the air campaign stretched resources in such a way to make many of those prosecuting it somewhat critical, and the build up of ground forces in Macedonia and Albania provoked considerable annoyance at the time on the part of commanders who felt they were not being given sufficient guidance for the preparation of their mission.

Three particular issues affected the nuances of the British policy-making elite. The first was that if unity and a strategy of low risk were to be paramount principles of this campaign, then a long haul was more likely than a short, sharp victory. 'Overwhelming force' could not be used because of the imperative political constraints. The USAF air commander in the operation, Lt Gen. Short has since said explicitly that NATO should 'go downtown from the first night so that on the first morning the influential citizens of Belgrade gathered around Milošević would have awakened to significant destruction and get a clear signal from NATO that we were taking the gloves off.'[16] The Chief of the Defence Staff, Sir Charles Guthrie, has made it clear that this was never the British view: '... that was never what we were trying to do and ... that was a step too far for quite a lot of the alliance. We have to think of alliance solidarity.'[17] Many British officials have since expressed their view that whilst they hoped for a short campaign, they did not expect one, unlike most of their US counterparts: in this respect the position was realistic. Secondly, and as a reflection of this, it was always felt in Britain to be foolish for the US explicitly to rule out a ground offensive as part of the operation. There was no doubt in British minds that a ground offensive would be a major undertaking that would have as many unintended as intended consequences. It could not, in any case, be mounted before the end of September at the earliest and then could not be guaranteed success. Nevertheless, the explicit ruling out of a ground offensive deprived the alliance of a key psychological element in its ability to keep the Serbian leadership guessing and gave comfort to Milošević in his – reasonable – view that NATO unity would crack since it lacked the will to force through its policy. Both the Chief of the Defence Staff and the current Minister of Defence, have made it clear that there was deep opposition in Whitehall to ruling out a ground offensive but accepted that British statements supporting the US position at the time had to be made because of the political realities of NATO unity.[18] Thirdly, there was some disquiet, privately expressed, among policy-makers in London regarding the range of targets which were struck during the bombing campaign. At least four different sets of targets were being pursued simultaneously by the NATO air action: the Serbian air defence system, which was never entirely overcome; strategic targets within Serbia and Montenegro which could contribute in the long term to the Serbian war effort; the leadership nodes within Belgrade, and the sources of personal income for some of the leadership around Milošević; and fielded Serbian forces in Kosovo who were engaged in ethnic cleansing. These were all different types of targets and the vicissitudes of the weather, as well as the ambiguities of the political objectives in the campaign, necessitated allied aircraft pursuing all of them simultaneously and switching to particular target sets as and when opportunity arose. British policy-makers had influence over the choice of targets only insofar as it had a role in the North Atlantic Council where general authorization for types of targets was given. But the day-to-day choice of targets was made through the Supreme Commander (SACEUR) to his regional commander in AFSOUTH, Naples. Not even the British Chief of Defence Intelligence knew which precise targets were selected on a given day until after they had been attacked. Although target selection had to be a military decision taken in the light of prevailing circumstances, there was evidence in many leadership circles in London that targeting was failing either to get to grips with Serbian forces in Kosovo, or to convey a sufficiently powerful message to Belgrade of allied intent to impose its will. More to the point, targeting decisions – let alone the targeting errors – were seen to be failing to win the public opinion battle. For this reason London was keen to dispatch the Prime Minister's adviser to NATO headquarters in Brussels to help coordinate the media campaign on the military effectiveness of the operation.

Domestic politics

There were no major, mainstream party political disagreements over the Kosovo crisis during the course of the bombing campaign, or indeed in the lead up to the action from October 1998 to March 1999. Two weeks before the air action began the Prime Minister was clearly in a mood to act decisively. His position demonstrated a sense that the Bosnia experience – perhaps even the appeasement experience – hung over the government's position. 'In Kosovo', he said, 'we will not repeat those early mistakes in Bosnia. We will not allow war to devastate a part of our continent, bringing untold death, suffering and homelessness.'[19] The day before the air action was initiated the Opposition offered 'wholehearted support for the British force who might have to take part in the NATO action.'[20] The only party leader to express even veiled opposition to the action was Alex Salmond of the Scottish National Party, who doubted that air operations would do more than steel the resolve of the target population as German bombing had steeled British morale during the war.[21] He was immediately attacked on all sides for his lack of support in the midst of a military operation in a way that appears to have damaged his party. General support continued throughout the campaign. In April the Opposition made it clear – in a neat but unconscious contradiction of Conservative support for the principles of sovereignty – that, 'We continue to support the Government. We continue to believe that it was right to take action against the regime that has inflicted so much terror on those whom it regards as its own citizens.'[22]

As in other allied countries, the Kosovo operation created some strange undercurrents. Overall opinion on the centre-left tended to be in favour of any action that could prevent ethnic cleansing, and that would deal decisively with an increasingly onerous dictatorship in Belgrade; conservative opinion was more naturally sceptical about wars of intervention in the name of humanitarianism, particularly if it seemed to be failing to get to grips with the human suffering on the ground. This near reversal of normal positions in the event of military action had the effect of dampening political criticisms during the course of the operation, although it also emphasized some powerful undercurrents of unease that it was generally regarded as unwise to vent during the course of the operation. There was bipartisan support for the position that Milošević was now beyond the pale. A similar bipartisanship was evident in the acknowledgement that NATO could not be humiliated now that it had begun decisive action and that the trans-Atlantic relationship must not again be put under the sort of pressure it had experienced in the Bosnia crisis during 1992–5. The only break in this bipartisanship during the course of the operation itself came from the government benches in the stance of Tony Benn and Tam Dalyell who argued that the operation contravened international law,[23] and from idiosyncratic Conservatives who argued that the operation was 'clumsy, wasteful and shambolic' with 'neither clearly defined objectives nor any measurable progress in attaining them'.[24]

A certain unease within Parliament found expression in criticisms of particular issues. The bombing errors that caused loss of life in Serbia, and the relatively inept way in which they were handled by the alliance, provided a major focus for criticisms that, however justified the action, it was clearly not working in the way NATO had intended. There was no party political divide on this question, but individuals in both major parties were outraged that such mistakes should occur, whilst NATO aircraft continued to operate predominantly above 15,000 feet and appeared unwilling to take normal military risks. The second issue that attracted regular criticism was the indecision over the objectives and the relationship between the means and end of the operation. The Liberal Democrats were more inclined to voice this criticism, because it did not compromise the principle that the operation was necessary and right, but capitalized upon the government's discomfort that it was failing to be sufficiently hard-nosed in its objectives.[25] There was little sympathy in the Conservative Party for the overriding fact that Britain was only one member of the alliance and, although not without influence in Washington, was in no position to dictate strategy.

A third issue that attracted criticism on all sides, though particularly among Labour and Liberal Democrat opinion, involved the use of cluster bombs by the RAF. It was grasped very early on that cluster bombs may not have been the right weapon to drop from 15,000 feet against objectives that require precision attacks and which, in any case, were mixed in with civilian facilities. Their anti-armour role was always accompanied by an anti-personnel capacity in that each weapon dispensed almost 150 individual bomblets. It was impossible to use such weapons in a discriminating way except on a traditional battlefield. In addition, the actual, as opposed to predicted, failure rate of cluster bombs was in the order of 5–12 per cent, whereby anything from 4000 to 10,000 bomblets were left unexploded on the ground, which could not but have the effect of creating further civilian casualties and collateral damage. Although the government would not be drawn on its choice of weapons or the targets allocated to RAF aircraft by the NATO planning process, the reported casualties from the use of cluster bombs was a growing theme throughout the campaign and eventually resulted in some angry exchanges between MPs and the Secretary of State for Defence in the Parliamentary Defence Committee.[26]

Fourthly, a number of Conservative and Liberal Democrat commentators focused criticisms on the effect of the Kosovo crisis and the implementation of the government's Strategic Defence Review of 1998. It was argued that the Kosovo crisis had undermined some of the assumptions of the SDR, and that its requirements would knock its delicately poised conclusions off track both in financial terms and in the extra commitments it would imply for the forces. The government replied that far from undermining the SDR, the Kosovo crisis validated the work that was done in that review, though the after-action reports by the National Audit Office, the House of Commons Defence Committee, and even the government's own Lessons of Kosovo Report indicated more equivocal conclusions.[27]

Interestingly, after the completion of the air campaign, Opposition criticism was limited to demands that a full enquiry be held to take 'a close and objective look after the event at the circumstances leading up to the military action'.[28] The Liberal Democrats questioned whether air operations had 'begun at the right tempo, and intensity'.[29] No one seriously questioned whether the operation should have been mounted at all.

Public attitudes

Given that the Kosovo crisis was far away from Britain and did not appear to have any strategic importance beyond the humanitarian principles involved, there was great public curiosity about the campaign but not an enormous amount of public interest at stake in it. But if the public was distanced from the events in Kosovo, it was also assumed to be fairly volatile in its acceptance of allied casualties or collateral damage on the ground, in pursuit of indirect objectives.

Nevertheless, there is some evidence that the media arguments about the campaign were more vociferous, and certainly more volatile, than were revealed in public attitudes. The media occupies a critical interface with domestic public opinion, and hence support, for military operations. Although debate continues over how far the media can shape public opinion – the consensus is that in the longer term it is less powerful than many of its critics normally contend – there is little doubt that the media in Britain are a major channel of communication between government and popular opinion in both directions.[30] This is why the images of NATO bombing errors were regarded by all concerned – and not least by the Serbian leadership – as politically of the highest significance. During the crisis some important and heated debates took place in the media about the role of news management and its effects on public support for military action.[31] Michael Ignatieff even characterized Kosovo as a new breed of 'virtual war' in Western perceptions, risk free and high tech, driven by the realities of the media rather than events in the theatre of operations.[32] Others, however, argued that this was to mistake the style for the substance.[33]

In fact the evidence indicates that the British public made some quite carefully graduated judgements of its own – albeit judgements affected by media images – as to the national interests at stake and the justification for losses in their pursuit. The Kosovo air operation revealed almost from the beginning that the majority of the public in Britain – around 70 per cent – did not expect the air action to succeed on its own, that a ground operation would sooner or later have to be mounted, and believed that there was a significant danger that it would lead to a more generalized conflict in the Balkans.[34] There was, if anything, a weary realism in the British public's view of the crisis. On the wider implications of the operation, there remained the majority of some 52 per cent in favour of pressing ahead in any case although where ground operations were anticipated the degree of opposition to doing so reached levels of around 40 per cent and seems to have forced a number of indeterminate opinions to oppose the operation.[35] As in the case of the original Bosnia operations some seven years previously, the British public displayed shades of opinion that were not averse to domestic casualties in the Balkans, or even to losses among British service personnel.[36] The public's opposition to losses is more when they are perceived to be pointless losses. Thus opinion is subject to some rapid fluctuations where, as in this case, there was not an overwhelming sense that the interests at stake were more than indirect or humanitarian.[37]

What was at stake here was an understanding on the part of the government that the 'CNN effect' was up against the 'body bag effect': one creates the 'something must be done!' syndrome; the other the 'why does it have to be us to do it?' effect.[38] In this, however, the Serbian leadership also adopted a strategy that deliberately tried to maximize the perception that it was a victim. This made the interaction between these two effects difficult to predict and for the government to influence.

In the event, the public's tolerance of the operation was never seriously questioned because NATO did not have to follow through with a dangerous and expensive ground operation and was eventually able to argue that its air campaign had 'done enough' to achieve the desired objective. More to the point, Milošević overplayed his hand as a 'victim' and in the event the Kosovo Albanians and the KLA appeared to be the principal victims. The British government never quite had to balance the 'CNN' and the 'body bag' effects since Milošević could not shake off the mantle of the dictator and the aggressor.[39] Nevertheless, there has been a clear recognition in official circles that this operation was a 'close run thing' and that public support for policies that may seem adventuristic – even in the service of humanitarian principles – cannot be taken for granted.

Notes

1. See, Martin Smith and Ken Aldred, *NATO in South East Europe: Enlargement by Stealth?* (Global Security Studies 1, London: Centre for Defence Studies, 2000).
2. See, Michael Clarke, 'Lessons for the British Military in Bosnia', *Brassey's Defence Yearbook 1994*, (London: Brassey's, 1994).
3. Tim Ripley, *Operation Deliberate Force: The UN and NATO in Bosnia 1995* (Lancaster: Centre for Defence and International Security Studies, 1999), pp. 207–44.
4. Department of Defence (DoD) Report to Congress, *Kosovo/OAF After Action Report,* 31 January 2000, p. 1.
5. Michael MccGwire, 'Why Did We Bomb Belgrade?' *International Affairs,* vol. 76, no. 1 (2000), pp. 39–61.
6. House of Commons Defence Committee, Session 1999–2000 HC 347, *Kosovo, The Lessons,* paras 23–36.
7. *ibid.,* para. 24.
8. *ibid.,* para. 29.
9. *ibid.,* paras 57–8.
10. House of Commons Defence Committee, Session 1998–9, *The Future of NATO: The Washington Summit,* HC 39, *Evidence,* Q.356.
11. *ibid.,* p. 147, Q.375.
12. *Kosovo: Lessons from the Crisis,* Cm 4724, Annex F.
13. National Audit Office, *Kosovo: The Financial Management of Military Operations,* HC 530, 1999–2000, June 2000, pp. 29–36.
14. Presidency Progress Report to the Helsinki European Council, *Strengthening of the Common European Policy on Security and Defence: First Measures on the Military Instruments of Crisis Management and Guidance for Further Work,* 24 November 1999, para. 13.

15. Gen. John Jumper, 'Kosovo Victory – A Commander's Perspective', *Air Power Review*, vol. 2, no. 4 (Winter 1999), p. 5.
16. Quoted by Lord Gilbert, HCDC, Kosovo, *op. cit.*, para 94.
17. HCDC, Kosovo, *op. cit., ibid.,* para. 82.
18. *Ibid.,* paras 74–83.
19. Speech by the Prime Minister, NATO's 50th Anniversary Conference, Royal United Services Institute, 8 March 1999.
20. *HC Debates* 23 March 1999, Col. 163.
21. *Financial Times,* 30 March 1999.
22. *HC Debates*, 19 April 1999, Col. 583.
23. *HC Debates*, 23 March 1999, Col. 169.
24. *HC Debates*, 19 April 1999, Col. 597.
25. *HC Debates,* 19 April 1999, Col. 583.
26. HCDC Session 1999–2000 HC 347, *Evidence*, Q.1214.
27. Cm 4724 *op. cit.,* National Audit Office, *op. cit.*
28. *HC Debates*, 17 June 1999, Col. 594.
29. *HC Debates*, 17 June 1999, Col. 604.
30. See the excellent book by Philip M. Taylor, *War and the Media,* (Manchester: Manchester University Press, 1998).
31. See, for example, John Pilger 'Acts of Murder', *Guardian*, 18 May 1999, and Ian Black, 'Bad News', *Guardian*, 19 May 1999.
32. See, for example, Michael Ignatieff, *Virtual War: Kosovo and Beyond* (London: Chatto & Windus, 2000).
33. Mark Mazower, 'War Seen on Television Still Sheds Blood', *The Times*, 6 April 2000, p. 17.
34. The Gallup Organization, *Poll Releases,* 30 March 1999.
35. *Ibid.*
36. Paul Dixon, 'Britain's "Vietnam Syndrome"? Public Opinion and British Military Intervention from Palestine to Yugoslavia', *Review of International Studies*, vol. 26, no.1 (January 2000), pp. 99–121. *Gallup Political Index*, December 1998.
37. Dixon, *op. cit.*, pp. 119–20. On the specific reactions, and volatility, with regard to casualties in Bosnia, see, *Gallup Political Index*, June 1995.
38. Karin von Hippel and Michael Clarke, 'Something Must Be Done', *The World Today*, vol. 55, no. 3 (March 1999).
39. See Lawrence Freedman, 'Victims and Victors: Reflections on the Kosovo War', *Review of International Studies*, vol. 26, no. 3 (July 2000).

CHAPTER SIX

French Perceptions

RICHARD MCALLISTER

Background

Both long-standing concerns and local, contingent factors played a part in French perceptions of Kosovo's troubles and the war. The former included France's tradition of pro-Serb sympathies; its determination to keep Russia 'on board' as far as possible; its desire to show itself worthy of its UN status and its preoccupation with US dominance within NATO and the need to reform Western defence institutions. The latter included its 'special relations' with the 'moderate Kosovar' leader Ibrahim Rugova – 'francophone et francophile', as *Le Monde* described him.[1]

Irritated by 'premature' German recognition of Croat and Slovene independence, and with the Bosnia experience freshly in mind, French opinion at the outbreak of war was described as 'bewildered', and split between three attitudes:

> (first) seeing in it an example of the unsolvable Balkan puzzle which has already cost us one war ...; (second) casting about to find 'friends' or to scapegoat enemies, from whence [comes] the re-emergence on the one hand of a visceral anti-Americanism and on the other a fear of the return of Germany to international prominence; (third) abhorring war itself and seeking always a negotiated way out, even when one of the parties piled up lies, provocations and a refusal to negotiate.[2]

Yet on the surface, the French *government* behaved throughout the Kosovo war much more like a 'reliable ally', and 'unexceptional Western power', than might have been expected. Much of this chapter will discuss this 'public face' of French conduct, and of French responses to the war and the country's *perceived* role in it. This may well not be the whole story, however; and French public sources themselves (if somewhat after

92

the heat of war) hinted as much. These hints are redolent of France's longer standing preferences and perspectives in the whole Balkan region, which themselves form an important backdrop to French actions and perceptions over Kosovo itself.

The issue raised in some quarters was this: whether beneath the appearance of compliance and co-operation, France had, perhaps for long, been playing its own 'double game' in regard to the former Yugoslavia. For instance, on 2 December 1999, an article in *Le Monde* by O. Remy asked why Serbia had so singled out France to be accused of hatching a 'plot' to assassinate Milošević. French emissary Bernard Kouchner had been described by the Belgrade publication *Politika* as 'Serbophobe': Serb Deputy-Premier Vojislav Šešelj accused France of being a 'tool of the Americans [in pursuit of] nazi objectives in Europe'.[3]

All of this might be thought an understandable reaction to the perceived 'treachery of an old friend'. However, Remy chose the term 'opaque' to characterize Franco-Yugoslav relations, long marked by 'tortuous accusations of espionage': yet also for him, the charge of 'recruiting Serb agents' (to kill Milošević) marked 'a new turning point'. He reminded his readers that France was seen as the 'black sheep' among Western powers and was viewed by many in Bosnia as pro-Serb, and that between 1992 and 1995, French troops had not, as he put it, 'distinguished themselves by moral or political courage': when; in 1995, Chirac had spoken of 'Serb barbarism' and 'saving Srebrenica', that town had promptly fallen.

Remy described 1995–9 as an 'era of suspicion', in which France's attitude was again 'controversial'. Notable ambiguous episodes included the recall of General Bachelet in December 1995 for denouncing the Dayton provisions on the 'reunification' of Sarajevo; the 'Gourmelon affair' of April 1998 (a French officer accused of siding with the Pale Serbs and transmitting documents to Radovan Karadžić); and the Brunel affair of November 1998 – again a French officer, at NATO Brussels HQ, who confessed to handing 'NATO Secret' documents on the bombing plans, to the Serb spy Jovan Milanović.[4] He recalled that Hague Tribunal Judge Louise Arbour had described the French SFOR zone as a 'sanctuary' for Serb war criminals; and asked whether General Bernard Janvier and Chirac's emissary (Prefect) J-Ch Marchiani had promised Ratko Mladić not to pursue Serb 'war criminals'. Whilst France had participated in the 1999 bombing, it had urged caution; and France had been accused in Kosovska Mitrovica of helping Serbia to *divide* Kosovo and of helping Serbia over the Trepca mining enterprises.

Thus, France was both accused by some in the West of being 'pro-Serb'; and attacked by Serbia: 'Something has changed in Franco-Serb relations, but what?' Remy asked: and his answer was telling: 'The problem with France' was that it 'spoke with different voices, it is hard to *decipher* (*décrypter)* the messages … Is it the Élysée and the government; or

Kouchner ... or the *obscure networks, close to business, the secret services, and the pro-Serb lobbies?*

France has a famed penchant for political *scandales* and *affaires* but, even operating a discount, these are useful reminders of murkier corners; such remarks have often enough been made about policy elsewhere, for instance, the *coulisses* of French African policy.[5] These straws in the wind may serve to remind us of where France was 'coming from', as the Kosovo crisis deepened.

Diplomacy (prior to war)

Foreign Minister Hubert Védrine was interviewed on 2 October 1998, after the passage of SCR (Security Council Resolution) 1199. Asked whether another UN Authorisation would be necessary prior to use of force, he replied that that could not be clear until the UN Secretary-General had reported on Serb compliance. He was asked, 'Is that because you wish, at all costs, to include the Russians in the decision-making, if there's military intervention?' His answer linked the need for Security Council unanimity to that of the Contact Group, and to continued Russian accommodation over Bosnia too. He characterized such unanimity as a 'geopolitical imperative for the future'.[6] He also stressed that things did not happen because of 'what America wants': it had been France and Britain that had driven the inclusion of the Chapter VII reference in the SCR, even if 'inside NATO, it is the US and France who are asking for *comprehensive studies covering every scenario'.*

A subtle shift was apparent after talks with Prodi in Italy on 6 October.

> Our shared position of principle ... is that, before any military intervention ... the SC must adopt a Resolution authorising that intervention. But in the specific case of Kosovo, on which a Resolution citing Chapter VII has already been adopted, we must ... keep a very close eye on the humanitarian aspect of the situation ... which can demand very rapid ... implementation of measures to deal with an emergency ...[7]

It later became clear that there had been, from Autumn 1998, close collaboration between France and the UK *in NATO,* including the joint presentation of operational plans and, from 30 January 1999, intelligence sharing.[8] Clearly, hosting Rambouillet and Paris also kept the issue centrally before the French public. Despite qualifications and hesitations, the French government lined up, perhaps more clearly than might have been expected, with NATO and 'the West'. This official alignment contrasted with more worried responses from much of the 'political class'; of a divided and somewhat confused public opinion, and of more general intellectual and media hostility to 'the war', which tended, following a long tradition, to see an 'American plot' behind almost everything.

Three 'special features' of the French 'governmental' situation were of *potential* importance:

1 *division* of executive powers – President/Prime Minister and Cabinet;
2 *cohabitation* of Left and Right;
3 *coalition* of parties within the governmental 'majority'.

In practice, the difficulties arising from the first and second were less serious than from the third: even the last did not greatly affect the conduct of the French government and, indeed, the first two probably helped maintain wide unity at the top; push dissent further to the political fringes and create, at least for a while, a broader basis of public acquiescence, even support, than there might otherwise have been.

The reasons for this are interesting. France was in the midst of its longest *cohabitation* (1997 until, prospectively, 2002) when the war started; also, like other European countries, it was preparing for the June 1999 European elections. *Cohabitation* meant, not presidential dominance in this supremely executive domain of war, but effectively co-decision between President and Prime Minister. Thus, most of the 'opposition' were bound to support the line of 'their' man, the President and most of the 'majority' were bound to support 'their' government. Hence the further result – *open* opposition to the line pursued by the 'co-habitants', who were careful to stress frequently the closeness of their views – was scattered and somewhat ineffective. Such opposition was pushed to the 'margins': on the left, the PCF and the far-Left groups; on the Right, the 'eurosceptic sovereigntists', such as Philippe de Villiers, leader of the Mouvement pour la France, and Charles Pasqua. These two, indeed, sealed a unity deal on 9 April, to present a 'common list' for the European elections. Kosovo was described as 'merely the pretext' for it: nevertheless, their communiqué was *entirely* devoted to the Balkans and to denouncing NATO's role: declaring, in a splendid irony for 'eurosceptics', that 'the EU should not rely on others (NATO; US) for the defence of its interests or the conduct of its policy. Independence is essential for Europe's future and for global balance.'[9] But Jospin's 'there is no alternative' line was widely supported: and the 'anti-' forces tended to lose ground.[10]

The war produced in the French population the same kind of soul-searching, about the country's role and identity, as evident at the time of the Gulf and the Maastricht debates. Many weighty voices either condemned the war or urged caution.[11] The war forced awkward choices: to take exception to NATO and American leadership meant to accept a European defence, an even larger surrender of 'sovereignty', a European defence industry, and higher defence spending.

After Rambouillet, Messrs Védrine and Cook were at pains to stress the 'indivisibility' of the two aspects of the 'agreements': the political package on the 'substantial autonomy' (not independence) of Kosovo; and the military, on the dispatch of an international military force.[12] But as the Paris talks began (15 March), the French press noted that nothing had progressed since Rambouillet, that everything pointed to an impasse, the KLA still not having 'signed up'. It was widely noted that the 'political' package, held to have been all but agreed at Rambouillet, appeared no longer so as the Paris talks started. That day the Kosovars signed up, however, and Védrine was quick to point out that 'the Yugoslav Republic was now on the spot'.[13] (The letter from Hashim Thaqi, head of the Kosovar talks delegation, sent in identical terms to Védrine, Cook and Albright, spoke of Kosovo as the 'ally' of the three. In effect, it sought to line up France with the others and widened the gulf between 'official' France and Belgrade.) Yet for several days, these developments had to take second place in the French media to the fallout from the 'Wise Persons' Report' on the misdeeds of the Santer (EU) Commission.

On 23 March, PM Lionel Jospin made clear before the National Assembly, France's basic stance: 'determined to play its full part' in any 'possible military action'. He added: 'The President of the Republic and the government *share* that determination.' But France agreed neither with the methods nor with the strategic and diplomatic aims of the KLA: 'We no more want a Greater Albania than we want a Greater Serbia.'[14]

Upon the declaration of war, *Le Monde*'s editorial declared this a 'historic turning point', the first time in its history that NATO, dedicated only to the defence of its members, had declared war on a sovereign European state. This it said was comparable neither to Kuwait, nor to Bosnia, which had called for assistance from a position of sovereignty. But NATO had *de bonnes, de très bonnes raisons, pour prendre d'aussi gros risques*. To do nothing at the outset would mean having to intervene yet more forcefully later. Success was not guaranteeed; the raids could give Milošević the pretext for more repression and lead to a ground war against a powerful Serb army. Right-of-centre *Le Point* made the same point: this was the 'first NATO attack against a sovereign state without UN SC agreement'. Left-of-centre *Le Nouvel Observateur* opined 'et pourtant il fallait intervenir'; 'one should not take sudden fright when for once one has chosen firmness'; *but* 'one cannot approve of a war if its result is dramatically contrary to the desired objective'.[15]

Acknowledgement that 'NATO was the only show in town' did not, however, equate to the view that it was ideal. At first criticism was fairly muted; but, especially once the bombing ended, debate resumed over the future shape of and burden sharing within Western defence.

This was, for most of the French defence and foreign policy establishment, part of a long process of argument, persuasion and adaptation. It was a debate that found increasing echoes and resonance in both the UK and Germany. 'Kosovo' in several ways gave a further push to the 'St Malo process' – of alignment of views on defence – with the British. In May 1999 came the joint Franco-German defence declaration at Toulouse. This was not a smooth process, and its success has been much debated over the past year.[16] Some tentative judgments are made in the concluding section of this chapter.

Opinion and perceptions during and after the bombing

Public opinion appeared, perhaps surprisingly, more ready even than the government to make sacrifices/have troops on the ground. It is important to distinguish *levels* of support from the *time profile* of support. The latter was, in the early phases, broadly similar to that in other Western states: after a couple of weeks of the bombing, it was *higher* than at the beginning. Support for air strikes in France was reported as 40 per cent on 27 March; 50 per cent by 7 April; and, significantly, support for use of ground troops (inevitably including French) was put at 68 per cent on 7 April (27 March n/a). This figure was virtually the same as that in the UK (66 per cent, 2 April).[17] French support for *air strikes* was thus below that of the US, UK and Germany, and above only that in Italy, but support for the use of ground forces was highest in France, and in marked contrast to lower support in Germany and the US for ground involvement *than* for air strikes. Much of the French public clearly believed that only a substantial ground presence could come close to achieving stated alliance aims, although they also thought such deployment highly unlikely. Later, of course, disillusion over the bombing set in in France as elsewhere, and support for the air campaign fell further.

There was some variation among polls: an end-March 1999 *Ipsos* poll gave 57 per cent of French pro the NATO air action; 59 per cent pro French *participation* in it. But CSA for *Le Parisien* showed opinion split evenly. Well into April, noted Patrick Jarreau, the 'no alternative' line propounded by Chirac (on 6 April) and Jospin (8 April on TF2) in unison was broadly approved; and parties that took a clear stand against it (PCF, FN) were losing ground, whilst PS, RPR, UDF gained support.[18]

Ipsos' poll of 2–3 April (published in *Le Point*, 10 April: sample size 966) showed increased support/satisfaction levels for both Chirac (+5 per cent to 67 per cent) and Jospin (+8 per cent to 65 per cent) with strong approval for Jospin amongst RPR supporters. Approval levels for 'pro-intervention' parties were up: PS +5 to 58; RPR +2 to 44; UDF +4 to 41); down for the 'anti-war' parties: PCF –3, to 30; FN –4, to 10).[19]

The National Assembly debated Kosovo on 25 March. The debate revealed some strange alignments. It was clear that much of the political class was unpersuaded about the wisdom of NATO's methods and their likely outcome. Thus Georges Sarre of the (left) Mouvement des Citoyens (MDC – Chevènement's party): 'military operations lacking a clear goal ... won't help resolve the crisis'; and François Bayrou, president of the centrist Union pour la Démocratie Française (UDF), worried about the worst outcome – the 'enforced serbianization' of Kosovo.

By contrast, the revolutionary of '1968', now leading Green, Daniel Cohn-Bendit (no less) backed the need for military intervention,[20] in common with Edouard Balladur of the neo-Gaullist Rassemblement pour la République (RPR): 'The response of the international community, and especially of the EU, was both legitimate and desirable.'[21] Again, divisions *within* parties were apparent: the *most* divided electorate, reportedly, was the '*Ecolo*' one (*CSA* for *Le Parisien*) – 'caught between pacifism and the defence of national minorities'.[22] For Philippe Séguin of RPR, in rare agreement with Bayrou, the barely coded message was that the fact that NATO was taking the lead showed how far 'Europe' had yet to evolve in this sphere: as long as that lasted, 'the Americans decide ... we are part of the action, but not at the level (of importance) that we ought to have'. Predictably, the left groupuscules characterized matters very differently: 'a new imperialist infamy', said Arlette Laguiller of *Lutte Ouvrière* (LO). And on the right, for de Villiers and Pasqua, it was a question of French status: the tradition of 'exceptionalism' was being destroyed: Pasqua spoke of the 'obliteration of France' (*l'effacement de la France*) and its alignment with the US; and Bruno Mégret of the Front National – Mouvement National (FN-MN) said Chirac and Jospin were 'at the heel of the Americans ... behaving like puppy-dogs'.

Jospin's intervention, on 26 March, however, might have been written in London or Washington. France had tried in every way to find a political solution. Belgrade had long opposed the legitimate rights of the majority of Kosovars. Thus military action, 'carefully weighed by the President of the Republic and myself', he stressed, was inevitable:

> We are not waging war on the Serb people, whose heroic past in the struggle against nazi oppression we remember ... We will not accept terrorism, nor support those who advocate a 'Greater Albania', but even less the militias who massacre the civilian population ... The strikes can stop at any time, if Milošević agrees to return to the table to conclude the Rambouillet agreements.[23]

Prior to parliamentary questioning of Védrine and (Defence Minister) Richard on 30 March, however, quite widespread disquiet and reservations were apparent among politicians and public alike. The Greens (les Verts) took the line that bombing was 'the lesser evil'; MDC and especially PCF (Parti Communiste Français) viewed it as 'useless and dangerous'.

The PCF was broadly united against any military action:[24] however, its position underwent much twisting and turning as the weeks passed. The Party at the beginning assumed that the French public was hostile, and pitched its message accordingly. It began with Robert Hue's 26 March declaration on RTL, 'Quelle connerie, la guerre!' On the same day, L'Humanité's headline was 'L'OTAN Go Home'. This same day saw the first of two anti-war demonstrations: represented were, for example, the PCF, the CGT, the LO, the LCR (Ligue Communiste Révolutionnaire), Mouvement de la Paix – and, embarrassingly, Serb representatives. The PCF then chose President Chirac's 29 March broadcast to solidify its anti-war position. On 30 March L'Humanité splashed across five columns – 'Five minutes to sell the war'. Claude Cabanes' editorial asked whether 'the White House had pulled the strings' – manoeuvring the European negotiators at Rambouillet in order to 'slam shut the diplomatic door and deliberately to begin the macabre dance of war'. The PCF, still convinced that there was widespread public hostility to war, launched a second 'day of action' on 1 April. It had to take care, however, that this was not again hijacked by pro-Serb groups, and thus laid down precise terms: these included 'an end to the massacres and ethnic cleansing pursued by Milošević'. Again unwelcome allies appeared: in addition to Didier Motchane, Vice-President of MDC, and various Paris Greens, were the 'No to War' representatives of the New Right. Such strange bedfellows meant that the PCF's heart was not in it, and the crowds were smaller too. There was no repeat, despite calls by left non-Communists for another demonstration on 2 June.

By 11 April, Hue, averring that he did not preach any visceral anti-Americanism, said for the first time that he favoured a co-ordinated European defence policy. And half the sales price of L'Humanité's 13 April edition went to aid Kosovar refugees.[25]

Many PS Deputies, at the outbreak of the war, were pinning their faith on the last-minute Russian mediation efforts. Alain Barrau (PS, and President of the Assembly's EU delegation) said that it was 'not unreasonable' to ask whether agreement could not have been reached by 'following up' the Rambouillet agreement: the questions raised by PCF leader Robert Hue were valid. J.-L. Bianco (PS), whilst averring that 'doing nothing would be worse', regretted that Parliament had not been consulted earlier, and that the juridical basis for the air strikes was so vague.

It was clear that views did not split on 'left-right' lines even within parties. The 'moderate' F. Loncle (PS) declared he opposed military action, which would not solve anything and would be 'counterproductive'; views akin to those of Yvette Benayoun-Nakache of the Socialist Left. It was widely reported that the doubts of such influential figures as Paul Quilès, of the National Assembly's Defence Commission, had disturbed the PM's friends much more than the criticisms of the PCF; and that Jospin's people were watching Laurent Fabius 'like hawks'; and on 10

April, *Le Point* spelled out the splits and divisions within the '*la majorité plurielle*'.[26]

On the right, matters were little clearer. The extreme confusion and infighting were part of the wider chaos that had characterized the politics of the right ever since the electoral debacle of 1997. If there was one major fault-line, it united on one side most 'eurosceptic sovereigntists' with the 'anti-war' position, whilst most 'pro-Europeans' – 'federalists' as their opponents called them – backed the 'official' line.

Whilst there was less division in the UDF and DL groupings, the RPR was very split, and important defections were to follow. Most significantly, Philippe Séguin, RPR President and head of its European election list, cancelled at short notice a broadcast scheduled for 7 April (on France Inter), so as not to have to devote all his speaking time to Kosovo, it was said. His position may be gleaned from an interview he gave to *Le Parisien*[27] (9 April), in which, whilst declaring his 'confidence' in President and Prime Minister, he queried the aims of NATO in the war. On 16 April 1999, Séguin resigned from both posts. Although his resignation message did not mention Kosovo specifically as a reason, his disagreement with the presidential/governmental stance over the war had long been clear: and his resignation coincided with US Defence Secretary Cohen's declaration that bombing could go on for 'many, many weeks'. The group's leadership had for such reasons hoped to stifle debate but considerable scepticism was expressed by other deputies including Nicole Catala, Jacques Myard and René Galy-Dejean.

The rest of the RPR, whatever the reservations of some of its leading figures, was *constrained* not least by having 'its' President (Chirac) advocating full participation. This did not stop Charles Pasqua (ex-RPR) making a joint declaration with Russian General Alexander Lebed in France, proclaiming that 'NATO operations in Yugoslavia are not bringing about any solution – neither military, diplomatic, nor political'.[28]

Cohabitation had promoted both unity of view between President and Prime Minister and also a swiftly constructed 'division of labour' between them. In this, the Prime Minister took charge of relations with Parliament directly, summoning leaders of party groups for briefings and meetings at the Matignon; whilst Chirac concentrated on lofty presentations to the French public via the media, following the precedent set by Mitterrand during the Gulf War.[29]

A classic French response was the production of petitions headed up by leading intellectuals and writers. In April there were two in particular, notable because first, they disagreed with each other; second, each included strange bedfellows from right and left; and third, both were 'anti-war' in their sentiments. One called for the end of 'aggression against Serbia'; the other appealed to the 'principles of self-determination' in favour of Kosovo whilst also calling for an immediate end to the bombing.

Thus there was no unity of voice, except against the war in general.

There was a good deal of heart searching in the months following the end of the bombing. Predictably, this concerned both domestic politics, and also trust in NATO and views about the desirable evolution of defence arrangements and institutions.

Védrine, interviewed on 1 September 1999, nonetheless claimed that European and international unity as a whole had been sustained. But a crucial lesson was that Europeans were too dependent on US military assets; and were aware of the value of 'moving towards greater autonomy as regards its foreign policy and defence ...'[30] As we see below, other voices supported this view.

He stressed that the war had aimed 'to restore the rule of law'; that the allies' strategy had been 'a coherent one', coming to 'a positive conclusion': he denied that France had adopted a 'different tone from that of the US and UK', and stressed again the 'no partition or independence' line. 'In the text ... presented by Ahtisaari, it is clearly reaffirmed that Kosovo belongs to the FRY. If we did anything else we could neither end this conflict [n]or guarantee the future.'[31]

French views about military co-ordination and 'Euro-defence'

At the start of the conflict, the immediate problem for France, (still) not a member of the NATO IMC (Integrated Military Command), had been how to dovetail its forces into the operation whilst ostensibly maintaining independent 'control'.

In truth, it had no choice. France took on NATO procedures, whilst claiming that 'operational control' remained with French Army Chief-of-Staff General J-P Kelche. Air, naval and land forces were under direct command of US Admiral James Ellis, C-in-C Allied Forces Southern Europe in Naples. By a fine irony, this was of course the very command that Chirac, in 1997, had argued should go to a 'European' (read French) national. French officers were attached to CAOC (Combined Air Ops Center) Vicenza, preparing and evaluating air strikes. France put at NATO's disposal some 40 varied aircraft, including those aboard the ACC *Foch. Foch* was itself escorted by two frigates, one British. All the French forces took their mission orders from Ellis and reported to him but, by what was described as a 'procedure peculiar to France', also to the COIA (*Centre Opérationnel Interarmées*) located beneath the Paris Defence Ministry, where the French Chief of Staff checked that missions, sorties, conditions of use, objectives and rules of engagement 'conformed to the decisions of the President of the Republic and of the French government' as Jacques Isnard delicately put it.[32]

Two points stand out: first, the (internal) 'dual control' under *cohabitation*: President *and* government, reflecting the classic constitutional ambiguity; second, that France was acknowledging that NATO 'is the only military tool (to hand) today'.[33]

That, however, was only the beginning of the story. A couple of weeks later, François Heisbourg of the Geneva Centre for Security Policy was writing about '*Three Lessons for France*'.[34] He too argued that there should be no succumbing to notions of 'partition' of Kosovo. France drew strategic conclusions from the Kosovo conflict. It 'could only confirm our country's desire to press ahead with European defence', wrote Heisbourg. If the Europeans had wanted to mount a serious land operation in Kosovo, they could have done so only if the Americans had taken the *initiative* or the *leadership* of it. It showed how tightly constrained the Europeans were: this relative weakness sprang less from budgetary constraints than from ill-adapted force profiles still derived from the Cold War. He took up again a theme common in French defence debate – that of 'being more atlanticist today, in order to be more European tomorrow':

> There is a paradox here. For France to play its full part as a pilot-country in the europeanisation of defence, it is vital for her to reintegrate fully into NATO ... First because at present we are in the worst of positions: our soldiers and airmen put themselves at risk for NATO orders over which we have no say at the military level. Secondly, because a NATO in which the Europeans 'hunt together' is one way of stopping the growing American tendency to act unilaterally ...[35]

In the new (global) situation, argued Heisbourg, nuclear weapons mattered far less, but public opinion and adequate channels for national representation – meaning a better defined set of relationships between executive and legislature in the area of external operations – mattered more. This was important if the executive were to sustain legitimacy for 'long-haul' operations such as Kosovo promised to be. For this, constitutional amendment would be needed.

The theme of defence capability and defence institutions was further aired by other French leaders. It was stressed by both Chirac and Jospin at the close of the Cologne European Council (4 June 1999). Here, for instance, is Chirac:

> Lastly, Europe has ... demonstrated a cohesion which, it has to be said, is fairly new. From the launch of the Rambouillet process to the mission by ... Ahtisaari, Europe has shown real solidarity and real political dynamism ... Europe today must provide itself with the *defence capabilities commensurate* with its responsibilities.[36]

The debate about *capabilities* required a parallel debate on defence *institutions*. There were several *post bellum* reflections from government sources. Védrine, interviewed in the October 1999 issue of *La Revue Socialiste*, reiterated that one vital 'lesson' was the urgent need to construct a 'European defence', signalled in the 'St Malo process', reinforced especially in the (French drafted) 'action plan' agreed at the June 1999 Cologne EU Council. The Foreign Minister showed that NATO remained a sensitive spot: '*We* were using NATO, not NATO using us' was the refrain.[37] But reintegration in NATO was not essential, he insisted. He portrayed the protracted debates and consultations inside NATO over strategy as give-and-take among equals, not as US insistence. This was not a view shared by most French commentators; it was contested by, for instance, Guillaume Parmentier, Head of IFRI's US section.[38]

Another reflection, sometimes unhappy in tone, came from the French Defence Ministry.[39] This complained that Operation Allied Force was essentially 'supplemented by a parallel and simultaneous operation managed at both levels by the United States without reference to NATO's Council, which was supposed to monitor the use of force by Alliance countries'.[40] Most opinion in France reverted to concern about US tendencies to unilateralism, and to worrying about how best to counter this. The debate returned time and again to the same issues: how far, and how, to reinforce specifically *European* defence capabilities and arrangements; how far to press instead for reform of NATO. A dominant theme was of the gap between 'real' and 'pretend' authority within NATO: whilst 'pretend' authority lay with the Council, 'real' authority lay with SACEUR (the American Supreme Allied Commander Europe).[41] 'Optimists' in the French policy community saw progress though: for Dumoulin, for instance, the Cologne summit had set forth the *objectives* and that at Helsinki indicated the *method.*[42]

Conclusion

The Kosovo war both reopened some old ideological splits within French politics, and also confirmed some more recent fault-lines. Such 'bipartisanship' as occurred at *governmental* level, owed a good deal to the timing, in the middle of a long *cohabitation.* But the war also revealed the constraints on French freedom of manoeuvre; and showed that, in trying to adapt coherently to the post-1989 world, France still had much 'unfinished business'. It appears, at the time of writing, that France will pursue both the 'St Malo process' and the objective of reforming NATO without breaking it in parallel, but that some uncertain noises will emerge as a result. One 'lesson' of Kosovo in France was that several of the fundamental foreign policy interests of most European states were very similar: the issue was how, in terms of both 'architecture' and capability, to give adequate expression to that near-identity of interests.

Notes

1. *Le Monde*, 31 March 1999, p. 15.
2. M.-F. Allain and A. Garapon (of the Kosovo Committee), *Le Monde*, 31 March 1999, p. 1.
3. 'France-Serbie: Le Mystère', *Le Monde*, 2 December 1999, p. 1.
4. *Le Monde*, 2 December 1999, p. 1.
5. See, for instance, R. Marchal, 'France and Africa: the emergence of essential reforms?' *International Affairs*, vol. 74 , no. 2 (1998), pp. 355–72.
6. French Embassy, London: *Statements* (hereafter SAC), 98/256, p. 8.
7. *Ibid.*, p. 2.
8. *Le Point* 1384, 27 March 1999, p. 80.
9. *Le Monde*, 11–12 April 1999, p. 7.
10. *Ibid.*, p. 13.
11. See, for example, articles by Marie-France Garaud and (Reserve) General Jean Cot, *Le Monde*, 27 March 1999, p. 18.
12. *SAC*, 99/104; *Le Monde*, 7–8 March 1999, p. 2.
13. *Le Monde*, 17 March 1999, p. 4.
14. *Le Monde*, 25 March 1999, p. 4.
15. *Ibid.*, p. 17; *Le Point* 1384, 27 March 1999, pp. 75–80; *Le Nouvel Observateur* 1795, 1–7 April 1999, p. 50.
16. See, for instance, the articles by Heisbourg; Howorth; Andréani; and Parmentier in *Survival*, vol. 42, no. 2 (Summer 2000); and by S. Croft *et al.*: ' "The good ship NATO" in difficult waters?' *International Affairs*, vol. 76, no. 3 (July 2000); A. Dumoulin, 'Les ambitions de l'Europe: d'après Kosovo aux indicateurs de cohérence', *Politique Étrangère*, no. 2 (2000), p. 485ff.
17. *The Economist*, 10 April 1999, p. 25.
18. *Le Monde*, 11–12 April 1999, p. 13.
19. *Le Point*, 10 April 1999; *Le Monde*, 11–12 April 1999, p. 7.
20. Parallels were drawn with '*son ami Joschka Fischer*': *Le Nouvel Observateur* 1795, p. 68.
21. *Le Monde*, 27 March 1999, p. 4.
22. *Le Nouvel Observateur* 1795: 1–7 April 1999: 68. Reporting how much Cohn-Bendit '*gêne les Verts*', the paper recorded a 'Dialogue with a Green':
    'Will you be at the Demo?' – 'Non'.
    'What's your position?' – 'Between Oui-mais and Non-mais.'
    'And Daniel Cohn-Bendit?' – 'Oui-Oui.'
    'Is that a problem for you?' – 'Oui'.
23. *Le Monde*, 27 March 1999, p. 4.
24. Even there, Geneviève Fraysse came out FOR NATO intervention – *Le Nouvel Observateur* 1795, p. 68.
25. *Le Monde*, 22 May 1999, p. 6.
26. Cathérine Pégard in the [right-of-centre] *Le Point* 1385, 3 April 1999, p. 7; 'Les divisions de la jospinie', *Le Point* 1386, 10 April 1999, p. 64.
27. *Le Parisien*, 9 April 1999.
28. *Le Monde*, 30 April 1999, p. 2.
29. Indeed, Chirac's '*redoublement*' was deemed necessary because his first

broadcast had been compared unfavourably to those of Blair and Schroder for lack of 'mobilizing zeal': Cathérine Pégard in *Le Point* 1485, 3 April 1999, p. 7.

30. *SAC*, 99/294.
31. *SAC*, 99/232, p. 15.
32. See J. Isnard in *Le Monde*, 31 March 1999, p. 4.
33. Isnard in *Le Monde*, 31 March 1999, p. 4.
34. *Le Monde*, 15 April 1999, p. 17.
35. F. Heisbourg in *ibid.*
36. *SAC*, 99/230, 4 June 1999.
37. *La Revue Socialiste*, October 1999, pp. 27, 38.
38. In *Survival*, vol. 42, no. 2 (2000), especially pp. 97, 101.
39. 'Les enseignements de Kosovo': *Analyses et Références*, November 1999.
40. G. Parmentier: *Survival*, vol. 42, no. 2 (2000), p. 100.
41. Parmentier, *ibid.*, 104.
42. *Politique Étrangère*, no. 2 (2000), p. 485ff.

CHAPTER SEVEN

German Perceptions

ADRIAN HYDE-PRICE

On 24 March 1999, four German ECR-Tornados took off from their base in Piacenza to participate in NATO's bombing of targets in the rump Yugoslav Federation. This event constituted a significant landmark in the history of the Federal Republic of Germany. For the first time since 1945, German military forces took part in offensive combat missions against a sovereign state. This historic watershed is all the more remarkable because it took place under a 'Red-Green' coalition government and without a clear UN mandate.

German participation in Operation Deliberate Force was a defining moment in the domestic politics of the new Germany and raised a number of important questions about this large and influential country's future role in Europe. The Kosovo war occurred at the very moment when the seat of government moved from its provincial setting on the Rhine to the metropolitan city on the Spree. The 'Berlin Republic', as many commentators noted, was thus 'born in war'. In addition, the tragedy in Kosovo erupted mid-way through the German presidency of the EU and the West European Union (WEU), and its chairmanship of the G8. This thrust the new Red-Green government to the forefront of international diplomacy. The fact that NATO was engaged in an intensive bombing campaign against a sovereign state at the moment when the alliance was planning its celebrations of its fiftieth anniversary also generated considerable reflection in Germany – given that postwar German national identity has been deeply marked by its multilateral *Einbindung* (integration). The Kosovo war thus raised fundamental questions about Germany's self-perception as a 'civilian power', and about the future role of the Berlin Republic in the reshaping of post-Cold War European order.

The background: German security policy in the 1990s

German participation in 'Operation Allied Force' is even more striking given its stance during the Gulf War. The Bonn Government refused to participate in Operation 'Desert Storm' against Iraq in 1991, a position strongly supported by public opinion. This reflected postwar Germany's response to German aggression in the Second World War. Postwar West Germany consciously pursued a policy that was multilateral and defensively orientated. The constitution (*Grundgesetz*), it was argued, limited the role of the Bundeswehr to collective territorial defence within the framework of Article V of the Washington Treaty. This gave rise to a strategic culture that was focused on deterrence not defence, and which reflected the prevalence of pacifist sentiments throughout the population. Not surprisingly, West Germany was often described as a 'civilian power',[1] consciously eschewing great power *Realpolitik* and military power projection in favour of political and economic goals.

The Gulf War represented the first major challenge to the comfortable domestic consensus surrounding German foreign and security policy. The peace movement enjoyed another lease of life, and proved itself a potent political force. White flags were often seen hanging out of windows, and the slogan 'No War for Oil' received a wide echo. The Kohl government distanced itself from these pacifist sentiments, but none-theless argued that the *Grundgesetz* forbade German participation in operation 'Desert Storm'. Instead, Germany provided financial support to the tune of $17 billion. This led to snide comments about Bonn's 'cheque-book diplomacy', and very real policy dilemmas for Germany's political elite. On the one hand, Germany prided itself on its role as a loyal ally of the US and a committed advocate of multilateralism. On the other, it sought to play a role as a civilian power committed to further international peace and co-operation. However, it became increasingly apparent that membership of multilateral organizations involved commit-ments and responsibilities for maintaining international peace which were incompatible with a policy of eschewing 'out-of-area' military operations. It was also clear that Germany's campaign for a permanent seat on the UN Security Council would fail unless it was willing to deploy the Bundeswehr in a wider range of military operations than hitherto envisaged.

In response to these pressures, the Kohl government followed a cautious, long-term strategy designed to gradually build-up public support for participation in 'out-of-area' operations. German troops participated in peacekeeping operations in Cambodia and Somalia; Germans participated in AWAC operations over Bosnia; and the Bundeswehr provided a contingent of troops for IFOR/SFOR. The constitutional obstacles to German military crisis-management were cleared by the Constitutional Court decision of July 1994.

This carefully calibrated strategy of committing troops to morally defensible peacekeeping or peace-support operations proved to be remarkably successful in preparing the ground politically for the Kosovo operation. Of particular significance in this respect was the change in attitude on the political left. Both Social Democrats and Greens started the 1990s as parties strongly marked by pacifist sentiments, and opposed to 'out-of-area' operations. Bosnia provided the learning ground: confronted by mass murder and ethnic cleansing, traditional pacifist ideas proved inadequate. The leading Green 'realo', Joschka Fischer, played a pivotal role on changing attitudes on the German left, declaring in 1995, after a visit to Bosnia, that military force was morally justified in order to stop genocide, and that German troops should participate in such humanitarian intervention.

The decision to participate in the air campaign

The decision by the German government to participate in the NATO operation has effected a sea-change in German domestic politics. It underlined once again that 'the fate of a country is decided in foreign policy rather than, for example, constitutional or social policy.'[2] CDU Chairman Wolfgang Schäuble argued that it brought 'a new seriousness' to the political debate in Germany – not surprisingly, given that issues of war and peace raise fundamental questions for any country.[3]

The Kosovo war constituted a defining moment for the Red-Green coalition. After months of a 'false-start', characterized by policy incoherence, intra-coalition wrangling and bureaucratic rivalries – culminating in the dramatic resignation of Oskar Lafontaine – the government faced its first real test. The coalition responded with unity of purpose that many commentators found surprising, given their previous disarray. Indeed, *Newsweek* declared that the Kosovo war had turned the Government 'from a bunch of bumbling amateurs to a bunch of determined hawks'.[4] The final decision to participate in operation Allied Force took 15 minutes, from the time of Clinton's telephone call to the final 'yes'.[5] The subsequent debate in the Bundestag was remarkable for its lack of controversy, with only the former East German Communist Party, the PDS (Party of Democratic Socialism) opposing the war. Indeed, some critics noted that more controversy surrounded a proposed law against graffiti-artists than the debate on German military action against Yugoslavia. German motivations for participating in the bombing campaign were threefold. First: a strong sense of responsibility towards its NATO allies. For the Red-Green government, the first lesson it learnt from Kosovo was how limited foreign policy options are. Particularly for a country like Germany, whose identity and national role conceptions are intimately bound up with multilateralism, foreign policy is constrained by international commitments to allies and partners. In the case of Kosovo, not to have participated in the NATO action would have fatally undermined the international position of the new Government, precipitating a major domestic political crisis.

Second, there was a strong sense of moral and political responsibility towards the humanitarian suffering in Kosovo. Such normative considerations are often overlooked in foreign policy analysis but they can have a very real political force. This is certainly true in the case of Germany, given the legacy of Hitlerism and the Holocaust. Postwar German identity has been constructed around a rejection of its totalitarian past. Confronted by pictures of appalling human suffering, ethnic cleansing and Serbian atrocities, many Germans felt that 'something must be done'. The brutality of Serbian military and police units was widely equated with the ruthlessness of German military and special policy units in the Second World War, and this time most Germans wanted to be on the 'right side'. Hence the broad support for the use of military force to stop ethnic cleansing and widespread human rights violations in Kosovo.

A third factor, less openly discussed, but no less important, was concern about a new wave of asylum seekers and refugees. This has been a sensitive political issue in Germany – as it has been throughout Western Europe, and has exposed the less attractive side of German politics, not least because it has fuelled the rise of racist and neo-fascist groups. Serbian ethnic cleansing in Kosovo threatened to precipitate large-scale migration into Western Europe, which the German Government wished to prevent. As Rudolf Scharping commented, the ghastly events in Kosovo pose a fundamental question: 'do we deal with force, murder and expulsion by tackling these problems at their source? Or do we watch passively and wait until their consequences come home to us?'[6]

The mandate issue

What is particularly remarkable about the German government's decision to commit the Bundeswehr to its first active combat missions is its dubious legal status under international law.[7] It had long been assumed that Bundestag approval for military crisis management would require a clear UN or OSCE (Organization for Security and Co-operation in Europe) mandate. The lack of such a mandate was criticized by many on both the left and the right. For a peace researcher like Ernst-Otto Czempiel, the lack of a UN mandate was the rubicon that both Germany and NATO crossed in Kosovo. He argued that it represented an attempt by the US and NATO to brand certain states as *Schurkenstaat* ('rogue state'), and to establish NATO as the dominant element in the European security order, rather than the EU or the OSCE.[8] On the other end of the political spectrum, former Cold War warriors like Alfred Dreggar, or Realpolitikers like Helmut Schmidt were also critical of the lack of a UN mandate.

On the other hand, other opinion formers on both left and right took a different stance. Karl-Heinz Kamp of the Konrad Adenauer Foundation (which is close to the CDU) argued that the mandate issue needed to be placed in its historical and political context. If the UN Charter was taken in isolation, then NATO's military action was illegal and the sufferings of the Kosovo Albanians a question of 'domestic affairs' of Yugoslavia. However, he argued that this question should be seen in the context of efforts to the reform the UN system and to make international law more relevant to the contemporary international security agenda. A choice needed to be made between a strict interpretation of the UN Charter and the duty to prevent human suffering. When a state violates its fundamental duty towards its citizens, namely to defend the life and freedoms of its citizens, it loses its right to sovereignty. Military measures aimed at preventing severe human rights violations are therefore fully in accord with the humanitarian norms of the UN, even in the absence of a Security Council resolution. In addition, Kamp argued, the UN Charter is not the only source of international law. The 1951 UN Convention on Genocide provided a legal basis for the NATO action.[9] Similarly, the SPD Minister President of Saarland, Reinhard Klimmt, argued that although NATO's intervention lacked clear legitimation under international law, it did accord to the 'spirit of international law'.[10]

Not surprisingly, Defence Minister Scharping also argued that it was wrong to assume that the UN Security Council was the only source of international law. Scharping argued that 'the UN Charter, the UN Security Council resolution on Kosovo last year, and the right to *Nothilfe* (emergency help) together provide a clear basis under international law.' At the same time, he argued, NATO had no desire to act as a worldwide intervention force. Rather, its concern was with security and stability in the Euro-Atlantic area.[11] Similarly, Karl-Heinz Kamp rejected suggestions that NATO's 'self-mandating' may be misused in order to provide NATO with a new role as self-appointed 'world policeman'. As an alliance of nineteen democratic nations, based on consensual decision-making procedures, he argued, NATO was not politically able to act in this way. The evidence for this was 'three years wavering and 200,000 dead in Bosnia.'[12]

Humanitarian intervention and the lessons of Srebenica

Closely bound up with the mandate issue was the question of humanitarian intervention. Does the international community have a right to humanitarian intervention? This question has proven particularly divisive for the German left – particularly since the shocking events in Srebenica.[13] The dilemma that Srebenica spotlighted for the left was whether the old rally cry *'nie wieder'* meant *'nie wieder Krieg'* ('never again war') or *'nie wieder Auschwitz'* ('never again Auschwitz')?[14] The problem for convinced pacifists like Christian Ströbele who rejected military intervention against aggression on principle is that 'they must in the end also reject and condemn the war against Hitler'.[15] Very few Germans have adopted this extreme pacifist position and, consequently, the moral dilemmas posed by military crisis management have faced most politically engaged Germans. These dilemmas have split both left and right, and generated new coalitions between erstwhile opponents – for example, between Egon Bahr, one of the leading architects of *Ostpolitik*, and conservatives like Alfred Dreggar and Karl Lamers, all of whom opposed military intervention.[16]

Domestic political consequences

The Kosovo tragedy had a major impact on German domestic politics and constituted the first real *Bewährungsprobe* (test) of the new Government.[17] It precipitated a reshaping of German domestic politics and provided the new generation of political leaders (the 'sixty-eighters') with their first major crisis.[18] Unlike the older generation, the 'sixty-eighters' have no direct experience of the Second World War or its immediate aftermath. They have grown up in a Euro-Atlantic 'security community' characterized by multilateral co-operation, welfare states and democracy. Not surprisingly, therefore, their response to the Kosovo war was markedly different from the generation of Helmut Kohl, Alfred Dreggar and Helmut Schmidt.

The first important domestic political consequence of the Kosovo war was to improve the political reputation of the Chancellor, Gerhard Schröder. During the election campaign, Schröder was admired for his Italian designer clothes and televisual skills. Critics, however, pointed to the lack of substance and content behind his sound-bites. The responsibility of leading his country into its first military campaign since 1945 demonstrated his leadership qualities and his ability to take tough decisions.

Similarly, Kosovo boosted the political capital of Defence Minister Rudolf Scharping. Previously seen as a rather dull and uncharismatic figure, his competent and unruffled performance during the campaign won him growing respect from colleagues and former critics. Last but not least, the Kosovo tragedy has witnessed the final transformation of the Green Foreign Minister, Joschka Fischer, from 1960s radical to a bulwark of *Westbindung* (Western integration) and continuity in German foreign policy. Before the September 1998 election, Schröder commented that Fischer would soon become the 'darling' of the international community. Fischer's energetic and constructive diplomacy during the course of the war certainly won him many plaudits and underlined his statesmanlike qualities.

While the Cabinet itself, by and large, remained united behind the bombing campaign, the war seemed at times to present a serious threat to the very survival of the Red-Green coalition. Both parties were closely associated with the 1980s peace movement, and contained sizeable pacifist elements. The SPD held a Special Party Conference (*Sonderparteitag*) on 12 April 1999 under the slogan of 'responsibility' (*Verantwortung*). Schröder give an impassioned speech, full of conviction and determination, in which he stressed Germany's *Verantwortung,* both to its NATO allies, and towards the victims of ethnic cleansing in Kosovo. At the same time, he stressed that pacifists had a home in the SPD. By the end of the conference, the majority of the party had united behind the bombing campaign. Opinion polls also showed solid and continuing support among SPD voters for NATO's intervention. However, the issue of deploying ground troops in combat roles remained highly controversial within the party and any decision to commit Bundeswehr troops to such an operation would undoubtedly have opened up deep fissures among Social Democrats.

The Greens found the Kosovo war much more problematic and much more divisive – not surprisingly for a party whose election programme contained an unequivocal rejection of using military means to enforce peace.[19] Most Green Bundestag deputies and a majority of Party members reluctantly supported the line of their Foreign Minister, but opponents of military intervention grew each week the bombing continued. Given their origins as an 'eco-pax' (ecological and peace) party, this is not surprising.[20] Despite the impassioned arguments of Fischer and other 'realos', the Greens have not found it easy to come to terms with the political and ethical dilemmas of military intervention. Opinion polls also showed a steady fall in support for the bombing campaign among Green voters as the war continued. While there was no major haemorrhage of Party members, there were mounting criticisms of NATO's targeting of Yugoslavia's economic, communications and transport infrastructure outside of Kosovo itself. The issue of a combat deployment of ground troops was even more divisive. If NATO had embarked on a ground campaign with German participation, the result might well have been a major split in the Greens and the collapse of the coalition. Although this crisis was avoided, the support of the Red-Green government for a NATO bombing campaign has left many Greens uncertain of their fundamental principles and values.

The 'loyal' opposition: CDU, CSU and FDP

With the exception of the PDS, all the opposition parties in the Bundestag gave their critical support to the NATO operation. The CDU, CSU and FDP all expressed broad support for the government's policy, although all three parties made clear their opposition to the combat deployment of ground troops. The CDU's support for the government's policy was not surprising. As Wolfgang Schäuble noted, as a political party that had long accepted the inescapable need to use military force in the last instance, the CDU had had fewer problems with the Kosovo intervention than the SPD, the Greens and parts of the FDP. However, Schäuble also warned against an exaggerated moralistic rhetoric, and stressed the need for new political and diplomatic initiatives involving the UN and Russia.[21] This approach was endorsed by the CDU Party Conference in Erfurt (26/27 April 1999), as was the Party's opposition to sending ground troops to fight in Kosovo.

CSU-Chairman Stoibler also supported the NATO bombing campaign but stressed his opposition to the use of ground troops, particularly given the severe implications of this for relations with Russia.[22] Some in the CSU and on the right of the CDU sought to make political capital from Kosovo by drawing a parallel between the expulsion of Germans from the east after 1945 and ethnic cleansing in Kosovo. Such views were also common in the letters pages of the conservative press, but did not find expression in the statements of CSU or CDU leaders.

Finally, the FDP has underlined their opposition to the use of ground troops as 'militarily risky and politically dangerous'. They also called on the government actively to push for the implementation of the Rambouillet peace plan, and for the Green and SPD critics of the bombing campaign to keep quiet, rather than giving support to Milošević.[23]

The PDS – between pacifism and anti-imperialism

The Kosovo crisis accelerated the reconstitution of the German left, a process that had been underway since the entry of the Greens into the Bundestag in 1982, and that received a further impetus by the electoral successes of the PDS. As the Social Democrats under Gerhard Schröder have moved to the centre and the Greens have abandoned much of their past radicalism, the PDS has sought to position itself as the only 'left opposition' in Germany.

The PDS was the only party in the Bundestag to oppose the NATO operation. They argued that the 'war' against Yugoslavia violated international law, and was an act of aggression by NATO, led by the US, against a sovereign state. Given their early reticence to condemn Serbian ethnic cleansing, and their support for national liberation struggles, their pacifist stance was not entirely credible. Their aim, however, was to strengthen their profile on the radical left of the party spectrum and to establish a political basis in western Germany amongst anti-war activists. As part of the PDS effort to construct an international network of left parties against NATO's 'aggression', the PDS Bundestag leader, Gregor Gysi, travelled to Belgrade on 13 April to meet Serbian political and religious leaders.[24] His handshake with Milošević led to subsequent taunts by Chancellor Schröder that the PDS had become the 'fifth column' of Serbia.

However critical Bonn politicians may have been of the PDS's anti-war stance, it certainly received a positive echo in Eastern Germany. Indeed, the Kosovo conflict has starkly exposed the deep divisions between the two parts of Germany. While 59 per cent of west Germans believed that NATO's bombs were serving humanitarian ends, only 38 per cent of easterners were of this view. In the west, 70 per cent supported the participation of the Bundeswehr in the Kosovo operation. In the east, only 41per cent were in favour, whereas 48 per cent were against.[25] Finally, as early as mid-April nearly two-thirds of East Germans wanted to see an immediate end to the air strikes.[26] The differences between the two parts of Germany reflected the legacy of two different socialization processes, and underlined what a long-term process it is to integrate East Germans into the political culture of the *Bundesrepublik*.

German diplomacy – the Fischer Peace Plan

In their coalition agreement, the Greens and Social Democrats had declared that 'German foreign policy is peace policy' (*Friedenspolitik*). Yet when faced with ethnic cleansing and atrocities in Kosovo, this 'peace policy' had been redefined to include air strikes. The dilemmas involved in this policy shift were reflected in the twin-track strategy adopted by the Red-Green Government. On the one hand, participation in the bombing campaign. On the other, intensive diplomatic efforts to find a solution to the crisis. A high-profile diplomatic role for the government also served a vital domestic political purpose, because only by demonstrating an active commitment to finding a political solution to the Kosovo tragedy could the government hope to contain opposition to the bombing campaign among sceptical Greens and Social Democrats.

Given its presidency of the EU, Germany played a pivotal role in negotiations to find a solution to the Kosovo war and to bring peace to the wider region. In early April, Foreign Minister Fischer announced a peace plan, which, it was hoped, would provide the basis for a new international diplomatic consensus. The German EU Presidency also took the initiative in developing a 'Stability Pact for Southeast Europe', along with more focused economic and financial aid for Albania and Macedonia.

Throughout the bombing campaign, a key concern of German diplomacy was to involve both the UN and the Russians in the search for an end to the war. In his capacity as President of the European Council, Chancellor Schröder invited the UN Secretary-General Kofi Annan to attend the informal EU Summit in Brussels on 14 April. The future role of the EU in a peace settlement for the Balkans was also extensively discussed during Annan's three-day visit to Germany. As regards Russia, the German government recognized that UN involvement in Kosovo would only be possible if the Russians could be brought 'back in the boat'. Moreover, they did not want the Kosovo war to undermine a co-operative security relationship with Moscow, which remained a key aim of German foreign policy. Consequently a key theme of German diplomacy was to engage Russia in the search for a peace settlement. All through April and May, a steady stream of German diplomats and political leaders travelled to Moscow to encourage the Russian government to play a positive role in the conflict. The German government also encouraged the Americans to intensify their dialogue with Moscow. Finally, the German government sought to use the G8 as a forum for building a political agreement with Russia. The success of this strategy was evident from the positive outcome of the G8 summit in Bonn on 5 May, at which a set of 'principles' were agreed for ending the conflict.

In the medium to long term, the Kosovo war is likely to have a significant impact on Germany's relations with its key Western allies. Bundeswehr participation in the Kosovo operation demonstrates that united Germany has overcome its earlier reservations and is now politically willing and constitutionally able to join its allies in military crisis management. This will certainly make Germany an even more important partner for the US, particularly in the context of NATO's New Strategic Concept. Yet at the same time, West European unease with the quality and direction of US 'leadership', coupled with a belief that the Europeans must do more for their own defence, has given renewed impetus to European defence and security co-operation. During the German EU Presidency, historic decisions were reached at the Cologne European Council meeting (3–4 June 1999) concerning the building of a European Security and Defence Policy (ESDP) within the framework of the EU's Common Foreign and Security Policy (CFSP). This initiative was followed up at the Helsinki EU summit (10–11 December 1999) which set a 'headline goal' whereby EU member states would, by 2003, generate military forces capable of carrying out the full range of Petersberg tasks, 'including the most demanding', in operations up to corps level.[27]

If the EU succeeds in meeting its ambitious targets and forges an effective instrument for collective military crisis management, this will transform the face of the European security order. It will also have implications for transatlantic relations, the future of NATO, and EU-

Russian relations.[28] At the heart of these interlocking processes of change will be Germany, a country that plays a key role in both NATO and the EU, and which enjoys a close alliance with the US and a strategic partnership with Russia. Thus the lessons that German policy-makers draw from the experience of the Kosovo war will have an important influence on the reshaping of European order.[29]

War and the Berlin Republic

On 19 April 1999, the Bundestag held its first plenary session in the redesigned and newly renovated Reichstag building in Berlin. The event marked another historical moment in the history of the Federal Republic, as the seat of government moved from provincial Bonn to the metropolitan city of Berlin.[30] The start of a new era in German history was an event heavy with symbolism, given Berlin's troubled history, and lingering concerns that the Berlin Republic might be more assertive and less Western-orientated than the Bonn Republic. In this context, it was particularly significant that inauguration of the Reichstag building as the official seat of the Bundestag took place at a time when German troops were, for the first time since 1945, engaged in offensive military actions against a sovereign state. As the headline in the *Tageszeitung* from 20 April ominously declared, *Im Krieg beginnt die 'Berliner Republik'* ('In war begins the "Berlin Republic"').

Bundeswehr participation in NATO's military intervention has raised serious questions about the role of Germany in the reshaping of European order and the future direction of German foreign policy. In particular, it poses a question mark over Germany's status as a 'civilian power'. In his book *Risiko Deutschland*, published in 1995, Joschka Fischer argued that it was certainly not in Germany's national interest to give up the dominant civilian character of its politics, and adopt a more assertive foreign policy.[31] Today, however, Joschka Fischer is a Foreign Minister in a coalition government that has deployed German military forces in combat missions abroad.

This demonstrates the ambiguities and dilemmas at the heart of postwar German foreign policy. On the one hand, the Federal Republic has been committed to shaping a European peace order in which military force and traditional *Realpolitik* have no part. On the other, it is aware of the international responsibilities that membership of the Euro-Atlantic community entails. Similarly, Germany, as a democratic *Rechtsstaat*, has striven to strengthen international law. On the other hand, it has argued that human rights cannot be seen as a matter of the internal affairs of sovereign states – notably in the context of the OSCE.

The dilemmas facing contemporary Germany reflect broader changes in the international system since the end of the Cold War. As Wilfred von Bredow, Professor of Politics at the University of Marburg, has argued, 'international politics has suddenly become considerably more ambivalent'.[32] New conflicts have emerged that are not amenable to simple solutions or black-and-white analyses. These dilemmas have resulted in a hybrid war in Kosovo, with a partisan-type war on the ground, fuelled by ethnic nationalism, and a high-tech war fought from the air by an alliance committed to post-national normative values. Faced with a complex and ambiguous international system, von Bredow argues, the danger exists of a political paralysis. Consequently, he argues, the changed international context places greater demands on the judgement and negotiating skills of political leaders, who have to operate in a context in which legal and moral dilemmas abound.

The ambivalences of post-Cold War Europe are embodied in the distinctive character of the Kosovo war. Wars have traditionally been fought for, or in defence of, territory, population or resources. The Gulf war was motivated by concerns for oil and international law. The Kosovo war was different. In his speech to the opening session in the Reichstag building, Chancellor Schröder quoted the Albanian writer Ismail Kadare: 'With its intervention in the Balkans, atlantic Europe has opened a new page in world history. It is not about material interests, but about principles: the defence of legality and of the poorest people on the continent. This is a founding act.' Kadare's words may be somewhat of a rhetorical exaggeration, and overlook German and Western concerns about refugees, NATO's credibility and instability in Europe's 'backyard', but there was certainly a new factor present in this war. Kosovo was an example of military intervention for humanitarian purposes – for which there are few historical parallels. In this sense, the Kosovo war – and the moral and political dilemmas it poses – may be the prototype for future conflicts facing the international community in the twenty-first century.

Conclusion

The Kosovo tragedy has forced Germany to confront two distinct but closely inter-linked questions that lie at the very heart of the reshaping of post-Cold War European order. The first concerns the role and utility of military force. One of the most difficult questions to answer is 'whether military power will be readied or employed to influence political developments in or near Europe, especially where the interests of the great powers are not fully engaged.'[33] The second is whether European order can continue to rest on the traditional principle of the Westphalian states system, namely sovereignty and non-intervention in the domestic affairs of states.[34] Does the 'international community' (however defined) have the moral and legal right to intervene in the case of large-scale human rights violations? These two questions have been obscured by endless debates on institutional architecture and NATO enlargement, but they are the key questions facing the reshaping of European order.

Given their traumatic history and their postwar identity as a civilian power, the Germans have been confronted with the moral and political dilemmas these two questions pose more starkly than many of their NATO allies. Most importantly, the German debate on Kosovo should reassure those who fear that Germany is seeking to escape from its past and emerge as a 'normal' Great Power. The German debate demonstrated a maturity and seriousness found in very few other countries – and certainly contrasted favourably with the public debate in the US or the UK. This reflects a learning process over many decades during which Germans have sought to address the moral and political questions raised by the use of military force. German postwar history has witnessed intense debates about rearmament, Wehrmacht war crimes, 'out-of-area' missions, missile deployments and humanitarian intervention. The cumulative impact of these debates has been to shape a German public discourse and political identity that is deeply conscious of the need to avoid simple answers to complex moral and political dilemmas. The number of convinced pacifists in Germany is small, but virtually all German politicians are aware of the complexities and moral dilemmas raised by Kosovo. As *Die Zeit* noted, 'traumas, scepticism and the political lessons of the last decades are certainly present in the collective consciousness.'[35]

The arguments for and against military intervention are not simply between opposed camps, but can be seen within parties, and to some extent, within individuals themselves. As the writer Peter Schneider has argued, both those for and against intervention 'find themselves in the same inner struggle' (*Seelenstreit*). 'This war is not suited for drawing sharp moral distinctions between "defenders of peace" and "good guys" on the one hand, and on the other, the power-hungry military, using any pretext to test their new weapons.'[36] For most Germans, Kosovo presents complex moral and political dilemmas that defy simple solutions.

Finally, is Germany still a 'civilian power', even after Kosovo? The concept of 'civilian power' is somewhat vague and loosely defined. Perhaps this partly accounts for its attractiveness to politicians and its frequent use in public discourse in Germany. Hans Maull defined a civilian power as a state that sought to pursue its foreign and domestic objectives primarily through political and economic means, and that was committed to multilateral co-operation and strengthening international law.[37] He did not, however, equate it with a pacifist renunciation of the use of military force under any circumstances. Rather, a 'civilian power' was expected to use military force only as a last resort, after the political and economic instruments of statecraft have failed. Even then, civilian powers are expected only to use military force multilaterally, on the basis of international law, and in a manner proportionate to the political goals. The Kosovo war demonstrated that the concept of civilian power needs further elaboration if it is to be analytically useful in exploring the moral and political dilemmas of military intervention for humanitarian purposes. In the case of Kosovo, both the status of the NATO operation under international law and the appropriateness of its targeting strategy raise difficult questions for civilian powers.

Nevertheless, the German public's response to the Kosovo war suggests that united Germany remains, at heart, a civilian power. This is evident from the overriding concern to stop human suffering; the desire to avoid collateral civilian casualties; the emphasis placed on using the Bundeswehr to build and run refugee camps in Macedonia and Albania; and the efforts of the Government to reach a negotiated settlement. Not only is the identity of the Berlin Republic still deeply marked by a civilian power mentality, in contrast to the Bonn Republic, it is now a 'normal' civilian power. The political reservations that the Bonn Republic had towards the use of military force for anything other than territorial defence under Article V of the NATO Treaty gave its 'civilian power' character a decidedly stunted and one-dimensional quality. The Berlin Republic is now willing to use military force for humanitarian purposes within a multilateral framework. It has therefore finally evolved into a 'normal' civilian power, comparable to other mature democracies in the Euro-Atlantic community. Kosovo has underlined this fact; it has not changed it.

Notes

1. Hans Maull, 'Zivilmacht Bundesrepublik Deutschland', *Europa Archiv*, vol. 47, no. 10, (1992), pp. 269–78.
2. *Frankfurter Allgemeine Zeitung*, 28 March 1999, p. 3.
3. Interview in *Die Zeit*, no. 17, 22 April 1999, p. 9.
4. 'Spoiling for a Fight,' *Newsweek*, 26 April 1999, p. 28.
5. Gunter Hofmann, 'Ist die Nation erwachsen?', *Die Zeit*, 31 April 1999, p. 6.
6. 'Greifen wir dort ein, wo die Spirale von Gewalt, Mord und Vertreibung ihren Ursprung hat? Oder schauen wir tatenlos zu und warten, bis alle Konsequenzen bei uns zu Hause ankommen?', Scharping interview, *Der Spiegel*, no. 13, 31 March 1999, p. 218.
7. The basis of the NATO operation in international law was widely regarded in Germany as highly ambiguous, and the bombing of Yugoslavia was certainly not regarded as a traditional example of humanitarian intervention. See Prof. Dr Ulrich Fastenrath, 'Intervention ohne UN-Mandate?' *Frankfurter Allgemeine Zeitung*, 22 April 1999.

8. Czempiel argued that the motives of NATO's political elite were 'die Nato als glaubwürdige Interventionsmacht zu etabilieren: Die Nato als ordnungspolitisch dominanter Faktor in Europa – jenseits von Europäischer Union und OSZE', interview in *Die Zeit*, 31 March 1999, p. 7. At a discussion meeting in the Frankfurt Peace Research Institute on 21 April 1999, the lack of a UN mandate was widely condemned, and NATO likened to a 'vigilante group'. 'Gefahr der Willkur', *Frankfurter Allgemeine Zeitung*, 22 April 1999, p. 4.

9. Karl-Heinz Kamp, 'UN-Charta nicht alleinige Richtschnur', *Focus*, no. 14, 1999, p. 30.

10. *Frankfurter Allgemeine Zeitung*, 26 April 1999, p. 6.

11. Scharping interview, *Der Spiegel*, no. 13, 31 March 1999, p. 219.

12. Kamp, *op. cit.*

13. Cora Stephen, 'Die Friedensbewegung und die neue deutsche Aussenpolitik', in Thomas Schmid (ed.), *Krieg im Kosovo* (Hamburg: Rowohlt Taschenbuch Verlag, 1999), pp. 269–78.

14. Jan Ross, 'Die Deutschen und der Krieg', *Die Zeit*, 31 March 1999, p. 1.

15. Peter Schneider, 'Eiserne Mienen', *Frankfurter Allgemeine Zeitung*, Feuilleton, 23 April 1999, p. 43.

16. Egon Bahr entered into a fierce debate with his former ally from the peace movement on the left Erhard Eppler, who supported intervention. Their open letters have been published in *Die Zeit*, no. 16, 15 April 1999, p. 7, and no. 17, 22 April 1999, p. 4.

17. 'Der erste Kriegseinsatz deutscher Soldaten seit 1945, den er [Schröder] zu Verantworten haat, beendet für seine Regierung die Phase des Übens und Ausprobierens,' *Frankfurter Allgemeine Zeitung*, 13 April 1999, p. 1.

18. Günter Bannas, 'Bewährungsprobe einer Generation', *Frankfurter Allgemeine Zeitung*, 3 April 1999, p. 1.

19. 'Militärische Friedenserzwingung und Kampfeinsätze lehnen wir ab', Election Programme, Bündnis 90/Die Grünen, 1998.

20. For a critical history of the Greens and foreign policy written from an 'insider' perspective see Ludger Volmer, *Die Grünen und die Aussenpolitik – Ein Schwieriges Verhältnis* (Münster: Westfälisches Dampfboot, 1998).

21. Interview in *Die Zeit*, no. 17, 22 April 1999, p. 9.

22. 'Bodentruppeneinsatz könnte zu drittem Weltkrieg führen', *Frankfurter Allgemeine Zeitung*, 13 April 1999, p. 7.

23. 'Opposition weiter zurückhaltend', *Frankfurter Allgemeine Zeitung*, 13 April 1999, p. 6.

24. 'PDS will Aktion der europäischen Linken', *Frankfurter Allgemeine Zeitung*, 13 April 1999, p. 6.

25. 'Stimmungsgefälle', *Frankfurter Allgemeine Zeitung*, 14 April 1999, p. 16.

26. *Stern*, no. 16, 15 April 1999, p. 34.

27. For details see François Heisbourg, *European Defence: Making It Work*, Chaillot Paper 42 (Paris: WEU Institute for Security Studies, 2000), pp. 6–7.

28. See Peter van Ham, *Europe's New Defence Ambitions: Implications for NATO, the US, and Russia*, Marshall Center Papers no. 1 (Garmisch-Partenkirchen: George C. Marshall European Centre for Security Studies, 2000).

29. These questions are discussed at greater length in Adrian Hyde-Price,

Germany and European Order: Enlarging NATO and the EU (Manchester: Manchester University Press, 2000).

30. Former Chancellor Kohl declared that this was comparable in historical significance as the 3 October 1990 (the day of German reunification). *Die Zeit*, no. 17, 22 April 1999, p. 7.

31. Joschka Fischer, *Risiko Deutschland: Krise und Kukunft der deutschen Politik* (Cologne: Kiepenheuer und Witsch, 1994), pp. 228–9.

32. Wilfred von Bredow, 'Der krieg im Kosovo und die Ambivalenz der Eindeutigkeit', *Frankfurter Allgemeine Zeitung*, 26 April 1999, p. 16.

33. Philip Zelikow, 'The Masque of Institutions', *Survival*, vol. 38, no. 1 (1996), pp. 6–18, (p. 7).

34. See Rudolf Scharping, *Wir Dürfen Nicht Wegsehen: Der Kosovo-Krieg und Europa* (Berlin: Ullstein, 1999), pp. 221–2.

35. 'Aber in kollektiven Bewußtsein sein Traumata, skepsis und die politischen Lehren der letzten Jahrzente präsent', *Die Zeit*, 31 April 1999, p. 6.

36. Peter Schneider, 'Eiserne Mienen', *Frankfurter Allgemeine Zeitung*, Feuilleton, 23 April 1999, p. 43.

37. See for example Hanns Maull, 'Germany and Japan: The New Civilian Powers', *Foreign Affairs*, vol. 69, no. 5 (Winter 1990/91), pp. 91–106, and Hanns Maull, 'Civilian Power: The Concept and its Relevance for Security Issues', in Lidija Babic and Bo Huldt (eds), *Mapping the Unknown: Towards a New World Order* (Stockholm: The Swedish Institute of International Affairs, 1993), pp. 115–31.

CHAPTER EIGHT

Italian Perceptions

MARTIN CLARK

There are many reasons why Italy was likely to oppose NATO's direct military intervention in Kosovo. To begin with, it was far too crude. Italian foreign policy, like her domestic parliamentary politics with which it interacts, is founded on a long tradition of ambiguity, inconsistency and mediation. Both at home and abroad, opponents are 'transformed' easily into supporters, and vice versa. Governments are always unstable coalitions of parties with differing interests and ethical positions, and deputies change sides and labels with bewildering frequency; over 100 did so between 1996 and 2000. The country ended both world wars on a different side from the one to which it was allied at the outset. During the Cold War Italy was very deeply divided, and tried in vain to keep a foot in both camps, East and West. In the Gulf War of 1990–1 the government's attitude towards the 'West' was lukewarm, and was clearly much resented in Washington.

This ambiguity is inevitable, for the Italians feel vulnerable. Like the Balkans, the Italian peninsula is in a key strategic position, and likely to be fought over during inter-power disputes. Furthermore, Italy has a tradition of military defeat, not just by the Allies in 1943 but also by the Greeks in 1940–1, by the Austrians in 1917 (Caporetto) and in various mid-nineteenth century battles, and even by the Ethiopians in 1896, not to mention during many earlier centuries of foreign occupation. Unlike Britain with its 'Falklands mentality', Italy is used to losing. In any case, since 1945 engaging in foreign wars has inevitably been seen as 'fascist'. Mussolini's regime in the 1930s launched a series of wars and overseas conquests, including that of Albania in 1939, which had the inevitable result after the Second World War of associating any military intervention abroad with fascism, and with ultimate disaster. So Italy has learned to remain ambiguous, to conciliate both sides where possible, to specialize in diplomacy rather than aggression, and to offer her services as a mediator. Moreover, it must always be remembered that Rome is the capital not only of Italy, but also of a worldwide Church with her own strong diplomatic tradition that is also committed to negotiation and to the peaceful settlement of disputes. The voice of the Vatican is always heard loudly in Italy. It may often be unwelcome to Italian politicians, but it can hardly be ignored.

Links with the Balkans have always been fairly close. It is, after all, only fifty miles across the Adriatic from Otranto to the Albanian coast, roughly the same as from Wales to Ireland. The sea can easily be crossed, on missions both legitimate and clandestine, and there have been many Albanian settlements in Southern Italy. Indeed, Albania's great nineteenth-century linguistic and cultural historian, Jeromin de Rada, was born there and lived there all his life. In 1896 Italy's future king, Victor Emanuel III (1900–46) married the daughter of the king of Montenegro. Albania gained independence in 1912 partly as a consequence of Italy's successful war against Turkey, and thereafter Italy made great efforts to have influence there. Italy helped build railways, founded newspapers and banks, won mining or forestry concessions, and bribed local notables.[1] Albania became an Italian protectorate, and in 1939 it was formally annexed and became part of the Italian Empire. It was from Albania that Mussolini launched his disastrous attack on Greece in 1940. The Italians remained in occupation until 1943. Albania was never a profitable or glamorous part of the Italian Empire, but it had been 'Italian' and some cultural and linguistic links remained, although not of course overtly during the long postwar years of Enver Hoxha's dictatorship. After 1991, however, these legacies unexpectedly revived. Albanian migrants flooded across the sea into Italy, attracted by the affluent society they could see every night back home on Italian television. Many were welcomed as cheap labour, but many others soon acquired a fearsome reputation. By the mid-1990s burglaries, drug smuggling, armed assaults and prostitution were all automatically (if wrongly) blamed on 'Albanians', particularly in south-eastern Italy where hundreds arrived clandestinely every week.

In these circumstances it was unlikely that Italy would wish to go to war on behalf of 'Albanians'. Many older Italians had very unfavourable wartime memories of the country, scene of one of Italy's most humiliating defeats; many others loathed and feared the Albanian immigrants, who were by far the most unpopular immigrant group. The whole 'humanitarian' appeal of the Kosovars' plight was likely to fall on fairly deaf ears in Italy. Moreover, most Italians were completely bewildered by recent events in ex-Yugoslavia, and had no wish to take sides. If anything, northern Italians had been brought up in an anti-fascist culture that looked back with pride to the Resistance of 1943–5. They therefore respected and liked the Serbs, who had given arms and assistance to some of the Italian partisan units; and Tito's regime had often been admired on the Italian left. Catholics, too, much preferred the Orthodox Serbs to the (mostly) Moslem Albanians. In short, Italy's historic links with Albania were real, but unhappy; the contemporary links were even unhappier.

As for NATO's strategy of relying on aerial bombing, this seemed to most Italians to be useless and unjustifiable, as the polls cited below show. There were few obvious military targets, so the bombing would kill large numbers of civilians. Above all, it would intensify the existing inter-ethnic conflict between Serbs and Kosovar Albanians, and might well result in thousands more refugees fleeing to Italy. This was the last thing any Italian politician wanted. It is very striking how the most urgent concern of the Italian government in the days before and immediately after the bombing began was the likely impact of a flood of 'Albanian' refugees.

The defence Establishment view – inasmuch as there is an Establishment in Italy, for the reality is a host of competing state agencies – was very different. Italy was a committed NATO member, derived great economic and security benefits from NATO membership, and had no choice but to be loyal to the alliance in wartime. The Kosovo crisis was seen as an opportunity for Italy to re-establish credentials as a reliable ally, after the doubts and hesitations of the Gulf War eight years earlier. In any case, NATO was bound to win. Italy, as ever, intended to be on the winning side. But it was not just a matter of loyalty, or at least of loyalty to NATO. The 'European' dimension was even more important. The Italians had imposed quite tough austerity measures on themselves throughout the 1990s in order to qualify for entry into the European single currency. They had succeeded, but they knew that their European partners, particularly the Germans, were still suspicious. The Kosovo crisis was, therefore, an opportunity to boost Italy's 'European' credentials as well as her NATO ones. Now the Cold War was over, Italy needed new protectors, in Europe; and 'Europe' had the great advantage of being popular, unlike NATO.

All this was a recipe for tension – between the various parties, between Parliament and government, and between Italy and her various allies. This tension was made more acute by the fact that the Foreign Minister, Lamberto Dini, was by no means a spokesman for the 'defence Establishment' view. On the contrary, he epitomized the traditional Foreign Ministry 'foot-in-both-camps' approach. He made serious efforts to avoid the war, was clearly always anxious to negotiate even during the war itself, and kept the Italian embassy in Belgrade open throughout hostilities. He also stated publicly that the Rambouillet agreements had been designed to be rejected by the Serbs, criticized both his government colleague, Defence Minister Scognamiglio, and Madeleine Albright very harshly, and condemned NATO's bombing campaign unequivocally. At one point in the war Milošević invited him to visit Belgrade, although he decided not to go after, as he diplomatically put it, discussions with the Prime Minister.[2] He could not be dismissed nor even disciplined, since he led his own tiny party which had nineteen vital votes in the Chamber. Similarly, the President of the Republic (and therefore head of the armed forces), Oscar Scalfaro, was an old-fashioned Christian Democrat whose lack of enthusiasm for the war was palpable.

Still, the basic choice had been made, inevitably. As a weak power with an unstable political system, Italy needed allies, and therefore needed to show support for her allies' actions, however little conviction or sympathy ordinary Italians may have felt. The government's task – or rather, the Prime Minister's task, because he could expect little help from his colleagues – was, therefore, to take part visibly in the war, and to mobilize as much public support as possible. The solution was to stress the 'humanitarian' aspect. On 28 March the government launched a relief agency, the 'Rainbow Mission', to help Kosovar refugees in Albania and Macedonia. It was supported by Italy's leading journalists, and collected over 130 billion lire (£45 million) from the public for relief work – not, perhaps, as much as might have been expected, given the publicity, but it helped greatly to diminish Catholic disapproval of the war. The other major argument used was, as so often in recent years, to emphasize the 'European' nature of the enterprise. Italy was portrayed as fighting alongside her 'European' partners, in a 'European' war fought for 'European' values. The US's contribution to the war's origins, and its overwhelming contribution to the war itself, were therefore constantly downplayed in official Italian pro-war rhetoric. This 'European' propaganda was never very plausible, and it became less plausible as the war went on.

Public opinion polls indicate that, at the outset, in late March 1999, most Italians, in a ratio of about 2:1, were hostile to the bombing campaign, although about a quarter of the population was undecided. By early April, as television reported nightly the horrors of ethnic massacre and the plight of the refugees, sentiment turned against the Serbs, although the war's opponents still outnumbered its supporters. During April support for the war increased further: by late April at least one poll found that a majority had come to approve of it. But two weeks later opinion had shifted back again: 42.2 per cent thought the war unjustified, 35.4 per cent justified, and the rest were undecided. War fatigue had set in, exacerbated by worries about the effectiveness and morality of bombing civilian targets, about whether the war could be won, by the numerous 'errors' in targeting, and by fears of a lengthy bloodbath if it came to a land campaign. Above all, the refugee issue continued to alarm the public. It was noticeable that the biggest 'shift back' in public opinion took place in the north-east and in the mainland southern regions – the areas where most of the refugees had gathered.[3]

It was also noticeable that popular anti-war feeling was muted. True, there were occasional protest demonstrations at the air base of Aviano, but they were token gestures. On the Adriatic coast, fishermen and tourist operators were not pleased when planes returning from aborted missions dropped their bombs into the sea (143 bombs in six zones by 20 May), but they were peripheral groups and could be safely ignored. By Italian standards, there were no massive demonstrations against the Kosovo war, unlike against the Gulf War eight years earlier; demonstrations took place, of course, but attracted about 100,000 people, instead of 400,000. There was no panic rush to stock up on sugar, no general strike – indeed, the railwaymen actually called *off* a strike because of the war – and only one terrorist assassination. There were also around 30 attacks on governing party branches, which caused little serious damage. There is a simple explanation for the fact that the protests were so half-hearted: the left was in power. If the opposition leader Silvio Berlusconi had been in government, the response would unquestionably have been very different. And the left was in power not just in Italy but also in Germany, France and Britain. The Kosovo war could be presented not just as 'humanitarian' or 'European', but as 'socialist'.

Perhaps that was why the most vocal opposition to the war came from Umberto Bossi's Northern League, but there were other reasons. The League was in the political wilderness. Two years earlier it had proclaimed an independent 'Padania' in northern Italy, with its own parliament and executive, but this scheme had led only to general derision. Now it needed a popular theme to win back support. Opposing the war was a wonderful opportunity. On 24 March Bossi denounced the 'Freemasons' war against the friendly Yugoslav people', and sent off three League members to observe the bombing in Belgrade. A month later he himself visited Milošević in Belgrade, and later claimed to have secured the release of Ibrahim Rugova. He naturally stressed the impact of thousands of Kosovar refugees on Italy, and warned of more to come.[4] His arguments often had distinctly 'northernist' overtones: Serbia was a civilized, Christian country, and the honest Serbs were forced to fight against the bandits and organized criminals at the southern end of their country. Italy was on the wrong side, as usual. Furthermore, the war was not 'European' at all, as the government was claiming, but simply yet another example of Yankee imperialism. Throughout the war he attacked NATO ('obsolete'), Clinton ('decadent'), and the shameful subservience of the Italian government to the Americans, worse than that of Mussolini to Hitler. All this had an obvious appeal, but less than expected. Even some of the League's members rejected it. Bossi was too demagogic, and still too isolated politically, to be a real threat. Nonetheless, he played successfully on the traditional anti-Americanism and anti-fascism of the left, as well as on the anti-refugee sentiment of the right; and he undermined the government's efforts to 'Europeanize' the war. The 'Anglo-American war' gave him an opportunity to re-enter the stage, and he seized it brilliantly. By June he had ditched his most ludicrous policy, an independent 'Padania', and was making overtures to Berlusconi to relaunch an effective alliance against the left – an offer that Berlusconi could not refuse.

The other major opponent of the war was, of course, the Pope. The Vatican has long held that a modern war can hardly be 'just', whatever the provocation, if only because of the technology likely to be used and its impact on civilians. Moreover, John Paul II is a Pole, who knows it is unwise to provoke the Russians. Above all, his ultimate ecclesiastical aim is to achieve a reconciliation between Rome and the Orthodox Churches of Eastern Europe and the Middle East, and he had long hoped that the Jubilee Year of 2000 might help set this process in train. This was a vital aim of papal diplomacy. He was, therefore, particularly anxious to avoid a 'Western' war against an Orthodox people, especially on the eve of the Jubilee. Early in May 1999 he made a long-planned visit to Romania – the first visit by a Pope to a predominantly Orthodox country since the Great Schism of 1054. While in Romania, he and Patriarch Teoctist issued a joint appeal for an immediate end to the war. Later papal statements, including harsh criticism of national Churches for not doing more to prevent the conflict, clarified his views. Horrified by the West's simple-minded moralizing, he insisted that *all* sides were blameworthy. In other words, the war was unjustified. Here was a real challenge to the official government line.

Yet the Vatican had to be careful. The Church, with a host of volunteer bodies (including many in Albania itself) devoted to caring for refugees, could hardly ignore the 'humanitarian' argument and the 'Rainbow' mission, whatever she may have thought of their use by government and NATO propagandists. Nor, of course, could the Pope risk finding himself accused, like his predecessor Pius XII, of failing to speak out against genocide. He made, therefore, strong diplomatic efforts to avoid the war, and to mitigate it once it had started. Mgr Tauran was sent to Belgrade on 1 April and saw Milošević, without success. Later papal efforts to secure a bombing truce over both the Catholic and Orthodox Easter celebrations were rebuffed by Clinton, as the Vatican complained in unusually uncompromising language.[5] Thereafter the Vatican continued to deplore both the ethnic cleansing of Kosovars and also NATO's bombing campaign, and its diplomatic efforts continued as well. The papal nuncio, like the Italian ambassador, remained in Belgrade throughout the conflict. The Vatican seems to have given much support to UN endeavours, or rather to have tried to spur the UN into action by statements and appeals that were surprisingly critical of UN hesitancy and weakness. Like the UN, the EU was also criticized for shamefully avoiding its responsibilities. War could and should have been avoided by a conference on the Balkans, and the European powers should have taken the initiative in calling one. Indeed, the 'European' theme was a striking feature of papal peace efforts. The Vatican was clearly uneasy at unchallenged American dominance,[6] insisted on the single, Christian nature of 'Europe', both east and west, and welcomed unification, both secular and religious.

Whereas the Prime Minister presented the war as 'European', the Pope regarded it as largely American and called on 'Europe' to end it.

But Italian politics were no longer dominated by the Christian Democrats, as they had been before 1993. True, their successors in the Italian Popular Party (PPI) were part of the coalition government, but the Vatican had distanced itself from Italian politics over the previous few years, and its occasional pronouncements on Italian themes were often resented rather than revered. The Church's impact on opinion about the war was, therefore, less than might have been expected, certainly less than it had been during the Gulf War eight years earlier. But the Church did express anti-war feelings openly, and insisted that bombing was no way to secure the reconciliation of ethnic conflicts. And on 'Europe' her view was not that different from Bossi's.

If the Prime Minister had to mediate between the defence establishment and public opinion, he also had to mediate among the government members themselves. Since 1996 Italy had been ruled by a 'centre-left' coalition, dominated by the ex-Communists of the 'Democrats of the Left' (DS) and by the ex-Christian Democrats of the Popular Party (PPI), but including various smaller parties, known collectively as the 'seven dwarfs' although sometimes numbering even more. Initially led by Romano Prodi of the PPI, since October 1998 the prime minister was the DS leader Massimo D'Alema, the first ex-Communist to lead an Italian government. D'Alema was cautious, competent, serious-minded and prosaic. His aim for some time had been for Italy to become, as he had put it, 'a normal country' with effective government and reasonable administration. But D'Alema's coalition majority was fractious, unstable and more 'pacifist' than the general population. Most of the government parties had a long tradition of anti-Americanism, or pacifism, or both. The DS itself still included many older ex-Communists hostile to NATO in principle, and with fond memories of Russians, Yugoslavs and the Resistance; despite recent efforts at modernization, the party's basic culture was still anti-fascist and anti-American. Some of its older leaders, like Aldo Tortorella or Pietro Ingrao, protested openly against government policy. Most DS members were unhappy and saw government policy simply as subservience to the US, enabling a US-dominated NATO to push into eastern Europe and the Balkans – a very widespread perception in Italy at this time, and not only on the left. What was true of the DS was even more true of Armando Cossutta's 'Italian Communists' (PdCI), founded only in 1998 after a split from 'Communist Refoundation'. The PdCI was still firmly committed to Marxist principles. It was in government for the first time with two key ministries, including the Ministry of Justice, and its votes in Parliament were essential to the government's survival. Cossutta himself had remarkably close personal links with eastern Europe,[7] and visited Belgrade on 6 April, during the bombing. The government coalition also included the pacifist Greens, opposed to any war, and the ex-Christian Democrats of the PPI, a 'lay but Catholic' party that was also opposed in principle to any war, and in practice was much influenced by papal pronouncements.

D'Alema clearly had his work cut out. His difficult task was to ignore the views of most of his own party, to conciliate the other coalition members enough to keep the government in being and to maintain his parliamentary majority, and at the same time to appear a reliable ally abroad and not to lose too much public support at home. And he had to do it virtually on his own, with little help from his Foreign Minister. As the first ex-Communist Prime Minister, the task was particularly important to him: it was vital to show that the DS could be trusted in government. Perhaps, too, he feared what might happen to him if he did not 'pass his examination'. His predecessor Giulio Andreotti, Prime Minister during the Gulf War, has always blamed the later criminal proceedings (for instigation to murder, and for Mafia membership) against him on the Americans, claiming that Washington was furious at his tolerance of regimes considered pariahs there, and at his revelations about the secret *Gladio* organization.[8]

The aim of government policy, therefore, was to appear neutral at home but warlike abroad. This was rather easier than it may seem. D'Alema's coalition partners may have disliked the war, but they disliked the opposition parties even more, and they disliked the prospect of early elections (in which they would lose badly) most of all. D'Alema could let them protest if they wanted to; he knew they would keep his government intact – they had nowhere else to go. In any case, most of the opposition parties were pro-war and at a pinch D'Alema could rely on their votes to survive. So his parliamentary majority was never in danger. Still, it was politically more sensible to conciliate his allies, to make verbal concessions that would allow them to save face and to support him in public. Hence the history of Italian government activities during the war is one of a series of apparent compromises with the minor coalition partners, particularly the PdCI and the Greens, designed to keep them on board the coalition government. In reality, neither party had the slightest intention of leaving, and the concessions to them were merely a charade – but an important charade, that had some influence on general public opinion as well as on parliamentary debates.

I have already mentioned the government's launch of the 'Rainbow' humanitarian mission, designed particularly to conciliate the Catholics, as well as the somewhat ambiguous role of Foreign Minister Dini. Another good example is the fact that at the outset of the bombing the Defence Minister promised that, although NATO planes could use Italian bases, *Italian* planes would only be used to defend Italian airspace. Only in mid-April did the Italian Air Force begin, apparently, to drop bombs itself, and only in mid-May was this officially admitted (or claimed). Even more strikingly, on 26 March a government-backed motion in the Chamber of Deputies called for the suspension of bombing and the resumption of negotiations – a device to enable the PdCI to support the government. In mid-May, as opinion was turning once more against the war, the government went further and proposed a motion in Parliament urging a bombing pause *in order to encourage* UNO approval of the G8 proposals. This was approved in the Chamber on 19 May by 308 to 189; even the left-wing opposition party Communist Refoundation voted in favour. In the closed world of Italian politicking, this was seen as a real victory for Cossutta and the Greens. The Italian parliament had voted a 'pacifist resolution' in mid-war, a clear expression of the country's increasing scepticism. D'Alema pledged the government to act accordingly, although of course NATO as a whole would decide the outcome. It is not clear how long this game might have continued. Certainly it would not have survived vast popular protests, nor a land invasion of Kosovo. The government could not rule out the possibility of a land war altogether, because NATO might have decided to invade despite the inevitable casualties; but even the PdCI and the Greens would never have swallowed that. Nor, for that matter, would Dini, who warned on 28 May that a land invasion was 'unthinkable', and that Italy would be 'constrained to dissociate herself' from any such move.[9] D'Alema was fortunate that the war ended just in time. So he succeeded in keeping his coalition intact throughout the war, but even so he had to pay a high cost. Most of his supporters were unenthusiastic at best, and many were disillusioned and disgruntled. Support for the government fell from 40 per cent of the electorate in early March to 34 per cent two months later. The government, and the left-wing parties in general, were seriously wounded by the war.

Three major political developments occurred during or immediately after the war, and demonstrate this outcome. On 18 April a referendum was held on whether to abolish the 25 per cent 'proportional representation' (additional member) element in parliamentary elections – that is to introduce the British/American 'first-past-the-post' system. Although overwhelmingly approved by those who voted, it failed very narrowly, by 0.4 per cent, to secure the necessary 50 per cent turnout, and so was unsuccessful. Perhaps this result would have occurred anyway, but it seems highly unlikely. The war had made the DS unable to mobilize its supporters. And for a month before the referendum the press had been full of war news, distracting everybody from more mundane concerns. This was bound to have reduced the turnout. In any case, the simple 'majoritarian', 'first-past-the-post' system was seen in wartime as too characteristic of the USA and the UK – the warmongering countries. The outcome was generally regarded as a victory for Bossi and for the 'old guard' parties of the political centre, and as a defeat for the DS, for Prodi's 'Democrats' and for Gianfranco Fini's 'National Alliance', although not for Berlusconi, who had supported the referendum but in an extremely lukewarm manner. Crudely, the anti-war parties won; the pro-war ones lost. Or, perhaps more accurately, the conservatives won and the institutional reformers lost, arguably their most serious defeat for eight years. The result discredited not only the electoral reformers, but the whole idea of 'institutional change by referendum'. It was noticeable that when a similar series of referenda were re-proposed the following year, the turnout was lower still. Italy's burst of reforming zeal, from 1991 to 1998, seemed to be over.

The second major event was the election of a new President of the Republic, by an electoral college of parliamentarians and regional representatives, when the seven-year term of President Scalfaro expired in May. The usual protracted bargaining and open political disputes were not tolerable in wartime, particularly as the President is head of the Supreme Council of Defence. In practice, the new President was chosen by Prime Minister D'Alema and by the leader of the major opposition party, Berlusconi. Carlo Azeglio Ciampi, seventy-nine years old, Treasury minister, former governor of the Bank of Italy and Prime Minister in 1993–4, was elected president at the first ballot. He was much respected internationally, was good at avoiding controversy, and was just the man to mediate effectively with the US and other major powers. His election was another success for Berlusconi, who had loathed Scalfaro, and it was another defeat for the reformers. Not only was Ciampi undoubtedly a man of the old guard; his election showed that the best way to secure a dependable head of state was to keep the electorate small. A direct election by the people, or a 'semi-presidential' system, as advocated by many reformers, might have rewarded a partisan candidate like the bellicose ex-judge Di Pietro rather than a natural conciliator.

Finally, on 13 June came the elections to the European Parliament, at which the parties might be rewarded or punished for their stance on Kosovo. There is little evidence either way: neither the pro-war parties, nor the anti-war ones, seemed to benefit noticeably. On the right, Berlusconi's Forza Italia did very well but Fini (pro-war) and Bossi (anti-war) did not. But among the government parties, the PPI won only 4.2 per cent of the vote compared with 10 per cent in 1994, and the DS also went down, from 19.1 per cent to 17.3 per cent. The European elections confirmed the previous opinion poll findings: the war had weakened the centre-left coalition as a whole. Within the month, in fact, the left suffered an even greater defeat, losing its traditional stronghold of Bologna in local elections. It had lost not merely voters, but its *raison d'etre*. It could no longer hope to push through reforms. D'Alema, a convinced reformer, had lost his role as well as much of his base.

Whatever his domestic preoccupations, D'Alema also had to appear a reliable ally. He had not made a good start in his relations with the US. In December 1998 he had stated publicly that US (and UK) bombing of Iraq was useless; and Italy also refused to extradite the Kurdish leader Ocalan to Turkey, despite some American pressure. On 7 February 1999, as the Rambouillet conference opened, D'Alema warned that wars could not be won by bombing alone; military action in Kosovo would require ground troops, would trigger civil war and would certainly bring a host of refugees to Italy.[10] Early in March D'Alema visited President Clinton in Washington and repeated these arguments, to no avail. According to D'Alema's own later account, the Americans clearly expected Milošević to yield at Rambouillet, and thought that bombing would work rapidly (as in Bosnia) if he did not. D'Alema was clearly horrified to find that on the eve of war they had not thought through the humanitarian implications at all, had not anticipated ethnic cleansing nor a mass exodus of refugees, and had made no plans to cope with this eventuality.[11] To make matters worse, on that same day a US court martial acquitted the USAF pilots whose fighter plane had flown into a cable car at Cermis, in Northern Italy, some months earlier, killing 20 people. The disaster had already aroused a great deal of anti-American feeling in Italy, and the acquittal made matters even worse, as did the US Congress' refusal, during the war, to offer any compensation to the victims' families. So D'Alema's visit was blighted, and Italian-USA relations remained distinctly cool. Announcing the verdict while D'Alema was in Washington was at best tactless, and was taken in Italy as an arrogant snub. After this episode D'Alema made strenuous efforts to broker a 'Bosnian-type' peace deal, but he received little response either in Moscow or in Western Europe: Jacques Santer's EU Commission was in its death throes, and Schroeder's German government had severe internal difficulties.

Yet, once the war started, Italian-US relations rapidly improved, despite some American doubts about D'Alema's various parliamentary man-oeuvres. Italy was, after all, the major base for NATO air operations. She became, at last, the 'huge aircraft carrier' that Mussolini had called her in the 1930s. Throughout the seventy-eight days of the bombing campaign US planes took off regularly from Aviano, in north-east Italy, and from eight other NATO bases. After the first three weeks the Italian Air Force flew regular sorties too, with 54 planes, more than the RAF. Washington had to recognize the value of Italian support, and the political risks that D'Alema was running to provide it. Moreover, Clinton did not want a land war either, so was not likely to mind any diplomatic efforts, such as D'Alema's unsuccessful peace proposals of 16 May, that might help get him off the hook. Above all, Italy now mattered, and might even be trusted. She was a 'front-line state', or could plausibly claim to be, and she had to be consulted more often on matters both military and diplomatic.

In mid-war Admiral Guido Venturoni was appointed chairman of Nato's military committee, and no-one objected.

D'Alema, who later in the summer wrote an apologetic book on the Kosovo crisis, was very proud of this prestige aspect. Italy, he proclaimed, had once more 'passed the test'. In 1998 she had been allowed to join the European Monetary Union; in 1999 she had gone one better, and joined the wider international club as a full member, for the first time. This argument continued to be heard in defence Establishment circles. Italy had not merely made her bases available. She had played her part in the 'Premier League', had won unaccustomed respect for her military prowess, had ended the war on the same side as she started, and had even secured some of the key jobs. Defence experts, and the prime minister, hoped that the successful war would provide a strong incentive to modernize the armed forces and equip them with the most modern technology; the money would come from abolishing conscription at long last. Italy would acquire the 'ability to act abroad' (*'capacità di proiezione esterna'*),[12] for the first time since Mussolini's day. Certainly Italy would have a vital role in post-war Kosovo and Albania; civil and economic development missions would benefit Italian firms and Italian trade.[13] Moreover, Russia had not been too affronted; UNO had, eventually, resumed its proper role. 'Europe' had proved disappointing, but it was soon being argued that the war simply proved the need for stronger European co-operation/integration in military and foreign affairs, long an Italian aim. Even the Vatican thought this desirable, if only as a counterweight to the USA.

But other aspects of the war proved more contentious. The 'European left', proclaimed D'Alema, had fought a 'moral', 'humanitarian' war (admittedly against the 'old left') and won, with virtually no loss of NATO life. The Kosovar refugees were able to return home. However, it was noticeable that after the war there was little triumphalism, little talk of 'victory' or 'heroism', and no call to 'rejoice'. The Italians are, after all, a sceptical people. They could see that Milošević was still in power and realized that the Serbs would nurse their grievances and eventually fight back. Few Italians thought the war had been fought for 'humanitarian' reasons. They knew that Italy had been dragged into the Kosovo war against her will, something that had never happened earlier. They accepted that war might possibly be a lesser evil in some circumstances, but a 'humanitarian' war was impossible: at the very least, such a war would have unforeseen consequences, like any other. Common prudence, too, dictated caution: NATO could not make war on every country that treated minorities badly. Hence many Italians, of all parties, were horrified by the new Western doctrine of 'limited sovereignty' – limited, that is, by 'human rights', as defined *ad hoc* by Western politicians. Such a doctrine was rightly seen as overthrowing international law, as destroying the UN, and as being a recipe for perpetual war. It was contested most strongly by the left, by lawyers, and by the Church (which, of course, opposed not 'limited sovereignty' *per se*, but the attempt to impose Western secular values on everybody else). As I have stressed, Italy has a 'mediating' tradition. She is not anxious to impose her values, let alone her allies' values, on other people. She tried that in the past and it did not work.

From late May 1999 onwards the Italian press was full of reports of the slaughter and destruction *in Serbia itself*, caused by the bombing. And from late June the press carried detailed and lengthy reports of 'reverse ethnic cleansing' (of Serbs by 'Albanians') in Kosovo, of KLA atrocities against Serbs and gypsies, and of the destruction of Orthodox churches and monasteries. These reports have continued very prominently to the time of writing (July 2000), partly because Italy sent 4200 men to join the UN KFOR troops in Kosovo, and there were thousands more on relief missions in Macedonia and Albania, particularly after September 1999. Hence there were plenty of Italian eyewitnesses to what was happening in the 'liberated' zones, and much press interest in their stories. Needless to say, the 'Rainbow' relief supplies of food and clothing were found to have been diverted to other hands, and used as a cover for arms smuggling. Above all, journalists reported that the troops felt they were presiding helplessly over ethnic cleansing and acting simply as stooges of the KLA, an organization devoted not only to ethnic warfare in Kosovo but also to gun-running and drug-smuggling in Western Europe. In February 2000 General Silvio Mazzaroli, deputy commander of KFOR, made a public protest about the situation, and had to be dismissed.

So D'Alema's pro-war 'humanitarian' propaganda was soon discredited. The war may have brought Italy some military and diplomatic benefits but it had also brought some real costs, and many of the political consequences were disquieting. They included increased public scepticism about the 'centre-left' government, about NATO and the US, and about 'Europe'. D'Alema's coalition collapsed in December 1999, and although he patched up another one, it only lasted four months. In April 2000 he had to resign, after a poor showing in regional elections. The many Italian critics of NATO complained that it had lost its original defence rationale and had become merely a bombing organization, to be used against any country of which the US disapproved. It had been unwilling to fight a real land war and had been unable to make peace, let alone to win it. As for 'Europe', it had proved uncertain and very divided on military and diplomatic issues, and had been ludicrously over-used as a propaganda slogan. Romano Prodi, the new president of the European Commission, had the advantage of being an Italian but he kept remarkably quiet during the war, seemed anxious mainly to avoid offending anybody, and was soon derisively known in Italy as 'Good King Wenceslas'. If the European Union had hoped to become the protector of Kosovo, it failed. It was obviously the US, not 'Europe', which had fought the war, and Russia, not 'Europe', which had brokered the peace. Moreover, the euro was making a less than impressive debut, and the middle classes were becoming worried about their savings.

The Italians had always felt vulnerable, but now they began to feel dangerously exposed. Italy was clearly near, if not in, the front line. She had managed to placate her main protector, the US, but she distrusted the Americans' judgement and knowledge; her other allies had proved unreliable, but she was very reluctant to rely on her own resources. Worst of all, Italy had allowed herself to be dragged into the Balkan quagmire. As the ex-colonial power in Albania, Italians remembered something of the region. They knew that internecine strife was interminable. If the Balkans were not worth the bones of a single Pomeranian grenadier, they were certainly not worth those of a Piedmontese *bersagliere.*

Notes

1. R. J. B. Bosworth, 'The Albanian forests of Signor Giacomo Vismara', in *The Historical Journal*, vol. 18 (1975), pp. 571–86. Cf. also the book of the future Italian Foreign Minister, A. di San Giuliano, *Lettere sull' Albania* (Rome: 'Giornale d'Italia', 1903). On de Rada, see the wonderful description in Norman Douglas, *Old Calabria* (London: Secker & Warburg, 1915), pp. 195–200.
2. *Corriere della Sera,* 11 June 1999.
3. R. Mannheimer, in *Corriere della Sera,* 27 March, 2 April, 26 April and 10 May 1999.
4. It is impossible to obtain accurate figures: many, perhaps most, Albanian immigrants are clandestine, and during the war they naturally claimed to be Kosovars. Official figures reported 12,736 Kosovar refugees in Italy by early June; *Corriere della Sera,* 5 June 1999.
5. 'The proposal advanced in this sense has been rejected'; in *Osservatore Romano,* 3 April 1999.
6. 'The epoch-making changes at this end of the century ... do not permit the United States to continue to act as the sole agent for the defence of common interests'; in *Osservatore Romano,* 2 April 1999.
7. Cf. C. Andrew and V. Mitrokhin, *The Mitrokhin Archive* (London: Penguin, 1999), p. 390. The publication of the Italian edition of this book in October 1999 aroused much public controversy, particularly about Cossutta's past activities.
8. G. Andreotti, *Cosa Loro* (Milan: Rizzoli, 1995), pp. 69–70.
9. *Panorama,* BBC TV, 28 May 1999.
10. 'Soldati nei Balcani', in *Corriere della Sera,* 7 February 1999.
11. M. D'Alema, *Kosovo* (Milan: Mondadori, 1999), pp. 19–20.
12. *ibid.,* p. 92.
13. In mid-2000 it was reported that 600 Italian firms were operating in Albania, and that Italy was Albania's largest trading partner; *Corriere della Sera*, 30 July 2000.

CHAPTER NINE

Perceptions in Central and South-Eastern Europe

RICK FAWN

March 1999 was a watershed in the security practice and thinking of central and south-eastern European leaders.[1] On 12 March, three former members of the Warsaw Treaty Organization (WTO) – Poland, Hungary and the Czech Republic – signed NATO's charter, to become members of the alliance. That day institutionalized a looming political divide within the region, previous co-operation agreements with NATO aside. Three other former WTO members, Slovakia, Bulgaria and Romania, which had also sought NATO membership, were now clearly on the outside. This was a blow to policies of the centre-right, pro-European integration parties that had replaced parochial, nationalist, leftist governments in 1998, 1997 and 1996, respectively.

March 1999 was of further significance to this region, of course, because of NATO's application of military force to Yugoslavia, a geographical neighbour to three of these states, and, in different measures, an historical, cultural or political friend or ally of most of them. Despite the potentially different political and strategic implication of NATO's military campaign for the six countries, the outlook and response of the governments were remarkably similar. For the three NATO members, the war was defined with terms such as a 'test' of their credibility as allies; for the other three, which were not members but hoped to become such, the bombing campaign presented an opportunity to prove their worth as potential future members. This was especially true of Slovakia where, since the end of 1998, the government had pursued an intensive, and successful policy of both reviving and reintegrating itself into the Visegrad co-operation of Poland, Hungary and the Czech Republic.

Difference in perspectives on the conflict generally, and NATO's use of force specifically, arose with divisions between the governing political elites in these countries and their publics. The non-member publics were generally opposed to the use of force, whereas the Polish and Hungarian populations were and remained generally supportive of the bombings. The Czech Republic presents an anomaly where not only public opinion and non-governmental actors opposed the war, but sections of the government were publicly divided.

The responses of each country will first be established in turn, starting with NATO members, followed by that of Slovakia, Bulgaria and Romania. Similarities and differences of perceptions of the conflict across this region will be offered in the conclusion. The chapter begins with Poland, the largest state in the region.

NATO's new members

Poland

Poland could have faced the greatest physical risks if the use of force in the Balkans resulted in an expansion of the conflict. Unlike other Central European states, Poland still bordered Russia at the Kaliningrad oblast. Disruptions to Western-Russian relations because of the conflict might have had geostrategic implications for Poland; the Polish government's careful nurturing of its policy towards Lithuania, Belarus and Ukraine could also have been jeopardized. Nevertheless, the Polish government's stand on the bombings was categoric. Polish Foreign Minister Bronisław Geremek held Milošević responsible for the crisis and declared that diplomatic means were 'exhausted'. All governmental bodies expressed their support for NATO's action.[2] Poland's first post-communist Prime Minister, Tadeusz Mazowiecki (who resigned as UN Special Commissioner for Former Yugoslavia after the UN failed to protect the 'safe havens') said Poland's 'political attitude' was that of a mature and loyal ally.[3]

Popular support was fairly strong for NATO's actions, although it slid somewhat in the course of the bombings. 51 per cent of respondents in a May poll felt the attacks to be justified, down from 55 per cent in April; 26 per cent were now opposed, a 4 per cent increase from the previous month.[4] A similar survey found 53 per cent in favour, as opposed to 51 per cent in April, and 35 versus 31 per cent were opposed.[5]

Some concern was expressed about the practicalities of a Polish response, such as the cost of sending combat troops. The head of the National Security Office cautioned that 'all our budgets and calculations relating to defences will fall through'.[6] Moderation of Polish support of NATO came from Polish Peasant Party (PSL) leader Jarosław Kalinowski; but he said on 20 April that Poland should be active in proposing diplomatic solutions to the conflict rather than overeager to commit its soldiers to operations in Kosovo.[7]

Clear opposition to the war came from disparate groups with relatively little political influence. The far-left grouping Polish Communists Proletariat (ZKP Proletariat), formed in 1990, opposed the NATO intervention, calling it a pretext for NATO to create military bases in the region.[8] The political council of the far-right National Democratic Party, unrepresented in the Sejm, also condemned the bombings.[9] Outspoken opposition came also from former Chief of the Polish Army General Staff, General Tadeusz Wilecki, who called NATO's policies towards the Balkans 'barbarous'. He said the actions contradicted international agreements and referred to a 'Clinton doctrine', which he compared to the Brezhnev doctrine.[10] Protests were made from the Warsaw Antiwar Committee, composed of about sixty mostly elderly people. Twelve of their members held a candle protest outside the US embassy in Warsaw on the first anniversary of the bombing. They called the bombings a 'disgrace' and likened the attack on Serbia to that against Poland in the Second World War.[11]

The position of the Polish government was hardly surprising. Despite see-saw changes in presidential and parliamentary elections throughout the 1990s, including the defeat of Solidarity hero Lech Wałesa by former junior Politburo member Aleksander Kwasniewski, successive governments pursued a policy of Western integration. Kwasniewski's letter to 140 Polish troops being readied to go to Albania to protect NATO Command expressed mainstream Polish sentiments about membership of NATO and Poland's role therein: 'day by day your task will be to raise the prestige of Poland's armed forces and the North Atlantic Alliance.'[12] And despite the problems with military funding and supply that Kosovo showed in the Polish military,[13] the government nevertheless found funds and decided in April 2000 to send an other 600 troops to the 800 already posted to Kosovo.

For Poland as a whole, Kosovo was a crisis that could prove the country's reliability and even enthusiasm as a new member of NATO. That attitude was also reflected in Hungary.

Hungary

The potential risks to Hungary from the conflict exceeded those to Poland. Hungary was alone among the new alliance members in directly bordering Yugoslavia, and each government since 1990 had made some claim to safeguard the wellbeing of the Hungarian diaspora, some 500,000 of whom inhabit Vojvodina in northern Serbia. Concern was expressed that both Hungary and its Yugoslav minorities might suffer as a consequence of the bombings. The daily newspaper *Nepszabadsag* noted that the important Taszar airbase in southern Hungary, which would be turned over to NATO use, was within range of Yugoslav weapons and might become a target.[14]

Hungarians in Yugoslavia had previously been relatively secure but were subject to new danger with the commencement of NATO bombing. A Hungarian commentator noted: 'Paradoxically enough, since the ethnic frenzy of Milosevich [sic] did not reach the ethnic Hungarians, the Hungarians of Serbia seemed to suffer less ethnic conflict so far, than the Hungarians in Meciar's Slovakia or Iliescu's Romania. It seemed they can really lose much, if Milosevich turns against them out of retaliation because of the Hungarian participation in the NATO operations.'[15] Clinton's envoy to the Balkans, Richard Holbrooke, announced in Hungary on 25 March that the safety of the minority could not be guaranteed.

Despite the risks, all major political parties backed the NATO action. The government's position, as in Poland, was that Milošević was to blame, and force was required and justified against him, even if the lack of UN Security Council authorization was regretted by some. The Hungarian Parliament had already rendered the country's airspace available to NATO in October 1998 but unlike other governments in the region, it extended this provision at the outset of the bombing campaign to make its own military airports and bases available to the alliance as well. The one qualification on this measure was that Hungarian military personnel were to be exempt from active participation in the conflict itself and that airstrikes would not be launched from Hungarian soil.

The alliance sought to address Hungarian security concerns, promising that Vojvodina would not be targeted. Clearly that was abrogated and targets that were often construed as purely civilian, such as Novi Sad's bridges, were bombed. This should have swayed Hungarian public opinion and perhaps even the government against the airstrikes. As NATO began hitting targets in Vojvodina, a survey found 54 per cent of respondents feared a spillover of the conflict into Hungary.[16] Sixty per cent of the population supported war at the outset, such numbers falling to 40 per cent as the war continued.

As in Poland, opposition in Hungary to the government's support of NATO was limited to marginal political parties. These were two small extremist parties that carried under 2 per cent of the electoral vote, the small nationalist party Magyar Iqazság és Élet Pártja (MIEP), and the Workers Party, which defines itself as a communist party, although not an 'extreme' party. It opposed the bombings outright, denouncing NATO's claim of protecting the Kosovar Albanian as a 'nursery tale', and arguing that NATO simply wanted to wage war for its own sake, and to gain experience for a future aerial and perhaps also a land war in Europe. The Workers Party charged that in attacking Yugoslavia NATO sought to eliminate the last 'left-wing social order' in the region.[17] In addition to these groupings, opposition was manifested in some intellectual circles, the noted author and former dissident György Konrád questioning the legitimacy of NATO's actions.

The economic effects of the conflict seemed relatively limited. While the conflict decreased tourism in Hungary by 5–10 per cent, and some Hungarian ships were stranded in Bulgaria and Romania due to the blocked Danube, the greatest losses were in trade with Yugoslavia, amounting to US$120 million annually, but only 0.5 per cent of Hungary's overall trade. As a Hungarian analyst commented: 'the Kosovo crisis did not shake the Hungarian economy and the losses so far were much lower than those of the Bosnian war and of the embargo against Serbia between 1992–95' which amounted to US$2.2 billion.[18]

Rather than being destabilized by the conflict, Hungary's strategic position seemed emboldened. When Hungary followed the EU's embargo on fuels to Yugoslavia, it imposed restrictions on the transit of such goods from Russia to Yugoslavia. This angered Russia, and the Russian Ministry of Trade threatened to demand compensation for damages to the Russian economy.[19] That did not bother the Hungarian government. Rather, Prime Minister Orban was delighted that his government could refuse entry to Hungary for two days to Russian forces seeking access to Kosovo, noting that for the first time in 100 years Hungary could control its eastern border. He also declared on a state visit to Toronto in November 1999 his willingness to have NATO nuclear weapons stationed on Hungarian soil.

Hungary seems intent on being, or becoming, a significant regional player. Polish analysts saw Hungary's increased strategic importance eclipsing that of their own country, as NATO's own objectives have begun to look southward to the Balkans and further to the Caucasus and Middle East.[20] In addition to contributing personnel to KFOR (as most countries in the region did), Hungary hosted meetings of Serb opposition leaders, such as the three-day conference of royalists and democrats in the Hungarian town of Szentendre where they agreed to co-operate to oust Milošević,[21] although that role would be surpassed by the mass protests that forced the Yugoslav leader's departure in October 2000. Budapest's regional role is reinforced by it serving as the home of some of the rebuilding efforts, such as the Danube Commission, founded in 1949, and now charged particularly with the unblocking of that river.

While the Hungarian government may not have expressed its role in the conflict in the same clear manner as the Poles in proving its alliance credibility, its actions did that for it and brought praise from NATO officials. Such unambiguous behaviour was not forthcoming from the third new NATO member, the Czech Republic.

The Czech Republic

The Czech Republic, as a successor to the turbulent history of Czechoslovakia, might have been expected to support its NATO membership and to accept the principle of humanitarian warfare. Czechoslovakia's dismemberment in 1938 gave the concept of the 'Munich syndrome', by which totalitarian diktats cannot be appeased, a principle governing Czechoslovak-born Madeleine Albright's own political thinking.[22] The Soviet intervention of 1968 was invoked in the autumn of 1998 by Western media as a counterexample of how to deal with Milošević.[23] With the exception of President Václav Havel, major figures in the Czech government were either ambivalent towards or even opposed to NATO's decision and also indifferent to the country's implied obligations of alliance membership.

Both Premier Miloš Zeman and Foreign Minister Jan Kavan distanced themselves from the NATO campaign, explaining that the decision to bomb was taken before the Czech Republic became an alliance member, and Kavan stressed initially that the Czech Republic was not at war with Yugoslavia and that it would not contribute to NATO's campaign.[24] While the Cabinet consented on 2 April to NATO's request for military overflights, it did not do so unanimously. Václav Klaus, leader of the opposition Civic Democratic Party and parliamentary speaker, routinely criticized the airstrikes. Early in the NATO campaign Zeman rejected the use of Czech forces in a ground operation, a statement that Havel called a default of alliance obligations. The lower house of the Czech Parliament voted to oppose the transit of NATO soldiers that might be used in Yugoslavia. Unlike other countries in the region, which agreed immediately to alliance requests for use of national airspace, the Czechs waited ten days before doing so. The government's obstruction of NATO efforts was highlighted when the parliamentary opposition centre-right parties of the Freedom Union (US) and Christian Democrats (KDU–ČSL) openly supported the airstrikes. The latter's Cyril Svoboda reprimanded the government, declaring 'We are fully-fledged NATO members, other countries have made pledges of solidarity with us, so we should also show solidarity with them.'[25] Czech political scientists wrote that the Czech position 'can only be judged as disgraceful' and noted that the Czech political and popular view was clearly different from that of countries in the region that sought NATO membership.[26]

Havel, however, was distinguished from all other key Czech politicians. He did not seek use of force from the outset; rather, he proposed in early March 1999 that a multilateral peace conference be held in Kosovo.[27] But once the NATO decision was taken, Havel expressed clear support for NATO's actions and blamed Milošević for the conflict, calling him 'unequivocally responsible'.[28] He further said in late April that Czech forces would participate in any ground operations in Kosovo, a statement that contrasted sharply with that of other governments in the region, and Kavan's statement at the Washington NATO summit that Czechs would not participate in a land campaign and would only contribute to a post-conflict peacekeeping mission.[29] Havel explained NATO's actions in terms of global responsibility and suggested that it might be the first war ever waged not for national interest but for 'principles and values', namely, out of concern for the plight of others.[30] His explanation made him one of the key intellectual proponents of the war and, consequently, also one of the targets of detractors, such as Noam Chomsky.[31]

Perhaps the biggest divide within the Czech political establishment arose between Havel and Jiří Dienstbier. Long-time personal friends, leading communist-era dissidents, signatories of and spokesmen for Charter 77, the two men also constructed Czechoslovakia's postcommunist foreign policy. While that foreign policy could be described as a mix of idealism, humanism and a measured but principled reliance on the use of force (such as Czechoslovakia's participation in the coalition against Iraq in the Second Gulf War),[32] Havel and Dienstbier fell out publicly over Kosovo. Dienstbier criticized Havel's stance on the conflict in Kosovo, while Havel replied that Dienstbier lacked sufficient knowledge of the issues, despite having been to the region several times, to hold a valid opinion.[33]

Elite division may explain why the Czech government produced a peace proposal with the Greek government. Announced on 25 May, it differed from the standing G-8 proposal by suggesting that NATO bombing be suspended before Serb forces withdrew from Kosovo and by not calling for the full removal of the Serb military thereafter.

As in Poland and Hungary, opposition was also expressed by non-governing parties and the public; the Communist Party (the only direct successor to a pre-1989 ruling party in the region not to change its name or rescind the core of its historical record), was particularly opposed, and organized egg-throwing rallies outside the US embassy in Prague. While mainstream Churches agreed that NATO intervention was necessary they still sought a peaceful solution. The leader of the Czech and Slovak Orthodox church, however, compared NATO's actions to that of Germany against Czechoslovakia in 1938 and claimed the war was waged primarily for the benefit of Western arms producers.[34]

Whereas the Polish and Hungarian governments interpreted the conflict as a test or opportunity to express their commitment to NATO, the official view in the Czech Republic was unsupportive of NATO. Havel, too, saw the conflict as a test of resolve, a fact that Albright told Kavan in Prague on 12 April. Havel publicly feared that the Czech Republic would fail this test and would scupper future alliance enlargement, stating 'I have information from very senior sources that these doubts' arose because of the attitudes of Czech politicians. Even Kavan, who eventually sought to project an image of solidarity among chief political personalities, observed Havel's concern, and declared 'the noises [made in the Czech Republic] may not arouse the feeling of solidarity, the attitude expected by NATO'. This position was particularly surprising, because Kavan expressed at the same time his desire that Slovakia be admitted to NATO.[35] Slovak behaviour in the conflict, the first of three hopeful new members of NATO, was strikingly different from that of its western neighbour.

The non-members

Slovakia

Slovakia may have been expected to express some Slavic unity with the Serbs; certainly the government feared that Slovaks might volunteer to enlist in the Serb forces in the name of Slavic unity, prompting the Slovak Defence Ministry to make fighting for another country without official permission a punishable offence.

The position adopted by the coalition government of Mikuláš Dzurinda was one of support of NATO. As with Bulgaria and Romania, this was at least in part to assist the overall foreign policy goal of European integration, a process stunted in all three countries by policies of the previous governments. The Slovak government's offer of the use of its air space to NATO, including particularly for mid-air refuelling, was taken as proof of Slovakia's commitment to the alliance.[36] The Slovak daily newspaper *Sme* commented on how Slovakia could show its renewed strategic importance, indicating that Austrian and Swiss neutrality disallowed NATO air traffic. Slovakia therefore provided the only air corridor in Central Europe between NATO and the Commonwealth of Independent States (CIS) and between north-western and south-eastern Europe.[37] As the bombing came to an end Dzurinda reconfirmed his government's position, saying that its policies were based on the ethics and morals of the civilized world.[38] It may be also that Slovakia's international image was enhanced when Foreign Minister Kukan was appointed (along with former Swedish Prime Minister Carl Bildt) the UN Secretary General's Commissioner for Kosovo.

The Slovak government's alignment with NATO was moderated slightly by concerns over the legality of operations. Following discussions with NATO Secretary General Javier Solana in late May, Kukan noted that Solana linked the cessation of air attacks to Serb military defeat rather than a UN resolution.[39] The government said its troops would not participate in ground operations once that possibility came to be discussed, although Slovak Foreign Ministry State Secretary Jan Figel also said military participation in Kosovo would be contingent on a UNSC resolution.[40] Despite such reservations, the government pressed on with its aims of meeting the perceived expectations of NATO.

Limited dissent could have been detected within the government. Ján Čarnogurský, a former dissident and post-communist Czechoslovak federal deputy Prime Minister, and Justice Minister in the Dzurinda government, seemed critical of the Slovak government's outright support of the NATO action. On 1 May 1999, for example, he called for communication with all sides and for negotiation and said that NATO had no comprehensive plan or final goals. He also stated that public opinion did not support the use of military force and that politicians risked losing popular support.[41]

Opposition clearly came from outside the government. The Movement for a Democratic Slovakia (HZDS), a national movement that ruled until autumn 1998, labelled NATO's actions 'barbaric' and called the government's granting of use of Slovak airspace to the Alliance without parliamentary consent unconstitutional.[42] The leader of the HZDS and former Premier Vladimír Mečiar, said that he was opposed to the division of a country's territory and the arming of groups that receive special military status and recognition at international discussions. These indirect references to autonomy or even independence for Kosovo (which was not granted) and the Kosovo Liberation Army take on significance for Slovakia because Mečiar added that there may be implications for Slovakia.[43] He intimated that the Kosovo war meant that the Hungarian minority in Slovakia may one day be armed, receive international backing and succeed in achieving de facto autonomy. Opposition MPs moved an unsuccessful motion of non-confidence against Kukan for his support of the bombings. The fiercely nationalist Slovak National Party declared that it would send aid independently to Yugoslavia, symbolically choosing Belgrade's Gynecological and Maternity Hospital, which had been bombed by NATO.[44]

Public opinion was divided on NATO's decision, and support declined because of the bombings. A Defence Ministry spokesman said support for NATO membership had fallen both among Slovak soldiers and the general public. A Ministry poll conducted in June showed support for NATO membership at between 30 and 40 per cent for soldiers and 34 to 35 per cent for the public, which was down from the figure of 52 per cent given by Dzurinda for two months before. The Defence Minister commented that NATO would gain more popularity with more investment from the alliance in Slovakia.[45]

Representatives of the 70,000 Slovaks in Vojvodina called NATO's actions 'aggression', claimed that it caused more damage than the fighting in the Second World War, noted that it might be southern Slovakia that is subject to such actions tomorrow, and recalled that Yugoslavia opposed the 1968 Soviet intervention in Czechoslovakia. Slovak-Yugoslavs were also reported as believing that NATO was using Yugoslavia as a testing and dumping ground for radioactive bombs.[46]

Overall, then, while popular opinion and opposition politicians were generally opposed to the NATO bombings, the official perception was that the war could and should expedite the Dzurinda government's efforts to achieve NATO membership. It was, at least, not as blunt as the Bulgarian government in its intentions.

Bulgaria

Perhaps no better than any of the six countries, Bulgaria provided a test of commitment to NATO. The country borders Yugoslavia directly and has a proportionately high amount of trade with it, and Bulgaria is routinely viewed as being culturally, religiously and politically linked to both Serbia and to Russia. In addition, Bulgaria's response to NATO's campaign was further tested by the accidental bombing of the outskirts of the country's capital in April.

Opposition to NATO's airstrikes was considerable in Bulgaria, but this did not divert the centre-right government of the Union of Democratic Forces from its aim of Western institutional integration. It had much to overcome, as the prospects of EU accession were hindered by poor economic reforms and other issues, such as the Kozloduy nuclear power station. The government seized the conflict as an opportunity to demonstrate its support for NATO, which included the offer of the use of its airspace before bombing began. The government's view, however, seems rather brazenly to have been that Bulgaria was paying for its entry into the Alliance. Premier Ivan Kostov told the Bulgarian Parliament in late March 1999 that NATO should admit Bulgaria as a member at the Washington Summit in the following month. Bulgaria's ambassador to the US, Philp Dimitrov was reported during the summit as saying that his country expects a 'clear message from NATO that accession is "but a matter of time"'.[47]

President Petar Stoyanov gave no indications of cultural links with Serbia or Russia, even though he used such terminology when expressing concern for the stability of Macedonia;[48] a newspaper editorial commented that 'hoards of volunteers will not go to Serbia to fight for their Eastern Orthodox Slavonic brothers',[49] although within a few days of 24 March at least 430 Bulgarians had registered and some had already left for Serbia as 'volunteers' to fight in the name of 'Slavic brotherhood'.[50] The Bulgarian government alleged that in addition to lobbying foreign embassies about the Yugoslav position, the Yugoslav embassy in Sofia was rallying Serbs living in Bulgaria against the country.

Rather than expressing solidarity with Russia, the Bulgarian government resisted Russian requests for overflights and land travel by Russian forces for the post-conflict peacekeeping mission. Russian government news agencies noted that Russia was the only country participating in Kosovo peacekeeping to have problems in requesting transit through Bulgaria.[51]

The left-wing political opposition proposed relinquishing newly-made commitments to NATO, but Stoyanov refused and suggested that the Bulgarian left should 'behave' like its counterparts in Romania, Hungary and Poland.[52] Opposition to the government's stands was expressed in the Bulgarian media. The newspaper *Pari* asked whether those who conducted NATO's war such as Clinton, Blair and Clark (the latter referred to as a *Gauleiter*) should not be considered war criminals, in part due to the mistakes made in the conduct of the war.[53]

The government's overall aims were critized as well; an editorial charged after the bombings that Bulgarian politicians were 'inadequate with regard to the national interest and unlikely to produce any perceptible benefit in the future' for the country following their stance during the Kosovo conflict. The commentary added that Bulgaria had 'no importance in European politics', that it was uniquely outside the 'limelight of European politics', and that 'we will be turned into a rear support base for NATO, without being an official member of the alliance, and that we will remain in this position for an indefinite period.'[54]

General opposition to the war and to Bulgaria supporting NATO was evident. Bulgarian media were clear in reporting that Stoyanov was going against public opinion, which he otherwise 'reveres'. His references to popular support for his position were reported as 'coming straight from the production line of the dreams factory',[55] and he denied the figure of 70 per cent of the population being opposed to the air war.[56] Stoyanov thus knew he lacked popular support and admitted that his backing of NATO's bombing campaign would 'lower rather than raise my rating'. But he also said it was only 'a small section of society' who opposed Bulgarian membership of NATO as 'people who want to live in the shadows, to be free to steal, to export capital, to commit crimes, and by no means want Bulgaria to be part of a community, in which there are rules, order, legality, mutual help, and co-operation.'[57]

Stoyanov also denied splits within the political leadership, declaring: 'It is not logical to seek any rifts in the positions of the parliamentary majority, the Government, and the President, because we all started, concluded, and won our election campaign with a strategic goal' of achieving NATO membership.[58] Rather, he called for political solidarity: 'everyone would have to toe the line', as one report put it, as Stoyanov called for 'all Bulgarian politicians to shoulder their political responsibility in the name of Bulgaria's future membership of NATO.'[59]

Opposition to the stand of the President and the government was evident in the Bulgarian media. Newspapers wrote that the country was being drawn into the conflict, with analogies being made to pacts with Nazi Germany. It was alleged during the airwar that NATO Commander General Wesley Clark requested from Bulgaria 'total rear support and supply for a possible ground operation in Yugoslavia'. This was accompanied by assertions that 'history repeats itself', comparing the present to March 1941 when the Bulgarian National Assembly over-whelmingly approved a pact with Nazi Germany turning over use of Bulgaria's air, land and sea. The same article alleged that the aims were the same now as during World War II: 'to banish the Russian bear to the Urals and get a hold of the Caspian Sea oil'. The article claimed, however, that Bulgaria's overture to NATO – granting use of its airspace on 5 May – came late, and should have been given when originally requested in October 1998, and the rewards will now be much less for 'the commodity' of Bulgaria's land and air.[60]

The key perception, then, for Bulgaria has been the extent to which its commitment during the conflict fulfilled the ambition of accession to Western institutions. Bulgarians expected an offer of EU accession, or at least accession negotiations, in return for their support of the alliance during the conflict. This was true also of membership of NATO. Opinion polls and journalists routinely showed this view, as evidenced by a press summary:

> All those polled see the prospective invitation [of EU membership] as a political reward for Bulgaria's support for the moves of Western countries during NATO's airstrikes against Yugoslavia. Though most Bulgarians disapproved of the government's position at that time, the latter's support for the Alliance significantly improved this country's chance of receiving serious compensation in the form of an invitation to open accession talks. The war was a test for Bulgaria's orientation which the country passed.

The position adopted by the government was seen in public opinion as accelerating Bulgaria's chances of being invited for accession talks.[61]

Indeed, numerous promises were offered by foreign leaders and officials. When Clinton visited Bulgaria on 22 November 1999 he told a crowd of 10,000 in Nevsky Square: 'I am told that during the recent war you could actually hear some of the bombs falling on Serbia from this square.' He continued 'Tonight, I hope the people of Serbia can hear our voices when we say if you choose as Bulgaria has chosen, you will regain the rightful place in Europe Mr Milosevic has stolen from you, and America will support you too.'[62] Forty-seven per cent of those polled in Sofia felt Clinton's visit was in recognition of Bulgaria's backing of NATO; 29 per cent said he came to establish US bases in the country.[63] (NATO has denied ever seeking to open facilities in Bulgaria.)

German Chancellor Gerhard Schröder visited Bulgaria during the airwar, declaring: 'Not only Germany but NATO greatly appreciates Bulgaria's solidarity, such as allowing NATO planes to overfly the country' and he said that Germany would make 'great efforts' to advance Bulgaria's membership of the EU.[64] The state-owned press agency BTA reported

147

that the new NATO Secretary General, Lord Robertson, 'expressed gratitude for the sacrifices Bulgaria and the Bulgarian people made during the Kosovo crisis in the name of partnership.'[65]

But the population was also realistic. As one domestic source observed, 'Bulgaria could hope for compensation for its unconditional support.' And Bulgaria was invited to begin accession talks, but the same report indicated that popular beliefs held that Bulgaria could not achieve membership until, most optimistically, 2010 or 2015, and perhaps even 2020.[66]

The expectation of some Western reward was also heightened by the economic costs to Bulgaria of the crisis. Fifteen per cent of Bulgarian trade was lost because the Danube was blocked. Bulgaria's main trade in oil, metals and cellulose – all too heavy to transport economically by land – used to ship through Yugoslavia and had to be redirected through Romania, and the closure of the Yugoslav shipping routes was estimated to threaten half the country's exports. The US ambassador to Sofia reassured the Bulgarian government that it would be compensated from economic losses caused by the NATO action.

Stoyanov was confident, at least, that his government's policies had raised Bulgaria's profile in the West. In a New Year's speech to Bulgaria's diplomatic corps, Stoyanov called the invitation to begin EU accession talks 'a logical result of the foreign and domestic policy of the Bulgarian government' and noted that Blair, Clinton, and Dutch Queen Beatrix visited the country for the first time in 1999.[67] Romania was in a similar political and strategic position to Bulgaria.

Romania

Whereas Bulgaria and Slovakia had not met criteria for membership talks with the EU and NATO in the 1990s, in the first six years of the decade Romania was sharply criticized by Western institutions for its lack of political development and democratization and consequently was rejected from the North Atlantic Cooperation Council. As with its Bulgarian and Slovak counterparts, the Kosovo crisis presented the centre-right Romanian government with an opportunity to advance its goal of European institutional accession.

Consequently, the Romanian government supported NATO, even though its position was to avoid the use of airstrikes, and granted the alliance unrestricted use of Romania airspace.[68] The Democratic Union of Hungarians in Romania (UDMR), a junior coalition partner in the government, was fully supportive throughout; indeed, UDMR Senator György Frunda was blunt about the practicalities of this measure. He likened it to the favourable response Poland, Hungary and the Czech Republic gave to NATO during the Bosnian war and which in turn, he said, favoured their future accession. Despite dissatisfaction with the situation of Hungarians in Romania, UDMR President Bela Marko nevertheless called for unity within Romania as it approached NATO's Washington summit.[69]

Romanian President Constantinescu, in a lengthy speech made as the bombing ceased, meant to reassure his population about the effects of war: 'we have passed a test with flying colours. This was a test in resolution and consistency regarding our alliances ... We have proved that we are capable not only of words but of deeds as well.' Constantinescu also indicated how Romania's economic and political position had improved as a result of its stance, stating that its relations with major international institutions had improved, including the EU and NATO and also the IMF and the World Bank.[70]

Even though the government intended to secure earlier accession – a popular objective – the government had to contend with strong criticism, even bombast, from the opposition Social Democracy Party of Romania (PDSR). When, for example, Tony Blair visited the country in early May while the airstrikes continued, first PDSR Vice President Adrian Nastase ridiculed the British Prime Minister's comments and said the visit might simply lead to further NATO requests for Romanian involvement in the conflict.[71] President Ion Iliescu of the PDSR, who was president from 1990 to 1996, objected to force being used against a sovereign state.[72] Iliescu, whose government was considered antagonistic toward the country's Hungarian minority, charged that the UDMR might take advantage of the Kosovo precedent to engage in separatism or secession within Romania.[73]

Parliament's post-conflict legislation allowing the transit of Polish and Czech troops participating in KFOR was also contested. Opposition Social Democracy Party MPs requested that it be struck down, contending that it broke Romania's Law on National Security because foreign troops are allowed transit only when in joint operations with the Romanian military.[74] The use of force by NATO against Yugoslavia, and the government's contributions to that effort, was generally unpopular, a situation noted by US Congressmen in a letter they wrote to Clinton concerning the economic losses suffered by the country from the war and its aftermath.[75] Public opposition may account for some moderation of the Romanian government's stand during the conflict. It made clear that it always preferred a negotiated outcome to conflicts; the Romanian Foreign Minister Andrei Plesu was one of several to suggest a cessation of bombing over Easter; and he explicitly ruled out use of Romanian forces in a ground war and denied the existence of plans to deploy NATO troops in Romania as part of a ground offensive against Yugoslavia.[76]

Romania fared no better than Bulgaria or Slovakia in receiving concrete reassurances about Western integration; its efforts, however, were similarly acknowledged.Visiting Romania in December 1999, Polish Deputy Foreign Minister Radosław Sikorski said that all NATO member states were impressed by Romania's handling of the crisis and that the Alliance recognized its assistance in co-ordinating air strikes and in making available its airspace. He added that this was in Romania's favour and benefited its drive for NATO membership.[77] The Romanian press reported that General Clark stressed that NATO understood the sacrifices that the Romanians had made both in Bosnia and Kosovo.[78]

Perhaps not as brashly as Bulgarians, Romanian officials also expected an indication on NATO membership at the Washington Summit. Romania's Ambassador to Washington Mircea Geonana commented: 'Romania felt the need to join NATO, not only because we want to take care of our security, but also because we felt, and feel, that we can contribute to the security of that region of Europe.'[79]

While accession was obviously not given, government officials were positive regarding alliance assessments of the country's stand and contribution. Foreign Ministry Secretary of State Mihai-Razvan Ungureanu reported that foreign diplomats had lauded Romania for its support of NATO during the conflict and its good positive contributions to peace and security in the region. He spoke of Romania's 'advanced level' of ties with the alliance and said that Romania would participate in activities to increase NATO's military inter-operability.[80]

The outcome of the conflict can be said to be similar for the three non-member states. But how did the conflict affect the region as a whole and what was its relevance for issues and perceptions of security?

Central and south-east Europe's new perceptions of security

The governing political elites of five of these states, that of the Czech Republic excepted, were united in the need to support NATO both rhetorically and practically, the latter expressed generally through granting access to airspace and to contributing forces to KFOR. The Polish and Hungarian governments saw the conflict as a test of their new alliance membership, a test they believed they passed successfully. In the Czech Republic, the elite divisions that were anomalous in the region, are perhaps best explained by contradictions in Czech foreign policy thinking throughout the 1990s. Havel, however, even feared that Czech irresolution and obstinence would not only fail the country in NATO's eyes but also imperil further NATO enlargement.

For the three non-member states the war was perceived not only as a test but also as an opportunity to accelerate their entry into NATO and possibly into the EU. The experience for those three in practice, however, has been rather different. And it is in this that the lasting but subtle perceptions of the conflict may be found. Despite regional expectations otherwise, Solana said on 17 June 1999 that Kosovo would not change the speed of NATO's open-door policy. While he said NATO would soon launch its Action Membership Plan, which would bring interested states closer to the Organization, he added that participation in KFOR (for Slovakia, but also generally) bore no relation to future NATO membership.[81]

In addition to alliance membership not being forthcoming, assistance to the region was also limited. The Stability Pact, presented initially as a panacea for south-eastern Europe, was seen by regional leaders to lack substance or even to be counterproductive. Hungary and Slovenia were excluded from the financial side of the Stability Pact, relegated to what was called the 'political' dimension, because they were already undergoing accession talks with the EU. Disappointed, the two countries were reported as consequently pushing for earlier EU membership,[82] which has also not been forthcoming. Romanian Prime Minister Radu Vasile was very positive after a meeting with Pact co-ordinator Bodo Hombach, but asked him for details of the economic benefits.[83] Bulgaria's Stoyanov was more blunt: at a meeting with his Romanian and Greek counterparts in November 1999 he proclaimed 'We esteem highly the Stability Pact, but we find this framework still void of concrete substance.'[84] EU candidate countries expressed fear, such as that by Slovakia's minister responsible for European integration Pavol Hamžik, that EU funds would be diverted from them to the reconstruction of Yugoslavia.[85]

While the post-conflict order provided by Brussels may have been unsatisfactory for the region, the conflict may have prompted greater co-operation and reliance within the region. The conflict drew Slovakia even closer to the other three Visegrad states, complementing the revival of that process begun the year before. The four countries jointly stressed that they provided a source of stability.[86] Within south-eastern Europe new forms of co-operation were expressed as well. Romanian President Constantinescu announced that 'Bulgaria and Romania will undertake to pursue an active policy of proposing investment projects' to generate investment. Constantinescu also said that relations between his country and Bulgaria were a model for others, and that relations between them and Greece were a model for regional security.[87] Bulgarian Premier Kostov told Lord Robertson that he aspired 'to continue developing military co-operation with NATO together with our neighbour to the north, Romania, within the context of the two countries' preparation for membership in NATO.'[88] A landmark decision was taken to build the Vidin-Calafat bridge between Romania and Bulgaria, partly because of the continued disruption to Danube shipping; Slovakia's Foreign Minister was also supportive because the measure would improve the region's transportation.[89]

A striking change in the region's perceptions of security regards Russia. It is ironic that NATO membership was conceived by former members of the Warsaw Pact as not just a generic security guarantee but also one particularly against Russia. Yet at no time does it seem that any of these six governments felt threatened by their eastern neighbour. Instead, many governments could be said to have stood up to Russia, as indicated by the denial of transit rights, even for an ostensibly impartial and internationally mandated peacekeeping mission. Certainly, the Russian Defence and Foreign Ministries were reported as 'stunned' that Hungary, Bulgaria and Romania denied use of their airspace to Russian forces participating in KFOR.[90]

The enduring, but unstated perception from the region must be the sway that NATO (and, by extension, general European integration) holds over the governments of central and south-eastern Europe. In all six countries some form of public opinion was overridden; in Poland and Hungary this was more marginal. In the remaining four countries, opposition was wider. Despite NATO's contradiction of its pledge not to bomb Hungarian-populated Vojvodina; despite stray missiles exploding in Bulgaria, despite few concrete offers of post-conflict financial assistance; and despite no statement of an accession timetable, all of these states lent their support to NATO and continue to view their stance positively and appropriately. To be sure, NATO warned Serbia not to endanger its neighbours; and Bulgaria, Romania, and Slovakia, along with Latvia and Lithuania, began EU accession talks in 2000. The gains to the region nevertheless remain unquantifiable and potentially deceptive. The perception of south-east European leaderships was almost certainly that rewards would follow their support of NATO. That governments are unwilling to admit such, not least in the face of domestic criticisms, further illustrates NATO's allure.

The military actions of NATO prompted all six countries to revise their perceptions of post-Cold War security. For the three new alliance members, the impositions on them from the bombings demonstrated that security carries costs and obligations; for the non-members, the actions provided an instrumental, perhaps even Machiavellian, means to improve their security environment by consenting to an operation with which they did not necessarily agree, which their populations generally opposed, and which may at best provide the desired security dividends only in the longer term.

Notes

1. The geographical terms used to describe this region are of course contested. This chapter covers the countries that constituted the non-Soviet members of the Warsaw Pact, excluding East Germany.
2. *RFE/RL Newsline II*, 25 March 1999.

3. *Le Monde*, 31 July 1999, in *Foreign Broadcast Information Service*. Daily Report. East Europe (hereafter cited as FBIS), 3 August 1999.
4. Pentor Institute poll, reported in PAP, 2 June 1999, in *FBIS*, 7 June 1999.
5. CBOS poll, PAP, 26 May 1999, in *FBIS*, 27 May 1999.
6. PAP, 19 April 1999, in *FBIS*, 20 April 1999.
7. PAP, 20 April 1999, in *FBIS*, 21 April 1999.
8. PAP, 25 April 1999, in *FBIS*, 27 April 1999.
9. PAP, 24 April 1999, in *FBIS*, 27 April 1999.
10. PAP, 26 May 1999, in *FBIS*, 27 May 1999.
11. PAP, 24 March 2000, in *FBIS*, 28 March 2000.
12. PAP, 28 April 1999, in *FBIS*, 29 April 1999.
13. *Polityka*, 18 September 1999, in *FBIS*, 23 September 1999.
14. *RFE/RL Newsline II*, 24 March 1999.
15. Béla Balgózci, 'The Impact of the Kosovo crisis on Hungary', Balkans Workshop, 1 July 1999 in Helsinki, at http://www.etuc.org/kosovo/New_-pages/congress3.cfm.
16. Mark Gillespie and Robert Manchin, 'Kosovo Air Strike Receive Support in Britian, Hungary', *Gallup News Service*, 30 March 1999, at http://www.gallup.com/poll/releases/pr990330b.asp.
17. *Nepsazbadsag*, 7 July 2000, in *FBIS*, 10 July 2000.
18. Balgózci, *op. cit.*
19. *ITAR-TASS*, 25 May 1999, in *FBIS*, 26 May 1999.
20. *Polityka*, 18 September 1999, in *FBIS*, 23 September 1999.
21. *The Toronto Star*, 15 November 1999.
22. Albright is quoted as saying 'my mindset is Munich'; *Guardian*, 6 December 1996.
23. William Pfaff wrote, for example, 'tolerating what Slobodan Milosevic is doing to "restore order" in Kosovo, because Washington relies on him to enforce the Dayton agreement, is like choosing Soviet order in 1968 over Prague's springtime. It is the sort of thing that ends badly.' 'Prague 1968 and the West's Toleration of the Kosovo Crisis', *International Herald Tribune*, 8 September 1998.
24. *Mladá fronta Dnes* and *Lidové noviny*, 26 March 1999.
25. ČTK, 26 April 1999.
26. Ladislav Cabada and Martin Ehl, 'The Kosovo Crisis and the Prospects for the Balkans', *Perspectives*, no. 13 (Winter 1999/2000), p. 27.
27. ČTK, 4 March 1999.
28. ČTK, 24 March 1999.
29. *Lidové noviny*, 26 April 1999.
30. Václav Havel, 'Kosovo and the End of the Nation State', *The New York Review of Books*, 10 June 1999.
31. Noam Chomsky, *The New Military Humanism: Lessons from Kosovo* (London: Pluto Press, 1999), especially pp. 87-9.
32. For a brief discussion, see Rick Fawn, *The Czech Republic: A Nation of Velvet* (Reading and Amsterdam: Harwood Academic Publishers, 2000), pp. 132-3.
33. *Mladá fronta Dnes*, 19 May and 12 June 1999.
34. ČTK, 2 April 1999.

35. ČTK, 13 April 1999. See also Deputy Premier Egon Lanský's comment: 'We are prepared to do our utmost for Slovakia's admission to the Alliance.' ČTK, 16 April 1999.
36. Michael Shafir, 'Yugoslavia: The Kosovo Crisis and the NATO Hopefuls', *RFE/ RL Newsline*, 26 March 1999.
37. *Sme*, 25 March 1999.
38. TASR, 17 June 1999.
39. TASR, 25 May 1999.
40. TASR, 1 June 1999.
41. ČTK, 1 May 1999.
42. *Sme*, 27 March 1999. This position was reiterated at the HZDS convention the following month. For accounts, see TASR, 18 April 1999.
43. TASR, 15 April 1999.
44. *Narodná obroda*, 24 January 2000.
45. ČTK, 30 November 1999; Dzurinda's figure from *Standart*, 17 June 2000, in *FBIS*, 21 June 2000.
46. Comments of Juraj Cervenak, chairman of the local government in Backa Petrovac, in ČTK, 13 May 1999.
47. Julie Moffat, 'Eastern Europe: Six Countries Seek NATO Membership Despite Balkan Conflict', *RFE/RL*, 22 April 1999.
48. *Trud*, 3 May 1999, in *FBIS*, 4 May 1999. He called Macedonia 'an absolutely fraternal country'. This may have been a reference to politics more than 'civilization', particularly as his views on the conflict were consistently presented as a clash between democracy and communism.
49. *Trud*, 2 April 1999, in *FBIS*, 5 April 1999.
50. Shafir, *op. cit.*
51. ITAR-TASS, 5 July 1999, in FBIS, 8 July 1999.
52. *Trud*, 3 May 1999, in *FBIS*, 4 May 1999.
53. *Pari*, 1 June 1999, in *FBIS*, 2 June 1999.
54. Evgeniy Gindev, 'Kosovo Crisis Showed Up Weaknesses of Our Politicians and Army', *Pari*, 16 June 1999.
55. *Pari*, 17 April 1999, in *FBIS*, 19 April 1999.
56. *Trud*, 3 May 1999, in *FBIS*, 4 May 1999.
57. *Trud*, 17 April 1999, in *FBIS*, 20 April 1999.
58. *Trud*, 17 April 1999, in *FBIS*, 20 April 1999.
59. AFP, 16 April 1999, in *FBIS*, 19 April 1999.
60. *Trud*, 5 May 1999, in *FBIS*, 6 May 1999.
61. BTA, 3 December 1999, in *FBIS*, 6 December 1999.
62. Marc Lacey, 'Clinton thanks Bulgaria for backing NATO attack', *National Post*, 23 November 1999.
63. BTA, 19 November 1999, in *FBIS*, 23 November 1999.
64. AFP, 26 May 1999, in *FBIS*, 27 May 1999.
65. BTA, 8 February 2000, in *FBIS*, 10 February 2000.
66. BTA, 3 December 1999, in *FBIS*, 6 December 1999.
67. BTA, 12 January 2000, in *FBIS*, 13 January 2000.
68. See the report of the Foreign Ministry's press conference given on Radio Romania on 24 March 1999, in *FBIS*, 25 March 1999.

69. Radio Romania, 21 April 1999, in *FBIS*, 22 April 1999.
70. Radio Romania, 11 June 1999, in *FBIS*, 14 June 1999.
71. Radio Romania, 4 May 1999, in *FBIS*, 5 May 1999.
72. Radio Romania, 25 March 1999, in *FBIS*, 26 March 1999.
73. Radio Romania, 21 April 1999, in *FBIS*, 22 April 1999.
74. Radio Romania, 17 June 1999, in *FBIS*, 18 June 1999.
75. Rompres, 20 March 2000, in *FBIS*, 31 March 2000.
76. Radio Romania, 1 June 1999, in *FBIS*, 2 June 1999.
77. Rompres, 9 December 1999, in *FBIS*, 12 December 1999.
78. Rompres, 2 March 2000, in *FBIS*, 3 March 2000.
79. Moffat, *op. cit.*
80. Rompres, 12 November 1999, in *FBIS*, 20 November 1999.
81. TASR, 17 June 1999.
82. Ladislav Cabada and Martin Ehl, 'The Kosovo Crisis and the Prospects for the Balkans', *Perspectives*, no. 13 (Winter 1999/2000), p. 24.
83. Radio Romania, 15 July 1999, in *FBIS*, 16 July 1999.
84. BTA, 4 November 1999, in *FBIS*, 20 November 1999.
85. TASR, 5 May 1999.
86. See the comments by Mazowiecki and Czech Deputy Premier for European Integration Egon Lanský, ČTK, 26 May 1999.
87. BTA, 4 November 1999, in *FBIS*, 20 November 1999.
88. BTA, 10 February 2000, in *FBIS*, 11 February 2000.
89. *Pari*, 30 August 1999, in *FBIS*, 31 August 1999.
90. Interfax, 4 July 1999, in *FBIS*, 6 July 1999.

CHAPTER TEN

Russian Perceptions

MARY BUCKLEY

The general picture delivered in the Western media of Russian responses to NATO's bombing of Kosovo was that they were extremely hostile, misunderstood the intentions of the leaders of NATO's member states (whatever their differences) and displayed an unthinking reflex loyalty to 'Serb brothers', wanting in moral judgement given the appalling atrocities of ethnic cleansing. The impetus for Russian involvement through President Boris Yeltsin sending Viktor Chernomyrdin as a peace envoy to Belgrade, despite huge criticism at home, appeared to be twofold: to please the West in order to obtain another tranche of IMF money and to be seen to be active again as a great power on the world stage, making a difference and meriting respect.

In fact, although the overwhelming majority of Russian political leaders, parties and citizens were highly critical of NATO's actions, there were variations in Russian understandings of the course of events in the Balkans, not one Russian 'view'. Although Yeltsin and his successive prime ministers Evgennii Primakov, Sergei Stepashin and later Vladimir Putin, as well as Foreign Minister Igor Ivanov and Defence Minister Igor Sergeev, and also the International Affairs Committee of the State Duma, all condemned NATO, their emphases differed. Yeltsin himself was not consistent throughout and there were visible differences between those in the Ministries of Defence and Foreign Affairs. Most vitriolic were Genadii Ziuganov, leader of the Communist Party of the Russian Federation (KPRF) and Vladimir Zhirinovskii, leader of the Liberal Democratic Party of Russia (LDPR). Both called for more drastic action to the point of military involvement, organizing lists of volunteers to fight. The legislature was quick to call for a military response, unlike the executive. Even reformers like Grigorii YavIinskii, leader of Yabloko, voiced their criticisms of NATO, although in Duma debates called for caution.

In a lively press, various shades of opinion were put, ranging from critical of NATO in *Argumenty i Fakty* from former President of the USSR, Mikhail Gorbachev and former dissident Aleksandr Solzhenitsyn, to more sympathetic from journalists such as Iuliia Berezovskaia and Genadii Sysoev writing for *Izvestiia* and *Kommersant*, respectively. Predictably, the most hostile journalism was found in *Pravda*, *Zavtra* and *Krasnaia Zvezda*. *Nezavisimaia gazeta* was highly critical. There were critical but also mixed views showing a willingness to publish debate in *Izvestiia* and in the magazine *Rossiiskaia Federatsiia Segodnia*, with the most bland reporting with some sympathy for the West in *Kommersant*. A content analysis of the Russian press shows diverse assessments of the significance of NATO's bombing, different recommendations to Russian leaders and competing conclusions about Russian defence policy and the fate of relations with Western governments.

Broader public opinion also showed some diversity, athough it was heavily weighted at 98 per cent 'against', contrasting with more divided populations in France and Germany.[1] Italians, like Russians, fell towards the critical end of the spectrum but by April support for NATO in Italy had increased, an upward trend being evident in Britain, France and Germany too but lacking in Russia.[2] Polls in April 1999 showed a steadfast 92 per cent of Russians against the bombing.[3] Only 2 per cent explicitly approved.[4]

Despite overwhelming opposition in Russia's political elites and population to NATO's campaign, and notwithstanding Russia's withdrawal from the Partnership for Peace, shunning of NATO's 50th Anniversary summit in late April, refusal to comply with NATO's oil embargo of Belgrade[5] and growing tensions in Russian/American relations to the point of attacks on the US embassy in Moscow,[6] once the bombing had ceased, opinion polls showed far more Russians ready to accept good relations with the USA than had supported NATO's bombing. Although there were still divisions in Russian assessments of the USA, the bombing had not irreparably damaged positive views of 'the West', even though strong negative sentiments persisted. Yeltsin, Putin's government, reformers and most centrists also wanted to mend East/West relations in beneficial ways, even if simultaneously declaring that the post-Cold War 'partnership' of Russia and the West no longer existed in its ertswhile briefly romantic form. Most were steadfast in their criticisms of what NATO had done, but pragmatic in their readiness to co-operate on other issues. Continued vitriol came from the communists and nationalists.

Once Acting President in January 2000, then elected President after March, Putin held a consistent position on the need to restore Russia's greatness but also tried to appear businesslike to Western leaders and bankers. On British television, Putin commented that it was harmful to see NATO as an enemy and that 'isolationism is not our way'. When asked if Russia could join NATO, he quipped 'why not?'[7] This went down badly in newspapers such as *Sovetskaia Rossiia* where it was noted that during NATO's bombing the Russian Defence Ministry had categorized that organization as 'criminal'.[8] In his book *First Person* (very much a public relations device), Putin declared 'I don't see any reason why cooperation between Russia and NATO shouldn't develop further; but I repeat that it will happen only if Russia is treated as an equal partner.'[9] Another repeated message, dating back to Brezhnev and earlier, was that Russia merited respect, as befitting a great power. Indeed, it was a central theme in the election materials of Edinstvo, or Unity, the movement to which Putin had given personal backing in the 1999 parliamentary election campaign.[10] This was reiterated in the 'new' foreign policy concept announced in July 2000. Co-operating with NATO was deemed constructive 'in the interests of security and stability on the Continent', but only so long as NATO did not threaten or use force or deploy forces, weapons or delivery vehicles on the territory of new NATO members.[11] The document also declared that the introduction of concepts of 'humanitarian interventionism' and 'limited sovereignty' into international practice was unacceptable. When announcing the document, Ivanov insisted that Russia would be 'tough' when necessary.[12]

Putin's pragmatism in domestic and foreign politics does not mean that NATO bombing of Kosovo or NATO's reaction to the Russian war in Chechnia ultimately made no difference to East/West relations.[13] Russia's 'new' military doctrine, friendship with China and India, and ongoing criticism of the US's favouring of a 'unipolar' world, topped with the 'new' foreign policy concept, are among the outcomes, although most were in the pipeline anyway, or at least on some agendas, now given added justification by NATO's bombing. Under Putin's leadership, Russia finally ratified START II and subsequently approved the Comprehensive Test Ban Treaty, tossing a challenge back to the USA not to violate the 1972 ABM agreement. In July 2000, Putin and Chinese leader Jiang Zemin spoke out again against US plans for a limited national defence system, holding that it would lead to 'distortions of the balance of power'.[14] Colonel General Leonid Ivashov also announced that Russia would not take part in military manoeuvres within the framework of NATO's partnership for peace, planned for 2000, claiming that some were a 'mere backdrop to the rehearsing of military action against Russia'.[15] The loud message from Putin is that Russia remains a nuclear power to be seriously reckoned with on the world stage, whatever her domestic economic and social problems.

Historical context

The perceptions of Russian leaders and public were set in a context significantly different from that of West Europeans. Just ten years earlier, the Russian 'empire' in eastern Europe had collapsed as revolutions

brought independence from the Soviet grip, a process unintentionally
facilitated by Gorbachev's encouragement of perestroika throughout
eastern Europe.[16] Also in 1989, the Soviet Union's first elected parliament,
the Congress of People's Deputies, came into existence heralding a
significant political break from the past, soon followed in 1990 by
elections to parliaments in the fifteen Soviet republics and the legalization
in November 1990 of political parties. The one-party state was crumbling
and nationalists in the Baltic States, Georgia and Ukraine demanded
independence. Complex and mutually reinforcing processes of social,
economic and political change from 1985 to 1991 culminated in the
disintegration of the Soviet state, finally accelerated by the failed coup of
August 1991, which had attempted to restore order, unity and maintain
the state.[17] Not only had the empire in Eastern Europe crumbled, but now
the Soviet state itself imploded, amid serious crises of legitimacy and
identity.

These developments did not augur well for international status and
prestige. Humiliation intensified as economic reforms resulted in a
widening gap between rich and poor, increased crime and the growth of
corrupt mafias, themselves intertwined with government and law-
enforcement agencies. Tensions between President Yeltsin and his
Russian Congress of People's Deputies over the nature of economic
reform and constitutional arrangements brought political crises in 1993,
culminating in Yeltsin's dissolution of Parliament and its subsequent
bombing.[18] The new presidential regime enshrined in the 1993 Constitution was meant to bring a more workable polity. Tensions, however,
between executive and legislature continued since the first two State
Dumas elected in 1993 and 1995 had strong anti-reform compositions.
The KPRF won a total of 48 seats in 1993, jumping in 1995 to 157.
Zhirinovskii's LDRP did unexpectedly well in 1993, gaining 64 seats, but
support fell to 51 in 1995.[19] The Presidential race in 1996 was a close one,
reflecting a divided society, with Yeltsin and Ziuganov in the first round
receiving 35.3 and 32 per cent of the vote respectively. Only a political
deal between Yeltsin and General Lebed before the second round, which
made Lebed Secretary of the Security Council, ensured Yeltsin's final
victory of 53.8 per cent.[20]

Disagreements over economic reform continued into the late 1990s in
an ideologically divided state. Dependence on IMF loans humiliated
communists and nationalists – the so-called Red-Brown alliance. The
economic crisis of 1998 was further testimony for critics of the ill-advised
economic policies of reformers. Moreover, Yeltsin's firing in March of
Viktor Chernomyrdin, Prime Minister of five year's standing, his
replacement with the unpopular Sergei Kirienko, then the sacking of
Kirienko in August to be replaced by Evgenii Primakov in September after
Yeltsin's failed attempt to reinstate Chernomyrdin, followed by the

removal of Primakov in May 1999 in favour of Stepashin, gave the impression of an erratic President bringing confusion and instability.[21] This heightened the feeling of uncertaintly, unpredictability, incompetence – in sum, a weak state. Public discourse talked of *obval*, or avalanche, implying insecure and sliding ground. The sense of instability did not abate when, in August 1999, Stepashin was fired too – a Prime Minister of under three months – replaced by the relatively unknown Putin.

The expansion of NATO eastwards had been yet another unwelcome development, adding salt to a series of accumulating wounds.[22] The accession of Poland, Hungary and the Czech Republic did not just mean erstwhile allies joining a former superpower enemy, but brought the added discomfort of NATO troops for the first time on Russia's western borders, even though there were promises from NATO about limited numbers and no weapons. Foreign Minister Ivanov declared that 'NATO expansion is a step in the wrong direction'.[23] Leaders in Moscow demanded no further expansion of NATO, especially concerned about the desire to join in Ukraine and the Baltic states.[24] Against this backdrop, NATO's bombing of the former Yugoslavia was seen as aggressive action in a part of Europe not previously in the US sphere, part of a broader process of expansion into the post-Soviet space, illegally bypassing the UN and casting the USA as unaccountable and arrogant world policeman.

The President and Government

In March 1999, prior to NATO's bombing, the priority of the Russian government had been to prevent such a course of action. Prime Minister Primakov commented that 'I hope there will not be any bombing' since this would have 'an enormous destabilizing effect' in Yugoslavia, Europe and the world.[25] Foreign Minister Igor Ivanov urged continued use of negotiating processes, which were 'far from exhausted'.[26] Defence Minister Igor Sergeev's message was more fraught. Early in the month, he emphasized how lessons in Yugoslavia required intense examination of how to increase Russia's military capabilities. He cautioned that, because NATO was considering sending in ground forces, 'the international arena is abruptly much changing'.[27] He added that NATO was about to confirm a new conception of itself as unable to use force without a resolution of the Security Council of the UN, but in fact was denying that organization a role.[28] Sergeev warned on 23 March that NATO bombing could generate 'another Vietnam, but this time in Europe'. The Ministry of Defence was watching closely and 'drawing up plans and taking steps which will boil down to increasing combat readiness.'[29] The next day ITAR-TASS revealed that the Defence Ministry was preparing proposals for the possible deployment of tactical nuclear weapons on the territory of Belarus in the event of NATO strikes.[30]

Once US Vice-President Al Gore had informed Primakov that strikes were unavoidable, Primakov told Russian television viewers that he refused to issue a joint statment with the Americans about the agreed postponement of his visit to the USA since this looked like collusion. From his plane, Primakov phoned Michel Camdessus, IMF managing director, to say that Kosovo was one problem distinct from talks with the IMF, not wanting loans to be jeopardized.[31]

Within government, then, different concerns were evident. Ivanov stressed diplomacy, Primakov emphasized talks and compromises with a separation from IMF loans, while Sergeev talked about the need for military preparedness. These were predictably different institutional interests of a foreign minister, prime minister and defence minister.

President Yeltsin's immediate reaction to NATO's bombing was to issue a statement on 24 March which recorded Russia's 'outrage' at 'undisguised aggression' and 'military adventurism'. Yeltsin argued that since the UN Security Council had not agreed to this course of action against sovereign Yugoslavia, then NATO was setting a dangerous precedent for 'reviving the policy of diktat' based on force and behaving like a 'world policeman'.[32] Yeltsin called off Prime Minister Primakov's visit to the USA, demanded an emergency meeting of the UN Security Council to try and bring an end to the bombing, recalled to Moscow Russia's Chief Military Representative to NATO, suspended Russian participation in the Partnership for Peace and postponed talks on opening a NATO military mission in Moscow. Settlement of issues in Kosovo, he insisted, could be reached 'only through negotiation'. He threatened that if conflict should spread, Russia reserved the right to take 'appropriate measures, including measures of a military nature'.[33] Primakov echoed these sentiments, pointing to 'gross violation' of the UN Charter and a tremendous threat to world stability.[34]

Marshall Sergeev's response was consistent with earlier statements. Speaking in Tajikistan in early April, he commented that 'the situation in the world might become more strained for a long time and seriously so' because it was becoming divided up again and 'NATO is assuming the role of international policeman'.[35] Sergeev, especially, was sensitive to NATO encroachment.

Foreign Minister Ivanov made more diplomatic statements. Quick to indicate that Russia would not take any countermeasures, as Yeltsin had hinted, he stressed that he did not wish to see conflict spread beyond the Balkans. The priority was to stop aggression by 'purely political means'.[36] When asked to comment upon Sergeev's remarks on military action, Ivanov refused to back them. He calmly noted the need to ensure 'Russia's national interest' to contain the conflict.[37] Yeltsin's bolder statement was in part to show his communist and nationalist opposition that he could talk tough, threatening but not actually intending to use force.

Even more distinct were the views of Andrei Kozyrev, former Foreign Minister from November 1990 to January 1996. Kozyrev criticized Primakov's about-turn in mid-air on his flight to the USA as tantamount to showing support for Milošević, whom Kozyrev characterized as a dictator who only understood force and ethnic cleansing. Kozyrev held that since the EU had endorsed NATO's military action, it was Russia who was out on a limb.[38] Having lost his job for his pro-Western sympathies at a time of nationalist strength in the Duma, Kozyrev represented a minority view.

After intially hostile reactions to the bombing, Yeltsin appeared publicly to vacillate. The paper *Segodnia* pointed out that one day his message was that Russia would pursue only diplomacy, the next that 'we will not allow Yugoslavia to be vanquished'. Threats and warnings of 'critical' moments from Yeltsin were interspersed with emphasis on diplomacy and non-military involvement.[39] In early April, Yeltsin announced that Russia would not supply Serbia with weapons and not get involved.[40] Then on 19 April Yeltsin made a typically confused statement: 'We will act with restraint. But we certainly cannot abandon Milošević.'[41] Milošević's request a week earlier to join the union of Belarus and Russia, relayed to Yeltsin via Gennadii Seleznev, speaker of the Duma, sent a frisson of concern through the world's press as Yeltsin responded favourably, allegedly announcing to Seleznev that Russian missiles were being re-targeted on the states at war with Milošević.[42] Officials at the ministries of Defence and Foreign Affairs were either silent or confirmed that no such orders had been given.[43] The chief of the General Staff of the Russian Strategic Missile Forces, Colonel General Anatolii Perminov, also said he had received no such order, but added that he would act immediately should he do so.[44] Once the re-targeting of missiles had been denied, greater calm ensued. Yeltsin's appointment of Chernomyrdin as peace envoy was more pragmatic and constructive, especially because he was respected in the West.[45] This move, however, was highly controversial at home. In taking NATO's peace plan to Belgrade, Chernomyrdin was accused of acting contrary to Russia's interests. This was levelled most explicitly by Marshall Sergeev and General Leonid Ivashov.[46] Sergei Stepashin, who in May had replaced Primakov as Prime Minister regretted, too, that through Chernomyrdin NATO was getting its way.[47]

The Legislature

Prior to the bombing, Duma speaker Gennadii Seleznev was more outspoken than Primakov and Ivanov. He did not, as Primakov, talk diplomatically of 'mutual concessions and compromises', instead declaring that 'we shall regard this as an act of aggression'.[48] The International Affairs Committee of the Duma condemned the air raids as 'irresponsible' and blamed NATO for bringing Europe 'to the verge of the most serious military-political crisis in decades'. Not taking Russia's interests into account, NATO 'has thus taken a hostile position with regard to the Russian Federation'. The Committee pressed president and government to make an 'adequate response' and to consider 'military assistance' to Yugoslavia. Co-operation with NATO was branded 'senseless'.[49]

The harshest language against NATO was expressed by communists and nationalists. As well as being leader of the KPRF, Ziuganov was chair of the People's Patriotic Union of Russia (*Narodno-patrioticheskii soiuz Rossii*, or NPSR), a red-brown alliance. In this latter capacity, Ziuganov signed in *Pravda* an announcement of the Presiduim of NPSR, declaring that NATO was consolidating 'an era of an aggressive world order' and that the 'USA is establishing a global dictatorship by neo-fascist methods' and NATO 'is returning us to the time of Hitlerism'.[50] This tragedy, moreover, was 'the inevitable result of the activities of pro-American groups in Russia's ruling elite.' Both Gorbachev and Yeltsin were branded 'general secretaries of the party of betrayal', controlled by world oligarchs. Russian television was depicted as providing 'ideological centres' for NATO agents.[51] The NPSR recommended Russian withdrawal from all agreements with NATO, an end to Russian sanctions against Yugoslavia, Iraq, Libya and Iran, the immediate despatch of weapons and volunteer brigades to Serbia, refusal to ratify START II, support for nuclear weapons in Belarus, and backing for a strategic Union of Russia, Belarus, Ukraine and Yugoslavia (even though Ukraine had not requested inclusion).[52] The final rallying cry was 'Brother Serbs, we are with you! There are 200 million Russians and Serbs.'[53] In late April, Ziuganov as leader of the KPRF repeated that Union with other Slavs would be a 'great political step'.[54] *Pravda's* headlines included 'Why do we need a second Vietnam?' 'Belgrade wants peace – NATO war'.[55] The patriotic and anti-semitic newspaper *Zavtra* exhibited much vitriol about 'vile' America, allegedly poised to attack Belarus and Russia from Serbia.[56] One headline read 'And it will bomb us too'.[57] Russian communists announced that there were 13,000 volunteers ready to fight in Yugoslavia alongside the Serbs and Zhirinovskii had a list of a further 5000.[58] Whenever interviewed, Zhirinovskii criticized the Russian leadership for its weak response.[59]

Meeting with heads of the twenty-one republics of the Russian Federation on 9 April, Yeltsin criticized the Duma for trying to draw Russia into the conflict by supplying military hardware and volunteers. He also observed that the Duma was issuing Yeltsin with an ultimatum – either declare Russia's military involvement or be impeached. The vote in the Duma, however, failed to impeach Yeltsin, falling seventeen votes short of the required 300. The only circumstance, now, under which

Yeltsin publicly admitted countenancing involvement was if America used ground troops and seized Yugoslavia to make it a protectorate.[60]

At the other end of the ideological spectrum from Ziuganov and Zhirinovskii, certainly not all economic reformers publicly endorsed Kozyrev's opinion. Grigorii Yavlinskii, for instance, blamed the US for events in Kosovo, noting that force was not being used intelligently.[61] He differed, however, from communists and nationalists, indeed from the majority in the Duma, on unification of Belarus, Russia and Yugoslavia, fiercely opposing it. He argued that it could lead to a threat of confrontation with nuclear powers, automatically exclude Russia from a peacekeeping role and undermine the Commonwealth of Independent States (CIS) because Russia would be seen as anti-Muslim. In the Duma, however, 293 voted in favour of union and only 54 against.[62]

Political commentators

Once so respected by Western leaders in international matters, but not quoted prominently in Western papers on this particular issue, Gorbachev, now over six years without a top post, immediately joined in the spate of condemnation. He praised Primakov for cancelling his US visit, accusing 'our partners' of casting off 'all restraint' and of putting Primakov in a vulnerable position. He added that the US could not use loans to Russia as a bargaining chip.[63] As the bombing went on, Gorbachev consistently criticized NATO for 'flouting international law, skirting the Security Council of the UN, even the members of the UN! Morals and conscience are unacceptable to NATO.'[64] Gorbachev also cautioned that the proposal to unite Russia, Belarus and Yugoslavia, needed serious discussion and a referendum.[65] Like Yavlinskii, he opposed it.[66]

Those in the literary intelligentsia contributed to the outcry against NATO. Solzhenitsyn passionately agued that:

> Having flung aside the UN, trampled on its members, NATO declared to the whole world and to the next century the ancient law of the Taiga: who is strong is absolutely right ... Before the eyes of humanity, a wonderful European country is being destroyed – and civilized governments are brutally applauding.[67]

Exhibiting a similar disgust, the writer Viktor Astafev pointed out that the US had never known serious war or bitter grief. He warned that just as God was punishing Russia for the evils of 1917 and after, so God would punish the USA for inflicting war.[68]

Amid these condemnations of the USA came the occasional voice that branded them misperceptions. Journalist Iuliia Berezovskaia argued that Russians mistakenly blamed the USA alone. Even the Russian educated public, she charged, overlooked the relevance of the European humanist tradition in motivating all European members of NATO and of the EU, which included Austria, Sweden and Finland, to approve of the intervention. These states, she insisted, were not puppets of American leaders. Rather,

> Europe was not burning with a desire to fight and, it is possible that she came too late to battle with the Milošević regime which, in the middle of the continent was waging violence on a peaceful population on ethnic grounds. Neither the French sympathy for the Serbs, the pacifist convictions of the German 'Greens' nor the traditional anti-Americanism of a significant part of the European elite has prevented recognition of today's common duty.[69]

Berezovskaia concluded that it was more terrible for ethnic cleansing to go unpunished than for changes to occur to Balkan borders. She argued that a defeat for NATO would be bad for Russia and that Russia only had the right to call itself a European state if it pressed Milošević into accepting NATO's plan.

Limitations of space prevent full discussion of other lively issues in the Russian press. These include Chernomyrdin's role as peace envoy, the accelerated arrival in Priština of Russian troops ahead of the Americans and British and the larger role of Russian troops in Kosovo. Suffice to note here that whereas some articles portrayed Chernomyrdin as Strobe Talbot's puppet in Belgrade,[70] even as playing a 'sinister role',[71] others by journalist Maksim Iusin in *Izvestiia* praised the 'diplomatic marathon' and contended that peace had come thanks to Chernomyrdin. Iusin held that Chernomyrdin's achievements were to make Russia's voice heard at a time when Russia was economically weak and suffering power struggles and to insist that Russian peacekeepers would not be under NATO command.[72]

Public opinion

Although 98 per cent of the population had opposed NATO's bombing, a nationwide survey showed that by August 1999 attitudes towards the USA were not overwhelmingly hostile. Conducted by VCIOM, it asked 1600 respondents: 'How on the whole do you feel about the United States?' While only 5 per cent responded 'very good', a much larger 44 per cent declared 'basically good'. Twenty-two per cent felt 'basically bad', 10 per cent 'very bad' and 18 per cent did not know. Although highly negative feelings outweighed very positive ones, 49 per cent overall were nonetheless positive. Lingering hostility post-Kosovo was therefore receding. When asked what Russia should now do, as Table 10.1 indicates, roughly equal percentages of 40 and 43 per cent respectively favoured

Table 10.1 Public opinion: Russia's relations with the West (18–21 August 1999)

	All replies %
Do you think Russia should now	
Strengthen mutually advantageous relations with the West	40
or	
Try to eliminate dependence on the West	43
Don't know	17

Source: Joint project of the Centre for the Study of Public Policy, University of Strathclyde and the Russian Centre for Public Opinion and Market Research at http://www.RussiaVotes.org/

Table 10.2 Public opinion: future relations with NATO (18–21 August 1999)

How do you think relations between Russia and NATO will develop after the Kosovo conflict?

	All replies %
Growth in tension, as in Cold War	17
Gradual normalization	52
Don't know	25

Source: Joint project of the Centre for the Study of Public Policy, University of Strathclyde and the Russian Centre for Public Opinion and Market Research at http://www.RussiaVotes.org/

strengthening relations with the West and eliminating dependence upon the West.

While Table 10.1 shows a population divided about what Russian leaders should do regarding relations with the West, Table 10.2 illustrates that simultaneously 52 per cent of respondents felt that relations with NATO would nonetheless normalize. A high 25 per cent, however, seemed unclear about the future, and 17 per cent feared a growth in tensions.

An earlier poll in June among urban residents showed that 29 per cent of city dwellers thought the peace plan devised with Chemomyrdin's help was a useful step whereas 24 per cent labelled it a difficult compromise that made peace possible. Fourteen per cent considered the terms humiliating for Yugoslavia and did not rule out more conflicts arising from it. Another 14 per cent saw the plan as just a cover for NATO aggression with the aim of separating Kosovo from Yugoslavia.[73] As many as 64 per cent of those surveyed felt that Russian leaders should work with Western states to bring about peace, while 21 per cent wanted to oppose attempts by NATO to bring an humiliating peace for Yugoslavia. Only 4 per cent believed NATO should solve the problem of Kosovo, with 43 per cent backing a UN solution and 44 per cent wanting to leave it to Yugoslavia to sort out. Although urban public opinion was divided, it supported a peaceful solution and generally backed working with Western states rather than against them.[74]

In January 2000, however, almost half of the Russians surveyed in a sample of 1940 felt that the USA was a 'substantial threat' to Russian security. Table 10.3 also shows how many Russians distinguished between the US and the European Union, with the latter considered to be much less of a threat. Non-Russian nationalities in the Russian Federation were portrayed as more dangerous. With the second Chechen war now raging, this was perhaps not surprising, especially since Russian propaganda held Chechens responsible for bomb blasts in Russian cities. European and US condemnation of Russian conduct in the war, in particular torture in 'filtration' camps, were dismissed in Russia as fine examples of a new Western double standard. Although the USA was dubbed a threat, 58 per cent interviewed thought that it was 'not very likely' for Russia to be attacked. Seventeen per cent said it was 'not at all likely', with only 4 per cent deeming it 'very likely' and 21 per cent pondering 'maybe.'[75]

Table 10.3 Public opinion: perceived threats to Russian security

Do you think that any of the following countries could be a substantial threat to the security of Russia?

	Per cent totally or somewhat approving
China	23
Germany	14
Iraq	24
USA	48
European Union	22
Non-Russian nationalities in Russia	43
Ukraine	9

Source: New Russia Barometer VIII, Fieldwork, 19–29 January 2000; N = 1940. At http://www.RussiaVotes.org/Mood_intnl_cur.htm nrb1

Table 10.4 Public opinion: sympathies in the Kosovo conflict

Last year there was a conflict in Serbia between Serbs and ethnic Albanians living in Kosovo. Do you sympathize with:

	Per cent
Serbs	19
Albanians	3
No sympathy for either	42
Not at all interested	36

Source: New Russia Barrometer VIII, Fieldwork 19–29 January 2000; N = 1940. At http://www.RussiaVotes.org/Mood_intnl_cur.htm nrb1

These expressions of fear of the US threat coexisted alongside reduced sympathy for the Serbs in Kosovo. Forty-two per cent of Russians surveyed felt no sympathy for Serbs or for ethnic Albanians in Kosovo and 36 per cent expressed 'no interest'. As Table 10.4 shows, sympathy for the Serbs was greater than sympathy for the Albanians, but not as huge as one might have expected. By 2000, the Chechen war was a key issue, much referred to in the December 1999 elections to the Duma and later in March in the presidential election. The topic of NATO intervention in Kosovo was less salient, having receded in prominence as the Chechen war dominated news and propaganda. But Russians still blamed the US for its conduct in foreign policy and in world affairs.

Implications for foreign and defence policy

During NATO's bombing campaign, Sergei Prikhodko, deputy head of the Presidential administration, told journalists that NATO's actions might now require 'changes to the Russian defence doctrine'.[76] Also during the conflict, the State Duma and Federation Council on several occasions looked at the state of Russia's armed forces. A Duma resolution called upon the President to convene the Security Council to reconsider aspects of military doctrine and to examine military reforms. People's deputies wanted increased funding for the military.[77] Co-operation between CIS states and Russia on military matters was also given fresh impetus.[78] Officials in the Defence Ministry met with the Ukrainian Defence Minister, Aleksandr Kuzmuk.[79] Plans to set up a unified regional group of forces on the territory of Russia and Belarus discussed earlier by Sergeev when visiting Belarus now appeared increasingly necessary.[80] On 29 April 1999, the Security Council met, chaired by Yeltsin, even though he had not led a meeting himself since July 1998. The agenda was classified, concerning the development of Russia's nuclear arms complex. *Kommersant* reported that those who were not members of the Security Council were asked to leave the room. Apparently, buying strategic bombers from Ukraine through barter and the extension of storage time for tactical nuclear weapons were discussed.[81]

While bombing continued there were calls for expansion of Russia's nuclear arsenal. Once it was over, the conciliatory commission approved a 26 billion rouble or $1.01 billion increase in defence spending for the budget in the year 2000. The chairman of the Defence Committee, Roman Popkovich, argued that it should be as high as 37 billion.[82] Michel Camdessus, IMF managing director, warned that 'we shall interrupt our support' if uncontrolled military spending occurred.[83]

In September 1999, the Russian Defence Ministry examined a draft of a new military doctrine, designed to replace an earlier one approved in November 1993. The press informed that fresh consideration was given to 'potential external and internal threats' that had not been a preoccupation of the previous doctrine.[84] Renewed concern about threats to Russia's national security interests, about expanding military blocs and about a disrupted balance of power underpinned the document.[85] Interviewed in *Krasnaia Zvezda* in October, General Valerii Manilov, who had worked on the document, commented that events in Kosovo indeed had a bearing on its contents, as had the contradiction in the modern world between the strivings for unipolarity and multipolarity.[86] The new doctrine was approved by the Security Council in early 2000 and decreed by Putin in April. Sergei Ivanov of the Security Council said that it was underpinned by a pessimistic view of the international situation due to 'growing threats' to Russia. NATO had become 'prosecutor, judge and executioner', disregarding the UN, OSCE and Russia. Because NATO wanted superiority, progress towards multipolarity was being rolled back. The US intent to build a national strategic missile defence system also undermined American claims that the 1972 Anti-Ballistic Missile (ABM) Treaty was really the cornerstone of US security.[87]

In the aftermath of the conflict, Russian leaders also displayed a heightened sensitivity to perceptions in other states of their status on the world stage and of their ability to deal with domestic security problems without Western involvement. When Russia launched a fresh bombing campaign in Chechnia after explosions in September 1999 in Moscow were blamed upon Chechen terrorists, Russian leaders rejected Chris Patten's offer of mediation with the Chechens in his capacity of new foreign affairs commissioner of the European Union. Similarly, Moscow was unresponsive to George Robertson, the new NATO secretary general, to whom Aslan Maskhadov, the Chechen President, had appealed. Predictably, Ivanov declared, 'This is an internal problem of Russia and no mediators are needed.'[88] Russian leaders would have responded this way *anyway*, whether or not the NATO bombing of Kosovo had taken place. However, Ivanov wanted to make clear that just because Russia had been a mediator with Milošević, this was not an acceptable pattern for the EU and NATO to follow regarding issues on Russian territory.

Western criticism of the war in Chechnia was viewed as misplaced, interfering, hypocritical and two faced. When, in early April 2000, the Parliamentary Assembly of the Council of Europe voted to initiate proceedings to suspend Russia and also to strip the Russian delegation of its right to vote, many Russian politicians again felt insulted.[89] They considered that this 'double standard' meant that Western leaders could bomb Kosovo and escalate a refugee crisis in another country, but that Russians could not deal with 'terrorism' within their own borders.

Conclusions

Different assessments of how Russia should react to NATO military action in a context in which people's deputies were anyway considering the impeachment of their sickly President for causing the disintegration of the USSR, heightened tensions between executive and legislature. Legislative exasperation with Yeltsin increased when he fired Primakov in May and then Stepashin three months later. Stories of corruption in the presidential 'family' and of the misappropriation of IMF loans did not bolster presidential credibility. Those in the Ministries of Foreign Affairs and Defence also exhibited marked differences in their readiness to advocate Russian military action. The President and his ministers, however, as well as deputies in the Duma, were all ready to reconsider Russia's military doctrine in the light of NATO's bombing campaign. Even if their reactions to NATO bombing had varied in emphasis and in recommendations, in 1999 they displayed unanimity on the need for spending and heightened Russian defence capability.

Although war in Kosovo led to tense relations between Russian leaders and their 'partners' in America and Europe, Yeltsin wanted to stay out of military conflict. Notwithstanding fresh talk in Russia, particularly from communists and nationalists, of a new Cold War, a European Vietnam and an American international policeman, once NATO bombing finally stopped, there was more readiness to repair relations than might have been expected from the vitriolic condemnations of March and April 1999. The government's desire to receive IMF loans was an important element behind this, but so too was the commitment to some normalcy and stability both in domestic and foreign affairs. Nonetheless, a fresh mistrust of NATO and of the US in particular, due to events in Kosovo, together with a feeling of greater vulnerability, meant that Russian nationalism strengthened at home and broad acceptance developed in favour of a new military doctrine. Kosovo had made a significant difference to Russia's relations with the USA and NATO.

In the twelve months following the bombing of Kosovo, citizens in the Russian Federation elected a new parliament and a new president. The new legislature and executive were committed more explicitly than before to defending Russian interests in a world that they insisted should be multipolar, not unipolar.[90] Greater harmony than before also now existed in relations between executive and legislature. A 'new' military doctrine enshrined Russia's renewed attempt to be assertive and respected on the world stage, looking for 'partners' beyond the West in China, Iraq and North Korea. Old allies were to be valued and new ones sought. A more pragmatic Putin, although loyal to the rhetoric of Russia's greatness, nonetheless announced cuts in troops (sparking controversy) and fired generals loyal to Sergeev.[91] He visited North Korea, made a positive impression on Western leaders at the Okinawa summit, and accepted an invitation to visit Quaddafi in Libya.[92] Although his image was tarnished by his handling of the sinking of the Kursk submarine, with Russia again humiliated before the world, Putin kept to the message that Russia meant to play a dynamic role in world affairs, promoting a multipolar system and opposing humanitarian intervention and the notion of limited sovereignty. Putin also finally recognized Vojislav Kostunica's electoral victory over Milošević, after indecision, while Ziuganov and Zhirinovskii lamented it.[93]

Russian interpretations of the significance of NATO's bombing fed into a debate about *national'nyi interes*, or 'national interest'. Although discussions about how this differs from *gosudarstvennyi interes,* or 'state interest' are conceptually muddled, leaders are nonetheless keen to define its priorities and parameters.[94] NATO bombing not only prompted Russians to rethink the state of international relations and to give added justification to the formulation of a 'new' military doctrine and 'new' foreign policy concept, but also to reflect upon what national interest is. Although relations with NATO members, in particular with the USA, have not been definitively damaged, they have been reconfigured and reassessed.

Viktor Kremeniuk has argued that the USA at the end of the Cold War exhibited a 'winner's syndrome', enshrined in articles such as that by Francis Fukuyama on the end of history, out of which developed an arrogance in foreign policy and a 'de-intellectualization'.[95] In his view, the Balkan crisis marked the 'end of one period' in world politics and the beginning of an immeasurably different one, 'more stern, dangerous and threatening'.[96] Whilst not all Russian academics and policymakers concur, many do.

MARY BUCKLEY

Acknowledgements

I am grateful to the Leverhulme Trust for a research grant from October 1999–June 2000 to work on political debates in post-Soviet Russia. Gratitude is due to the Carnegie Trust for the Universities of Scotland and to the British Academy for research trips to Moscow and to the Kennan Institute for Advanced Russian Studies of the Woodrow Wilson Center for a short term fellowship in April–May 2000.

Notes

1. *The Economist,* 10–16 April 1999, p. 25.
2. In Germany, when 64 per cent in the west of the country were 'for', only 40 per cent were in favour in the East.
3. *Argumenty i fakty,* no. 14, (April 1999), p. 4.
4. *ibid.*
5. *Izvestiia,* 27 April 1999, p. 1.
6. *Vremia MN,* 26 March 1999, p. 1.
7. *Izvestiia,* 7 March 2000, p. 2.
8. *Sovetskaia Rossiia,* 7 March 2000, p. 1.
9. Vladimir Putin, *First Person* (London: Hutchinson, 2000), p. 179. Putin commented that Russia could consider joining NATO if it transformed itself, 'but not at this moment'; *ibid.,* p. 177.
10. See *Vremia Edinstva,* no. 2, 2 December 1999, p. 3; *ibid.,* no. 4, 16 December 1999, p. 2.
11. *Nezavisimaia gazeta,* 11 July 2000, p. 1.
12. *ibid.*
13. For perspectives on Russia's place in the world, consult Sergei Karaganov, 'New Foreign Policy', *Moscow News,* no. 9, 8–14 March 2000, p. 5.
14. RFE/RL, *Newsline,* vol. 4, no. 129, 7 July 2000, p. 2.
15. *ibid.,* p. 3.
16. Karen Dawisha, *Eastern Europe, Gorbachev and Reform: The Great Challenge* (Cambridge: CUP, 1990).
17. Richard Sakwa, *Gorbachev and his Reforms, 1985–1990* (Hemel Hempstead: Philip Allan, 1990); Mary Buckley, *Redefining Russian Society and Polity* (Boulder CO: Westview, 1993).
18. Richard Sakwa, *Russian Politics and Society* (London: Routledge, 1996), 2nd edition, pp. 116–55; Archie Brown, 'The October crisis of 1993', *Post-Soviet Affairs,* vol. 9, no. 3, (July–September 1993), pp. 183–95.
19. *Rossiiskaia gazeta,* 28 December, 1993; *Segodnia,* no. 104, 1993, p. 1; Stephen White, Richard Rose and Ian McAllister, *How Russia Votes* (Chatham NJ: Chatham House Publishers, 1997).
20. White *et al., op. cit.,* pp. 241–70.
21. For discussion of these governments see A.A. Dantsev, *Praviteli Rossii i XX vek* (Rostov-na-Donu: Feniks, 2000), pp. 388–415.

22. For the argument that NATO expansion was tragic, see Aleksandr Avdeev (First Deputy Minister of Foreign Affairs), 'Doktrina NATO otstala ot zhizni,' *Rossiiskaia Federatsiia Segodnia,* no. 6, (1999), pp. 53–5.
23. *Kommersant,* 12 March 1999, p. 4.
24. *Segodnia,* 21 March 1999, pp. 1 and 3; *Ivestiia,* 12 March 1999, p. 1.
25. BBC, *Summary of World Broadcasts* (hereafter *SWB*), 23 March 1999, SU/3490 B/4.
26. *ibid.*
27. *Krasnaia zvezda,* 9 March 1999, p. 1.
28. *ibid.*
29. BBC, *SWB,* 25 March, SU/3492 B/2-B/3.
30. *ibid.,* B/3.
31. BBC, *SWB,* 25 March 1999, SU/3492 B/1-B/2.
32. *Rossiiskaia gazeta,* 26 March 1999, p. 2.
33. *ibid.*
34. *ibid.*
35. *Krasnaia zvezda,* 8 April 1999, p. 1.
36. *Vremia MN,* 26 March 1999, p. 2. For official responses, see *Diplomaticheskii Vestnik,* no. 4, (April 1999), pp. 3–7, 9–46; *ibid.,* no. 6, (June 1999), pp. 7–18; *ibid.,* no. 7, (July 1999), pp. 5–18; *ibid.,* no. 8, (August 1999), p. 39; *ibid.,* no. 2, (February 2000), pp. 3–13, 65–6.
37. BBC, *SWB,* SU/3492, 25 March 1999, B/5.
38. *Segodnia,* 25 March 1999, pp. 1–2. For diverse views, see *Rossiiskaia Federatsiia Segodnia,* no. 12, 1999, pp. 40–2; *Rossiiskaia Federatsiia Segodnia,* no. 14, (1999), pp. 4–6; and *Obshchaia gazeta,* 15–21 April 1999, p. 1.
39. *Segodnia,* 20 April 1999, p. 3.
40. BBC, *SWB,* 10 April 1999, SU/3505, B-1.
41. *Noviye Izvestiia,* 20 April 1999, p. 1.
42. *Segodnia,* 10 April 1999, pp. 1–2.
43. *ibid.*
44. BBC, *SWB,* 10 April 1999, SU/3505 B/1.
45. Egor Gaidar, Boris Nemtsov and Boris Fyodorov, as leaders of the newly formed Just Cause, travelled to Belgrade, attempting through 'people's diplomacy' to bring NATO, Yugoslavia and Russia to the negotiating table. Nemtsov argued that involvement of the Russian and Serbian Orthodox Churches and the Catholic Church was important. See *Argumenty i fakty,* no. 13, March 1999, p. 5. *Nezavisimaia gazeta* noted that the Russian Foreign Ministry had disassociated itself. Ivanov commented that the visit was a 'personal' one, not representing government nor president but Anatolii Chubais said it did enjoy Yeltsin's backing. See *Nezavisimaia gazeta,* 30 March 1999, p. 4.
46. *Kommersant,* 9 June 1999, pp. 1–2.
47. *Nezavisimaia gazeta,* 8 June 1999, pp. 1 and 6.
48. BBC, *SWB,* SU/3492, 25 March 1999, B/4.
49. *ibid.,* B/7.
50. *Pravda,* 26–29 March 1999, p. 1.
51. *ibid.*

52. *ibid.*
53. *ibid.*
54. *ibid.*, 20–21 April 1999, p. 1.
55. *ibid.*, 26–29 March, p. 1; *ibid.*, 8 April 1999, p. 1; *ibid.*, 23–26 April 1999, p. 1.
56. *Zavtra,* March–April 1999, pp. 1 and 4. *Zavtra* criticized America, NATO, Yeltsin, Yavlinksii, Kozyrev, Ivanov and even Sergeev: *Zavtra,* March–April 1999, p. 1. Aleksandr Prokhanov lambasted Yeltsin for playing Ghenghis Khan and ridiculed Zhirinovksii, the Jewish Congress, Putin and Luzhkov: *Zavtra,* April 1999, pp. 1 and 3. In May 1999 *Zavtra* carried the slogan 'Glory to Serbia!'.
57. *ibid.*, April–May 1999, p. 2.
58. *Argumenty i fakty,* no. 14, April 1999, p. 4. The paper discussed the views of a psychologist on why Russians were offering to fight. Volunteers were not limited to the Serbian side. There were around 20 million Muslims in the Russian Federation. Some in Kazan volunteered to help Kosovo Albanians. President Shaimiyev urged caution, noting that this could be destabilizing for Russia: *Kommersant,* 14 April 1999, p. 2.
59. *Rossiiskaia Federatsiia Segodnia,* no. 13, 1999, p. 2.
60. BBC, *SWB,* 10 April 1999, SU/3505 B/2.
61. *Segodnia,* 25 March 1998, pp. 1–2.
62. *Noviye Izvestiia,* 17 April 1999, p. 2.
63. *Segodnia,* 25 March 1999, pp. 1–2.
64. *Argumenty i fakty,* no. 15, April 1999, p. 4.
65. *ibid.*
66. *ibid.*
67. *ibid.*
68. *ibid.*, no. 14, 1999, p. 3.
69. *Izvestiia,* 16 April 1999, p. 4.
70. *Nezavisimaia gazeta,* 8 June 1999, pp. 1 and 6.
71. *Sovetskaia Rossiia,* 10 June 1999, p. 1. For views on Chernomyrdin as peace envoy and on the consequences of the war, consult *Rossiiskaia Federatsiia Segodnia,* no. 13, 1999, pp. 2–5. See, too, 'Plan Chernomyrdina', *Kommersant,* 24 April 1999, p. 1.
72. *Izvestiia,* 10 June 1999, p. 1. For an upbeat article on the peace agreement with a photograph of a smiling Igor Ivanov and Madeleine Albright, see Gennadii Sysoev's 'Rossiia i NATO dogovorilis' o mire: v Iugoslavskoi voine nastupil perelom', *Kommersant,* 7 May 1999, p. 2. See, too, Gennadii Sysoev, 'NATO prekratis bombit' Iugoslaviiu,' *Kommersant,* 30 April 1999, p. 3; Gennadii Sysoev, 'Nashi mirotvortsy voidut v Kosovo vmeste s NATO', *Kommersant,* 28 April 1999, p. 2.
73. *Noviye Izvestiia,* 10 June 1999, p. 1; *The Current Digest to the Post-Soviet Press,* vol. 51, no. 23, (7 July 1999), p. 4.
74. *ibid.*
75. New Russia Barometer VIII, http://www.RussiaVotes.org/Mood_intnl_cur.htm nrb1.
76. BBC, *SWB,* 10 April 1999, SU 3505 B/3.
77. *Nezavisimaia gazeta,* 28 April 1999, p. 5.
78. *ibid.*

79. *ibid.*
80. *ibid.*
81. *Kommersant,* 30 April 1999, p. 1.
82. RFE/RL, *Newsline,* vol. 3, no. 199, 12 October 1999.
83. *ibid.,* vol. 3, no. 2000, 13 October 1999.
84. *Nezavisimaia gazeta,* 13 October 1999, p. 3.
85. *ibid.*
86. *Krasnaia zvezda,* 8 October 1999, p. 1.
87. *Segodnia,* 15 March 2000, p. 4.
88. *Guardian,* 8 October 1999, p. 18.
89. *Noviye Izvestiia,* 8 April 2000, pp. 1-2.
90. Views among scholars are divided. See Karaganov, 'New Foreign Policy,' *op. cit.*
91. *Guardian,* 12 August 2000, p. 1; *Kommersant,* 1 August 2000, p. 1.
92. *Nezavisimaia gazeta,* 2 August 2000, pp. 1 and 6.
93. RFE/RL Newsline, vol. 4, no. 194, Part I (6 October 2000), pp. 1-2.
94. *Polis,* no. 1, 2000.
95. V.A. Kremeniuk, 'Vneshniaia politika SShA na rubezhe vekov', *SShA: Kanada: Ekonomika, politika, kul'tura,* no. 5, 2000, pp. 4-6.
96. V.A. Kremeniuk, 'Rossiia – SShA: pervye uroki Balkanskogo krizisa 1999g', *SShA: Kanada: Ekonomika, politika, kul'tura,* no. 1, (2000), pp. 4-6.

CHAPTER ELEVEN

Perceptions in the Commonwealth of Independent States

SALLY N. CUMMINGS

Introduction

The Commonwealth of Independent States (CIS) was established in December 1991 in the aftermath of the demise of the Soviet Union.[1] It was intended to maintain formal cohesion among the post-Soviet states, but has by many accounts been a failure.[2] This chapter is concerned with the perceptions of Kosovo as expressed by the leaders of the CIS states excluding Russia. Only two of these states – Belarus and the Ukraine – were involved in the diplomacy connected with the crisis. The others played a reactive role, and in some cases that reaction was marginal, since many of these fledgling states were consumed with domestic crises of their own. Nevertheless, their responses to events in Kosovo revealed their views of the norms and rights of the international community, their relationships with each other and the wider world, and their own attitudes towards issues of state-building, autonomy and sovereignty. For some, Kosovo was a reminder of the hegemonic role the US plays in the world, and of the way membership in the USSR, or allegiance to Russia thereafter, was important in maintaining a bipolar balance. For others, it signalled hope that the international community would become similarly involved in their crises. On 27 March 1999 Moldovan President Petru Lucinschi summarized this range of reactions by warning that Kosovo 'generates a realistic danger of conflict expansion to neighbouring states and creates an undesirable precedent for European and world security through the polarization of states' positions.'[3]

It was clear from the 2 April 1999 summit meeting of the CIS that there would be no single 'CIS perception' of the situation in Kosovo. Russia and Belarus were determined to push through an anti-NATO, pro-Serbian resolution, even if it meant violating CIS rules of procedure. During the pre-summit negotiations over the agenda, a number of countries, particularly Ukraine, Moldova, Georgia, Azerbaijan, Kazakhstan and Uzbekistan, had exercised their right to veto the proposed discussion of a joint statement on the Serbia-NATO conflict. As a result, the item did not even figure on the official agenda. Nevertheless, the Kremlin and Russia's Foreign Ministry announced on the eve of the summit that Russia and Belarus would raise the issue regardless of the official agenda, and Russian Foreign Minister Igor Ivanov inexplicably expressed his 'confidence that the Presidents will condemn NATO's aggression against Yugoslavia'. In the event, no joint statement was issued, and most countries insisted on citing their individual positions, which in all cases differed substantially from the Russian-Belarus stance.

The wide difference among viewpoints is perhaps not surprising in light of the formation of GUUAM. This organization, with its 'unpronounceable acronym', was established in 1997 by Georgia, Ukraine, Azerbaijan, and Moldova as a counterweight to Russia, particularly in the fields of energy and transport. Uzbekistan became the fifth member during NATO's 50th anniversary celebrations in April 1999.

Belarus

Belarus allied itself firmly with the Serbs, severing all ties with NATO and its member states. The complaint by Russia's Yegor Gaidar that by dropping bombs on Yugoslavia, NATO was bombing Russian democracy, demonstrates an attitude that was even more prevalent in Belarus, claimed Belarus analyst Jan Maksymiuk.[4] The official Belarus position echoed that of Russia but was more extreme, and its invective against the West far stronger; President Lukashenka even accused *Russia* of being too soft on NATO. On victory day, Lukashenka condemned the 'hegemonic plans' of the US, which he accused of seeking 'the role of global policeman'.[5] The coverage offered by the official Belarusian press contained virtually no reports on the problem of Albanian refugees and, consequently, no reference whatsoever to the reason for NATO's intervention in Yugoslavia. One official explanation stated that Yugoslavia could be found guilty only of desiring to exist 'according to its own laws'. Addressing the residents of flood-stricken villages in Brest Oblast, Lukashenka explained NATO's intervention in Yugoslavia even more simplistically: Yugoslavia was being attacked because it was one of the 'richest regions [where] people mine gold and other precious metals.'[6]

Through the official propaganda machine of Belarus, NATO's air strikes in Yugoslavia became a powerful stimulus for President Alyaksandr Lukashenka's idea of 'Slavic unity' and reintegration with Russia.

What had seemed a far-fetched idea when first voiced by ultra-nationalist Serbian Deputy Premier Vojislav Seselj in Belarus in May 1998 had in fact materialized only one year later: the Yugoslav Parliament in April applied for membership in the Belarus-Russia Union and was supported in its bid by both the Russian State Duma and the Belarusian legislature (which was subservient to Lukashenka). The course of action advanced by Luka-shenka's propaganda campaign had three major pillars: the Belarus-Russia Union should counterbalance NATO; both Belarus and Russia, while remaining sovereign states, should delegate extensive executive powers over military and economic policies to the Union leadership; and the Belarus-Russia Union should help Yugoslavia militarily. During his visit to Cuba in September 2000, Lukashenka called for the formation of a three-tiered force to oppose 'world monopolarity' – that is, the US and NATO. In his vision, the core of that force should be a centralized Russian state; Belarus and such ex-Soviet republics as might wish to join the bloc, as well as Cuba, would form a second tier and China a third. Lukashenka had hoped to emerge as an international player as a result of Kosovo, and indeed following the crisis he held top-level meetings with China, Lybia, Iraq, and North Korea. But these hopes were dashed when Vladimir Putin replaced Boris Yeltsin as Russian President, since, unlike Yeltsin, Putin does not countenance Lukashenka as head of a Union state.[7]

To put the Belarusian reaction in perspective, however, remember that Belarus had already *de facto* severed relations with the West as a result of its dismal human rights record. Unlike Russia, which could not risk jeopardizing much-needed financial assistance by a rupture of its relations with the West, it had little to lose by taking this extreme stance.

Moldova

Moldova did not have the luxury of such an unequivocal reaction. Its geopolitics, history and economic interests demanded that its leadership maintain balance in its statements about Kosovo. On 21 April 1999, Lucinschi expressed fears that NATO bombings of chemical industry facilities would result in an ecological disaster.[8] Early in the conflict the Foreign Ministry expressed concerns about the possible outflow of refugees and economic chaos.[9] According to Ukrainian Defence Minister Boris Tarasyuk, the Danube used to carry 24 per cent of Ukrainian transport merchandise.

Even though the Foreign Ministry had admitted two days previously that NATO had been 'forced' to act,[10] Moldova's President Lucinschi did not take long to declare Moldova neutral, explaining that its foreign policy doctrine demanded this stance:

Moldova believes that maintaining this situation poses real threats to the peace in the region … as a neutral country and a part which is particularly interested in consolidation of the regional security, [Moldova] has repeatedly voiced for a peaceful and exclusively political settlement of the Kosovo crisis.[11]

The political situation of Moldova's leaders regarding Kosovo was further complicated by the fact that the crisis coincided with Moldova's local elections, the presidential race, a nationwide referendum, and the ongoing Transdniester conflict. In an interview with *Rossiyskaya Gazeta* on 19 May 1999, Lucinschi again emphasized that his was a 'neutral state', and that constitutionally Moldova could not belong to defence pacts. His dealings with NATO during the Kosovo crisis simply amounted to 'cooperation and ties', which Lucinschi defended thus: 'We cooperate with the NATO Partnership for Peace Programme only, but it does not mean that we should not take part in the Washington summit … We do not seek to join the North-Atlantic bloc, and our cooperation with NATO is restricted only to the Partnership for Peace programme.'[12] He further explained that the summit was also attended by representatives from fellow CIS members Armenia and Tajikistan. The Moldovan Defence Ministry on 7 July 1999 confirmed that Moldova would take part in NATO peacekeeping operations, provided NATO would cover costs.[13] The leadership's cautious statements represented an attempt to accommodate its country's sharp regional and political divisions over Kosovo.

Criticism of the West was widespread. Moldovan Communist Party leader Vladimir Voronin asked:

Why do not the world gendarmes – US and NATO – make air strikes on China to resolve its Tibet problem, or on India to defend its Kashmir province, or Israel conflicting with Palestine, or on Great Britain with its Northern Ireland problem?[14]

Transdniester Cossacks, who fought on the side of the Tiraspol separatists in the 1992 clashes, announced on 26 March that they were ready to send volunteers to Yugoslavia to fight with the Serbs.[15] In the above-mentioned interview with *Rossiyskaya Gazeta*, Lucinschi revealed that the leadership was often being 'reproached for a strictly pro-Western orientation'. The controversy in Moldova over the Kosovo crisis was partly shaped by the possible implications of Kosovo for Transdniester. Lucinschi, however, stated that his

initial position is that the Dniester region is part of the Republic of Moldova with a high level of autonomy … It is impossible to project the situation in Kosovo onto the Dniester region. There is a different reality in our country. First of all, there is no ethnic aspect. (… 40 per cent Moldovans, 27–8 per cent Ukrainians and Russians). Second, we do not resolve our relations by force.

The Transdniester leadership also opposed future NATO involvement; Vladimir Atamanyuk, first deputy supreme council chairman of this non-recognized republic, argued that the Russian and Ukrainian military observers' presence was more than adequate. He added that any changes to peacekeeping structures would be highly destabilizing.[16]

However, the Transdniester Union of [Retired] Commissioned and Non-Commissioned Officers warned that Moldova intended to 'solve the Transdniester problem' using NATO's 'Yugoslav blueprint'.[17]

Ukraine

Ukraine's political and economic situation was similar to Moldova's with respect to Kosovo. But the Ukrainian elite overrode popular anti-NATO discontent over Kosovo, even if it insisted that it was in fact pursuing a balanced foreign policy. This reaction was partly due to the strongly pro-Western orientation of certain establishment and right-wing political actors.

Ukrainian President Leonid Kuchma insisted that Ukraine was sticking to its normal balanced foreign policy stance, offsetting the interests of Russia and the West. Speaking at the ceremony dedicated to Victory Day, he noted that in solving the Balkan crisis Ukraine could not and must not be involved militarily or politically on any one side: 'Ukraine is obliged to express its position on a number of issues ... although our position differs from that of the United States.'[18] He condemned NATO bombing[19] but, unlike Belarus, did not sever ties with NATO or its member states; the vitriol coming from Moscow and Minsk was conspicuously absent in Kiev. Like the leaders of Russia and Belarus, Kuchma criticized the NATO position on legal grounds, but in his case this one element was the main focus of his criticism. He acknowledged that there was a humanitarian crisis in Kosovo (although Ukraine was too poor to accept refugees),[20] but he argued that this did not justify the use of force, and certainly not force devoid of UN backing. Like Georgia's Shevardnadze, Kuchma called primarily for a strengthening of the UN and the Organization of Security and Cooperation in Europe (OSCE). He pushed from the beginning for a peaceful resolution of the crisis and, most significantly, proposed a three-point peace plan to the international community: synchronous cessation of military activities by NATO and Yugoslavia; provision for the return of refugees; and a peace conference.[21] He advocated maintaining Yugoslavia's territorial integrity but granting broad autonomy for Kosovo.[22] This position was largely backed by prominent members of the Foreign and Defence Ministries. Ukraine's Parliamentary Assembly Delegation Chair Boris Oliynyk stated: 'we do not vindicate the Serb side as there can be no angels or devils when it comes to discussing ethnic conflicts.'[23] Kuchma rejected overtures from Belarus to join the Slav Union on the grounds that the Union was simply 'a political measure for settling the Kosovo problem'.[24]

Kuchma was fighting against popular and party feeling, which was strongly anti-NATO. One opinion poll cited 31 per cent of Ukrainians against NATO bombing. Just 11 per cent of respondents blamed Yugoslav President Slobodan Milošević for the conflict.[25] The communist-dominated Parliament called for an immediate halt to bombing and argued that military and humanitarian assistance should be sent to Belgrade. It denounced NATO armed actions against Yugoslavia, suspended Ukraine's participation in NATO's programmes and suggested that the president and the government resubmit Ukrainian-NATO documents for ratification.[26] Chairman of the Ukrainian Supreme Council, Oleksandr Tkacenko, told his Slovak counterpart that the 'Ukrainian parliament does not agree with the Ukrainian government – it condemns the war in the Balkans and wants to contribute to a peaceful solution to the problem.'[27] The following day Oliynyk also demanded that Ukraine recall its ambassador from Washington and that the Cabinet step down for promoting co-operation with the US and NATO, decrying NATO's 'scorched-earth tactics'.[28] Petro Symonenko, head of the Communist Party, called for Parliament to reconsider Ukraine's relations with NATO. After an emergency Cabinet session devoted to the Kosovo crisis, Deputy Prime Minister Oleksandr Chaliy called the use of force in Yugoslavia 'inadmissible' without the consent of the UN Security Council.[29] Although Crimean Prime Minister Serhiy Kunitsyn stated that it was unacceptable to compare Kosovo with the ethnic situation in Crimea, the Crimean Parliament speaker, Leonid Hrach, stated that attempts by Crimean Tatars to assert their self-identity might lead to a NATO-backed Ukrainian government military clampdown.[30]

In the face of all this anti-NATO feeling, Kuchma justified his visit to the 50th anniversary summit as a trip intended 'not to celebrate ... but to resolve Ukraine's problems.'[31] This stance was part of Kiev's overall portrayal of Kosovo as an issue divorced from the country's general foreign policy direction. Tarasyuk stated in an interview on 20 May 1999 that the Kosovo crisis and 'the different perception of the methods to solve it ha[d] not affected Ukraine's attitude to NATO and the Partnership for Peace', insisting, 'We distinguish between two matters.'[32] He did not always maintain this decoupling of foreign policy issues, however: 'To sever relations with NATO would mean to sever relations with the European Union ... I shall not permit the isolation of the Ukraine.'[33]

These perceptions of Kosovo reflected Kiev's dilemma: it could not get too close to the West and too far from Russia, or it would face a possible security vaccuum. Kuchma opposed Ukraine's adopting a 'one-line', Westward-looking stance: 'We must not turn our back on either our neighbours or our past,' he stressed.[34] On the eve of the crisis, he added that joining NATO was 'not on the agenda'.[35] Volodymyr Horbulin, head of the Ukrainian National Security and Defence Council, asserted that the 'Russian factor' would definitely figure in the country's relations with the alliance.[36] On 27 April 1999, Ukrainian Defence Minister Oleksandr Kuzmuk told journalists that Russia and Ukraine had 'no differences on issues of implementing a programme for settling the situation in the Balkans.'[37] Kuchma emphasized on 18 June 1999 that a settlement in Yugoslavia would be impossible without Russia and Russian peacekeepers. Yet the president suggested, at a conference of Ukrainian ambassadors, that new principles should be worked out for a partnership with NATO that took account of Ukraine's non-aligned status and prevented the country from becoming a buffer between NATO and Russia.[38]

Azerbaijan

The Azerbaijani leadership, specifically the Presidency and Foreign and Defence Ministries, was unequivocally pro-Western and pro-NATO. Here it was also backed by some pro-presidential parties, such as Etibar Mammadov's Party for National Independence of Azerbaijan. Like its Ukrainian counterpart the Azerbaijani leadership faced both popular and parliamentary opposition to its position on Kosovo. Opposition parties criticized the leadership for being slow to react to the crisis. Musavat Party leader Isa Gambar said that Kosovo would set a 'bad precedent'. The United Communist Party of Azerbaijan described the bombing of Yugoslavia by NATO planes as 'aggression' and an 'attack on peace and peace-loving forces'.[39] But this opposition was far less pronounced than in the Ukraine.

At the 2 April CIS meeting, Azerbaijan restated an earlier offer to send an elite platoon to the former Yugoslavia as part of the Turkish contingent under NATO command and to offer its military bases to NATO. That position prompted Lukashenka to describe Azerbaijan as 'the most pro-NATO among the CIS countries'.[40] In July, at Baku's US Embassy in celebration of Independence Day, he stated regarding NATO's action: 'We support this. It is very good that the operation is already producing real results. The USA has once again shown the whole world that it does great deeds to protect human rights.'[41]

Azerbaijan's foreign policy advisor, Vafa Guluzade, called NATO a 'progressive organization' and said that his country would like to join NATO as a fully-fledged member.[42] Deputy Foreign Minister Araz Azimov defined Azerbaijan's relations with NATO as 'an integration partnership'.[43] As early as 26 February 1999 the Foreign Ministry agreed to send an Azeri unit and attach it to a Turkish battalion to assist war avoidance efforts.[44]

On 25 March the Foreign Ministry informed the US State Department that it would send a specially trained unit of the Azeri army to Kosovo under NATO once the bombing had stopped. (This stance differed from that of Ukraine, which agreed to send peacekeeping troops only under the UN's aegis.)

Yet the Azerbaijani leadership's position contained contradictions. Kosovo, it said, demonstrated the need to preserve the territorial integrity of the state. Said Foreign Minister Vilayet Quliyev: 'Azerbaijan's attitude to the conflicts [Chechnya, Kosovo and Nagorno-Karabakh] is based on the principle of a nation's territorial integrity.'[45] Adherence to this principle would seem to call for sympathy to the Serb cause. The solution offered by the international community to Kosovo – autonomy but not independence – partly extricated the Azerbaijani government from this predicament. The eventual outcome prompted Azerbaijani president Heydar Aliev to state the following during NATO's 50th anniversary celebrations:

> We believe that the best solution would be to ensure the territorial integrity of all Yugoslavia, but extend autonomy to Albanians of Kosovo within Yugoslavia ... There are many similar autonomous countries throughout the world. We are ready to grant Armenia the highest standards of autonomy that exist in other parts of the world. But, undoubtedly, we need to talk and negotiate the details with them. But I would say this is almost equivalent to extending independence to Nagorno-Karabakh.[46]

The Kosovo crisis elicited further analogies to other conflicts in which Azerbaijan was involved. Foreign Minister Gulizade called directly for NATO's 'humanitarian intervention' in the Caucasus, since 'if NATO forces were deployed in our regions the Armenians would have to leave the territories of our republic which they have occupied.'[47] Azerbaijani Defence Minister Safar Abiyev advised NATO to participate in the peacemaking process between Azerbaijan and Armenia as soon as possible.[48] The intensity of the Nagorno-Karabakh conflict caused civilians from both sides to flee their homes ahead of advancing enemy troops.

Armenia

Parallels with Nagorno-Karabakh also shaped the content of the Armenian leadership's statements on Kosovo. While Baku emphasized territorial integrity, Yerevan stressed the 'rights of peoples to self-determination'. In a 25 March 1999 statement, Armenian Foreign Ministry acting spokesman Ara Papyan expressed concern at NATO's recourse to force but added that 'Armenia has always stood up for the rights of peoples to self-determination.'[49] Armenian Foreign Minister Vardan Oskanyan stated in an interview with Armenian television that his country 'has a similar problem in the shape of Nagorno-Karabakh'.[50] The Washington correspondent of the Azerbaijani news agency Turan quoted Oskanyan as having called on NATO to bomb the Azerbaijani capital Baku in the event of NATO involvement in the Karabakh conflict. Oskanyan reportedly stated: 'If NATO is to get involved (in Nagorno-Karabakh), it must first bomb Baku … We did the job of NATO. What NATO has just done in Kosovo, Armenia did earlier: we stopped Azerbaijani aggression.'[51]

The Armenian leadership, including President Kocharyan, had rejected a 'common state' for Azerbaijan and Nagorno-Karabakh. It promoted neither Nagorno-Karabakh's union with Armenia nor its independence. It seems that territorial integrity of existing states was thus not a principle for the Armenian government – indeed, Armenia was the only one of twelve states present at the April 1999 CIS summit to reject the insertion of a clause on the inviolability of borders. All the other presidents wrote an affirmation of this principle into the summit's otherwise vague, declarative 'concluding' document.

A closer look at the Armenian leadership's position on Kosovo and its lessons for Nagorno-Karabakh reveals more similarities with that of Azerbaijan. Armenian commentator Emil Danielyan argued that the Armenian side had been insisting all along on an 'unconventional' solution, whereby Karabakh's status would fall short of outright independence but would not involve any subordination to the authorities in Baku – like Kosovo within Serbia.[52] Some Armenians, such as former National Security Minister and chief Karabakh negotiator David Shahnazarian, argue that even if Kosovo achieved its independence it would not set a precedent for Nagorno-Karabakh because Armenia is not democratic. Shahnazaryan is, however, clear on the general implications of Kosovo for Armenia's foreign policy direction: 'The West tries to bypass the norms it has defended for 50 years … There is nothing much Armenia can do about it except to take this into account when formulating foreign policy.' [53] According to Nagorno-Karabakh's de facto Foreign Minister, Naira Melkumyan, Kosovo was an aberration: 'We are not going to hold negotiations between autonomy and a common state. We are going to hold negotiations between independence and a common state.'[54]

The Armenian leadership encountered greater domestic opposition to Kosovo than either its Ukrainian or its Azerbaijani counterpart. Its support for NATO was muted in comparison with that of Azerbaijan; nevertheless, to a population with clear pro-Serb sympathies and a stake in 'strategic partnership' with Russia, the leadership's descriptions of NATO action as 'alarming'[55] and 'quite a serious and dangerous precedent'[56] seemed mild at best. This fact was quickly pointed out by the leader of the Union of Constitutional Law, Grant Khachatryan.[57] The Communist Party's objections were the most vitriolic; they demanded that Clinton be tried.[58] Significantly, however, in both Armenia and Azerbaijan, the anti-NATO political voices were far from confined to leftist parties. Many of the opposition parties could not understand Armenia's participation in the NATO's 50th anniversary celebrations.

The outcome of Nagorno-Karabakh relieved the administration of this contradiction. The Armenian leadership supported Kosovar Albanians in the same way that it defended the Nagorno-Karabakh Armenians, thereby overriding popular and opposition party sympathy for the Serbian people. The Armenian government also went against its commitments to the strategic partnership with Russia, a fact that some internal voices decried as a betrayal. The Armenian leadership was sensitive to the Russian stance, stressing that its support of NATO (albeit muted) did not affect Russian-Armenian relations. However, it was reassured by its growing alliance with the US-Turkey axis – which had resulted partly from the 1998 Armenian change in government. Deputy Defence Minister Vahan Shirkhanyan stated that Armenia did not intend to join the alliance but that it would participate in Partnership for Peace exercises.[59] On balance, Armenia's reaction was not as strong as that of Azerbaijan or its other neighbour, Georgia.

Georgia

Unlike in Armenia, pro-NATO sentiments prevailed among the Georgian population. Georgian President Eduard Shevardnadze, while calling the NATO action regrettable, said that the alliance had no choice since it was faced with 'ethnic cleansing and extreme separatism'.[60] Part of the reason for the popular support for this position was that Shevardnadze portrayed Kosovo as an almost identical situation to Abkhazia: the Serbs, he maintained, ethnically cleansed the Kosovar Albanians just as the Abkhaz had ethnically cleansed the Georgians; CIS peacekeepers would need to be replaced with an international peacekeeping force just like the one in Kosovo;[61] the use of force concept NATO adopted in April 1999 as a result of Kosovo could and should be applied to Abkhazia;[62] and the Kosovo solution of autonomy, not independence, should be applied to Abkhazia. According to Shevardnadze all these reasons justified NATO's action. Shevardnadze doggedly insisted that these parallels with Abkhazia be acknowledged by the international community.[63] In 1999 he sought first US-NATO and then UN backing of this perception.[64]

In April 1999 in Washington, Georgia's President told a press conference that his and Clinton's opinions had coincided: 'President Clinton', he said, 'believes that the same crime happened in Abkhazia as in Kosovo.' Shevardznadze stressed that the US president had agreed with him that 'ethnic cleansing and genocide should not remain unpunished irrespective of where they take place – in Abkhazia, in Kosovo or in any other country.' He openly stated that the reason he backed NATO was because he viewed Kosovo as equal to Abkhazia and expected the international community to do the same; NATO, however, subsequently categorically insisted that it would not intervene in the Caucasus. With mounting frustration, Shevardnadze condemned what he called the inattention of the international community to his problems.[65]

Like Azerbaijan, Georgia was less bound by its relations with Russia than the Ukraine or Armenia. Also, like Azerbaijan, it was confident that its future lay with the West. But unlike Azerbaijan, Georgia was ambivalent about its willingness to join NATO during the conflict. Its view on NATO membership developed over time. While on 5 March Shevardnadze admitted that Georgia was unlikely to be admitted to NATO,[66] on his return from the US he told a press conference that Georgia was actively seeking membership in NATO and that he had asked the Secretary-General Javier Solana to accelerate the process.[67]

In all this, Georgia wanted the respect of the international community. The Georgians, like the Ukrainians, felt snubbed when their peace proposals were not acknowledged – they accused the G-8 meeting of adopting Ukrainian proposals without recognition.[68] Georgia also blamed the UN for the failure to prevent the crisis in the first place. Shevardnadze called for the creation of a standing UN peacekeeping force, limitations on the right of permanent members of the Security Council to exercise vetoes, and an increase in the number of members in the Council.[69]

Georgia also threatened Russia that the US would intervene on its behalf as it had done in Kosovo, but, like Azerbaijan, it found its expectations of the US to be overrated.

Although the Georgian leadership encountered less internal opposition than did its Caucasian neighbours, it did face some regional opposition to its own perceptions of the Kosovo crisis. Abkhazia's *de facto* Foreign Minister Sergei Shamba ruled out any comparison of Abkhazia and Georgia to Kosovo and Serbia – even while conceding that something of a parallel could be made back in 1992–3, when tens of thousands of people of various nationalities had to flee to occupied Abkhazia as a result of Georgia's military aggression.[70] Ajarian leader Aslan Abashide stated that Georgia's reactions contradicted its balanced foreign policy and by so doing threatened to destabilize Georgia.[71]

Central Asia

In Central Asia the reactions to the Kosovo crisis remained primarily in the remit of the presidencies and, to a lesser degree, the foreign ministries. Less press coverage of Kosovo was found in this region than elsewhere. The Muslim heritage of these states did not automatically make them defend the Kosovar Albanian cause.

Kazakhstan was the first to react, albeit in a contradictory manner. On 25 March 1999 Kazakhstan's Russian Ambassador, Valerii Nikolaenko, quoted Foreign Minister Kasymzhomart Tokaev as saying that Kazakhstan supported Russia's position. On the same day its Foreign Ministry stated that the use of NATO force marked 'a transition to military methods in resolving the Kosovo crisis, which has escalated international tension', and called for 'employing appropriate mechanisms of the United Nations and the OSCE'.[72] The next day the Ministry toned down its statement and simply called for the withdrawal of Serbian forces from Kosovo.[73] President Nursultan Nazarbaev's first official reaction to the crisis came on 16 April 1999 when he pronounced that his country 'fully supported the Russian position' on Kosovo, and 'solidarized' with Russia in its call for an end to bombing.[74] After the bombing of the Chinese embassy in Belgrade, Nazarbaev sent a condolence telegramme to the Chinese leadership stressing that the tragic event was 'a logical consequence of the endless military actions' of NATO.[75] The Kazakh Communist Party accused the US of acting as a 'slayer'.[76] By the time the 50th Anniversary NATO summit had concluded, Nazarbaev modified his tone again: he called for the withdrawal of Serbian troops and their replacement by the UN. The 50th anniversary celebrations revealed Nazarbaev's intentions to get closer to the US; Clinton and Nazarbaev agreed to discuss their countries' strategic partnership in the Autumn of 1999.

Kyrgyzstan's official position bore similarities. Kyrgyzstan's Defence Minister stated on 25 March 1999 that his country was 'in total solidarity' with Russia and that its reaction should be viewed in the context of its membership of the CIS.[77] Simultaneously, Kyrgyzstan's President Askar Akaev sought ties with NATO. Neither Turkmenistan nor Uzbekistan commented extensively on the crisis, but in general the former adhered firmly to its policy of neutrality and the latter pursued its close relations with the US.

Unsurprisingly, the most outspoken reaction against NATO action came from Tajikistan.[78] This country's leadership has been proppped up by the Russian military since its civil war at the start of 1992. Tajikistan alone quietly supported Russia and Belarus in placing Kosovo on the agenda of the 2 April 1999 CIS summit meeting. Earlier in March, the Tajik Foreign Ministry had condemned NATO attacks on the grounds that they were doing 'tremendous political and emotional damage' to the cause of peace, democracy and stability.[79] This stance was vehemently supported by the ethnic Russian community in Tajikistan. The country's Coordinating Council of the 'Slavic Union' of ethnic and public-cultural organizations strongly accused Western politicians of trying to establish 'their world order'.[80]

Conclusions

In sum, three main lessons may be drawn from these case studies. First, neat dichotomies are not possible. It is not accurate to speak of a Slav state reaction, of a Caucasus reaction or even – given theses states' geographic distance from the conflict – of a Central Asian reaction. Kosovo confirmed what has been known for some time: that the CIS members are developing significantly different foreign policies.

The variety of reactions to the crisis is dictated largely by geopolitics. Many of these states were engaged in a delicate balancing act between Russian and US influence (and, indirectly, that of Iran and Turkey). Armenia's reaction reflects the fact that the US recently shifted support from the Azeri-Turkish axis to Armenia; in response, Russia stepped up its role in the peacekeeping efforts of the Caucasus. Kazakhstan's geographical position, sandwiched as it is between China and Russia, explains its mixed reaction.

The attendance (or otherwise) of each state at the 50th NATO anniversary celebrations in April 1999 was a political statement of its own geopolitical realities. As demonstrated, some leaderships were hard-pressed to justify participation to their constituencies. The range of reactions of these states to Kosovo also underlines the weakness of the CIS as an institution. The documents and discussions at the 2 April summit meeting illustrate the absence of the rule of law in intra-CIS relations and the risks inherent in CIS security arrangements. This situation vindicates Georgia's quest for security arrangements outside the CIS.

The alignment of CIS or GUUAM was not always a predictor of how particular states would react. For example, why did Azerbaijan send its Minister of Defence to the CIS Ministers of Defence summit meeting on 2 April? Why did Kazakhstan participate in both exercises – the only state to do so? Apparent contradictions such as these arise partly because these alignments are constantly in flux; during a top-level Ukraine NATO Council session, Kuchma stated that the 'tragic events in Kosovo compel us to re-think virtually the entire-post-confrontational architecture of European security'.[81] It is also true that perceptions reflect not only geopolitics but also such issues as national identity, domestic constraints and the role of individuals. In particular, many of these states have shown – and the example of Ukraine particularly comes to mind – how presidencies were able to override domestic anti-NATO sentiment if they felt that a Western stance was in their national interest. This phenomenon also revealed how official perceptions of the crises in these states were primarily shaped by elites, and how the executive dominated the foreign policymaking process.

Second, the CIS states differed in opinion over how best to handle issues of humanitarian rights and self-determination. Much more so than in the West, the debate at both the elite and the popular level was dominated by the legal ramifications of intervention. In most states, there was little media coverage of the plight of the Kosovar refugees; in any case, many of these states, notably those of the Caucasus and Tajikistan, had experienced their own refugee crises – which they felt had been blatantly ignored by the international community. Moreover, as newly sovereign entities themselves, these states were in no hurry to endorse a new world order based on human rights rather than sovereignty. The region saw its share of discussions about how such interventions could be avoided in the future, with Georgia and Ukraine seeing reform of the UN as the main solution. The young states could be somewhat comforted by the fact that the West, which still follows a Westphalian-based system that is archly conservative and reluctant to see the formation of new states, did not draw its intervention to its logical conclusion; Kosovo was not granted independence but only autonomy.

The 2 April 1999 CIS summit meeting demonstrated that each state had a different attitude about how sub-national units should be handled. Baku's resistance to the notion of a 'common state' indirectly helped two other countries represented at the CIS summit: Georgia, which had been under Russian pressure to accept that scheme in Abkhazia, and Moldova, which had undermined its own negotiating position after accepting the 'common state' in a key document on the principles of settling the Transdniester conflict.

Third, and indirectly, the post-Kosovo position of the West on this kind of intervention has not emerged any more clearly. The crisis highlighted how NATO's policy towards all these states, but in particular towards the Caucasus and Central Asia,[82] remains contradictory and piecemeal. At a meeting of the Azerbaijani, Georgian and Armenian presidents on 25 April 1999 in Washington, chaired by US Secretary of State Madeleine Albright, the NATO foreign ministers told the three presidents that Kosovo was not a model for the resolution of conflicts.[83] On the same day at the Ukraine-NATO Council meeting, President Bill Clinton said that NATO doors remain open to new members regardless of where they are located, if they are able and prepared to accept membership commitments.[84] Speaking in Warsaw in late June 1999, Kuchma expressed fears that the Kosovo crisis would weaken Europe's interest in Ukraine. Russian ultranationalist Vladimir Zhirinovskii saw dire implications for the West's involvement in the region. He predicted in June 1999 that NATO would soon use armed force in the Ukraine and the Transcaucasus to defend minority rights in the face of persecution. He believes that the economic interests of Western European countries and the US were behind many regional conflicts and that 'the West will be supporting uprisings by national minorities' in the coming ten to twenty years.[85] This position is extreme; nevertheless, it is hard to deny that the potential for armed international intervention in the many ethnic and territorial disputes of the CIS states has substantially risen since Kosovo.

Notes

1. On 8 December 1991 the heads of state of Belarus, Russia, and Ukraine signed an agreement on the creation of the CIS. On 21 December, in Almaty, heads of state of eleven former republics signed the declaration that incorporates the five central Asian states, as well as Armenia, Azerbaijan, and Moldova into the CIS. Georgia at this stage declined to attend but joined in 1994.
2. See, for example, the informative Martha Brill Olcott, Anders Åslund and Sherman W. Garnett, *Getting it Wrong: Regional Cooperation and the Commonwealth of Independent States* (Washington DC: Brookings Institution Press, 1999).
3. Infotag News Agency (hereafter Infotag), 29 March 1999. Online at http://www.mldnet.com/infotag/infotag.html.
4. Jan Maksymiuk, 'While Europe looks elsewhere', Radio Free Europe/Radio Liberty (hereafter RFE/RL) *Newsline*, 17 May 1999.
5. Radio Racyja in *Transitions Online*, 10 May 1999. Online at http://www.tol.cz/.
6. Maksymiuk, 'While Europe looks elsewhere'.
7. *The Jamestown Foundation Monitor*, 6 September 2000. Online at http://www.jamestown.org.
8. Information Telegraph Agency of Russia (hereafter ITAR-TASS), 20 April 1999. Online at http://www.itar-tass.com/
9. ITAR-TASS, 22 March 1999.
10. ITAR-TASS, 25 March 1999.
11. Basa Press News Agency, 27 March 1999. Online at http://www.basa.md/.
12. ITAR-TASS, 29 April 1999.
13. ITAR-TASS, 7 July 1999.
14. Infotag, 4 May 1999 in *Transitions Online*, 6 May 1999.
15. RFE/RL Newsline, 29 March 1999.
16. RIA News Agency, 12 June 1999. Online at http://www.ria.ru/.
17. RFE/RL *Newsline*, 29 March 1999.
18. Interfax News Agency (hereafter Interfax), 6 April 1999. Online at HTTP://www.interfax-news.com/
19. The Ukrainian Foreign Ministry's statement of 25 March 1999 voiced deep concern over the use of military force against a sovereign state. Interfax, 25 March 1999.
20. Interfax, 13 May 1999.
21. For further details of Ukraine's three-stage peace settlement, see ITAR-TASS, 20 April 1999.
22. Interfax, 13 May 1999.
23. ITAR-TASS, 27 April 1999.
24. Interfax, 10 April 1999.
25. Socis Gallup service, which conducted a poll among 1200 Ukrainians. Interfax, 20 May 1999.

26. ITAR-TASS, 6 May 1999.
27. Telegraphic Agency of the Slovak Republic (hereafter TASR), 5 May 1999. Online at http://www.tasr.sk/.
28. ITAR-TASS, 27 April 1999.
29. RFE/RL Newsline, 26 March 1999.
30. Intelnews, 7 April 1999. Online at http://www.brama.com/intelnews/.
31. ITAR-TASS, 21 April 1999.
32. *La Libre Belgique*, 20 May 1999.
33. Interfax, 10 April 1999.
34. Interfax, 15 July 1999.
35. Interfax, 24 March 1999.
36. *Rossiyskaya Gazeta*, 20 April 1999.
37. ITAR-TASS, 27 April 1999.
38. Interfax, 15 July 1999.
39. Turan, 25 March 1999.
40. *The Jamestown Foundation, Fortnight: A Biweekly on the Post-Soviet States*, vol. 5, no. 7, 9 April 1999.
41. Turan, 5 July 1999.
42. Interfax, 27 May 1999.
43. RFE/RL *Newsline*, 27 May 1999.
44. Interfax, 4 March 1999.
45. Interfax, 16 November 1999.
46. *Azerbaijan International*, Summer 1999, vol. 7, no. 2.
47. *Rossiyskaya Gazeta*, 13 July 1999.
48. ITAR-TASS, 16 June 1999.
49. RFE/RL *Newsline*, 26 March 1999.
50. Snark News Agency (henceforth Snark), 27 March 1999.
51. Turan, 30 June 1999.
52. Emil Danielyan, 'Armenia Watches for an Unconventional Spin in Kosovo Settlement', in *Transitions Online*, 22 July 1999.
53. See Danielyan, *ibid.*, 22 July 1999.
54. Snark, 20 July 1999.
55. Presidential Aide Aram Sarkisyan on 24 March 1999. See Noyan Tapan Information Centre (henceforth Noyan Tapan), 25 March 1999. Online at http://noyan-tapan.am/.
56. Armenian Foreign Minister Vardan Oskanyan. See Snark, 1 July 1999.
57. Noyan Tapan, 12 April 1999.
58. Noyan Tapan, 28 May 1999.
59. RFE/RL *Newsline*, 7 May 1999.
60. ITAR-TASS, 24 April 1999.
61. Interfax, 19 May 1999.
62. Interfax, 24 May 1999.
63. Interfax, 26 July 1999.
64. *Tbilisi Gergian TV1* in Georgian, 4 July 2000 in *FBIS-SOV*, 5 July 2000.
65. ITAR-TASS, 21 September 1999.
66. RFE/RL *Newsline*, 5 March 1999.
67. RFE/RL *Newsline*, 30 April 1999.

68. ITAR-TASS, 10 May 1999.
69. RFE/RL *Newsline*, 30 April 1999.
70. ITAR-TASS, 19 July 1999.
71. Interfax, 7 April 1999.
72. Interfax-Kazakhstan, 25 March 1999.
73. RFE/RL *Newsline*, 26 March 1999.
74. Interfax-Kazakhstan and ITAR-TASS, 16 April 1999.
75. Interfax, 11 May 1999; Interfax-Kazakhstan, 9 May 1999.
76. Xinhua News Agency, 11 May 1999. Online at http://202.84.17.11/en/.
77. ITAR-TASS, 25 March 1999.
78. RFE/RL *Newsline*, 26 March 1999.
79. Interfax, 25 March 1999.
80. ITAR-TASS, 2 May 1999.
81. Interfax, 25 April 1999.
82. See Robin Bhatty and Rachel Bronson, 'NATO's Mixed Signals in the Caucasus and Central Asia', *Survival*, vol. 42, no. 3. (Autumn 2000), pp. 129–46.
83. Turan, 26 April 1999.
84. Interfax, 25 April 1999.
85. Interfax, 23 June 1999.

CHAPTER TWELVE

Chinese Perceptions

MICHAEL YAHUDA

Kosovo and in particular the 7 May 1999 bombing of the Chinese embassy in Belgrade proved to be a defining moment in terms of China's domestic politics and its foreign relations. In domestic politics it proved to be the last hurrah of the leftists who tried and failed to reverse the path of economic reform and openness to the West. It also highlighted the strengths and weaknesses of China's particular form of nationalism. In foreign relations it heightened Chinese suspicions of American 'hegemonism' and of American policy towards China. Kosovo underlined Chinese feelings of vulnerability to an American adversary on whom they were nevertheless dependent for providing a degree of regional order that was necessary for security and for deepening their engagement with the international economy. Kosovo also provided an opportunity for the Chinese to develop a fresh approach to problems of humanitarian intervention. But above all Kosovo showed that despite Chinese pride in their growing weight in international affairs, they still had a long way to go before they could become a power of global significance to be treated as an equal by the most powerful.

The exposure of China's relative weakness

Despite the enormous noise that China's leaders generated over the Kosovo issue, they found that despite their best endeavours they were unable to change the course of the war, or to play a role in the process that led to its conclusion. Thus the Chinese had to relent on their initial insistence that the bombing had to stop before they would entertain the negotiation of peace moves at the UN. They also had to backtrack from their declared intention of becoming a primary player in the Balkan peace process.[1] Moreover, even though they turned the affair into an issue with the US, China's leaders found that they were unable to secure the unreserved apology that they wanted, or extract concessions from the US on other matters. Although they suspended exchanges with the US on trade negotiations, human rights talks, arms control and military visits, these were all resumed by the end of the year without any marked advantage having accrued to the Chinese side. Although the Chinese leaders made much play of the significance of the strategic partnership with Russia and of the development of multi-polar relationships, they could not alter the fundamental way in which their country was structurally tied in to American dominance in East Asia.

Since the legitimacy and indeed survival of the Chinese regime depends to a large part on being able to ensure continued economic growth and development, China's leaders cannot risk disengaging from the international economy without putting the further development of the domestic economy in jeopardy. Foreign trade accounts for more than a third of the country's GNP and the foreign related part of the economy is the main engine of economic growth and provides best economic practice. In 1998 the US absorbed more than $70 billion or 38.7 per cent of China's total exports with a balance of trade in China's favour of $56 billion.[2] The US is also seen in China as a principal source of advanced technology. But over and beyond that the US structural economic power has served China's interests well: US support has enabled China to benefit from favourable treatment from international economic financial organizations such as the World Bank and the IMF.[3] More broadly, the US has been responsible for providing the conditions in the Asia-Pacific within which the Chinese economy has been able to flourish since China embarked on the road of economic reform and openness more than twenty years earlier. In addition to shaping the rules and the character of the international political economy of the region, the US has also provided the terms of strategic stability in the region. It is the pattern of America's bilateral security arrangements with many of the countries in the Western Pacific that has largely determined the security environment within which China's leaders have been able to find the 'tranquil international environment' that they claim is necessary for the country's economic development. That is not to say that China's leaders do not feel constrained by the US, notably over the Taiwan issue, but they also recognize that whatever their problems in conducting relations with the US, they are in no condition to withdraw from or to seriously challenge the economic and security systems over which the Americans preside in the Asia-Pacific. As we shall see, the Kosovo affair, if anything, reinforced that condition.

Beijing also found that its stance was not echoed by others in east Asia. Muslim countries that may have shared Beijing's misgivings about American unilateral interventionism were nevertheless more sympathetic to the plight of Muslim Albanians at the hands of Christian Serbs. Others, more concerned about the possible damaging effects for them and the region of a breakdown in Sino-American relations, sought to reduce the severity of Beijing's reaction to the bombing.[4] Thus, even within its own region, China was unable to find significant support for its view.

Why did Kosovo have such an immediate impact upon China?

Given that weakness, the question arises as to why China's leaders reacted in the way that they did and why Kosovo and the bombing of their embassy had such an enormous impact within China. In retrospect it is possible to advance several reasons as to why Kosovo affected the Chinese so strongly. First, it occurred at a time when China's leaders and the country at large felt slighted by Washington after having been elevated to almost equals the previous summer by the agreement between the two presidents to build a 'strategic partnership'. Second, it was the culmination of official propaganda since Tiananmen and the collapse of the Soviet Union to the effect that the US has sought in various ways to undermine China's independence and to prevent it from assuming its rightful place as a major world power. Third, it showed how deeply set were the xenophobic nativistic nationalist sentiments, despite two decades of opening to the outside world. Fourth, it arose from a sense of insecurity by a regime that was fearful of its loss of control within China as a consequence of the massive and rapid economic changes and by a people caught up in rapid social change.

However, these are all reasons that turn on sentiment and emotion rather than on rational calculation of interest and strategy. To understand how this came about it is first necessary to look at the way the Kosovo issue grew and then erupted in China. The intensity of the Chinese response to Kosovo, especially as aroused by the bombing of the embassy in Belgrade, came as a surprise to most people. After all Kosovo was a very distant place of which Chinese would have known even less than Chamberlain's compatriots knew of Czechoslovakia at the time of Munich in 1938. Although the emotional intensity of the Chinese was to a degree officially inspired, there is no doubt that it was keenly felt by even those who had hitherto been sceptical of most of the exhortations of the Propaganda Department of the Party. Interestingly, the most vociferous at the outset were students from the prestigious universities who had access to the Western accounts of developments in the Balkans and were not prisoners of the official media. For example, on the day after the bombing Western residents observed some students at Peking University charging across shouting 'kill Americans!'. It must be added that no American was killed. Most Westerners stayed discretely out of sight and were not molested.

The impact of the war against Kosovo was already significant in China before the bombing of the Belgrade embassy. But its significance was largely confined to official circles and what may be called the 'attentive public'.[5] From the outset the government regarded the NATO attack on Yugoslavia as illegitimate and unwarranted. Not only did it lack a UN mandate, but it was portrayed as part of a new 'strategy for global intervention' by American-led NATO. As early as 25 March when President Jiang Zemin was completing a European tour, he demanded an 'immediate end' to the air strikes, while the editorial in the organ of the Party's Central Committee, *The People's Daily*, accused NATO of 'flagrantly using barbaric military force to interfere in Yugoslavia'. Noting that the ethnic conflict in Yugoslavia had ancient roots, the editorial blamed the recent violence in Kosovo entirely upon 'illegal Albanian armed forces' and, unlike most of the rest of the world, it deemed the Serbian actions as 'entirely appropriate and legitimate'. Perhaps, getting to the heart of the matter from China's point of view, the editorial noted: 'There are many countries with problems involving ethnic minorities. If we encourage division, won't the world fall into chaos?' This reflected Chinese concern that Kosovo might serve as a precedent for more general Western intervention elsewhere, perhaps even in China's sometimes violent ethnic conflicts in Tibet or Xinjiang or even Taiwan.[6]

The official Chinese reaction must be seen in the context of the profound disquiet in which the high point of Sino-American relations that had been reached during President Clinton's visit to China less than a year earlier had rapidly deteriorated. In no time, old issues of unfair trade practices, human rights violations in China were joined by new American accusations of Chinese spying and stealing of nuclear and missile secrets, of Chinese illegal campaign contributions and of continued proliferation of weapons of mass destruction. Meanwhile Chinese strategists portrayed the enlargement of NATO and the extension of its influence in the 'partnership for peace' into Central Asia as not only aimed at Russia but also as part of a design to contain China. They linked the NATO development with the enhancement of America's alliances with its partners in the western Pacific and in particular with the projected TMD (Theatre Missile Defence) to cover Japan and possibly Taiwan.

The Chinese official press and television coverage of Kosovo focused entirely on the Serbian account of events. The military actions of NATO were compared to those of Nazi Germany and the Yugoslav President, Slobodan Milošević, was depicted as an anti-imperialist hero. The plight of the Kosovo Albanians was overlooked to such an extent that ambassadors from several Muslim countries made (unofficial) representations in Beijing.[7] Interestingly, Beijing's media coverage and the general hardline stance on the NATO air strikes evoked strong criticism from leading foreign affairs scholars within China. In mid-April scholars from official think tanks warned that the media coverage was inciting anti-Western sentiment in China that ultimately would undermine the nation's openness policy. Moreover, they worried lest the current approach would damage China's national interest by weakening relations with the West that were imperative for China's development. There was also concern that leftist and conservative elements within the Party were using the crisis in the Balkans to undermine the efforts of President Jiang Zemin and Premier Zhu Rongji to improve relations with Washington. While supporting the government's opposition to NATO's military action, they urged that a more balanced view be taken towards the ethnic conflict itself.[8]

It was the bombing of the Chinese embassy on the night of 7 May that vindicated the concerns of these scholars. Ironically, many of them too were swept up in the emotionally charged Chinese response. Immediately, Chinese scholars began to advance a whole host of conspiracy theories to explain what was regarded as a deliberate act by the American leadership.[9] That response has to be understood within the context of the particular way in which patriotism had been promoted by the top leadership and the longstanding strength of the appeal of nationalism to successive generations of modern Chinese.

The distinctive character of Chinese patriotism (*aiguo zhuyi* – literally, love-statism – which is best translated as state-nationalism) is its promotion of China and its people as particular victims of modern history and its portrayal of the Communist Party as the unique and indispensable saviour of the country. In this view China is entitled to special treatment by the international community as it regains the status of a world power at least the equal of any other. However, the official view also claims that there are hostile forces headed by the United States that seek to deny China its rightful place in the international community. These are portrayed variously as seeking to prevent China from regaining the remaining territories allegedly lost during the 'hundred years of shame and humiliation' and/or to bring about unwanted changes within the country so as to deny it a separate independent domestic system. Popular, as opposed to official, nationalism is no less sensitive to claims of entitlement. But when these have not been forthcoming popular nationalists have had a habit, at least since the disappointment with the post-World War settlement of 1919, of turning against their own government for not demonstrating sufficient strength against the foreign foe.[10]

Matters were not helped when Premier Zhu Rongji, China's leading economic reformer, had his package of concessions for China's entry to the World Trade Organization (WTO) turned down by President Clinton when he visited the US in April. It was a personal humiliation at a time of great sensitivity in Sino-American relations in both Beijing and Washington. Even worse was the publication by Washington of Zhu's proposals on the Internet, as that aroused domestic opposition from those who stood to lose most.

It is against that background that the Chinese reaction must be understood. The bombing of the embassy was not seen simply as a mistake, but as a deliberate attempt to humiliate the country. Some 400,000 (largely student) demonstrators attacked Western embassies and American consulates within the first twenty-four hours of the outrage. But the government sought to ride out the storm it had played a part in unleashing, in part by facilitating the early demonstrations and then controlling them. At the outset the government insisted that the focus of public anger should be directed primarily at the US (hence the use of the term 'US-led NATO'), that no one should be physically attacked and that Western commercial operations should not be affected. All three were observed, even though a few McDonalds and Pizza Hut outlets were attacked as symbols of America. The government was able to bring the demonstrations to an end within five days.

The impact on domestic politics

As China's scholars had predicted, Kosovo provided the leftist and conservative forces with an opportunity to try to slow down the reforms and to drive a wedge between China and the West. The fragile consensus that Premier Zhu Rongji had mustered in support of the proposed package of concessions in support of China's bid to gain American acceptance for entry to the WTO had broken down even before the bombing of the embassy. He and Jiang had prevailed in the Politburo against those who opposed Zhu's visit to the US in April only to find that he had been humiliated by President Clinton. This enabled those economic interests who had most to lose from entry to the WTO to raise their objections once again. Moreover the failure of Zhu's visit strengthened suspicion of American policy towards China. Zhu's humiliation by Clinton took place just after the US had confirmed the expansion of its defence co-operation with Japan, which was seen in Beijing to dovetail with the extension of NATO's out-of-area operations in support of the new doctrine of humanitarian intervention. Thus the bombing of the embassy was seen as both a punishment of China for supporting Serbia and as a warning that it too was vulnerable.

That provided the opportunity for a coalition opposed to the reforms and to the opening to the West to try and reverse the course of China's policies. The coalition was made up of three broad groups. These included, first, the remnant leftists and state centrists, some of whom who were concerned about the non-socialist character of the reforms and the erosion of communist ideology and power that they entailed and others who might be called traditional Soviet-style bureaucrats concerned to maintain their status and control. Second, the disparate sets of economic interests who had most to lose from entry to the WTO. Third, hardliners, in the military especially, who felt China was sacrificing too much of its national dignity by becoming excessively dependent upon the US.

The high point of their public activities was the return to Beijing of the bodies of the three Chinese who had been killed in the bombing of the embassy. Li Peng, who ranked second in the Party hierarchy and who headed the National People's Congress, and General Chi Haotian, the Minister of Defence, went much further than the other leaders in attacking America in declaring that 'the whole Chinese people is united in hatred of the common enemy'.[11] However, they were seen to have over-reached themselves especially as they had no alternative economic programme with which to lift the economy out of its deflationary cycle in the short term or to address long term development. Moreover, it was readily apparent that China was neither sufficiently wealthy nor technologically sophisticated to modernize its armed forces through self-reliance or even through arms purchases from Russia so as to impose its will in the Taiwan Strait against American opposition. China's 1998 military budget was between $12 billion and $35 billion (the lowest and highest Western estimates) as against the American equivalent of $278 billion. Thus China's leaders soon accepted the olive branches sent by the American Administration. By the end of May (before the end of the American-led bombing of Serbia) China's official media reported statements by American leaders of their wish to resume constructive engagement.

Despite the failure of the leftist hardliners to reverse the policy of reform and openness, Kosovo and the embassy bombing left their mark on Chinese politics in other ways. Premier Zhu Rongji never again recovered the high standing that he had previously enjoyed. Even though an agreement was duly reached in November with America over China's entry into the WTO on substantially the same terms that Zhu had offered in April, Zhu's position in the hierarchy had already been damaged as some of his own associates had been demoted from key posts in favour of others with closer ties to Jiang Zemin.[12] It was a more chastened and insecure government that now had to address the question of further reform.

At a more general level of politics, the eruption once again of a more xenophobic and nativistic style of nationalism has once again introduced an element of volatility and uncertainty. As noted earlier, the leadership bears a measure of responsibility for having fostered a brand of state nationalism that portrays China as a victim and as still vulnerable to hostile external forces. In many respects it is a rather barren kind of nationalism as it offers little vision of the kind of society that the future may hold or of what may be offered to others in terms of new international norms. It is a nationalism that plays on a sense of resentment and a consequent entitlement. At a time of great social change within China, when the old bounds of community are fast eroding, nationalism may exercise a greater appeal as an 'imagined community' to use Anderson's distinctive term. But the parochial barrenness of China's state nationalism may be seen as potentially dangerous at home and as provoking uncertainty abroad about the implications of China as a rising power.

Thus although the leftist and conservative challenge may have been reversed, the result has not been a triumph for the reformers. Rather there has emerged a state of unease in which China's leaders recognize that they have no alternative but to proceed with the reforms despite the social disruption that they entail. At the same time they recognize that, although they must enter the WTO, they will be vulnerable to accusations of having allowed in excessive foreign influence. They will also be mindful of the domestic dangers of appearing to be weak in front of foreign countries, notably the US. Thus the impact of Kosovo has been to underscore the domestic pitfalls of deepening China's integration into the international economy and international society. Yet Kosovo also demonstrated that China had no alternative but to continue to deepen that process of integration.

The perspective of the military

It is important to recognize that like the military elsewhere, the Chinese military encompass a range of interests and views, but again, like those elsewhere Chinese military officers and analysts are obliged to consider 'worst case scenarios'. Moreover, the Chinese military have had less exposure to the Western world than their civilian counterparts as a consequence of the length of the application of the Western sanctions against military exchanges with China because of the events in Tiananmen Square. That sanction lasted well into the second half of the 1990s. As a result military analysts tended to underplay the domestic sources of foreign policy in Western democracies and in the US especially. Instead they tended to see underlying purposes and well-thought-out strategies behind policies that were often driven by disparate domestic political pressures. Thus Chinese military publications tended to see policies driven by American domestic politics as evidence of a grand American strategy to keep China down and prevent its reunification with Taiwan.[13]

One of the leading experts on the Chinese military has identified three groups within the People's Liberation Army (PLA): a majority that supports a cautious approach to the West; a small minority that supports better relations and political liberalization, and a large and growing minority that believes the US seeks to weaken China.[14] Clearly Kosovo will have strengthened the ranks of the third group. There was a military dimension to the challenge posed by the leftists that argued against the longstanding official view that the dominant trend in international affairs was still 'peace and development'. But it was unsuccessful.[15]

As in the case of the Gulf War, Chinese military observers were impressed by the high-tech weaponry of the Americans and veteran generals were quoted in the *People's Daily* as demanding that the PLA be equipped with modern weaponry and that the national defences should be strengthened.[16] The official military budget was duly increased by a further 10 per cent, but that was in line with previous annual increases and it is unclear what proportion, if any, of that was as a response to Kosovo. A stronger case could be made for the Taiwan factor as the key issue driving China's military modernization, including the emphasis upon missile development and deployment. Indeed some military journals also warned about the dangers of getting involved in a counterproductive arms race such as that which had crippled the former Soviet Union.[17] They also noted that the Americans were not getting things all their own way as Europe was divided about Kosovo and that, in any event, Serbia survived to fight another day. Indeed one year on, one of China's most significant military journals took heart from the enormous difficulties that American-led NATO was experiencing in Kosovo, seeing this as evidence of the limitations of this kind of warfare.[18]

In sum, the military response to Kosovo was mixed and rather paralleled that of the civilian side. A small group sought to use the episode to bring about a fundamental change of policy, but failed. More broadly, Kosovo had the effect of deepening the rather negative view taken of the US while recognizing that it was necessary to continue to be engaged with the sole superpower. Kosovo may also have strengthened the military's claim to speed up the process of modernization and the acquisition of advanced weaponry from Russia, but the Taiwan factor may well have done so anyway. China's military were once again impressed by America's capacity to wage a successful high-tech war, but the element of surprise with which they observed the Gulf War was less evident.

The impact on foreign relations

Beyond identifying some of China's structural weaknesses as a global power, the impact of Kosovo on China's foreign relations was less enduring than might have been thought. Kosovo did not change any of the key characteristics that shaped China's foreign relations, nor did it evoke new policies, except for a temporary sharpening of relations with the USA. Typically, the key problems of Kosovo were narrowed down from a Chinese perspective almost exclusively to the concern with the alleged hegemonic behaviour of the US. From the outset, China's leaders made it clear that their primary concern was not with NATO as such, but rather with the US. They received reassurance about this from no less a person than the British Prime Minister, who affirmed that the principles involved in the Kosovo intervention did not apply to Asia.[19] Thus China's leaders sought an apology and compensation from the US alone and in the end it was the US alone that offered China both. Since China resumed normal exchanges with the US within a matter of months, notably after the meeting between the two presidents at the APEC summit in early September, Kosovo soon receded from a high ranking in the agenda of US-China relations. Nevertheless the Chinese later still claimed to be dissatisfied with the American apology and with the American punishment of the perpetrators of the bombing.[20]

For a while it seemed as if the 'strategic partnership' between Russia and China that had been declared in 1996 might acquire a new significance. But although the two sides appeared to co-ordinate their approach to the Kosovo issue in the UN, this proved to be less substantive in practice. While each side was keen to play up their joint opposition to 'American hegemonism' their respective approaches to the Balkans differed too greatly in practice. Russian historical and geopolitical interests as well as ethnic and religious affinities were directly involved in an issue that, for China, was more a matter of principle and hurt pride in a distant conflict in which China had little or no immediate interest. Thus, unlike China, Russia was a direct participant in bringing the war to an end and in despatching troops to participate in the peacekeeping. More broadly, much of the foreign policy of each of these huge countries was driven by domestic concerns and by their respective drastic economic needs. These differed markedly, so that although they both shared an antipathy to the unipolarity of the US, they nevertheless looked to the US to play a constructive role in their respective economic development. Despite the realist perspectives of both sets of leaders, balance-of-power considerations were insufficient grounds on which to base policy in the complex post-Cold War world of interdependencies and globalization. Moreover neither had been able to generate the necessary degree of trust in the other to establish a sustained united front even for diplomatic purposes.[21] Within these constraints, however, Kosovo did bring the two closer together as they began to share more points in common in their opposition to the US.

The only dimension of foreign relations in which the impact of Kosovo may said to be still present is the continual Chinese objection to humanitarian intervention, in which the concern for human rights is elevated above the principle of state sovereignty. The Chinese government has stipulated that humanitarian intervention can only be allowed if it is authorized by the UN and sanctioned by the government of the relevant state. That of course would rule out intervention against a government that was involved in committing atrocities against its own people or one that was adjudged to be grossly violating the rights of ethnic groups. Thus China's Foreign Minister, Tang Jiaxuan, in addressing the UN General Assembly on 22 September, voiced his government's objection to the notion that active intervention was needed when civilian populations were at risk whether or not the government of the relevant state approved. Without naming the authors of these views, such as Secretary General Koffi Annan and President Clinton, Tang argued that any deviation from respect for sovereignty and non-interference in another country's affairs would lead to a new form of gunboat diplomacy that would 'wreak havoc'. He then used the example of Kosovo to drive home his point:

> The outbreak of war in Kosovo has sounded an alarm for us all ... A regional military organisation, in the name of humanitarianism and human rights, bypassed the United Nations and took military action against a sovereign state. It created an ominous precedent in international relations.[22]

However, it cannot be argued that it was the example of Kosovo that made China's leaders take this view. As China began the policy of economic reform and openness that led to many interdependencies with the outside world, Deng Xiaoping resurrected the 1950's doctrine of the Five Principles of Peaceful Co-existence. These explicitly dealt with state relations only and they demanded recognition of diversity between political systems, sovereignty and non-interference. At best Kosovo intensified the Chinese commitment to these principles.

Conclusion

In what sense then may Kosovo be described as a defining moment for the People's Republic of China? Following from the above analysis, it would seem that Kosovo served to point up two dimensions of significance in this respect. First, Kosovo demonstrated the limited parameters within which either China's fundamental domestic or foreign policies could be changed. Second, Kosovo underscored how China's insecurities have placed its government in opposition to the aspect of globalization that elevates concern for the human rights of the individual (or large numbers of individuals) over and above state sovereignty.

The fall of Milošović sent a shiver of alarm to China's leaders as yet another dictator was toppled by popular protest. But President Jiang Zemin presented a picture of outward calm by sending a warm message of congratulations to Kostunica once it was clear that his election to the presidency had been accepted. China's Defence White Paper issued just two weeks later duly repeated the standard Chinese official view of

Kosovo. In essence the Chinese reaction confirmed how far removed China was in practice from developments within former Yugoslavia. China's leaders were principally concerned with the implications for them of Western and especially American actions rather than with specific outcomes in the distant Balkans.

From the longer term perspective, China's nationalist-minded elites will have had their distrust of the US deepened. American leaders will have a more difficult task in persuading their Chinese counterparts of their benign intentions. That will make the long-standing problems on the agenda of Sino-American relations such as Taiwan, human rights, arms control, and proliferation, intellectual property rights and projected missile defence systems even more difficult to handle. If that were to result in the two sides discussing their relationship in terms of interest rather than partnership (strategic or otherwise) that could lead ironically to more easily managed relations. However, the abiding legacy of Kosovo for China will be the way it has cast light on the deep contradictions the country faces as its communist government seeks to shore up its rule by encouraging economic growth that necessitates painful economic reform at home and ever-deepening engagement with an outside world whose norms and procedures continually threaten to undermine the basis for Communist Party rule.

Notes

1. See, Brian Knowlton, 'US Rebuffs China on Bombing Halt', *International Herald Tribune*, 12 May 1999.
2. That is according to American figures. Chinese figures suggest a surplus of something less than a half of that. But in any case, both sets of figures show that access to the American market is clearly highly important for China. For discussion of these figures see, N. Lardy, 'Normalizing Economic Relations with China', prepared for The National Bureau of Asian Research, 21 May 1997.
3. For example, China has received more low interest loans and has been the beneficiary of more projects sponsored by the World Bank than any other country. Indeed the World Bank has regularly described China as its best customer.
4. Michael Richardson, 'Asian Nations Seek to Temper China's Anger', *International Herald Tribune*, 11 May 1999.
5. This is a term normally applied to a sector of public opinion in Western democracies, but it has become appropriate in China with regard to the tens of thousands who regularly follow international affairs from sources far broader than the official media. There is lively comment on Internet chat circles that, according to members of think tanks in Beijing, is monitored by the top leaders.
6. Eric Eckholm, 'Beijing Assails Air Raids', *International Herald Tribune*, 26 March 1999.

7. As told to the author by a diplomatic source.

8. Cary Huang, 'Scholars condemn policy on air strikes', *The Hong Kong Standard*, 21 April 1999.

9. See for example, Reuters, 'Conspiracy theories at full Throttle' in *South China Morning Post*, 17 May 1999 or Wang Jian in the Chinese Naval journal, *Jianchuan Zhishi* of 2 June in BBC *Summary of World Broadcasts, The Far East (SWB)* FE/3558 G/3-G/8, 11 June 1999.

10. There is an extensive literature on Chinese nationalism. Perhaps the most notable are Jonathan Unger (ed.), *Chinese Nationalism* (London and New York: M. E. Sharpe, 1996) and Lowell Dittmer and Samuel S. Kim (eds), *China's Quest for National Identity* (Ithaca NY: Cornell University Press, 1993). See also my, 'The Changing Faces of Chinese Nationalism' in Michael Leifer (ed.), *Asian Nationalism* (London: Routledge, 2000) pp. 21–37.

11. See, 'Sino-American Tensions' in *Strategic Comments* (London: IISS. vol. 5, no. 5, June 1999).

12. Willy Wo-Lap Lam, 'Zhu on slippery slope', *South China Morning Post*, 15 August 1999.

13. See for example, David Shambaugh, 'The insecurity of security: the PLA's evolving doctrine and threat perceptions towards 2000', *Journal of Northeast Asian Studies*, vol. 13, no. 1 (Spring 1994), pp. 3–25 and Phillip C. Saunders, 'China's America Watchers: Changing Attitudes Towards the United States', *The China Quarterly*, no. 161 (March 2000), pp. 41–65.

14. Michael Swaine, *China: Domestic Change and Foreign Policy* (Santa Monica CA: RAND Corporation, 1995), pp. 31–34.

15. Saunders, *op. cit.*, p. 63.

16. 'Veteran generals demand world-best weapons', *The Hong Kong Standard*, 16 May 1999.

17. See the article by Wang Jian in the naval journal *Jianchuan Zhishi*, cited in note 9.

18. Sa Bawang, 'The Past Not Forgotten is a Guide for the Future,' *International Strategic Studies*, vol. 57, no. 3 (July 2000), pp. 36–41.

19. He communicated this to the Chinese Vice Premier Qian Qichen during the latter's brief stopover in London *en route* to South Africa on 14 June. Information to the author supplied by a source in the Foreign and Commonwealth Office.

20. On 9 April 2000 the *Washington Post* reported that the CIA had just fired one intelligence officer and reprimanded six managers for errors that led to the bombing of the Chinese embassy in Belgrade. But the following day a spokesman for the Chinese Ministry of Foreign Affairs dismissed the American investigation and the punishment of the alleged perpetrators as unsatisfactory.

21. For accounts of the limitations of the Sino-Russian partnership, see Jennifer Anderson, *The Limits of Sino-Russian Strategic Partnership*, Adelphi Paper No. 315 (London: International Institute for Strategic Studies, 1997) and Shiping Tang, 'Economic Integration in Central Asia: The Russian and Chinese Relationship', *Asian Survey*, vol. XL, no. 2, (March/April 2000), pp. 360–76.

22. Barbara Crossette, 'China Resists UN's Call For Active Intervention', *International Herald Tribune*, 24 September 1999.

CHAPTER THIRTEEN

Perceptions in the Middle East

ROLAND DANNREUTHER

The war in Kosovo elicited a confused, contradictory and essentially muted response in the Middle East, at least in contrast to the crisis in Bosnia that had ended five years earlier. The essential problem was that the war did not conform to the normal stereotypes of Western intervention. Air strikes were not this time directed at Arabs and Muslims; rather, they were being used in defence of the rights of Muslim Kosovars against a Serbian Christian onslaught. It was this seeming paradox that was at the heart of the divided response in the Middle East. This chapter reflects these divisions by separating the countries of the region into three main groupings – the pro-NATO activists; the anti-NATO and pro-Yugoslav militants; and those countries expressing a significant degree of ambivalence. These divisions are rough and inexact and do not reflect the fact that within countries there was often a considerable division of opinion, but they do indicate the general tensions and main factors behind the positions taken by the countries of the region.

The pro-NATO activists

Turkey, as the sole NATO member in the region, was determined to demonstrate its fidelity as a member of the alliance and to defend without reservation the necessity of military action against Yugoslavia. The situation of Kosovo was seen as a continuation of the conflict in Bosnia where, as Prime Minister Bulent Ecevit pointedly argued, 'civilised Europe witnessed the massacre of innocent people, including women and children. No one can defend the continuation of such a situation ... the same goes for the situation in Kosovo.'[1] Turkish F-16 planes participated in NATO air operations; Turkish air bases were authorized for use by NATO forces; and Turkey contributed a 1000-man force for the post-conflict peacekeeping operation. During the course of the conflict, the Turkish government also stated that it would be willing to contribute forces towards a ground offensive, if NATO decided upon this option.

In the Turkish population generally, there was a genuine element of shock and distress over the developments in Kosovo and the government's pro-NATO and anti-Serb stance was warmly welcomed. The hostilities in Kosovo coincided with the 700th anniversary of the founding of the Ottoman Empire and popular sentiment supported a sense of historic obligation to come to the aid of their former loyal Ottoman citizens. This sense of responsibility was also strengthened by the ties of kinship that continue to connect many citizens of Turkey with this region. The Ottoman connection was frequently alluded to by Turkish leaders, with, for example, Ismail Cem, the Defence Minister stating that 'Kosovo is part of our history. We share a common culture, history and faith with the Kosovar Albanians and Turks ... Both in Bosnia and Kosovo, Turkey sought for the traces of our history not to be erased.'[2] Ecevit could also not avoid remarking that 'for 524 years, Kosovo remained under Ottoman rule and lived in security all this time without suffering any pain.'[3]

The Turkish government did, though, exercise considerable caution in limiting the involvement of Turkish forces in the NATO actions. Government officials stressed that Turkish planes were only engaged in defensive operations and that, unlike the case in Bosnia, Turkey was not an advocate for a ground offensive within NATO councils. This restraint was to become a major political issue in the run-up to the elections on 18 April and opposition parties assailed the government with slogans such as 'History will never forgive Ecevit' and 'Ankara has a heart of stone'.[4] Tansu Ciller, the leader of the True Path Party, gave her own emotional response by stating in an interview that 'I feel ashamed today. I feel ashamed as a Turk. Why are we not in Kosovo? Why is Turkey, which has the second largest army in NATO, not in Kosovo.'[5] Ecevit's strategy to deflect this internal criticism was to focus attention on the generosity of the Turkish government, and by implication the Turkish people, to the needs of the expelled Kosovar refugees. In contrast to the more circumspect European response, Turkey swiftly opened its doors to receiving up to 20,000 refugees on Turkish territory in addition to establishing Turkish-funded camps in Albania and Macedonia. The government's focus on the refugee crisis, which deflected media attention away from the more problematic military campaign, achieved its desired political objective with Ecevit and his party gaining a convincing victory in the April elections.

There were a number a factors that dictated the cautious politico-military strategy towards Kosovo. First, there was a real fear that the conflict in Kosovo could escalate more broadly in the region, most notably undermining the fragile peace in Bosnia. The intensity of the Russian opposition to the campaign also raised fears in Ankara that a

'Serb-Orthodox axis' was emerging that would drive 'Turkey towards a polarisation that might be far more dangerous than that of the [Cold War] ideological polarisation.'[6] These broader geostrategic factors were combined with concerns over the precedents being set by NATO's overriding of the principle of non-intervention. Throughout the campaign, Turkish officials regularly had to defend their policies towards the Kurds, especially as many European opponents to the war stressed the double standards of NATO in coming to the aid of the Kosovars but not the Kurds. As well as arguing that the analogy between the Kosovars and Kurds was totally erroneous, Ankara stressed that the NATO campaign was not seeking to undermine the territorial integrity of Yugoslavia but only to reverse the genocidal policies of the Milošević government.

Turkish moderation and restraint was also directed at projecting Turkey's international image and status. Turkish leaders sought to demonstrate their loyalty and commitment to Western policies and made pointed comparisons to the anti-Western opposition of Russia and the ambivalence of the rest of the Muslim world. In relation to the Europeans and the European Union, Ankara emphasized its strategic utility and fidelity so as to undermine European desires to decouple from NATO and to strengthen Turkey's credentials as an EU candidate member. The final acceptance by the EU of Turkey as a candidate country in December 1999 was seen in Ankara, at least partially, as a consequence of its self-perceived mature role during the Kosovo crisis.

No other countries in the Middle East took as proactive and intensive engagement in the Kosovo war as Turkey. But, the Arab Gulf states, at least in terms of rhetorical support for NATO and provision of humanitarian aid, were not far behind. With the memory of the Gulf War still ever present, there was a more open advocacy than in Ankara for NATO to engage in a ground offensive. Thus, Prince Khaled bin Sultan, Saudi Air Force commander during Operation Desert Storm, argued that 'we must encourage the Americans and their allies in NATO to stay the course … We must remember the situation eight years ago when air strikes against Iraqi troops forced them to withdraw. A land attack was necessary to finish the job.'[7] For the elites of the Gulf states, the NATO attacks on Serbia were also of value in demonstrating to their publics, who were becoming increasingly sceptical about the moral validity of the regular US-UK air attacks on Iraq, that the West could also act impartially in defence of Muslims under threat of attack from European Christians. In this vein, the Gulf media relished highlighting the ambivalence of the rest of the Arab world in failing to support the US and NATO, who were depicted as valiantly defending fellow Muslims in Kosovo.

Of all the states in the Gulf region, the United Arab Emirates probably went furthest in providing concrete support for the US and NATO. Along with the other Gulf states, the population of the UAE raised large amounts in humanitarian aid, with one UAE citizen donating over $1.8 million.[8] The UAE went further, though, in setting up their own refugee camp, which was generally recognized to be highly efficient, in the northern Albanian town of Kukes and in being the only Gulf state to make a contribution to the post-conflict peacekeeping force.[9] In addition, the UAE built an airstrip near to Kukes that was ostensibly to facilitate relief supplies but was also in practice used to supply US weapon systems for the KLA.

Amongst the other Arab countries that offered consistent support to NATO, mention should be given to the traditional pro-Western countries of Egypt and Jordan. The leaders of both countries offered their fealty to Washington and were the only Arab countries to withdraw their ambassadors from Belgrade. In Cairo and Amman, the pro-government press remained broadly consistent in its support for the NATO campaign with the Egyptian *al-Ahram* confidently predicting that 'history will record President Clinton's courageous and humanitarian position on the refugee crisis caused by Serb criminals in Kosovo'.[10]

However, as the NATO campaign progressed longer than expected and faced increasing difficulties, the more independent press began to be critical of NATO and the US and could not disguise some satisfaction at the West's apparent impotence. Doubts were raised over whether NATO should have overruled the UN and whether, in reality, US and European interests were truly motivated by concern for the Kosovars or by other objectives. Also, given the centrality of the Arab-Israeli conflict for these countries, there was regular commentary on the perceived double-standards of the West in acting so forcefully against Serbia but not against Israel. By the middle of the campaign, there was generally far greater ambivalence and the argument became more common that 'the world, and particularly Arab countries, [should] abandon the one-sided view of the war and condemn both sides, in order to achieve a balanced view that may be more constructive'.[11] As during the Gulf War, the official stance of these pro-Western Arab governments in support of the US and the West came under increasing pressure from the more deeply rooted anti-American and anti-Western sentiment amongst the general population.

Anti-NATO militants

For the Arab countries that have traditionally had more difficult and confrontational relations with the West there was no such compunction in directly condemning the NATO attacks. For Syria, Iraq, Libya and Algeria, whose regimes remain committed to a rejectionist Arab nationalist stance, there was little equivocation about asserting the illegality of the NATO air strikes on the basis that these attacks had not received the authorization of the UN Security Council. Thus, the Algerian government decided to 'condemn the NATO's states' choice of the use of force against Yugoslavia and call for a diplomatic solution to the Kosovo crisis'.[12] The fact that these radically inclined governments were also willing to give implicit, and in Iraq's case explicit, support for the Yugoslav government was one indication of how the Arab response to Kosovo differed from its response to the Bosnian crisis. In that earlier conflict, the Arab world had managed to maintain a degree of consensus in support of the Muslim Bosnian government and in condemnation of the Serb/Yugoslav authorities.

In Bosnia, though, it had been possible for the Arab and Muslim world both to support the Muslim cause and to condemn the West for not failing to avert the massacre of Bosnian Muslims. In Kosovo, the nature of the conflict was more problematic and, once Yugoslavia itself came under direct Western attack, the radical group of Arab states, who themselves have been the recipients of similar types of Western punishment, felt duty-bound to offer their sympathy to Belgrade and to demonstrate a certain solidarity with a new member of the US-defined grouping of 'rogue' states. The consequence was that the suffering of the Kosovars was almost completely neglected as the common experience of perceived US aggression, double-standards and imperial hegemonism was constantly evoked.

For these radical states, the actual developments within Kosovo was of far less importance than how the example of Kosovo shed light on their own more parochial concerns. As a group who feel a deep sense of victimhood in relation to the West, NATO's intervention into Kosovo was primarily depicted as an illustration of the injustice and arrogance of the West. For Algeria, its anti-NATO stance was principally dictated by the fear that the precedent set by NATO in Kosovo could potentially be extended to Western intervention in Algeria's internal affairs and its continuing internal civil war.

For Syria, the principal thrust of its reporting was to highlight the lessons that the Kosovo conflict offered about the US failure to secure a comprehensive Arab-Israeli settlement. Thus, Syrian commentators argued that NATO had caused more, not less, suffering for the Kosovar Albanians and that it showed that 'if the US is really seeking comprehensive peace in the Middle East, in Kosovo, in Africa, it needs to articulate a long-term vision of peace, and offer that vision before sending bombs and missiles across frontiers.'[13] Likewise, the double standards argument was continually brought out as a reason to distrust the sincerity of NATO's actions since: 'Isn't it a flagrant contradiction that the US supports the Kosovar refugees, but doesn't act on behalf of the Palestinian refugees?'[14]

Syrian criticisms of the US and NATO attacks were, though, surpassed in their virulence by the condemnations issued from Baghdad. The Iraqi authorities almost completely ignored the fate of the Kosovars and gave unconditional support to the Yugoslav government. The main concern in Baghad was to illustrate how again the West was seeking to undermine the territorial integrity of other states – this time Yugoslavia – following the example of the continuous Western attempts to fragment Iraq over the previous nine years. Iraqi support for Yugoslavia was also translated into extensive politico-military co-operation between the two countries, which had its roots in Yugoslav support for the Iraqi war effort against Iran in the 1980s. In 1997, there was a secret bilateral agreement that resurrected this relationship.[15] Just before the start of the NATO campaign, a high-level Yugoslav delegation, headed by Major-General Ceković, visited Baghdad and received from the Iraqis detailed information on the air combat tactics of their common enemy.[16] In exchange for this information, the Yugoslav authorities were willing to trade military spare parts and access to other military technology.

It is one of the ironies and flaws of US policy that defining a set of outcasts or 'rogue states' of the international community creates a degree of solidarity between such states who would otherwise have almost nothing in common. The Iraqi and Yugoslav regime found themselves not only with a certain mutual affinity but with very similar strategic needs. The long experience of Iraq in facing US air attacks provided an invaluable resource for the Yugoslav military planners, which certainly contributed to their relative success in maintaining an air-defence capability throughout the war and in protecting their forces in Kosovo from comprehensive destruction. A more interesting question is whether Milošević's willingness to test US and NATO resolve was influenced by the success of the Iraqi regime in maintaining its hold on power despite facing over a decade of a Western-imposed military siege. Whether the West will have a more satisfactory solution to the 'Iraq' of the Balkans will almost certainly be the major challenge in the search for a long-lasting settlement in the region.

The ambivalent countries

The final two Middle Eastern countries to be considered are Iran and Israel who both demonstrated a certain ambivalence about the conflict in Kosovo. This categorization is not dictated by the similarity of their responses, which were different on a number of counts, but by the fact that both countries faced a similar challenge to reconcile the conflicting foreign policy objectives in relation to the Kosovo war.

For Iran, the basic dilemma was to reconcile its pragmatic but strategically important relationship with Russia and its ideological role as a self-proclaimed leader of the Muslim world. As an avowedly Muslim state with a formally universalist state ideology, it could not ignore the plight of the suffering Kosovar Muslims under attack from Serb forces. In addition, in its role as chairman of the Organization of the Islamic Conference (OIC), Iran had an ideal institutional platform to project itself as guardian and leader of the Islamic world and to undermine the challenges of other contenders to this role, such as Saudi Arabia and Turkey. For the new leadership of President Khatami, the Kosovo conflict also provided an opportunity to demonstrate Iran's more moderate and mediatory international role, which reflected Khatami's emphasis on co-operation rather than Khomeini-style confrontation. The Kosovo crisis was, for Khatami, a good illustration of the need for his pet notion of 'a dialogue of civilisations' – an idea to which the UN General Assembly had agreed the year 2001 would be dedicated.[17] The pro-Muslim and anti-Serb stance was also driven by the legacy of Iran's earlier forceful diplomatic engagement in Bosnia which had led to considerable political, economic and military support for the Muslim Bosnian government.

However, Tehran had to balance its political and ideological support for the Kosovo cause with the primacy it accorded to preserving good relations with Moscow. From the mid-1990s onwards, Russia had emerged as Iran's most important external ally and their interests had converged on many issues – their common perception of being under a US-directed policy of containment and their growing foreign policy co-operation on regional security issues, such as in the Caucasus, Central Asia and Afghanistan.[18] In the Kosovo context, Iranian support for Russia's specifically anti-NATO stance was initially relatively unproblematic and Khatami joined Russia in arguing that the NATO air strikes were 'illegal' and that 'the current steps taken against Yugoslavia would not benefit the oppressed Muslims of Kosovo but would only serve the interests of major powers who were seeking to impose their domination over the Balkans'.[19] But, Iran's stance was increasingly challenged within the Muslim world as Russia adopted a more stridently pro-Serb posture. Pakistan, in particular, criticized Iran for not activating a more forceful role for the OIC. Tehran responded to this by reconstituting the OIC contact group which had been originally established during the conflict in Bosnia.[20] The OIC contact group met in Geneva on 7 April and issued a strongly anti-Serb statement, but this was the limit of consensus as the statement failed to make even a single reference to the NATO air attacks. Instead, the most that could be agreed on was that the OIC 'expressed regret that the UN Security Council had not been able to discharge its responsibilities', and called somewhat vainly for the 'strong resolution of the Muslim states to settle the crisis'.[21]

Iran continued through the conflict to seek to reconcile its pro-Muslim stance and its relationship with Russia. Indeed, it even tried to make a virtue of this balancing act, arguing that 'Iran's independent policy' could be seen when 'part of the Iranian stance blaming NATO may be close to the stance held by Russia while part of Iran's stance attacking the Serbs is not accepted by the Russians'.[22] Iran also had to show that it was still a major supporter of the Muslim cause in the Balkans. Although there was some evidence that Iran did supply some arms to the KLA, this was officially denied by the Foreign Ministry who argued that the cases of Bosnia and Kosovo were fundamentally different. For domestic and international consumption, the relative lack of direct military support for the Kosovars was compensated, as in most other Muslim countries, through emphasis on the generosity of Tehran in providing humanitarian support to the Kosovar refugees.[23]

In the end, Khatami's government generally managed to pursue a reasonably consistent and successful policy towards Kosovo. The pragmatic orientation of the government was preserved despite the attempts of the conservative factions within Tehran to utilize the conflict to enforce a more stridently anti-Western stance. The chairmanship of the OIC also offered Iran an institutional platform to demonstrate both its putative leadership of the Muslim world and the pragmatic and reconciliatory nature of its international diplomacy. The Russian relationship was also not undermined, though the problem for Iran of Russia's increasing antagonism with parts of the Muslim world was left unresolved. Later in the year, Iran was again to come under criticism from the rest of the Muslim world for its initial strong defence of Russia's offensive against Chechnya which included Kharrazi confirming 'Tehran's willingness to undertake effective collaboration in the struggle against terrorists to destabilize the situation in Russia.'[24]

It is perhaps rather invidious to include Israel in the same category as Iran as a country that remained essentially ambivalent over the course of events in Kosovo. There were some similarities, however, most notably over the role that Russia played in the strategic thinking of the Israeli government, though there were naturally a number of differences. Generally, the Israeli population was deeply shocked by the fate of the Kosovar Albanians which reflected their own Jewish experience of deportations and genocide. The Israeli government and people offered significant amounts of humanitarian aid, although it was noted in Washington that such generosity was exceeded by some of the Gulf states, such as the UAE and Kuwait. But, unlike most of the Muslim world, there was also some sympathy with the Serbs, who historically offered resistance to Nazi Germany. This pro-Serb stance was most strongly found among the right-wing Israeli constituency, who also expressed concern over the precedent being set by NATO of intervening on behalf of secessionist Muslims.

This sense of disquiet with the NATO attack was to find its most high-ranking advocate in the person of the then Foreign Minister Ariel Sharon, who has the deserved reputation as one of the most maverick of Israel's political elite. In private comments he was reported to say that 'the moment Israel supports the pattern of action we are witnessing in Kosovo, it could be the next victim. Israel must not grant legitimacy to forceful intervention of the type that NATO states, led by the United States, are employing in a bid to impose a solution in regional conflict.' Sharon continued by stating 'today they strike in Kosovo: tomorrow they could attack Israel should Israeli Arabs in the Galilee claim autonomy.'[25] In a subsequent public interview, Sharon went further to warn that 'the free world must look forward and see dangers in the future if a large bloc of Islamic states should develop what it is possible to call a Greater Albania. In my opinion, this can lead to unrest in Europe … lasting many years.'[26] He also noted that there were links between the 'Albanian underground in Kosovo and other terrorist organisations'.[27]

The Israeli Prime Minister Benyamin Netanyahu officially distanced the government from Sharon's comments and formally supported the NATO action. But, Netanyahu did not disavow Sharon's statements and stressed that the government was 'speaking with one voice'. It also took almost a week after the start of the NATO attacks for the government officially to support NATO and there were government-sponsored leakages of secret reports that Iran was arming the KLA. The US was, to put it mildly, not pleased with this demonstration of insubordination from one of its more junior allies. When Sharon visited Washington in mid-April, Madeleine Albright was visibly upset and the State Department's spokesperson pointedly noted that Albright had spoken to Sharon 'about his stand on Kosovo and his equally un-American position on Jewish settlements on the West Bank'.[28] In the aftermath of this visit, the US administration went as far as it is possible, without breaking the formal rules of non-intervention in the domestic politics of other states, to indicate to the Israeli electorate that they should not re-elect Netanyahu back into power in the forthcoming elections.

Israeli–US relations were also strained during the Kosovo conflict by the intensive and controversial attempt by the Israeli government to construct a closer *rapprochement* with Russia. During the period surrounding the conflict, Sharon visited Moscow three times where his views on the situation on Kosovo were naturally warmly welcomed. The Russian Foreign Minister, Igor Ivanov, made a visit to Jerusalem in mid-April. The official purpose of this flurry of diplomatic activity was for Israel to convince Russia to curb the flow of ballistic missile technology flows to Iran. Jerusalem argued that US policy to this end had proved to be unsuccessful and that a bilateral Israeli-Russian agreement would be more productive. The unofficial but more plausible reason for these diplomatic *démarches* was the upcoming electoral campaign and the resolve of Netanyahu to solidify his support among the 680,000 Russian-speaking Israeli constituency. Sharon actually betrayed this ulterior motive in an interview with William Safire in the *New York Times* on 8 April when he stated 'if I can get another 3 per cent of the electors who came from the CIS to support Bibi [Netanyahu], we will win the elections, and the Russian immigrants want relations with Russia to improve.'

In the end, these manoeuvres by Netanyahu and Sharon towards Russia did not achieve their short-term political objective as the opposition leader, Ehud Barak, won a convincing electoral victory on 17 May. Barak had been consistently critical of the government's ambivalent support towards the NATO campaign and, like most of his colleagues from the military, was concerned about the damage that the tilt to Russia could cause to US-Israeli political and military co-operation. Under Barak, the traditionally close US relationship with Washington has been restored. However, the brief Israeli honeymoon with Russia did indicate that, in the post-Cold War period, there were increasing areas of potential convergence between the two countries. The large Russian-speaking Israeli constituency, which represents one sixth of the overall population, continues to have an affinity with their former homeland. There are one million Jews remaining in Russia who could be a future source of immigration. The potential for military and other co-operation between Israel and Russia also remains unexplored.

Conclusions

Despite the variety and range of responses and perceptions in the Middle East to the Kosovo conflict, there was nevertheless a certain convergence in the widespread and genuine sense of empathy for the fate of the Kosovar Albanians. The ethnic cleansing undertaken by the Serb forces touched some sensitive emotional chords. For the Arabs, there was the memory of the dispossession and expulsion of the Palestinians; for the Jews, there was their own long experience of deportations and pogroms. The fact that Kosovo was part of the Ottoman Empire engendered a certain nostalgia for the loss of the inter-ethnic toleration that had been one of the empire's major achievements. For the Muslim world more generally, the sight of Muslims fleeing from Christian invaders evoked the whole history of perceived Christian hostility to the Muslim world – from the expulsion of the Muslims from *al-Andalus* to the crusades and to the later European colonial conquests, including the implantation of the Jewish state in Palestine.

Yet, this common sense of support for the Kosovars did not translate into a common or even consistent regional policy, which had been far more apparent in the case of Bosnia.[29] Only a minority of states were willing to provide unconditional support for the NATO campaign. For most states, and to a greater extent amongst the peoples of the region, there was an instinctive dislike and distrust of the West seeking to bomb its way to victory and its preference for the use of force rather than diplomacy. The failure to obtain UN authorization was a major factor that contributed to this lack of Arab and Muslim support for the NATO attacks. But, there were other factors too, most notably the precedent that the campaign in Kosovo might set for undermining the principle of territorial integrity. There were some, such as the Palestinians and the smaller Gulf states, who positively supported the potential creation of a mono-ethnic Kosovo state. The majority of states were far less relaxed, with Turkey, Iran, Iraq and Israel (to name just a few) deeply concerned that such a precedent might lead to NATO and the West supporting secessionist movements within their own states.

The role of the US in the NATO campaign also divided the Arab and Muslim world. Throughout the region, there was a general conflation of the US and NATO with only a few countries, such as Turkey, differentiating between the roles played by the US and Europe. Again, some countries welcomed the projection of US hegemonic power, such as Turkey and the Gulf States who have directly benefited from US tutelage. The majority reacted in a more traditional anti-US and anti-Western manner and regularly used the double standards argument to question the sincerity of the US's purported objectives over Kosovo. It is interesting, also, the extent to which Russia played a critical role in Middle East diplomatic activities was clearly disproportionate to its actual geopolitical influence in the region. Iran, Israel, Saudi Arabia and Syria all expended significant political resources in seeking to revitalize their relationship with Moscow. Sharon justified this by telling his compatriots that: 'The Russians are coming back to the Middle East – you should know that – and we are taking a responsible approach towards that.'[30] Even if Russia has neither the economic capability nor political will to 'return' to the Middle East, there are certainly a substantial number of countries in the region that would welcome such a return so as to weaken US hegemony.

Finally, despite the rhetoric in favour of the Kosovar Muslims, there could be detected a certain *ennui* or weariness in the diplomatic responses from the region, which lacked conviction or even a great sense of urgency. Much of the activity that did take place was driven more by the exigencies of regional rivalry than by concern for the fate of Kosovo, as the competing hegemonic claimants used the opportunity of an international crisis to assert and legitimate their claims for regional ascendance. Otherwise, there was a pervasive sense of 'Balkan fatigue'. However strong the emotional and historic links, Kosovo is not perceived to be part of the Middle East and there was a visible exasperation that, for over a decade, the West had become embroiled in a European problem at the expense of their engagement in the Middle East. This sense of neglect might seem paradoxical as Western intervention in the Middle East has normally been viewed as the main cause of the problems of the region. But, for most states and peoples in the Middle East, the only fate worse than US and Western intervention is US and Western neglect or disregard of the region's multiple problems. Thus, a large part of the commentary of the Middle Eastern press sought to provide parallels between Kosovo and the problems of the Middle East and implicitly to argue that the main lessons which should be learnt from Kosovo must be applied with vigour in pursuit of a comprehensive settlement of the multiple long-standing conflicts and tensions in the Middle East.

Notes

1. Turkish TV, 25 March 1999.
2. News Conference with Ismail Cem, Turkish News Agency Anatolia, 25 March 1999.
3. Turkish TV, 2 April 1999.
4. Quoted in Leyla Boulton, 'Turkey Aims to Aid Mulsim Brethren', *Financial Times*, 8 April 1999.
5. Turkish TV, 15 March 1999.
6. Statement by Bulent Ecevit on Turkish TV, 28 March 1999.
7. Reuters, 7 April 1999 as quoted in *Saudi Gazette*, 7 April 1999.
8. For report on the fund-raising in the Gulf states, see Delinda C. Hanley, 'Muslim Countries Send Huge Shipments of Aid to Kosovo Refugees', *Washington Report on Middle Eastern Affairs*, July/August 1999 at http://www.washington-report.org/backissues/0799/9907006.html.
9. JoMarie Fecci, 'Construction of Camp, Field Hospital and Airport', *Washington Report on Middle Eastern Affairs*, July/August 1999 at http://www.washington-report.org/backissues/0799/9907006.html.
10. *al-Ahram*, 7 April 1999.
11. *Al-Arab al-Yawm*, 19 April 1999.
12. Government announcement on Algeria Radio, 25 March 1999.
13. Fuad Mardoud in *Syria Times*, 3 April 1999.
14. Turqi Saqi in *Al-Ba'th*, 10 June 1999.
15. *Al-Hayat*, 1 April 1999. A Brazilian newspaper claimed that Iraq had given Milošević the Five Ray mid-range air-to-air missile system, which had been specially adapted by Brazilian experts to equip Iraqi jet fighters; see *O Estado de Sao Paolo*, 30 May 1999.
16. Reuters, 31 May 1999.
17. For more extensive discussions of Iran's post-Khomeini foreign policy, see Mehdi Mozaffari, 'Revolutionary, Thermdorian and Enigmatic Foreign Policy: President Khatami and the "Fear of the Wave"', *International Relations*, vol. 14, no. 5, (August 1999), pp. 9–28; and Jalil Roshandel, 'Iran's Foreign and Security Policies', *Security Dialogue*, vol. 31, no. 1, (March 2000), pp. 105–17.

18. For discussion on the Russian-Iranian relations, see Roland Dannreuther, 'Is Russia Returning to the Middle East?', *Security Dialogue*, vol. 29, no. 3, (September 1998), pp. 345–58.
19. Report of Khatami's meeting with the new Armenian ambassador on Iranian TV, 27 March 1999.
20. The OIC contact group consisted of Iran, Maylasia, Pakistan, Turkey, Morocco, Senegal, Egypt and Saudi Arabia. Bosni and Herzegovina and Qatar were observers.
21. Report of OIC meeting, Iranian News Agency (IRNA), 8 April 1999.
22. *Tehran Times*, 13 April 1999.
23. In this regard, Iran set 13th May as a 'Day of Solidarity with the Muslim Kosovars'.
24. *Iran Daily*, 26 September 1999.
25. Israel Radio, 2 April 1999.
26. Reuters, 6 April 1999.
27. *ibid.*
28. Reported in Eugene Bird, 'Acrimonious Albright–Sharon Meeting is a Domestic Political Plus for Israeli Hardliners', *Washington Report on Middle Eastern Affairs*, June 1999 at http://www.washington-report.org/backissues/0699/990621.html.
29. For an analysis of the Arab and Muslim response to the Bosnian conflict, see Tarek Mitri, 'La Bosnie-Herzégovine et la solidarité du monde arabe et islamique', *Monde arabe: Maghreb Mashreq*, no. 139, (January–March 1993).
30. Sharon interview on Israel TV, 9 April 1999.

CHAPTER FOURTEEN

European Security after Kosovo

JOANNE WRIGHT

The conflict in Kosovo was as shocking as it was tragic. For some, this was a 'just war' against a genocidal regime. It was about reordering international relations, especially in Europe, to reflect norms of human rights rather than the sovereign rights of states. It was a war fought by a democratic alliance, which maintained its consensus and nerve. It was a war in which the Europeans re-established at least some of their self-confidence in the wake of Bosnia. And, from one side's point of view, it was a casualty-free war that demonstrated the utility of 'smart' weapons and an air campaign.

Yet for others, this was a war in which international law and the UN were flagrantly ignored in order to pursue a vindictive campaign designed to demonstrate power. It was a war perpetrated by a hegemonic power (and a willing lackey) which rode roughshod over both its allies and alternative international opinion. It was a war where the Europeans conceded mastery to the US in their own backyard. And far from being a successful, high-tech and comparatively risk-free war, it was an ill-conceived, cowardly strategy that only increased the misery among the very people it was supposed to be assisting.

While selective evidence can be found to support these views, Kosovo is best seen as confirming rather than initiating several important trends. Although some of these trends predate the end of the Cold War, it was the previous conflicts in the former Yugoslavia, especially Bosnia, that brought them to centre stage. Kosovo highlighted the problematic aspects of these trends and prompted some reordering of priorities. There is no doubt that Europe's key security institutions, NATO and the EU, now see themselves not only as promoters of human rights but also as defenders, and even though this too predates the Kosovo conflict, Kosovo has revealed the difficulties and inconsistencies of such an approach. The end result of any security architecture based on inconsistency, especially between rhetoric and capability, will be a security atmosphere riddled with insecurity and a lack of trust. This could have profound implications for European security and international relations.

This chapter will proceed by outlining the trends in European security that Kosovo confirmed. For analytical purposes, these trends can be divided into two broad groupings, but in conceptual as well as policy terms there are strong interlinkages. The first grouping can be categorized as the 'expansion of Europe' and included here is the enlargement of both NATO and the WEU/EU. The second group of trends can be categorized as the 'expansion of activity'. Included in this category would be the broadening of both NATO and the EU's security mandates. Not only does Kosovo highlight problems inherent in these trends, but it also illustrates how important it is that institutional goals, capabilities and norms are mutually reinforcing.

The expansion of Europe

The expansion of both NATO and the EU was established as the key issue in European security soon after the end of the Cold War. Although NATO has now enlarged and the EU is well on the way to doing so, it has not been a smooth process. Significant difficulties became apparent, which the Kosovo conflict has shown remain unresolved. Four problems in particular stand out: relations with Russia; in what order individual countries should be admitted to membership and what security guarantees should be offered; the notion of flexibility; and institutional leadership in Europe.

The details of NATO enlargement do not need to be retold here, but it is clear that the Soviet Union/Russia figured largely. The balance appeared to be tipped in favour of expanded membership in the summer of 1993, when Russia recognized Poland's right to join NATO and stated that such an action would not be against Russia's interests.[1] In order to assuage Russian sensitivities that NATO expansion would relegate Russia to a secondary status in European security, NATO agreed to give Russia a 'special relationship' that was ultimately reflected in the Russia-NATO Founding Act signed in Paris in May 1997. As part of the Founding Act, NATO also committed itself to stationing neither nuclear weapons nor significant numbers of troops on the territory of the new members, which were now known to be Poland, the Czech Republic and Hungary.

There is no doubt that the conflict in Kosovo did put strains on relations between NATO and Russia (see Chapter 10). As Antonenko points out:

> [i]mmediately after the airstrikes began, Russia suspended its participation in the Founding Act and PfP, withdrew its military mission from Brussels, terminated talks on the establishment of NATO's military mission in Moscow, and ordered the NATO information representative in Moscow to leave the country.[2]

There were also reports that Russian anger over the airstrikes against Serbia had prompted Boris Yeltsin to announce plans to develop a new class of tactical nuclear weapons.[3] There were a number of Russian concerns articulated during the conflict, but the greatest was what sort of precedent NATO might have set, and how this might increase its own internal stability and the stability of its near abroad. These fears were fuelled by the fact that of all the Commonwealth of Independent states, only Belarus and Tajikistan sided unambiguously with Russia. The rest either supported NATO or did not voice condemnation (see Chapter 11). However, it is important not to overestimate the role of Kosovo in NATO-Russian relations.

To begin with Russia is widely accredited with playing a vital diplomatic role in ending the conflict.[4] Even though this may have been the case, overall Russia did not emerge with much credit from the Kosovo crisis. Its policy response was confused and inconsistent and it appeared indifferent to human suffering. Indeed, Levitin goes as far as to call Moscow's response to the Kosovo crisis 'a sustained fiasco'.[5] It is also worth noting that even though relations were undoubtedly strained, co-operation between Russia and NATO was quickly restored after hostilities ended.

NATO's relations with Russia will continue to be an important and difficult area of European security. However, these difficulties existed before Kosovo and remain largely unresolved. They relate mostly to continued domestic instability in Russia, problems in its 'near abroad', ballistic missile defence and the place that Russia occupies in the general security architecture. Kosovo revealed that Russia's own military capacity was well below that of NATO, but this too was known before the conflict. Where Kosovo may have its greatest direct impact on NATO's relations with Russia is in respect to further NATO and EU *de facto* if not *de jure* expansion.

It was always clear that not all countries that wished to join NATO would be granted NATO membership at the same time. Those not included in the first enlargement were encouraged to maintain and increase their links with NATO via the Partnership for Peace (PfP) programme. Although this created a clear expectation that there would be a second wave of expansion, the Balkan states were not the front runners. The Kosovo conflict has shifted the focus of NATO and the EU southwards. The German Deputy Foreign Minister, for example, says that the 'crisis in Kosovo has made south-east Europe strategically the most important region in Europe'.[6] Analysts seem divided on just what Kosovo means in terms of NATO expansion, but either way there are implications for European security. At the centre of the debate is the NATO troops that were dispatched to Albania, Macedonia and Bulgaria, and just what they might signify.

On the one hand, there are those who consider the promises given to those states bordering Serbia at the Washington Summit in April 1999, as a type of *de facto* membership. As Kay argues, these promises, while not legally binding, were nonetheless interpreted by the states to whom they were made as representing an ongoing NATO commitment to their territorial defence.[7] If this is the case, then it leaves NATO with two problems. First, it will create some disappointment in the Baltic states who were singled out as the next potential entrants, but now find themselves in the same category as the Balkan states. Second, the stationing of NATO troops in Albania, Macedonia and Bulgaria does appear to create the impression that NATO is in a better position to defend them than the three new full members who have limits on the numbers of NATO troops stationed on their territory.[8]

On the other hand, there are those who believe that the damage to NATO-Russian relations caused by Kosovo will prevent further enlargement. François Heisbourg, for example, says '[w]e are afraid to push the Russians over the brink, afraid not to have them on board when we need them, so NATO enlargement is over.'[9] Similarly, Robert Hunter, former US Ambassador to NATO, is quoted as saying '[b]ecause there is more desire to work with Russia, we are going to see less enthusiasm to enlarge NATO.'[10] If this is the case, then similar problems occur and there is a risk of creating a divided Europe and some sort of NATO concession of a Russian sphere of influence.

The EU, too, made additional promises to the Balkan states that raise some significant questions. What is of interest here are the problems that might be caused by an EU taking in more members to the contentious area of defence, the relations between NATO and the EU and institutional leadership in Europe. Again Kosovo did not cause these problems, but it has had some impact on them.

The European Union is moving towards a situation where it will absorb the West European Union (WEU). However, the WEU has a clear mutual defence obligation, which raises two problems. First, not all EU countries are members of the WEU, and second there is the link between the WEU and NATO.[11] In relation to the first problem, the EU has adopted the principle of flexibility whereby those countries who wish may opt out from both mutual defence obligations and particular peacekeeping or peace-enforcement operations without preventing others from acting. It can perhaps be assumed that no Balkan state would wish to opt out of additional defence guarantees or the opportunity to contribute to other security operations on a case-by-case basis, and if this happens the problems already inherent in flexibility are magnified.

Flexibility can be seen to have many advantages, but it is also a difficult security arrangement to manage and the potential for unpredictability and mistrust is high. Doubts can emerge about the commitment of all members of institutions to the security concerns, if not necessarily the defence, of some states. One small example of this occurred during 1996 when Italy and Greece pushed for military assistance in relation to the Albanian refugee crisis but were not supported by allies in either NATO or the EU. A potentially much more serious example was Germany's assertion that although it would not prevent others from doing so, it would not commit any ground troops to Kosovo without a prior peace agreement.[12] Although this problem also applies to NATO it is accentuated in the case of the EU by its operational reliance on NATO. So any member requesting EU assistance has to calculate not only who and what might be offered by EU members, but also what the reaction of non-EU NATO members might be.[13] Any expansion of Common Foreign and Security Policy (CFSP) membership will increase the range of security issues and the geographic area that the EU could be asked to become involved in, and thus raise further the potential for mistrust and uncertainly to develop.

Like Bosnia, Kosovo showed that the Europeans lacked both political leadership and military capability. Politically the Europeans were not able to set the agenda of any possible peace settlement. As Eyal points out, at the Rambouillet talks in February 1999, the British and French preference was that consideration of Kosovo's constitutional position would be postponed. But without any prior consultation, the US promised the Kosovar Albanians a referendum on independence.[14] While noting that individual Europeans played some role in the diplomacy ending the conflict, Buchan also emphasizes the lack of the EU's political presence when he says that it 'was solved by classical concert diplomacy involving the US and Russia'.[15] Even within the EU consensus was not always apparent. Belgium, France, Greece, Italy and Spain all expressed concern about the legality of NATO's actions.[16] Austria went even further and denied NATO access to its airspace because of the lack of a specific UN Security Council resolution.[17] Germany and Italy were prepared to break ranks on the issue of continuing the bombing campaign, and there were some physical attacks against NATO targets in Greece.[18] Tensions were also reported between Germany and Britain and France on the question of refugees and for most of the conflict Britain remained largely isolated on the question of ground troops.[19] But perhaps most damning are those criticisms that the EU was scared to lead either because it feared that without the US it would not be taken seriously or because it feared a repeat of the Bosnian experience.[20] Building the confidence to exercise strong political leadership will be a protracted process for the EU. In the short and medium term, it is more likely that the EU will try to strengthen its institutional links with NATO, including joint summits.

One of the major factors limiting the EU's ability to exercise political leadership is not only its lack of autonomous military capabilities but also the shape of those capabilities that it does have. Expanding military options and types of operations considered to be security related is another feature of post-Cold War Europe. Indeed, Kosovo is an example of such a security operation. But it has also revealed how poorly thought out and resourced such expansions have been to date.

The expansion of activity

To coincide with the Rome Summit in November 1991, NATO published its *New Strategic Concept*, which widened the type of security mission that NATO would include in its operational mandate as opposed to its 'consultation' mandate.[21] The Alliance's lastest *Strategic Concept*, announced during the Kosovo conflict, continues this trend. Under the heading of 'security challenges and risks', it talks of

> [e]thnic and religious rivalries, territorial disputes, inadequate or failed attempts at reform, the abuse of human rights and the dissolution of states [which can] lead to local and even regional instability. The resulting tensions could lead to crises affecting Euro-Atlantic stability, to human suffering, and to armed conflicts. Such conflicts could affect the security of the Alliance by spilling over into neighbouring countries, including NATO countries, or in other ways, and could also affect the security of other states.[22]

There were also some hints that NATO might in some circumstances adopt a global rather than regional role.[23]

The EU's expansion into the realms of defence and security is more complex. Like NATO, the EU has expanded the type of issue that it is willing to regard as a legitimate matter of security concern. As part of the Maastricht Treaty, the EU agreed to designate the WEU as its security arm, which it could request to undertake action on behalf of the EU in areas such as peacekeeping and humanitarian missions, the so-called Petersberg Tasks.[24] The fact that the WEU has few resources was thought to have been at least partially solved by the Combined Joint Task Force concept (CJTF) whereby NATO would lend the WEU its resources. Although this concept was reinforced in NATO's latest *Strategic Concept*, it remains problematic. Two difficulties stand out, which have been confirmed by Kosovo. First, there is the issue of a capability gap between the Americans and the Europeans, which, even with NATO willingness, could severely limit the Europeans' room for manoeuvre. And second, there is the issue of whether a distinction between defence and the Petersberg Tasks is either possible or desirable. Before discussing these problems, however, we need to address the weaknesses in both NATO and the EU's approach to non-Article 5 missions as revealed by Kosovo.

Despite George Bush's 1992 warning to the Serbs that the US would be prepared to deploy military force in Kosovo and the lesson learnt from

224

Bosnia that the careful and co-ordinated use of force could produce results, NATO was stunningly unprepared for the actual application of force in 1999. This can be demonstrated in two major areas. First, NATO has failed to overhaul its decision-making mechanisms to cope with non-Article 5 missions. As General Sir Michael Jackson tells us

> NATO's machinery for the decision making which produces activation orders, force generation, states of command, operational funding is outdated – it has not been revised since the Cold War. Frankly it is not up to the job and could do with a thorough review.[25]

In their *Kosovo After Action Review,* Cohen and Shelton, admit that a NATO priority must be to:

> Enhance NATO's contingency planning process for non-Article V operations; develop an overarching command and control policy and agree on procedures for the policy's implementation; and enhance procedures and conduct exercises strengthening NATO's political-military interfaces.[26]

This is the case if NATO wishes to back up its claims to be more than just a collective defence alliance.

Second, there was NATO's choice of a bombing strategy and there are a number of issues here that reveal the disparity between NATO's rhetoric of an expanded security mandate and its ability to act in support of this mandate. There are many who believe that the bombing strategy was chosen because NATO lacked the political cohesion or will to utilize other military means that would have heightened the risk to NATO personnel.[27] The key means here was ground troops. At various points during the conflict the US, Greece, Germany, Italy and Hungary all expressed severe reservations about, or refused to consider, ground troops. And early in the conflict the alliance itself declared that there was no intention to use ground troops.[28] The bombing campaign thus represented the 'lowest common denominator of risk' strategy, not the most appropriate or flexible one.[29]

The bombing campaign also revealed great weaknesses in NATO's planning and intelligence-gathering operations. Several commentators have noted NATO's erroneous assumption that only a few days of bombing would be needed to bring about the desired capitulation of the Serbian regime and how unprepared it was when this did not happen.[30] If NATO was serious about expanding its mandate to include human-rights-type issues, then bombing by itself was an inappropriate strategy. It exerted very little pressure on Serbian troops on the ground and allowed the Serbs to practise the very sort of hit and evacuation tactics for which the Yugoslav army had long trained. It also left NATO with no alternative to hitting large fixed targets with the associated risks of error and civilian casualty.[31] Thus the strategy chosen did not match NATO's claim to flexible responses in support of a wider security mandate. But the bombing campaign also raises further and interesting issues about capabilities that have ramifications for the future of European security.

The capability gap between the Europeans and the Americans first became apparent in the Gulf War of 1991. A decade later, according to Pond, the size of the military (and leadership) gap was still such as to 'shock the Europeans'.[32] Cohen and Shelton also reveal that the

> gaps in capability that we confronted were real, and they had the effect of impeding our ability to operate at optimal effectiveness with our NATO allies ... The lack of interoperable secure communications forced reliance on non-secure methods that compromised operational security.[33]

Plans to try and close this gap predate Kosovo. In 1998, the US sponsored the idea of a Defence Capabilities Initiative, which was officially adopted by NATO at its April 1999 Washington Summit.[34] However, this will only be the start of the debate as Kosovo has shown that difficult issues about weapons technology and procurement, burden sharing and doctrinal issues remain to be resolved.

The fact that, as far as NATO was concerned, Kosovo was a casualty-free conflict is bound to focus attention on expensive, 'smart' weapons as well as refocus attention on transportation capabilities. Some US defence officials were reportedly angered by Europe's reliance on the US in these areas and one is quoted by Cook as stating

> Europe is going to have to stock up. During the war, we were beset with requests for smart weapons from countries that didn't have any. We were lucky as a nation we had a reasonable amount of surge capability. But you can't count on that in the future; our surge capacity may be nil. Future conflicts are going to be come-as-you-are ... if you didn't order in peacetime, you don't get to play in wartime.[35]

Not only does this hint at further burden sharing arguments, but it shows that the Europeans could leave themselves without or woefully short of the sorts of weapons crucial for modern conflict. This would also leave NATO and the EU lacking in the capabilities needed to back up their claims to a wider security mandate – especially because there are no indications that a rise in European defence spending is in sight. Kosovo is likely, however, to prompt more European countries to engage in military restructuring and to push European strategic and tactical logistical capabilities even higher up the procurement agenda.[36] One of the most interesting consequences of Kosovo will be to cause more questioning of the division between defence capabilities and peace support operations.

For a while after the Cold War both the EU and NATO seemed to accept an implicit division of labour whereby NATO would retain primary responsibility for defence and the EU, through the WEU, would assume responsibility for other types of security. This has been understood by many as the defining characteristic of the WEU's link to the EU and the basis of its distinction from NATO.[37] This continues to be the case, especially for the neutral members of the EU. Finland and Sweden, for example, have reiterated that defence discussions within CFSP are acceptable only if they relate to crisis management and not mutual defence.[38] On the surface this seems to be accepted by the key European defence actors, Britain and France, with their constant references to strengthening the European Strategic and Defence Identity (ESDI) and the primacy of NATO in defence.

Nonetheless, the steps taken by these two countries to improve their defence co-operation after Bosnia have been stepped up since Kosovo, and have been generally welcomed by other EU members. At the Cologne Summit, held just as the conflict in Kosovo was ending, the British changed their previous position and agreed to the EU absorbing the WEU. The following month the British and Italians proposed a 'convergence criteria' of EU defence capabilities aimed at assisting member states to improve their capabilities.[39] In November 1999 the British and French proposed the establishment of a 60,000 strong European rapid reaction corps, which it would be able to deploy within 60 days and sustain for up to one year. This proposal was accepted by the EU Council in its December Helsinki Summit, although again it was stressed that this corps would be limited to the Petersberg Tasks.

These proposals, if they come to fruition, have some interesting and potentially difficult consequences. First, the move towards building up capabilities and the increased references to defence co-operation do seem to indicate an awareness on the part of the Europeans that a split between defence and other types of security operation is not as easy or desirable as they had thought. Again the first indications of this emerged from Bosnia where it was realized that had NATO been called upon to evacuate the United Nations Protection Force (UNPROFOR), it would have required a hard-edged war-fighting capacity. It would have been a similar situation had ground troops been deployed to Kosovo. This leaves a dilemma for the Europeans. Unless they develop high-intensity capabilities, they run the risk of only being able to undertake 'gendarmery' type operations and continuing to rely on the US for short-term operations requiring the overwhelming use of force. Yet, if they develop such capabilities they run the risk of alienating and perhaps even decoupling the US from European security. The US has already expressed concern about the Cologne proposals with Strobe Talbott declaring that the decisions at Cologne 'could be read to imply that Europe's default position would be to act outside the Alliance whenever possible, rather than through the Alliance'.[40] This dilemma does serve to focus attention on the role of norms within both European and international security.

Norms, values and European security

Developing a European security order which includes norms of using force to protect human rights is incredibly difficult, and carries with it a number of risks especially in relation to consistency and credibility. There are signs that both the Americans and the Europeans are aware of this and are backing away from viewing Kosovo as anything other than a 'one-off'. Such a situation will cast doubt on all alliance structures in Europe.

The fact that NATO achieved its 'victory' without loss of life was immediately branded by some as an illustration that past restraints on the use of force in the international system have been lifted. As Robinson has argued, the fear of casualties that acted as a deterrent to embarking on military action has 'been eliminated and the temptation to use force has correspondingly increased'.[41] This is too simplistic. It is more accurate to say that the reluctance to take casualties has been reinforced by Kosovo. Alternative opinion suggests that Kosovo was a 'post-heroic' war that 'will erode public support for the military essence of an Alliance that has shown itself to be incapable of using its extremely expensive armed forces in a real fight'.[42] The implication here is that unless 'others' are willing to risk casualties or unless the conflict is resolvable with cruise missiles, no action will be taken. If so, there is little credibility to claims of expanded security mandates.

There can be little doubt that NATO action in Kosovo represented a 'significant departure from international order based on the UN Charter.'[43] There are claims that this 'criminal act' violating internal sovereignty and international law will encourage other states to act in a similar way, with Russia being the first to do so in Chechnya.[44] On the other hand, there are those who see Kosovo as a continuation of a trend in international law and norms that does not regard internal sovereignty as absolute. As the Secretary General of the UN is quoted as saying, '[e]merging slowly … is an international norm against the violent repression of minorities that will and must take precedence over concerns of sovereignty.'[45] The Canadian Foreign Minister goes even further when he suggests that 'Kosovo is a clear example of how military power can support human security objectives.'[46]

Human rights concerns were the primary justification offered by NATO and its members. NATO's Secretary General talked of a 'military campaign to avoid a humanitarian tragedy'.[47] Cohen and Shelton also talk of humanitarian motivations and the need to avoid a humanitarian crisis.[48] In addition, during the conflict, there was considerable discussion about the 'Blair Doctrine' of military intervention in support of human rights.[49] Such an option is not only incredibly risky, but it is not supported by Blair's key allies within either NATO or the EU.

The most obvious risk inherent in a security policy that includes or emphasizes human rights is the loss of credibility associated with an inconsistent approach. Both NATO and the EU have already implicitly conceded that the human rights of the Kosovar Albanians are more important than those of, say, the Turkish Kurds or the Chechens in Russia. By not being able to prevent continuing ethnic violence in Kosovo, NATO and the EU also leave themselves vulnerable to charges of 'opportunistic' support for human rights. By promoting military intervention in support of human rights as a doctrine rather than as a matter of political judgement, NATO and the EU become prime targets for manipulation by separatist groups hoping to draw them into conflicts. Such a situation certainly has more of a destabilizing potential than stabilizing potential for European security generally and for NATO and the EU in particular.

Finally, promoting a human rights doctrine requires strong political leadership and unwavering alliance commitment, neither of which were present during the Kosovo conflict. As McElvoy argues:

> [w]e need a generation of political leaders who believe Europe is not just about quotas and qualifed majority voting, convergence criteria and communiqués, but something more profound – the preservation of a way of life, the duty of care for a peaceful order throughout the continent. We are still no closer to that.[50]

It is also noteworthy that there has been some 'back-tracking' on the significance of NATO's intervention in Kosovo in the months after the conflict. Far from hinting at a global role for NATO, Madeleine Albright stressed that NATO is a European and transatlantic institution, not a global one.[51] She, and several European leaders, also argued that Kosovo has to be seen as a 'special case', not a precedent, and that intervention should be the exception not the rule.[52]

On the other hand, there is no doubt that Kosovo did cause many of Europe's leading, and relatively new, political leaders to re-examine their own values and norms. This re-examination of values and how they relate to institutional goals and capabilities may be the most important legacy of Kosovo. As such it is to be welcomed as an improvement on the post-Cold War security debate which has focused too much on institutional design.

Conclusions

It would be difficult to argue that Kosovo has revealed much new about European security. Difficulties in relations with Russia, difficulties in relation to NATO and EU expansion, problems with the CFSP and especially weaknesses in European leadership and military capabilities were all well known before Kosovo. Similarly, although Kosovo represents an extreme example, it is far from being the first military intervention against the sovereign integrity of a state or in support of human rights. However, that is not to say that Kosovo is without importance for European security or international relations generally.

Kosovo has shifted the attention of both NATO and the EU southwards, and this has a number of important implications. It makes any further NATO expansion more difficult and will cause a re-examination of just what NATO's commitment to new and potential new members should be. Any expansion will test NATO's credibility as well as its relations with Russia, as will any decision to delay or stop expanding. For both organizations, Kosovo was also a very difficult exercise in maintaining consensus, and has illustrated some of the potential pitfalls with flexibility as a practical and conceptual approach to security problems.

Kosovo also revealed beyond any doubt that despite almost a decade of talking about non-Article 5 missions, the EU and NATO remain unequipped to deal with them in terms of organizational structure and military hardware. As far as the EU is concerned, Kosovo has strengthened the position of those who argue that the distinction between Article 5 and non-Article 5 missions has been overdrawn as both a concept and a basis for defence procurement. This, in turn, raises very difficult issues for the EU in regard to its neutrals, its relations with NATO and the US – not to mention its taxpayers.

Most fundamentally, however, the Kosovo conflict must cause NATO and the EU to consider just what sort of security organizations they want to be, what sort of commitment they want to offer all the peoples of Europe and what sort of relationship they want to have with the UN. At present, institutional design and security capabilities do not match the rhetoric of commitment to a wider security agenda that includes human rights. Such a situation is not sustainable without risking the basic credibility of security institutions and this would have implications beyond Kosovo, NATO, the EU and indeed Europe.

Notes

1. S. Croft, J. Redmond, G. Wyn Rees and M. Webber, *The Enlargement of Europe*, (Manchester: MUP, 1999), p. 30.
2. O. Antonenko, 'Russia, NATO and European Security after Kosovo', *Survival*, vol. 41, no. 4 (1999–2000), p. 131.
3. T. Whitehouse, 'Yeltsin ups the nuclear ante', *Guardian*, 30 April 1999, p. 14.
4. See for example, S. Grey, M. Campbell, A. Todorović, J. Carr-Brown and C. Meyer, 'Surrender', *The Sunday Times*, 6 June 1999, p. 19 (Features); E. Yesson, 'NATO and Russia in Kosovo', *RUSI Journal*, vol. 144, no. 4 (1999), pp. 20–6

and W. Cohen and H. Shelton, 'Joint statement on the Kosovo After Action Review', US Department of Defense, at http://defenselink.mil/news/Oct1999/b10141999_bt478-99.html.

5. O. Levitin, 'Inside Moscow's Kosovo Muddle', *Survival*, vol. 42, no. 1 (2000), p. 138.

6. Quoted in S. Bates and A. Brummer, 'War in Europe: Frontline States could get EU Status', *Guardian*, 28 April 1999, p. 3.

7. S. Kay, 'After Kosovo: NATO's Credibility Dilemma', *Security Dialogue*, vol. 31, no. 1 (2000), p. 76.

8. D. Buchan, 'A tethered superpower', *Financial Times*, (London Edition), 27 July 1999, p. 19. See also Kay, *op. cit.*, p. 77.

9. Buchan, *op, cit.*

10. Buchan, *op. cit.*.

11. Ireland, Finland, Austria and Sweden are EU members but not WEU members.

12. See *The Economist*, 22 May 1999, p. 20; I. Karats and A. Marshall, 'War in Balkans: No Ground Troops says Schroeder', *Independent*, 19 May 1999, p. 6 (News); and D. Macintyre, 'Ever so Carefully, Mr Blair Clears the Way for a Ground Invasion', *Independent*, 28 May 1999, p. 3 (comment).

13. See J. Wright, 'The Dangers of Flexibility in NATO and the WEU/EU', *Contemporary Security Policy*, vol. 20, no. 1 (1999), pp. 111–29.

14. J. Eyal, 'Kosovo: killing the myths after the killing has subsided', *RUSI Journal*, vol. 145, no. 1 (2000), p. 21.

15. Buchan, *op. cit.*

16. C. Guicherd, 'International Law and the War in Kosovo', *Survival*, vol. 41, no. 2 (1999), p. 26.

17. 'NATO Politics', *Financial Times*, (London Edition) 25 March 1999, p. 19, (Leader).

18. P. Betts, 'Italians Demand End to Bombing by NATO', *Financial Times*, (London Edition), 27 March 1999, p. 4; P. Wintour, 'War in the Balkans: Americans get tough', *Observer*, 18 April 1999, p. 18 and H. Smith, 'War in Europe, Angry Greeks hit NATO', *Guardian*, 30 April 1999, p. 3.

19. I. Traynor, A. Travis and L. Ward, 'War in Europe: German Fury at "Mean" Britain', *Guardian*, 30 April 1999, p. 3 and S. Castle, A. Grice and M. Dejevsky, 'Blair Left Isolated on Ground War', *The Independent*, 17 May 1999, p. 1.

20. See J. Rielly, 'Lessons of Kosovo …', *Financial Times*, (London Edition) 25 March 1999, p. 18.

21. These new security actions are generally referred to as non-Article 5 missions in that they do not necessarily invoke Article 5 of the North Atlantic Treaty concerning collective defence.

22. http://www.nato.int/docu/pr.1999/p99-065e.htm, paragraph 20.

23. *ibid.*, paragraph 24.

24. These are also sometimes referred to as non-Article 5 missions.

25. M. Jackson, 'KFOR: The Inside Story', *RUSI Journal*, vol. 145, no. 1 (2000), p. 18.

26. Cohen and Shelton, *op. cit.*, p. 11.

27. See *The Economist*, 12 June 1999, p. 17; S. Jenkins, 'A Victory for Cowards', *The Times*, 11 June 1999, p. 24; Eyal, *op. cit.*, p. 25; P. Robinson, 'Ready to Kill but Not to Die', *International Journal*, vol. LVI, no. 4 (1999), pp. 671–82; and N.

Cook, 'War of Extremes', *Jane's Defence Weekly Feature*, at http://www.janes.com/defence/features/kosovo/extremes.html, p. 2.

28. See L. Freedman, 'NATO's Search for a "Goldilocks" War', *Independent*, 26 May 1999, p. 4 (comment).
29. J. Markus, 'A Distant Trumpet', *Washington Quarterly*, vol. 22, no. 3 (1999), p. 7.
30. *The Economist*, 12 June 1999; Eyal, *op.cit.*, p. 25 and T. Judah, 'Kosovo's Road to War', *Survival*, vol. 41, no. 2 (1999), p. 3.
31. See *The Economist*, 12 June 1999; Freedman, *op. cit.*; Cook, *op. cit.*; Jenkins, *op. cit.*; and Eyal, *op. cit.*, pp. 25-7. The risk of error was compounded by NATO's 'high-fly' order (no flying below 15,000 feet) and intelligence failures such the bombing of the Chinese embassy.
32. E. Pond, 'Kosovo: Catalyst for Europe', *Washington Quarterly*, vol. 22, no. 4 (1999), p. 80.
33. Cohen and Shelton, *op. cit.*, p. 11.
34. See Cohen and Shelton, *op. cit.*, p. 12 and M. Oakes, *European Defence: From Pörtschach to Helsinki*, London: House of Commons Library, Research Paper 00/20, 2000, pp. 22-3.
35. Quoted in Cook, *op cit.*, p. 6.
36. *ibid.* See also Pond, *op cit.*, pp. 83-4.
37. See Western European Union, *WEU Contribution to the European Union Intergovernmental Conference of 1996*, WEU Council of Ministers, Document 1492, Madrid, 14 November 1995, Option C2 and Assembly of the Western European Union, *Organising Security in Europe – Political Aspects*, Assembly of the Western European Union, Document 1509, 26 January 1996, paragraphs 21-4.
38. Oakes, *op cit.*, p. 16.
39. Buchan, *op. cit.*
40. S. Talbott, 'America's Stake in a Strong Europe', RIIA, London, 7 October 1999, quoted in Oakes, *op. cit.*, p. 28.
41. Robinson, *op cit.*, p. 675.
42. 'Monitor: NATO divisions', *Independent*, 22 May 1999, p. 6 (Features).
43. Guicherd, *op. cit.*, p. 19.
44. See B. MacIntyre, 'American a Land Never to Die For', *The Times*, 26 June 1999, p. 20; R. Fisk, 'What is the Point of NATO?', *Independent,* 13 May 1999, p. 5 (comment); E. Said, 'It's Time the World Stood up to the American Bully', *Observer,* 11 April 1999, p. 19.
45. Kofi Annan quoted in O. Bring, 'Should NATO take the lead in formulating a doctrine on humanitarian intervention?', *NATO Review*, vol. 47, no. 4 (1999), p. 3 (Web edition).
46. L. Axworthy, 'NATO's new security vocation', *NATO Review*, vol. 47, no. 4 (1999), p. 5 (Web edition).
47. J. Solana, 'NATO's success in Kosovo', *Foreign Affairs*, vol. 78, no. 6 (1999), p. 114.
48. Cohen and Shelton, *op. cit.*, p. 4. See also Kay, *op. cit.*
49. See B. Macintyre, *op. cit.*
50. A. McElvoy, 'The Leaders of Western Europe Fiddle while the Continent Burns', *Independent*, 26 May 1999, p. 3 (comment).
51. Buchan, *op. cit.*
52. *ibid.*, and Guicherd, p. 29.

CHAPTER FIFTEEN

Kosovo: Geopolitics, Geostrategy and Geoeconomics

JOHN ERICKSON

The Kosovo crisis and NATO's attendant Operation Allied Force set off geopolitical turbulence and triggered geostrategic shockwaves and, as yet, neither shows signs of subsiding. Whether the circumstances of the Kosovo imbroglio embodied fundamental change of themselves or were rather the catalyst for it is open to dispute, but it is likely that the global reaction may prove in the long run to be more significant than the action itself.

The 1991 Gulf War literally fired warning salvoes about the form of 'international community intervention', inculcating preliminary lessons of which perhaps the most potent and the most pertinent was drawn by India's Defence Minister: 'Don't fight the United States unless you have nuclear weapons.'[1] The image of NATO in particular and the West in general in 'expeditionary mode' has been globally unsettling, to some unnerving. Unilateral intervention, whatever its 'humanitarian' guise or gloss, has not sent the most reassuring signals to a world already undergoing geopolitical transformation and geostrategic restructuring. Russia and China had previously declared their opposition to NATO's enlargement eastwards, expressed a certain apprehension at NATO's 'out of area' extension of its activities and rhetorically denounced a suspected covert strategy of global intervention in the service of 'American hegemonism'.

The 'Kosovo effect' reinforced Russia's suspicions of NATO as a self-mandating organization, intensified resentment of American hegemony and blighted the prospects of developing a working partnership with the US, leaving Russia stranded strategically where neither co-operation nor confrontation is a fully workable option. Russia and China, the latter outraged by the bombing of its Belgrade embassy, embarked on their own preliminary moves to reshape partnerships and transform align-ments through what some quarters claimed to be a 'grand Eurasian strategic design'. However, Moscow's initial fervour espousing a potential multi-polar coalition designed to counter the global influence of the US has cooled of late. Nevertheless both Russia and China, each in her own way, appear to be fully persuaded that they are committed to a protracted geostrategic contest in a 'post-Kosovo environment': a world of deteriorating international arms control regimes – a world of 'vital interests' increasingly associated with 'active geopolitical factors'.

Geopolitics resurgent

Geopolitics, its previous none too salubrious reputation now virtually forgiven and largely forgotten, is not only resurgent but some would argue rampant: a thoroughly modern ideology in the form of a 'relegitimized' theory of geopolitics.[2] Its manifestations are many and varied, although few escape the criticism that much, like its progenitor, is 'romantically absurd, intellectually sloppy', the appeal 'mythic', promising 'uncanny clarity and insight' in a complex world.[3] Its usage is diverse, most common when referring to a particular region or a specific problem. The issue here is the identification of geopolitics with grand strategy.

'Geopolitics as grand strategy' provided one of the key elements, some would argue *the* key element, in Western containment policy during the Cold War. Colin Gray has asserted that the 'overarching vision of US national security was explicitly geopolitical', one directly attributable to Mackinder's 'heartland theory', the source of the idea of 'containment'. Given intellectual substance by Yale professor Nicholas Spykman, Dr Henry Kissinger enlisted geopolitics in the service of 'the tactical conduct of statecraft', at once devious and ruthless, aiming to surround post-Soviet Russia with 'Western-backed states with strong and strongly anti-Russian official national identities and programmes'.[4]

That the symbiosis of geopolitics with grand strategy remains a serious enterprise was demonstrated at the end of June 2000 with the convening of a 'Mackinder Forum'. Significantly among its sponsors was The Strategic and Combat Studies Institute of the British army. General Sir Rupert Smith, NATO Deputy SACEUR addressed the forum by developing the theme of 'Geopolitics: A Tool for Strategic Analysis'.

Geographical contexts cannot be dismissed; indeed, for some, geography lies at the heart of international relations, but a central preoccupation is with the concept of 'space', some of it virtual, some real, its cruciality extending to 'information space', 'geo-economic space' and presumably applicable to the novel notion of 'geoproperty'.[5] If nature abhors a vacuum, geopoliticians and geostrategists do so with a vengeance, alternately afrighted or fascinated by it. In the absence of a specific strategic rationale prompting NATO's policy of enlargement to the east it has been argued that 'geopolitical imperatives' dictated this policy.[6] This is but the first stage. What has prompted policymakers, strategists and assorted geopoliticians to return to the 'Mackinder thesis', the concept of the Heartland, theoretically the commanding geographical redoubt in global politics, is that the Caspian and Central Asia lie at its epicentre.

The geostrategic centre of gravity has shifted and continues to shift, not as was widely advertised, in the direction of the Pacific Rim but rather towards the Caspian, the Caucasus, the eastern Mediterranean and thence the Balkans. Not only has this become a geostrategic highway, but its importance is further emphasized by the combination of geostrategy with geoeconomics involving the exploitation and transportation of huge oil and gas reserves. The geostrategic significance was underlined by US Presidential candidate George W. Bush on 19 November 1999, who spoke pure geopolitics in describing Europe and Asia as 'the world's strategic heartland', referring in particular to the significance of Eurasia, where Russia and China are transitional powers.

The picture that emerges is one in which the US has a 'vital interest', geostrategically expressed, in projecting power into Central Asia, occupying vacant 'space' in order to forestall Russian investment and to prevent a return to Cold War policies. In this context it has nevertheless been argued quite persuasively that the geopoliticians aiding and abetting the policymakers have erred quite grievously.[7] Stereotyped application of Mackinder's theories represent the US as an 'island power', an adjunct to the land-mass of Eurasia, hence the geostrategic imperative of preventing the formation of an anti-American Eurasian alliance, ensuring that no great power or coalition of great powers can dominate or endanger what Governor George W. Bush called 'our friends'.[8] Washington's Caspian energy policy acts as the geoeconomic complement to this predisposition. It challenges Russia's claim to an energy monopoly in the region, promoting an east-west 'energy corridor' linking the Caspian with Turkey, excluding Iran as a trans-shipment point for the export of oil and gas and by implication eliminating similar export traffic across Russian territory.

The expressive device of 'the game' has not lost its appeal. The whole context of geopolitical/geostrategic imperatives is frequently projected as 'a game of global control'. Inevitably the 'great game' of the nineteenth century has been resurrected as the 'New Great Game', this time in Muslim Central Asia involving great powers and regional powers: the US, Russia, Iran, Turkey, Saudi Arabia and Pakistan. The imperative of US policy in this region is to avoid 'giving a free hand to Moscow in order to bring about stability in Central Asia'.[9] The function of the geopolitical and geostrategic aspects of this 'game' is to keep inter-state conflicts 'at a manageable level', which will nevertheless generate 'a highly complicated version' of the 'new Great Game'. One such complication is that, viewed geostrategically and geoeconomically, Central Asia has steadily become an 'extension of the Middle East' involving Middle Eastern actors, Turkey, Saudi Arabia, Iran, each bent on enlarging its political influence. Iran is able to exploit its geographical proximity to Muslim Central Asia, not to mention its 'role model' as an Islamic republic, one that is Shiite amidst Sunni predominance. Muslim Central Asia must perforce settle the issue of its Islamic identity.[10]

Like Kosovo, Russia's latest war in Chechnia has added a further complicating factor in relations between Russia and the West. The priority Russia accords to stemming the flow of supplies from Georgia to Chechen rebels runs foul of Washington's association with Georgia. Neither can afford to 'back down'. Complication extends also to Turkey, bent on gaining influence in Central Asia and the Caucasus. Turkey is concentrating most immediately on Georgia and Azerbaijan, with whom it has had a long-standing association. But Russian assertiveness in Chechnia intrudes on Turkey's chances of implanting itself in the Caucasus. Though publicly critical of Russian actions in Chechnia, Iran has acted warily lest it damage the strategic Iran-Russia relationship, a stance that exposes a potentially dangerous contradiction between foreign and domestic policies.

All have become entangled in the pipeline noose. The existing system for the Caspian region is insufficient for the planned production. Russia built the Tengiz-Novorossiisk line from Kazakhstan to exploit Central Asian oil fields, but sections of the Baku-Novorossiisk line must be rerouted to skirt Chechnia. Turkey had already pointed to the disadvantages of this route, the possibility of sabotage by Chechen insurgents, then limitations of the port facilities of Novorossiisk, congestion in the Bosphorus and the potential danger to Istanbul. The US favours multiple choices and faces multiple difficulties. A pipeline running from Baku to Ceyhan, coupled with those routed to Baku-Supsa and Burgas-Viore, cost aside, would insure American and Turkish interest in Georgia, but would run certain security risks, most immediately in the Caucasus and the Balkans. The Burgas-Viore line envisaged pumping oil to be delivered by tanker to a Bulgarian port and thence through Macedonia to Albania, not the most peaceful and settled of environs.

The US has yet to produce the necessary money. It has yet to solve the geopolitical/geoeconomic conundrum of influencing Caspian oil development at large, edging closer to Iran, shoring up Georgia's independence and promoting Turkey's interests, keeping Russia at arm's length. The American 'multiple pipelines strategy' in the Caspian is itself a recognition of the limits on American power and a realization that it will be no easy task to loosen Russia's grip on pipeline routes for the export of oil and gas. Yet an obvious solution, routing pipelines southwards (through Iran or Afghanistan) well out of Russia's reach, has so far been foreclosed to the Americans by their own policy of imposing sanctions on Iran, an embargo already breached by Britain and France.

The geoeconomics of oil exploration and exploitation are further complicated with an infusion of straight geopolitics, the American pursuit of the Partnership for Peace programme, thrusting NATO's fingers deep into the Caspian region. How far NATO will ultimately go is a question of immediate moment to the Russians and growing preoccupation for the Chinese. They have expanding economic and strategic investment in Central Asia and the Caspian region, not least to secure essential energy supplies.[11] What might portend for Russian–Chinese relations will inevitably become one of the key questions in the 'New Great Game' in Central Asia.

American policies in the Caspian are dominated by the geostrategic imperative of constraining Russia, countering the Russian strategy of preserving and consolidating its regional pre-eminence and sustaining dominance of this geostrategic preserve as a matter of Russia's vital 'national interest'. Caspian energy supplies are not in themselves the *fons et origo*, the summation of the pattern of evolving relationships since, in global terms, these reserves play a 'marginal role': 4–7 per cent compared with 65 per cent in the Middle East.[12] What impels US strategy is the search for what Anatol Lieven describes as 'the Kemalist path' to promote democracy, market economics and pro-Western geopolitical orientation in 'post-Soviet space'.

Not surprisingly Turkey's model of secular democratic capitalism is perceived by the US as a prescription that would fit admirably within former Soviet states to ensure future benign development, though no single 'model', be it Turkish secularism or Iranian Islamicism, is ever likely to prevail within Central Asia. Expectations that the free market will act to produce political liberalization resulting in market-orientated democracies are likely to be disappointed. What has failed in post-Soviet Russia is not likely to succeed in the turbulent politics and ethnic clashes of the Caspian and Central Asia. Market reforms do not *ipso facto* generate reform at large, indeed they are frequently the harbinger of widespread corruption. None of this appears likely to eliminate protracted international confrontation and geostrategic competition in this huge geostrategic/geoeconomic conflict zone: the focus of American intrusiveness, Russian assertiveness, and Chinese possessiveness. Given this admixture of interests and enmities, the unilateral triumph of an American-engineered military, political and economic system seems to be far from assured.

Geopolitika Russian style

What was once ideological anathema in the former Soviet Union, namely geopolitics, the meat and drink of Western 'military adventurers', has been avidly embraced in post-Soviet Russia. Gone are the demonization and the denunciation of a pseudo-science, a heinous capitalist instrument designed solely to promote militarism and chauvinism among the masses.[13] Alfred Mahan, Halford Mackinder, even Karl Haushofer have been restored to the public domain, resulting in a near-obsessive preoccupation with geopolitics. The reasons are not far to seek. The collapse of Communism ushered in a huge crisis of identity and a challenge to post-Soviet Russia's security requirements of historic dimensions. The disappearance of the Warsaw Pact violently disrupted Russia's strategic surety in the west, forcing a strategic withdrawal on an unprecedented scale. Falling back from Prague to Smolensk placed Russia in a position uncannily like that which pertained three centuries ago. The Moscow Military District was transformed from 'the deep rear' into Russia's advanced western defence line.[14]

Even in the first stage of its enlargement NATO, 'a not clearly friendly military alliance', was closing on Russia, bringing Moscow within more immediate range of missiles and aircraft. Almost at one blow post-Soviet Russia has been transformed from a 'geopolitical extrovert' into a 'geopolitical introvert', a degradation sufficient for many to question whether in fact Russia can any longer be regarded 'functionally as a great power'.[15] A shrunken Russia has lost heavily in both the geostrategic and geoeconomic stakes. The unfavourable prospect has been clouded even further by the demographic factor where rising mortality outstrips the birth rate.

The result has been simultaneously despair and defiance. Inevitably neo-imperialist geopolitical phantasmagorias appeared, in which Vladimir Zhirinovskii figured prominently, proposing nothing less than the Russian pacification of Eurasia, eliminating that well-spring of war, pestilence and turbulence, the TransCaucasus, Iran, Afghanistan, Turkey, all brought to heel by Russia.[16] In a more serious vein, attempts have been made to link the geopolitical approach with the issue of Russia's national security in an attempt to generate 'a general theory of geopolitics and national security' (*obshchaia teoriia geopolitiki i bezopasnost'*). In brief, the argument runs that any attempt to formulate a concept of Russia's 'national security' without a 'systematic analysis of geopolitical factors' is pointless. Such an approach expands the concept of 'national security' but in so doing the nature of 'the threat' is amplified, a 'threat spectrum' emerges which involves diverse political, military, informational, economic and ecological factors.

This association of geopolitics with fundamental definitions of Russia's national security is no mere academic exercise, coming as it does from Rear Admiral V. S. Pirumov, Vice President of the Russian Academy of Natural Sciences, head of the Academy's section for geopolitics and security. Two significant innovations marked this approach: the first the formal revival or 'rehabilitation' of 'the geopolitical approach', the second the use of the term 'national security' (*natsional'naia bezopasnost*). The latter never formed part of the Soviet political lexicon, its present usage thus marking a fundamental break with the ideologically driven Stalinist model of the state.[17] This leads to an inescapable and necessary conclusion that: 'geopolitical space' has been transformed for Russia, presently consisting of 'a mixed and unstable conglomerate of states', 'geopolitical space' to which 'the zone of Russia's vital interests' will be confined at least to the year 2010.

The 'threat spectrum' is spread over political, military, environmental and ecological factors, even damage to the gene pool. The term that resounds and reverberates through all these discussions is 'space' (*prostranstvo*), not only that but 'great space' (*Bol'shoe prostranstvo*) which Russia must establish around itself. Enter Gennadi Ziuganov, author of *Geografiia pobedy Osnovy rossiiskoi geopolitiki*, published in 1997, elaborating and celebrating a new concept designed to bring comfort to an embattled Russia on the geostrategic defensive. The 'victory' Ziuganov proclaims is to be found not in history but in geography, in 'space' rather than in time. 'Control of space' is vital and must be considered a Russian 'vital interest'. Specifically, and here Ziuganov displays his best neo-Mackinderian style, Russia's 'main geopolitical aim' must be to ensure control of the Heartland (*hartlend*): 'only the attainment of this objective will guarantee the basic national security of our [Russian] state'.[18] Ziuganov recommends the path to 'control' through what he calls 'interstate union', possibly a form of confederation, Russia (itself), Belarus, Kazakhstan, Kyrgyzstan, Tajikistan and Armenia being the prime candidates, with Ukraine, Georgia and Moldova on the fringes. Not surprisingly Latvia does not fall within this orbit.

For Dr Kissinger and his interpretation of geopolitics in the context of statecraft this would simply amount to a reinvigoration of what he identified as 'Russia's dominant geopolitical thrust', the assertion of great power status designed to restore Russian pre-eminence in territories formerly under its control.

Ziuganov sets out in search of the 'geopolitical interests' of the Russian state. Some would have it that this is a nonsensical proposition when 'the Russian state' does not actually exist. Russian government statements and those emanating from various elites take a strictly pragmatic view. They cite central and eastern Europe, the Near East, Asia-Pacific, but high, if not highest on the list, regions of the Commonwealth of Independent States (CIS), as comprising Russia's strategic geopolitical interest. Complex geopolitical manoeuvres are enmeshed with geoeconomic competition in Russia's contiguous 'great space', but it is within the CIS regions that all three instrumentalities of 'control of space', variants of political, military and economic power converge.

The 1997 'National Security Concept', while downgrading the immediate geostrategic threat, referred in thinly veiled terms to 'a number of states' (and foreign intelligence) bent on undermining Russia's territorial integrity. This was no doubt an oblique reference to Zbigniew Brzezinski's advocacy of turning Russia into a loose confederation, further Russian fragmentation enhancing international security by weakening Russian military potential and suffocating its imperialist ambitions.[19] The 1997 Concept perceived this Russia as 'an influential Europe-Asian state', in which isolation from the Asia-Pacific region would be unacceptable because Russian 'national interests' were involved there. Russia constituted a geopolitical force, distinguished from the West, defining its interests within contiguous 'great space'. What could be neither concealed nor disguised was the waning of Russia's global influence, an unfortunate corollary being the inability of institutions such as the UN, CSCE, even the CIS, to halt the march towards a unipolar world only responsive to the will and whims of 'one national capital'. No prizes for guessing which capital.

What acted as the 'geopolitical detonator' in the first instance was NATO's planned enlargement to the east, accompanied by vigorous, sustained and fruitless Russian objections. The 1997 Concept made its opposition plain and unqualified, classifying NATO enlargement as a threat to Russia's national security. Early, if naive, Russian expectations that NATO would simply fade away failed to materialize. Russian designs for a pan-European security system never got off the ground. The idea of the Organization for Security and Co-operation in Europe (OSCE) acting as an over-arching 'security agency' fizzled out. Negotiations between NATO and the Russian Federation acknowledged, in principle at least, Russia's international importance and significant role in European security affairs. However, none of this had any effect on NATO's plans to enlarge itself. If this was perceived as a solution to Europe's security requirements, General Lebed mocked it as the equivalent of 'carrying out brain surgery with a chisel.'[20]

Not only the enlargement process but NATO itself was increasingly portrayed as an instrument of American hegemony in Europe and the world, the instrument of 'global military control over international space'.[21] Without further ado Lieutenant General Leonid Ivashov, head of International Military Co-operation in the Russian Defence Ministry, identified NATO as the external threat to Russia's security in the west from the West. NATO's 'open door policy', possibly culminating in the 'big bang' approach of rapid, all-inclusive enlargement starting with Slovakia, a programme 'well studied and *geopolitically based*', bears directly on several dimensions of Russia's own stated and perceived 'national security interests'.[22]

With the 'geopolitical detonator' already primed, the explosion came with Operation Allied Force, NATO's bombing campaign directed against Yugoslavia in 1999. General Ivashov interpreted the NATO bombing as only 'the beginning of a new division of the world through the use of force', observing sardonically that NATO, 'acting with the noblest of intentions', might henceforth use force to reconcile other antagonists, 'bring democracy to Belarus, Iraq and Syria', intervene in Kashmir or Nagorny Karabakh. Rhetoric apart, there was no doubting genuine Russian concern over the emergence of NATO as a self-mandating organization and the manoeuvres that short-circuited the UN.

The Russian Army's dash into Priština was almost certainly an exercise in the growing pragmatism that marks much of the military's attitude. Much more opaque is Russia's actual role in the quasi-resolution of the Kosovo crisis and the reaction of President Milošević.[23] Even before the Kosovo crisis, Operation Desert Fox, the December 1998 air strikes against Iraq, had been deemed sufficient cause for what Defence Minister Marshal Sergeev called 'a correction to our [Russian] approaches to the problems of international security'. Yevgenii Primakov went even further, declaring that 'the entire system of international security' had been prejudiced, a statement that heralded his quest for a new strategic partnership, a 'multi-polar coalition' implementing a 'geostrategic imperative' involving Moscow, New Delhi and Beijing.

The Kosovo crisis galvanized the Russian architects of the grand Eurasian strategic design, reviving the concept of 'Russo-Eurasia' and affirming its global mission. This geopolitical/geostrategic credo has been set out in greatest detail by Aleksandr Dugin in *Osnovy geopolitiki. Geopoliticheskoe budushchee Rossii,* a massive 900-page work, compiled with the assistance of 'scientific consultant' Lieutenant-General P. N. Klokotov, lecturer in the Chair of Strategy, General Staff Academy. The volume is directed to the attention of 'all those decision-makers in the most important spheres of Russian political life – business entrepreneurs, economists, bankers, diplomats, political analysts'.[24]

Dugin is ruthless in dismissing the rhetoric of the 'geopolitical interests' of the Russian state, arguing that *de facto* this 'Russian state' does not exist and freely admits that Russia has been a loser, 'vanquished', in the global geopolitical conflict.[25] Russia has been felled by a 'totalitarian ideology – liberalism', of which the US is the global quintessence. Geography nevertheless comes to Russia's aid, emplaced as it is within the Eurasian Heartland. 'Eurasianism' (*Evraziistvo*) as never before is 'our future. Our imperative. Our common task', one already delineated by Russian 'Eurasianists' Nikolai Trubetskoi and Petr Savitskii, Russian ethnologists, structural linguists and sociologists.[26] The geostrategic imperative demands the establishment of a 'continental Eurasian bloc', a zone of continental strategic control that presupposes 'Russo-Eurasia's' geopolitical expansion to the south, to the Caspian and Central Asia, the investment of the Caucasus.

The global realignment generated by the Kosovo crisis has proved in practice to be extraordinarily difficult to resolve in favour of 'Russo-Eurasia', a fact recently recognized by President Putin. What hopes rested in establishing supposed 'co-operation and partnership' with the US have long since been dissipated. Russian weakness rules out confrontation, the very same condition inhibits effective partnership. The dash for multipolarity, the Primakov plan for a grand coalition embracing Russia, India, China and others, perceived by some as using the Eurasian heartland as the 'launch-pad' for a global anti-Western movement, has meanwhile slowed down. Putin has literally shifted Russia's ground within these geostrategic and geoeconomic perturbations, simultaneously looking south and west.

To the south Russia's dependence upon CIS energy and raw materials resources will increase, making Russian access to and control over these reserves and markets a Russian 'vital interest', all underlined in the Russian Security Council report outlining a dependence that will increase by the year 2005. Russia must persist in retaining as much as possible of CIS energy resources for its own purposes, a position that has inserted a competitive element into the hitherto co-operative relationship between Russia and China in Central Asia.

United in efforts to check Islamic extremism, Russia and China are in competitive mode as China inserts itself into the region's energy politics, specifically into two of the four major oil fields in Kazakhstan. The Chinese economy is hungry for energy. Kazakhstan seeks to diversify its oil export routes, the bulk of which presently pass through the Russian pipeline network on to Samara. A second line due to come into operation in 2001 will also pass through Russian territory. Kazakhstan exports oil to China via a rail link, while a proposed pipeline from western Kazakhstan to Xinjiang in China would provide one secure land route for Chinese energy imports and free the rail link for trade. Russia contemplates another variant, a Tomsk–Beijing oil pipeline and a gas pipeline from Irkutsk passing through Mongolia, further strengthening the Russian monopoly of export routes and increasing its hold over Kazakhstan.[27]

While Russia fends off intruders from the west and the east into the Caspian region and Central Asia, Russia's 'great space', the term 'strategic partnership', which was earlier applied to relations between Russia and China, is increasingly used to describe an expanding relationship between India and Russia. These newly refurbished relations are, however, fraught with difficulties and contradictions. In view of the unresolved tension between New Delhi and Beijing, Russian arms sales to China must be set against closer Russian military co-operation with India, foreshadowed in Primakov's visit to India in late December 1998.

Moscow has assured New Delhi that arms sales to China will not be allowed to damage Russo-Indian relations. India meanwhile proposes to buy 300 T-90 Russian battle tanks, 40 SU-30 aircraft, the refurbished aircraft carrier *Admiral Gorshkov*, possibly Russian submarines and multiple missile systems. China has already acquired the former Soviet aircraft carried *Kiev*, more an 'anti-submarine cruiser' with a flight deck, the core of a potential carrier battle group and an important element of a 'power-projection navy'. Moscow clearly lends its military aid for the transformation of India from a regional power into a fully fledged international actor. What this reaffirmation of Indian–Russian military co-operation, which dates back to Marshal Zhukov's visit to India in the 1950s, will mean for further Russian sales of advanced weaponry to China remains to be seen.[28]

President Putin's new geostrategic gambits carry considerable risks. The complications and contradictions in the Moscow–New Delhi–Beijing triangulation are self-evident. Putin's diplomatic trawl through the former Soviet Union's clients, Iraq, North Korea and Vietnam among them, gave rise to Chinese misgivings, especially in the case of the latter two. Nevertheless, Putin asserts Russian influence in areas of vital American interest. This stance is not quite the Primakov strategy of 'multipolar coalition' designed to counter American power globally, nor is it full-blooded 'Eurasianism'. On the contrary President Putin has adopted or reverted to a 'Russia first' strategy, asserting Russia's 'national interests', emphasizing economics, assigning prominence to a policy of 'Russia in Europe', adopting a moderate tone over Russian–American relations, stressing 'Russia in Europe'.[29] Here Moscow has not neglected to exploit the doubts and misgivings over American plans for national missile defence, suggesting a joint Russo-European response to missile defence based on a different technical solution serving Europe's security interests rather than those of America only.[30]

The rapid Russian ratification of the START-2 strategic arms reduction agreement and the Comprehensive Test Ban Treaty (CTBT) was construed outside Russia as a conciliatory move but it was also one with the potential for ambush, confronting America over the issues of the ABM Treaty and the Test Ban Treaty. Simultaneously the new Russian military doctrine, rushed to completion in view of events in Kosovo, humiliating indifference to Russia's position, an unpredictable NATO, reinstated nuclear 'first use' in defence of Russia's vital national interests.[31] 'Kosovo represented a watershed for Russia..[32]

The Kosovo operation demonstrated unequivocally that advanced conventional weapons (PGMs) have 'consequences practically indistin-guishable from nuclear weapons', illuminating Russia's conventional weakness and necessitating 'closer attention to its nuclear advantages'. What response could Russia make in the event of an American 'punitive strike' using conventional cruise missiles to enforce a particular policy or resolve a disagreement by force? Acquiesce or resort to nuclear weapons? The idea of using land-based and sea-based *tactical* nuclear weapons as a countermeasure had already been tentatively explored even before Kosovo. In April 1999 the Russian Security Council debated the development of low-yield tactical nuclear weapons, possibly reintroducing nuclear warheads to land-based missiles and artillery.

Most immediately in the wake of Kosovo a major Russian military exercise *Zapad-99* planned in 1998 suddenly acquired, in June–July 1999, a 'nuclear scenario', simulated use of nuclear-armed air-launched weapons, nuclear support for Russian troops 'restoring the situation' in the Kaliningrad *oblast,* in order to repel a NATO attack with forces matching those deployed against Yugoslavia.[33] The unstable and essentially transient nature of this 'nuclear solution' has been dramatically demonstrated by the acrimonious dispute between Defence Minister Marshal Sergeev and Chief of the General Staff Anatoli Kvashnin, the latter arguing for the subordination of strategic land-based missiles to the army, cutting launchers from 756 to 150 by 2003, eliminating sixteen or seventeen missile units, producing only two rather than ten TOPOL-M strategic missiles per year.[34] Maintaining a first-strike capability against America is patent nonsense. A much smaller force adequately serves deterrence.

Kvashnin's proposal serves two aims: increasing the influence of the General Staff over Russian land-based ICBMs (countering Sergeev's recent proposal to reduce General Staff influence) and diverting money to Russian conventional forces whose condition was 'rapidly deteriorating', even as the threats to which they must respond increase. Chechnya is a grim illustration. So far Russian policy will retain nuclear weapons but whatever the outcome of the Sergeev–Kvashnin clash, the 'nuclear solution' alone cannot compensate for failure to modernize Russian conventional forces. The Russian high command has also to establish precisely what role nuclear weapons might perform, a debate dangerously complicated if infused with perceptions of US/NATO as 'the threat' and growing suspicions of American plans for national missile defence.

The inherent ambiguity in Russia's various postures, military, political, geopolitical, geoeconomic, is evidently deliberately contrived to position Russia as favourably as possible within the turbulent realignment in the global balance of power. If post-Soviet Russia under Yeltsin was a 'geopolitical loser', Putin is intent on ensuring that in post-Yeltsin Russia this is no longer the case.

'The China Tangle'[35]

The 'accidental' bombing of the Chinese embassy in Belgrade during NATO's air campaign against Yugoslavia understandably left China incandescent with rage. No truly satisfactory explanation for this 'accident' has yet been forthcoming. Beijing remains unconvinced by tales of 'error piled on incompetence piled on bad judgement in a variety of places'.[36] Even before the Kosovo crisis China had made its presence felt in the Balkans. In late January 1999 Macedonia proceeded to recognize Taiwan, whereupon Beijing abruptly severed diplomatic ties with Skopje and, as a permanent member of the UN Security Council, promptly vetoed a renewal of the mandate for the UN Preventative Deployment Force in Macedonia.

Like Russia, China voiced concern over NATO's enlargement. China might not in practice object to an enlargement in the west, which preoccupied the Russians, but the enlargement of NATO's role to cover activities beyond the borders of its member states, the potential globalizing of NATO, was of real concern to Beijing. If NATO insists on 'out of area' extension of its activities to include the Middle East, then the Chinese are concerned that this commitment might reach into Asia. This would be the culmination of a strategy of global intervention on behalf of the United States. The 'Kosovo precedent', armed intervention overriding national sovereignty, might well be applied to other ethnic disturbances or outright civil war in other climes. Like Russia, China also sees NATO's long arm reaching into Chinese 'geopolitical space' in Central Asia through the Partnership for Peace programme, yet another cloak or guise for 'American hegemonism'. Russia and China jointly oppose America's national missile defence plan.

All this would suggest strong communality of interest between Russia and China, sufficient to provide the cement for a strategic partnership, if not actual alliance. 'Strategic partnership' was in the air during the latter days of President Yeltsin in a distinct phase of warming up in Russian-Chinese relations. It was a relationship lauded by President Jiang Zemin, expressing common Russian and Chinese detestation of a unipolar world dominated by 'hegemonism and power politics'. Yeltsin's policy faltered through undue reliance on his Chinese 'partner' and inability to match Chinese economic and political achievements. Primakov's grand tripartite coalition dissolved into thin air. As a device to cajole or coerce the US Yeltsin's 'partnership' failed dismally. Russia offered only arms and oil. Moscow's supply of arms will now be subject to considerations of India's security. China makes provision for its energy requirements in competition with Russia in Central Asia. Both Russia and China compete for foreign investment.

President Putin is presently modifying Russian priorities in the Russian-Chinese 'co-operation-competition' relationship. India rather than China is now favourite candidate for the much-vaunted 'strategic partnership'. Not surprisingly China closes ranks with Pakistan and makes overtures to Iran. In the 'pipelines battle' Russia has successfully deflected American attempts to control oil and gas exports, directing them westwards, but in Central Asia China is intent on implementing the eastward orientation of export routes, challenging Russia's political and economic 'vital interests' in this region. Purported Russian-Chinese co-operation to oppose Islamic fundamentalism has nonetheless facilitated heightened Russian military presence in and closer ties with Central Asian states. Still further east illegal Chinese migration into the Russian Far East is not merely a population shift but Chinese returning to historically Chinese territories.

China inserted itself subtly into the contest to control and command post-Kosovo global realignments. China's State Council had already advertised a new concept of security based on 'mutual trust', implicitly challenging the American view that alliances were the foundation of stability in East Asia, an opening move in a protracted geostrategic contest, intensified by American plans for missile defence systems to protect Japan, South Korea and Taiwan.

China also neatly inserted itself in the geopolitics of eastern Europe, Ukraine and TransCaucasus, simultaneously scouting in western Europe, missions divided between Li Peng, Chairman of the Standing Committee of the People's Congress and Prime Minister Zhu Ronghi. Li Peng ostentatiously visited Belgrade, denouncing 'barbaric' NATO, deliberately bypassing Moscow. What Li Peng thus communicated both to applicants for NATO membership and to potential adherents of Moscow was that neither choice need be foreclosed, given China as a 'third force', a force to be reckoned with in a multi-polar world. This could only fall on deaf ears in Slovenia, Croatia and Slovakia but sounds more beguiling in Ukraine. China's contacts with this major regional power deploying significant military force are increasing, co-operating in anti-Russian intelligence, training Chinese intelligence officers in Kharkov, eyeing Ukrainian-built aircraft.

The other port of call, Azerbaijan on the fringes of NATO, could nevertheless play a useful role in China's energy policy. Li Peng's rhetoric in Belgrade made it clear that NATO was a declared enemy, any emergent NATO geostrategic colossus, anathema. Should that materialize, China would perforce reconsider its position and align with Russia to counter a global threat. Prime Minister Zhu Rongji deployed his talents in Western Europe, his mission to garner support for Chinese entry into the World Trade Organization (WTO), simultaneously displaying a Chinese disposition to work with Europe and the West.

That geostrategic hobgoblin haunting the West, full-blooded Russian-Chinese alliance, has yet to materialize. Neither party presently wishes to bring this about, neither party at this juncture wishes to antagonize the US. The coolness between Moscow and Beijing may persist, temporarily moderated at the G-8 and the Shanghai Five summit meetings, but the competitive mode will predominate, even intensify short of outright rupture. Only if there is to be a serious onslaught on 'hegemonism', an overt challenge to American global dominance, will the hobgoblin materialize, the inescapability of a Russian-Chinese formal alliance, but that eventuality presently seems remote for all the warm words exchanged between Moscow and Beijing. China is intent on the purposes of its own power.

We are conceivably witnessing only an opening round in the battle for the world. The advent of 'humanitarian warfare', that most bizarre of oxymorons generated by Kosovo, has prompted questions and misgivings, fears over what it might portend.[37] None of this has been lost on the theorists and practitioners of geopolitics. Filip Tunjic, wise in the ways of geopolitics, Senior Adviser at the Centre for Strategic Studies, Ljubljana, put the issue at its most stark. 'Are we walking from peace to war?' Given the prevalence of what he describes as 'the geopolitical burden' he is not sanguine about the prospects for peace. Neither am I.

Notes

1. Quoted in Samuel P. Huntington, 'The Clash of Civilisations', *Foreign Affairs,* vol. 72 (Summer 1993), p. 46.
2. For an indispensable analysis of 'practical and popular geopolitics', 'geopolitical reasoning and statecraft', structural geopolitics, 'critical geopolitics' as a deconstruct of stereotyped geopolitical conceptions, see Gearoid O. Tuathail (Gerard Toal), 'Understanding Critical Geopolitics: Geopolitics and Risk Society' in Colin S. Gray and Geoffrey Sloan (eds), *Geopolitics, Geography and Strategy* (London: Frank Cass, 1999), pp. 106–24.
3. See Christopher J. Fettweis, 'Sir Halford Mackinder, Geopolitics and Policy-making in the 21st Century', *Parameters,* US Army War College, vol. 30, no. 2 (Summer 2000), pp. 58–71; also David Newman (ed.), 'Boundaries, Territory and Postmodernity', *Geopolitics,* special issue (Summer 1998); also Filip Tunjić, 'War and Geopolitics – Really Together Again?', *Journal of Slavic Military Studies,* vol. 12, no. 2 (June 1999), pp. 89–109.
4. Anatol Lieven, *Chechnya: Tombstone of Russian Power* (Yale UP, 1998), p. 382.
5. Explored in Geoff Demarest, *Geoproperty, Foreign Affairs, National Security and Property Rights* (London: Frank Cass, 1998), applying 'property theory' in the context of human rights struggle.
6. See John Hillen and Michael P. Noonan, 'The Geopolitics of NATO Enlargement', *Parameters,* vol. 27, no. 3 (Autumn 1998), here p. 32 on a 'geopolitically informed and enlarged NATO'; for one of many critical views James H. Wyllie, 'NATO's Bleak Future', *Parameters,* vol. 28, no. 4 (Winter 1998-9), pp. 113–23.
7. Largely the burden of Fettweis's article, bent on 'debunking the fundamental assumptions of geopolitics', suggesting a 'prolonged investigation into the utility of all geopolitical theory'.
8. Governor George W. Bush, Republican Presidential candidate, speech 19 November 1999: Eurasia has the next six largest economies after the US, the next six largest military budgets.

9. See M. E. Ahrari with James Beal, *The New Great Game in Muslim Central Asia,* National Defense University, Washington, McNair Paper 47 (January 1996), p. 7.

10. *ibid.*

11. For an excellent map of oil and gas pipelines, detailed analysis of the strategic environment, strategic perspectives of major players, John McCarthy, 'The geo-politics of Caspian oil', *Jane's Intelligence Review,* vol. 12, no. 7 (July 2000), pp. 20–25.

12. John McCarthy, on revised figures for Caspian reserves, *ibid.,* p. 20.

13. For example, I. A. Modzhoryan, *Geopolitika na sluzhbe voennykh avantyur* (Moscow: Mezhdunarodnye Otnosheniia, 1974).

14. See Alexei Arbatov, 'Russian Security Interests and Dilemmas: An Agenda for the Future' in Alexei Arbator and Abram Chayes, *Managing Conflict in the Former Soviet Union, Russian and American Perspectives,* CSIA Studies in International Security (Cambridge, MA: MIT Press, 1997), pp. 411–58, here p. 418.

15. See Timothy W. Luke and Gerard Toal, 'The Fraying Modern Map: Failed States and Contraband Capitalism', *Geopolitics,* vol. 3, no. 3 (Winter 1998) under 'The Russian Twilight Zone' and 'The Chechen Twilight Zone', pp. 25–29; also Yuri N. Afanas'ev, 'Seems Like Old Times? Russia's Place in the World', *Current History,* 93/985 (October 1994) – 'A unitarian state? A multinational empire?' Russia seeking 'a new Russian place' must be first identified and then defined: here pp. 408–9; on Russia and Russian identity *Obozrevatel* Moscow 1994 (5–8) Special Issue 'Natsional'naya doktrina Rossii (problemy i prioritety)', p. 494ff.

16. For perceptive comments on Zhirinovskii, see Mark Yoffe, 'Vladimir Zhirinovsky, the Unholy Fool', *Current History* 93/585 (October 1994) pp. 324–6; see V. V. Zhirinovskii *Ocherki po geopolitike,* (Moscow: n.p. 1997).

17. See Rear Admiral V. S. Pirumov, 'Nekotornye aspekty metodologii issledova-niya problem natsional'noi bezopasnosti Rossii v sovremennykh usloviyakh' under 'Geopoliticheskie Prognozy' in *Geopolitika i bezopasnost,* Moscow 'Arbizo', 1993, pp. 1–17. Translated by Robert R. Love, *Journal of Slavic Military Studies,* vol. 7, no. 3 (September 1994) pp. 367–82.

18. See 'Geopoliticheskie ochertaniya budushchei Rossii', in G. Ziuganov, *Geografiya pobedy,* (Moscow: n.p., 1997), pp. 245–62, outlining a three-phase strategy to recover 'the natural geopolitical status of Russia'. Under the rubric of 'control' Ziuganov specifies military control, political control, economic control, communications control, demographic control, information control, civic-cultural control.

19. Zbigniew Brzezinski, 'A Geostrategy for Eurasia', *Foreign Affairs* vol. 76 (September/October 1997), pp. 37–50 suggesting loose confederation as a solution to the 'Russian problem'. As early as 1986 Brzezinski had outlined 'a geostrategic framework' for the conduct of the 'US – Soviet contest' emphasising 'the struggle for Euroasia' and also outlining US 'geopolitical priorities'; see Chapters 2 and 6 in Zbigniew Brzezinski, *Game Plan* (Boston, New York, 1986).

20. Quoted in Benjamin S. Lambeth, *The Warrior Who Would Rule Russia* (RAND, Santa Monica, 1996), p. 49.

21. For one of many similar statements, 'Rasshirenie NATO kak faktor reanimatsii blokovoi strategii i bezopasnosti Rossii' in R. G. Yanovskii and Yu. I. Deryugin (eds), *Armiya Rossii: Sostoyanie i Perspektivy*, Moscow ISPI RAN, 1999, pp. 25–37. For 'a fictional monologue' but nonetheless a penetrating analysis of Russian attitudes to NATO expansion, Colonel Frederick P. A. Hammersen, 'The Disquieting Voice of Russian Resentment', *Parameters*, vol. 28, no. 2 (Summer 1998), pp. 39–55.

22. '9 NATO Candidates Pledge To Join in a "Big Bang" Bid', *International Herald Tribune*, 20–21 May, also 'NATO Growth Spurt Unlikely by 2002', 23 May. Ukraine is not mentioned. On Ukraine's security role in Europe, David E. Albright and Semyen J. Appatov (eds), *Ukraine and European Security*, (New York, NY: St Martin's Press, 1999), pp. 125–205.

23. 'We conclude that Russia played a central role in causing Milošević to concede', Foreign Affairs Committee House of Commons Fourth Report KOSOVO 23 May 2000, Volume I Report and Proceedings, 'What was Russia's role in the Kosovo crisis?', xlii–xliii.

24. Originally published, *Osnovy geopolitiki*, Moscow 1997. Tatyana Yevgeneva in Kurt R. Spillmann and Andreas Wegner (eds), *Russia's Place in Europe A Security Debate*, (Bern, 1999), discussing Russia's 'profound identity crisis' argues that 'backward-looking orientation' provides models for confrontation (against the West). Dugin's work attests to this attitude, 'combining crudely simple theories with patriotic, messianic thoughts'. See pp. 59–70, here 69–70.

25. Aleksandr Dugin, p. 689.

26. *ibid*, pp. 648–9.

27. Contrary to some expectations an agreement to build the Tomsk–Beijing oil pipeline failed to appear among the documents signed on 18 July at the meeting in Beijing between President Jiang Zemin and President Putin.

28. Details in *East Asian Strategic Review 2000*, Tokyo, National Institute for Defense Studies, 2000, under 'Russia's Arms Exports and East Asia', China, India, South Korea, Malaysia, Vietnam, pp. 262–7. By way of retrospect on Soviet–Indian relations, see N. Galay, 'Zhukov in India', *Bulletin of the Institute for the Study of the USSR*, vol. 4, no. 4 (April 1957), pp. 3–9.

29. Russian foreign policy doctrine, 22 pages, signed by Putin 28 June, published Moscow, 10 July 2000, a revision of the 1993 document. The approach is 'pragmatic', eschewing global, superpower attitudes, emphasizing Russian 'national interests', promoting conditions for Russian economic growth, the 'broad integration' of Russia into the world economic system, pursuing a 'multi-polar' world, opposing American plans for a national missile defence, responding if necessary with 'adequate measures'.

30. See 'Cohen Parries Russia's Attempt to Split NATO,' *Aviation Week and Space Technology*, 3 July 2000, p. 34. US Defence Secretary William S. Cohen mentioned the possibility of co-operation with Russia on boost-phase intercept technology as a defensive system. At the prompting of Richard Perle boost-phase intercept appears to be Governor George W. Bush's preferred and declared solution for a missile defence system.

31. Russia's National Security Concept, published *Nezavisimoe voennoe obozre-nie*, 14 January 2000: Draft Military Doctrine, *Krasnaia Zvezda*, 8 October

1999, approved Security Council 4 February 2000, *Nezavisimoe voennoe obrozrenie,* 11 February 2000. Also Charles J. Dick, 'Russia's new doctrine takes dark world view', *Jane's Intelligence Review,* vol. 12, no. 1 (January 2000), pp. 14–19. For an excellent background study Deborah Yarsike Ball, 'Spurred by Kosovo, the Russian military is down but not out', *Jane's Intelligence Review,* vol. 11, no. 6 (June 1999), pp. 16–18.

32. Nikolai Sokov, *Russian Strategic Modernization Past and Future,* (Lanham MD: Rowman & Littlefield, 2000), p. 170.

33. Nikolai Sokov, *op. cit.,* p. 171. The Russian Northern Fleet also held exercises 'coinciding' with NATO air operations directed against Yugoslavia, the Far Eastern Military District carried out a 'strategic command post exercise' between March 29–April 4, planned in December 1998 but carried out immediately after the start of NATO air strikes in Yugoslavia. The Far Eastern military exercises were marked by the first deployment of the S-300 MPU1 surface to air missile (SAM) system, attacking air and ground targets.

34. 'Putin Scolds Generals He Demands a Halt to Public Brawl Over Russian Strategic Missile Forces', *International Herald Tribune,* 15–16 July 2000, citing figures published in *Izvestiia,* 15 July 2000. Kvashnin's ambitions regarding the Russian General Staff (and himself) are by no means new: see James H. Brusstar, 'Russia's Peacetime Battlefield', *Strategic Forum,* NDU/INSS Washington DC, No. 144, 8/1998, pp. 1–4. Sergei Rogov, Director, Institute USA and Canada, bitterly criticized Kvashnin and the incompetence of the General Staff, and its low professional level as demonstrated in the Chechen wars. The 'Kvashnin plan' enables the Pentagon to plan a first strike and avoid nuclear retaliation. Rogov accuses Kvashnin of reducing the Russian deterrent 'to the level of Indonesia'.

35. With acknowledgement to Professor Herbert Feis's original work, *The China Tangle: The American Effort in China from Pearl Harbor to the Marshall Mission* (Princeton and Oxford: Princeton UP/Oxford UP, 1953).

36. See 'Lack of Targets Led to the China Embassy Raid', *International Herald Tribune,* 18 April 2000. Chinese suspicions were aroused since the American attack actually destroyed the Defence Attaché's office and the Embassy 'intelligence cell', but Pentagon officials disclosed that the entire building was targeted throughout. They argue that evidently one or two missiles did not explode.

37. For examples of serious misgivings over NATO's Kosovo operation, see Philip Hammond and Edward S. Herman (eds) *The Media and the Kosovo Crisis* (London: Pluto Press, 2000), especially Chapter 5 R. Keeble, 'New Militarism and the Manufacture Warfare'. Also Tariq Ali (ed.), *Masters of the Universe? NATO's Balkan Crusade* (London: Verso Press, 2000).

CHAPTER SIXTEEN

Perceptions of Kosovo's 'Refugees'

JOANNE VAN SELM

Introduction

The main focus of discussion about NATO intervention in Kosovo was on the justness of the intervention, the means used, and the targets hit. The need to protect the Kosovar Albanians from the Milošević regime was the motive given for military intervention. However, the nature of the intervention, and the discussion surrounding its moral justification or legitimacy in international law obscured the main refugee law and policy issues involved. It was, put simply, often unclear whether the NATO states were attempting to protect *people* who were or might become 'refugees', or attempting to protect themselves and their populations *from* those same people as 'refugees'. The perception of all asylum seekers as illegal immigrants, scrounging off the more-or-less flourishing Western European welfare states, had taken hold for policymakers and populations alike since the mid-1980s. If *all* asylum seekers could be said to be undeserving, then the Kosovar 'refugees', who needed to seek asylum in order to become recognized refugees, must logically also be undeserving. However, if the Kosovar population was so undeserving, why go to great expense, and risk the lives of NATO fighters to protect them? (No-one was about to explicitly say that the great expense and risk was to protect 'us' from 'them'.) The confusion in perception of 'refugees' sewn by the NATO intervention and rhetoric of March to June 1999 may have an impact on the way refugee protection in conflict situations is conceptualized and organized in the future.

An understanding of the terminology involved in refugee protection is key to the argument presented here about the pivotal role the perception of the Kosovar 'refugees' could play in European and global management of refugee crises. The political debate about who exactly could be considered a refugee under the definition, which was established by the

1951 Geneva Convention and 1967 New York Protocol, might appear to be merely about semantics. However, once the legal terminology is tampered with by political debate, the popular perception of the meaning of words such as 'refugee', 'asylum seeker' and 'displaced person' can make semantics a matter of life and death, or at the very least of dignified existence or the creation of an underclass.

Perceptions are central to the argument that Kosovo could herald changes in refugee protection. If the 'refugees' were perceived as a burden then we could anticipate a downward turn in protection readiness and standards. If the perceptions were more positive, then we could expect an upturn in the willingness to protect. This upward turn would be dependent on the uniqueness of the perceptions of the Kosovar case. However, in anticipation of future cases, governments might take steps to avoid future chaos such as ensued in the wake of the massive displacements of 1999.

Much of the discussion of perceptions of 'refugees' must be anecdotal and generalized, and even if drawn from reliable media, open to question. The images of 'refugees' from Kosovo became tied into the Western propaganda about the justification both for intervention, and for keeping the majority of the Kosovar population close to 'home'. The images were also part of the Serbian propaganda surrounding the NATO intervention. It therefore became difficult to know what was 'true' and what was, at the very least, 'convenient'. For example, when Kosovars proclaimed to the watching TV cameras that they preferred to stay in Albania, that may well have been the case, but it was also useful to European states that preferred not to host the 'refugee' populations themselves.

Terminology

According to the 1951 Convention Relating to the Status of Refugees, amended by the 1967 New York Protocol, a *refugee* is someone who:

> owing to a well-founded fear of being persecuted for reasons of race, religion, nationality, membership of a particular social group or political opinion is outside the country of his nationality and is unable or, owing to such fear is unwilling to avail himself of the protection of that country; or who, not having a nationality and being outside the country of his former habitual residence as a result of such events, is unable or, owing to such fear, is unwilling to return to it.

Having been acknowledged as a refugee according to this definition, either by UNHCR or a host state prior to resettlement under agreed programmes, or after judicial procedures on seeking asylum in a host country, a person is, according to the Convention, guaranteed rights equal to nationals in some areas, and to other resident non-nationals in other areas of life in the country of residence. A recognized refugee also has access to refugee travel documents. The essence of recognition of the individual under the Convention is that a state offers protection, and that protection by a host state is recognized and respected by other states.[1]

If an *asylum seeker*, that is someone who has applied for protection in a host state, is not granted refugee status, there are in essence two alternatives. One is the granting of a status with fewer rights. These lesser statuses of protection vary from country to country and are not governed by an international standard. The other alternative is rejection of protection, which in turn could have two outcomes. One is deportation, either to the country of origin or another state, or if this is impossible or undesirable, for example because no state agrees to accept the deported person, then the person may be forced into remaining illegally in that state in which he or she had sought protection. In fact, if the state of origin will not accept the deportee, this may be an indication of the real need for protection, or at least be sufficient to file a new asylum claim.

At the time of the NATO intervention, an estimated 200,000 Kosovar Albanians were *internally displaced persons* (IDPs). The refugee definition stipulates that a person must be outside his or her country of origin. An IDP could be described as in every way like a refugee, except that no international border has been crossed. Those Kosovars who sought safety in Montenegro remained IDPs, as they remained within the Republic of Yugoslavia. Those Serbs who fled Kosovo after NATO troops' entry and headed to the rest of Serbia or to Montenegro were also IDPs.

One of the statuses referred to above as somehow less than refugee status is *temporary protection*. There has been no international agreement on what this category implies. Generally it could be described as a period of protection with an attached time limit. Refugee status is temporary in that it is expected to end, but the end results from invocation of the Convention's cessation clauses. For many Cold War refugees this took forty years. When granting temporary protection, European governments aim to avoid individual status procedures for massive influxes and the lengthy procedures attached to cessation of refugee status by indicating time limits, and limiting rights, from the beginning. They are often seeking return as the ideal solution after a period of protection, although much protection, temporary or otherwise, often culminates in longer term residence and potentially naturalization.

What the 'refugees' perceived

Two areas of perceptions will be examined. First: what might the 'refugees' have thought of the NATO intervention? Second: what might they have thought of their reception and protection? The perceptions of Kosovar Albanian 'refugees', rather than Serbs or Roma, will be foremost in view of being the most prominent group in the available media.

Although it is difficult to put oneself in the place of the Kosovar Albanian population in 1998-9 it might not be impossible, given hindsight and the range of reports available. One can imagine a sense of distrust that the outside world would do anything, reinforced by knowledge, often first hand, of how the West had failed to act in Bosnia. Thousands of Bosnians were in Kosovo by 1998. Alongside Bosnian Serbs, and some displaced Moslems, were Krajina Serbs displaced during the wars of 1991-5, and settled by the Milošević government in the Kosovo province, in an effort to increase the Serb minority. Those Serbs would probably also perceive the West as an unlikely protector. When they started to move after the bombing campaign, as vengeful Albanians returned, Serbs did not seek protection *en masse* in the West, but were also deterred from seeking the protection of families or friends within Serbia. The governing regime feared that knowledge of these Serb displacements would undermine the notion of victory over NATO and the UN, which had now been forced to enter Kosovo.[2]

When the NATO intervention started Kosovar Albanians were heard expressing gratitude. However, many lost their lives or loved ones due to the imprecision of the precision bombing, as well as during the forced marches to borders with neighbouring states. The NATO refusal to acknowledge some mistakes at the time must have left another sort of perception than gratitude with many people. Some Kosovar Albanians expressed a gratitude that was tinged with horror. The horror stemmed from the knowledge that more killings (as reprisals) would be carried out because of the attack, for which they had so much longed.[3]

Whether the Kosovar Albanians were displaced by a centrally planned, Serbian policy of deportation, NATO bombing or localized Serb reactions to the bombing has, since March 1999, been a hotly disputed topic. Many interview-based studies concluded that the 'refugees' were victims of mass deportations. One study using statistical data on border crossings and the geographic origin of 'refugees', which it compared to the geographic location of NATO bombing attacks of the same time period, likewise concluded that deportations rather than NATO bombing caused the size and direction of the exodus.[4] Another study suggests those deportations were rather more spontaneous, centrally organized, retaliation against NATO than a plan already underway, or localized actions.[5] A further interesting vision of the displacements is that the Kosovars sought to leave the province clear of Albanians so that NATO could bomb without fear of harming those they were (nominally at least) trying to protect.[6] The reasons for displacement are not only interesting for the discussion on the justification of the intervention; they are absolutely central to decisions about refugee status in protecting states.

For those who had feared for their lives at the Milošević regime's hands, who had feared persecution for reasons related to religion and political opinion (recall the refugee definition), the gratitude felt towards the NATO states who had intervened extended also to their 'protectors'. These included, initially, the neighbouring states that offered them initial shelter (Albania and Macedonia),[7] those organizations on hand to protect them (UNHCR, NGOs, ECHO), and those states that set up camps in the two neighbouring countries, as well as NATO's soldiers offering humanitarian assistance. The gratitude persisted in spite of the chaotic nature the protection often took on. For many there was surely satisfaction simply at being away from a day to day fear of harassment, arrest, torture and persecution. However, after a few days or weeks the perceptions of the camp surroundings and life as a 'refugee' in a relatively poor state must have altered, with thoughts turning to a desire to return or move on. Many 'refugees' in Albania were reported as being angry and reluctant when told to move further south for safety's sake. The most precious and useful belonging many people owned by that point was a tractor, often their means of escape. But tractors could not be taken to the camps UNHCR helped establish further from the borders. The perception of losing control over normal day to day decisions and desires must have been strong.

In Albania the 'refugees' were received as kin. However, some tensions existed amidst the generous response, in part harking back to recent historical tensions between the kin Albanian populations. During the Cold War isolation of Albania, the Kosovars had been perceived as better off, sparking jealousy amongst the Albanians in Albania. At the same time the more isolated and 'really Communist' Albania was perceived in the West as a more likely place from which people might need asylum. Yugoslavia was seen as more West-leaning and less likely to produce refugees. Where Kosovars sometimes pretended to be Albanians during the Cold War to seek refugee status in the West, Albanians sometimes claimed to be Kosovar, in seeking entry to the West during and after the NATO intervention.

In Macedonia the Kosovars were greeted rather differently. While welcomed by many of their kin (staying with host families was very common), the arrival of tens of thousands of Albanians in a country already dealing with a precarious ethnic balance and difficult minority situation was perceived a potential security threat. Macedonia was, in the words of one article, caught 'in The Middle'.[8] A majority Slav state, it was serving as a NATO base. It was also an obvious country of first asylum for 'refugees', whether they were choosing their own port of exit from Kosovo, or deliberately directed to the Macedonian border by the Serb leaders, intent on spreading the conflict one way or another. Macedonia sought international solidarity: it sought Western states that would accept evacuees, to relieve the pressure on this politically precarious state. When such solidarity was not immediately forthcoming, and as UNHCR sought to ensure that Macedonia lived up to its international commitments in not returning would-be refugees to a place in which they risked persecution and violence, the Macedonians closed the borders. This created TV pictures that would dramatically impact Western public perceptions. The outcome of this action was ultimately the development of a Humanitarian Transfer Programme, moving 'refugees' from Macedonia to Albania, and a Humanitarian Evacuation Programme, evacuating Kosovars to temporary protection in other states.

Many Kosovar Albanians had said they wished to remain close to home, hoping for an early return. By 5 May 1999, IWPR (the Institute for War and Peace Reporting) was reporting that poor conditions at the Stenkovec Camp in Macedonia were causing some to seek to move on out of the region.[9] For these Albanians and many Slavs from or in the Kosovo region, smugglers were the only means to fulfil individual desires to reach safer, calmer places where they would potentially have more opportunity for a relatively prosperous lifestyle. Relatively few tried this route, but of those who did many found that smugglers were not the lifeline they can be, but also included criminals seeking profit out of the misery of others combined with the strict rules against entry imposed by the West European states.[10]

The first 'refugees' to be evacuated from Macedonia on the evacuation programme, on 6 April, underwent a further traumatic experience. The first evacuations took place to Norway and Turkey: they were chaotic, with people not knowing where they were going, and being separated from family members. Some in the media described these first movements to protection countries as 'chain deportations'.

Attitudes to return were surveyed by the Institute for Policy and Legal Studies, Tirana and the American Association for the Advancement of Science. Using interviews and statistical sampling in eight camps in Albania the researchers found that all the 'refugees' wanted to return immediately, but many expressed concerns about the conditions they required for them to return. Security was the primary concern, then food and water, transportation and housing or shelter. Many were willing to wait if recommended to do so by UNHCR. Some were also adamant they would not go to areas where Russians had a role: this surprised the researchers as it was a spontaneous response, rather than being one of options given in the questionnaire. Ultimately the return from Macedonia and Albania was sudden, massive and against the advice of UNHCR.

In the countries to which Kosovar Albanians were evacuated, the temporarily protected were often reported to be grateful for the reception and protection they received, but desperate to go home. One man in the Netherlands was reported as saying, 'Thank you, but I won't be staying.'[11] At the end of the bombing campaign and when protecting states and parts of their populations started calling for return, a significant number of Kosovars (in most states at least a quarter of those protected) tried to stay, either illegally or by filing asylum claims. For some the psychological trauma of 'return' to destroyed houses and towns, in the presence of international peacekeepers and under the guidance of a UN protectorate, was too much. Real safety was where the Albanians now found themselves: in Germany, the Netherlands, the UK and other Western states. However, how truly comfortable (and also sometimes how safe) they could be, depended to a large extent on the evolving perception host populations had of them. At the same time, the more widespread return would be, the more chance there might be of the public and politicians seeking to alter policy approaches, and ultimately legislation, to allow for more generous protection in conflict situations in the future. If uncomfortable 'refugees' are more likely to return, then the host population might, in this context, be expected to try to make 'refugees' as uncomfortable as possible – a notion that is at odds with normally expected standards of humanitarianism and non-discrimination in Europe.

Ultimately, the issue of protection and policy is not determined by the perceptions 'refugees' entertain, but by the perceptions of the 'refugees' entertained by their host population. The labels attached to them are an indication of these perceptions. The perceptions that policymakers have of public perceptions of the 'refugees' and their treatment are the deciding factor in further 'refugee' protection, even if states in principle have to live up to a range of international protection and human rights commitments.

Perceptions of the Kosovar 'refugees' by Western governments and host populations

Prior to the NATO intervention, Kosovar Albanians arriving in Western Europe, often after a boat journey across the Adriatic to Italy and then by road onward to Germany, Switzerland, and the UK (primarily) were most often perceived by policymakers, the media and wide sections of the population alike as illegal immigrants. The increasing reports (whether verified or not) of massacres and terror in the province invoked a sense that the situation must be somewhat unstable and thus 'sad', but not a sense that those affected should seek sanctuary elsewhere. The fact that the Serbian government was clearly not protecting all those in the province of Kosovo did not affect this widespread perception. Some received the protection of non-return, but asylum was rarely forthcoming.

Once the NATO bombing campaign started on 24 March 1999, an

often-heard cry in the West was 'what are we going to do to help'. The sense that 'they can't all come here' was to an extent balanced by the flood of offers of individual hospitality. In many ways, the population and the media were ahead of the governments in their outpourings of generosity. Governments perhaps had a wary eye on the future, but populations were demonstrating that they, and the media they influenced and which influenced them, were in favour of refugee reception. The 'CNN effect' had a lot to do with the inspiration of such sentiments. The scenes of chaos in Albania and Macedonia inspired the sense that something had to be done. In particular those scenes of the burning of passports on the borders, of trains disgorging their human cargo, and the displaced stumbling along railway tracks heading for safety, but occasionally meeting closed borders, were reminiscent for many of scenes from the Second World War. In analysing the outpouring of goodwill, the *Los Angeles Times* pondered the way

> Heavy television coverage of white people with Western clothing, fleeing a European war zone being pummeled by US warplanes raises issues of race, evokes images of World War II, stirs patriotism and comes at a time when American pocketbooks are bulging.[12]

The scenes of chaos were perhaps inevitable, because NATO had informed UNHCR only three days prior to the bombing that it was going to intervene and the agency should anticipate some 100,000 'refugees' leaving the province for Albania and Macedonia.[13] As an estimated 200,000 people were internally displaced at that time, it seems almost predictably unbelievable that any international organization with experience of displacements in the Balkans (which both NATO and UNHCR had) should find the figure of 100,000 'refugees' credible. Particularly if, as was suggested, advance knowledge of 'Operation Horseshoe' was a motivation for intervention, it seems the organizations should have been able to make higher if not ultimately accurate predications of the scale of displacements. Whether the 'horse shoe' operation was really planned or really effected is not the most material point here. If a very large-scale plan to depopulate the province was thought credible in the West, then massive displacements should have been anticipated with or without NATO intervention. However, if NATO states did expect these displacements they seem to have thought they would be internal, not refugee movements, and that Milošević would soon cave in, meaning that whether his regime was forcing displacement, or people were running from NATO bombs, the cause of displacement would soon be removed.

In a sense therefore, NATO, its member states, the EU, US and UNHCR brought upon themselves the confusion that reigned in the European, American, Canadian and Australian populations' perceptions of the 'refugees'. Where 'refugees' had been portrayed in the media and by policymakers as 'scroungers' and undeserving for the past decade (in Europe perhaps more so than in the traditional immigration countries) the 'refugees' were now deserving of NATO protection. Perhaps this was because the Kosovars became, on TV and in reality, refugees in the sense that everyone understands the term 'refugee'. They were seen as moving in massive numbers, being protected in harsh but safe conditions close to home, and thus the popular perception of them as refugees indicated they should and would move on to 'better' protection elsewhere. And since they were European, and therefore 'close', they should move on to protection in Europe and traditional reception states.

They became tangible and recognizable via the media, and especially television, images. Families were singled out. They were followed in their anguish in the camps; in their joy on arrival in the state of the TV crew following them; in the perplexing circumstances of being offered gifts of, for example, old clothes and toys; and in their uncertainty of what to do once they were expected to leave again, and go back to Kosovo, still followed by TV cameras.[14] They were 'just like us' except they came from a place where the government refused to protect them, and in fact expelled them.[15] Unless, that is, one follows the thoughts of the Serbian propaganda machine cited in the *Salt Lake Tribune* as claiming that the Kosovo 'refugees' were paid actors, employed by NATO at the sum of $5.50.[16]

The chaos of the so-called protection initially offered to the victims of Milošević (and the protecting NATO forces) meant television pictures would be transmitted inspiring compassion. That compassion turned the displaced of Kosovo from illegal immigrants into 'refugees' in the eyes of populations around Europe and its allies. No longer 'bogus asylum seekers' the Kosovo Albanians became genuine refugees, for all but the governments who would decide on their status. For those governments the majority of Kosovars, whether admitted under the Humanitarian Evacuation Programme organized by the UNHCR out of Macedonia, arriving spontaneously or being transferred from previous illegality or waiting, fell under programmes of temporary protection.

The hastily constructed Humanitarian Evacuation Programme is another area in which the lack of advance planning became apparent. The UNHCR-commissioned independent evaluation of the UNHCR's activities in the Kosovo crisis charges the organization with a lack of contingency planning. The report's authors claim that more planning was needed for 'burden sharing', with richer, more distant states relieving the pressure on neighbouring states, who might see their own security called into question through the protection of significant numbers of the displaced. UNHCR responds that it cannot, politically speaking, co-ordinate such contingency planning, which may anyway have the effect of leading neighbouring states to shirk their own Convention responsibilities.

The evaluation suggests that UNHCR should have given more and earlier attention to the probability that the refugees would not be admitted to a potential country of asylum, and that alternative protection strategies should have been explored. UNHCR is concerned that contingency planning which assumes that states will not comply with their responsibilities to receive and host new arrivals, particularly in mass influx situations, runs the risk of becoming a self-fulfilling prophecy. At a time when the commitment of states to the institution of asylum appears to be in decline, that risk is real and dangerous.[17]

The legal and political arguments about first asylum and burden sharing are not so important to this chapter as the fact that the requirement populations placed on their governments in Western Europe to act became all the stronger precisely because no such arrangement was in place. If burden sharing had been preconceived and enacted, there would have been no need for Macedonia either to close its Blace border post or to make very loud and public threats to withdraw its support for NATO's presence within its territory (NATO being initially there to maintain stability in the face of Macedonia's own precarious position, ethnically and geographically). If displaced Kosovars had been moved on to other states from the beginning, there would have been fewer protests by Macedonia's Slav population, which formed only a small majority, and felt threatened by the sudden larger presence of ethnic Albanians, fresh from the conflict with Slavic Serbs in Yugoslavia.

There are very few measures of political or ethnic instability, prior to a conflict actually breaking out, which could be called objectively reliable. In the area of minority issues, the Organization for Security and Cooperation in Europe (OSCE) established the position of a High Commissioner on National Minorities in 1992. The sole incumbent to date, former Dutch Foreign Minister Max van der Stoel, has undertaken quiet diplomatic efforts in a number of countries with significant minority populations, including Macedonia. Mr van der Stoel has not used his mandated ability to issue early warning of a conflict situation: he is not prone to 'crying wolf'. In the situation of the massive influx of 'refugees' to Macedonia, however, Mr van der Stoel did issue a formal warning on 12 May 1999 that 'unless the international community significantly increases its efforts to help the country ... a destabilisation could occur.' Van der Stoel is not mandated to comment on Macedonia's closure of the border, and his visit to the country on 9–11 May 1999 did not coincide with dates of border closure. However, this is a clear argument supporting the perception that neighbouring states could not cope with the massive influxes without the threat of further instability. These perceptions translated also into the thinking that those people who were so like 'us' were still suffering in camps, and were suffering even more if they could not make it to the camps.

The perception garnered by the sight on television screens of Kosovars stopped short of the Macedonian border being turned back into the land from which they were trying to flee, triggered a sense of helpless recognition in a general public whose emotions had been touched by films such as *Schindler's List*. While Western Europe was tired of all the 'refugees' it could not face the idea of allowing scenes reminiscent of the Second World War being enacted live and for real on news programmes.

Kosovar Albanians thus seem to have been perceived by European and other populations as needy victims: as 'real refugees'. This concurred largely with the view presented by the fact of NATO bombing. However, it flew in the face of the past decade of restrictionist views towards all 'refugees', and governments, often accused of short-termism, seemed rather to be looking towards the medium term by granting only temporary protection while talking of 'refugees'.

Another facet of this medium-term thinking by governments was the approach called 'reception in the region'. According to this strategy, the 'refugees' could be protected by any given state while actually being on the territory of Albania or Macedonia. Thus camps were set up, notably by the Italian, Austrian and Danish governments. These camps often seemed to be vying for the prize of most luxurious. No investment was spared in the attempt to ensure the displaced were comfortable in Albania and Macedonia, and thus not seeking the path to Italy, Austria, Denmark and other states.[18] Other deterrence strategies employed included the claim that states had 'done enough already', either through involvement in the NATO actions, or through past deeds of protecting Bosnians, or by converting the already present, and until then 'unwanted' immigrants from Kosovo into 'our refugees'.[19] The US expressed the desire to accept some 10,000 Kosovar Albanians at its Cuban base, Guantanamo Bay, regularly used for the reception and processing of asylum claims from the Caribbean region, though this option was not ultimately used.

The American public, like the European public, seemed prepared to be open-hearted in a way which took policymakers by surprise. The French authorities were overwhelmed with offers of shelter in private homes.[20] Appeals in many countries raised millions of dollars, some spent on camps in Macedonia and Albania, some on reception in more distant states. Refugee aid workers and some journalists were left wondering why and how, making comparisons to the amounts of money, as well as time and attention, devoted to African refugees.[21]

Somehow, the public had leapt, unexpectedly, ahead of governments in their will to protect the Kosovars. While governments worried about signals linked to ethnic cleansing, and longer term potential problems about return, integration and xenophobia, the public desire seemed simply to be to protect the people. The government reaction was largely predictable, the public's was not. However, the public's reaction was perhaps in retrospect superficial. Anyway, at the time, the long-term intensity of xenophobic reaction apparently held more influence over European asylum policy-makers than the short-term depth of feeling for Kosovars.

Just weeks after the Kosovo intervention, as Chechnya lay in ruins with comparisons to Kosovo abounding, and as massive displacements amid violence occurred in East Timor, aid workers were again wondering why Kosovo had been so different. Yet that very wonderment showed that the aftermath of the perceptions of refugeehood in the Kosovo crisis might have some effect on future crises.

Once the intervention was over and NATO troops and UNMIK administration were on the ground in Kosovo, people from the province, as from elsewhere in Yugoslavia, who arrived in Western Europe became smuggled illegal immigrants (scroungers) once again. They had to turn to smugglers once the evacuation programmes came to an end. And for those who had been protected it was time to return. The return to Kosovo from Albania and Macedonia was the most rapid and massive 'refugee' return ever recorded: 600,000 people returned in just a few days. From states further afield the return process was somewhat slower, in spite of often attractive return packages, offered under the auspices of the International Organization for Migration, which generally co-ordinates return programmes. By June 2000, most EU states had seen some 75 per cent of the numbers of people accepted on the evacuation programme return to Kosovo. (The statistics are unclear as the return programme also included spontaneous arrivals and people previously seeking refuge in the EU states in question, so the figures, when compared to the evacuation programme figures, will not always really be as 'successful' as they look.) Some states had, however, seen returns far exceeding the programme arrival figures, indicating that their efforts to encourage return had taken many non-quota Kosovars back to the province too.[22]

Whether the province was really safe for return, and lived up to those conditions the Kosovars interviewed in camps had set, remains open to question. The NATO Secretary General, in his report *Kosovo One Year On*, asserts that the murder rate, while still too high, is down from 500 per week in July 1999 to five per week. However, Lord Robertson says that to allow the 1.35 million people (550,000 internally displaced and 800,000 from Albania, Macedonia and other states) who had returned home to remain there, a lot still needs to be done, not least the deterrence, through NATO presence, of further acts of persecution.[23]

Conclusions

After the Kosovo crisis, in May 2000, the European Commission submitted a draft directive on temporary protection to the Council of Ministers of the European Union.[24] Where previous Commission proposals on temporary protection had been based on the Bosnian experience, Kosovo influenced this one. The content of this directive was discussed in advance by Justice and Home Affairs Commissioner Vittorino with the member state governments. It involves a two-year period prior to assessment for Convention refugee status and does not focus on return so much as on the need for protection. It draws on the experience of Kosovo, particularly the notion that return can be effectuated rapidly, and that 'refugees' do not all stay for ever. However, it does not deal with issues such as the need for quota evacuations if solidarity with neighbouring states is to be displayed, or indeed if some measure of simple solidarity between EU states is to be enacted.[25] Neither does it deal specifically with the notion that, to bring about return, the EU states may in fact need to put themselves and the organizations they are committed to on the line. If populations perceived the need to protect the 'refugees' of Kosovo it was in part because they saw that the NATO governments were risking the future of the continent's security establishment on this conflict. The stakes were not only humanitarian and refugee protection stakes: the very nature of the post-Cold War security architecture in Europe was on the line. However, the conflict having seen a NATO winner (at least on paper) the question on which this chapter is centred is: will refugee protection win too?

Prior to the intervention few Kosovars were receiving refugee status, or more protection than non-removal on technical grounds. Yet one year after the intervention the NATO Secretary General wrote:

> organized acts of violence, repression, provocation, and retribution continued on both sides, particularly on the part of Serb forces and paramilitaries. In its December 1999 report – Kosovo/Kosova As Seen, As Told – the OSCE Office for Democratic Institutions and Human Rights (ODIHR) estimates that as many as 350,000 Kosovars, overwhelmingly Albanian, but including some Serbs, were displaced from their homes by the end of 1998.[26]

Would such displaced persons now, with the experience of the Kosovo intervention, be more likely to be protected farther afield? Probably not. Might NATO be inspired to intervene again on such a scale? Maybe – but that depends on the circumstances. Would the possibility of massive refugee displacements inspire intervention again? Maybe, again dependent on circumstances. Would the EU and other Western states be ready to offer meaningful protection on a short time basis to massive numbers of 'refugees'? If the temporary protection proposal on the table after Kosovo is accepted, then this could be the strongest 'maybe' in this list. For governments now know that in spite of the xenophobic sentiments often voiced about immigration and refugee protection some crises can strike a chord in popular perceptions, and then populations expect governments to act and to protect. It may have been NATO's intervention that caused this outpouring of goodwill in the Kosovo case; it may have been the 'just like us', 'real refugees' or CNN factors. However governments and international organizations cannot afford the chaos again in a case that strikes a chord. So at least the next case may well be met by a more co-ordinated and protective response – especially if it happens to be in Europe. For the post-Kosovo cases of Chechnya and East Timor have already demonstrated that public sympathy for 'refugees' is a fickle thing, yet its legacy may live on, for a brief period at least, in EU policymaking on refugee issues.

Acknowledgements

I am very grateful to Susan Martin, Director of ISIM for her comments on this chapter, and to both her and Andy Schoenholtz also of ISIM for discussions on this subject. Responsibility for the chapter remains my own.

Notes

1. Throughout this chapter the word refugee will be used without inverted commas where it refers to those people recognized as refugees by states. It will be used with inverted commas ('refugees') where it refers to people who in everyday language would be called refugees, but who may not have been recognized formally as such, but rather have another status, or no status, even if they are in a 'refugee-like situation'.
2. Milenko Vasović, 'Serb Refugees Rejected by Belgrade', War Report at http://www.iwpr.net, 23 June 1999.
3. War Report, 'Waiting in the Dark in Pristina', 29 March 1999.
4. American Association for the Advancement of Science, *Survey of Kosovar Refugees Project: Survey of Refugees' Attitudes about Return,* 14 June 1999, at http://www.aaas.org.
5. K. M. Greenhill, 'People Pressure: the Coercive Use of Refugees in the Kosovo Conflict', paper presented at the 2000 Annual meeting of the American Political Science Association.
6. This type of view might support a perception on the part of Kosovar Albanians that the NATO states should take them in to protect them – after all, according to this logic, NATO would want them away from the province. F. Nazi, 'Cleansing Kosovo', War Report, 31 March 1999.
7. For simplicity's sake I will refer to the Former Yugoslav Republic of Macedonia (FYROM) as Macedonia in this chapter.
8. I. Rusi, 'Macedonia In The Middle', War Report, 23 March 1999.

9. I. Rusi, 'Stuck in the Macedonian Mud', War Report, 5 May 1999.
10. G. Ignic, 'The Black Market to Nowhere', War Report, 13 May 1999.
11. *Volkskrant*, 26 April 1999, p. 5.
12. 'Outpouring of Goodwill for Refugees Amazes Officials', *Los Angeles Times*, 23 May 1999.
13. Confidential interview with an official involved.
14. The Dutch nightly TV news magazine NOVA followed a family like this, as did the *Volkskrant* newspaper. This pattern was repeated in other Western states. In some senses this seems like the news media following the 'reality' TV seen in the formula shows such as 'Big Brother' and 'Survivor'.
15. M. J. Gibney, 'Kosovo and Beyond: Popular and Unpopular Refugees', *Forced Migration Review*, vol. 5 (August 1999), pp. 28–30.
16. Whether the $5.50 was per hour, day, week or for the duration of the displacement was not mentioned.
17. *The Kosovo Refugee Crisis: An Independent Evaluation of UNHCR's Emergency Preparedness and Response* (Geneva: UNHCR, February 2000), at http://www.unhcr.ch/evaluate/Kosovo/unhcr.htm (cited from Appendix D).
18. T. Porter, 'Coordination in the Midst of Chaos', *Forced Migration Review*, 5 August 1999, pp. 20–3.
19. Elspeth Guild, 'The United Kingdom: Kosovar Albanian Refugees' in J. van Selm (ed.), *Kosovo's Refugees in the European Union* (London: Pinter, 2000), pp. 67–90. The UK employed this latter strategy, quite unsuccessfully. The government announced it would accept a quota of 10,000 refugees who, incidentally, were already there. One month before the end of the intervention the UK introduced a new quota of 1000 per week, and did, in four weeks, actually take in some 4000 people.
20. S. Lavanex, in J. van Selm (ed.), *Kosovo's Refugees in the European Union* (London: Pinter, 2000), pp. 162–88.
21. T. C. Miller and A. M. Simmons, 'Refugee Camps in Africa and Europe are a World Apart', *Los Angeles Times*, 22 May 1999.
22. IOM at http://www.iom.int.
23. Lord Robertson of Port Ellen, Secretary General of NATO, 'Kosovo One Year On: Achievement and Challenge', at http://www.nato.int.
24. European Commission, *Proposal for a Council Directive on Minimum Standards for giving Temporary Protection in the Event of a Mass Influx of Displaced Persons and on Measures Promoting a Balance of Efforts between Member States in Receiving such Persons and Bearing the Consequences Thereof*, at http://europa.eu.int/eur-lex/en/com/dat/2000/en_500PC0303.html.
25. 'Conclusion' in J. van Selm (ed.), *Kosovo's Refugees in the European Union* (London: Pinter, 2000), pp. 189–209.
26. Robertson, *op. cit.*

CHAPTER SEVENTEEN

The Concept of Humanitarian Intervention Revisited*

JAMES MAYALL

The last decade of the twentieth century opened and closed with wars that were ended as the result of international interventions. Operation Desert Storm, which ousted Iraq from Kuwait in January 1991, was an American-led, predominantly Western military campaign. But it was mounted with a mandate under Chapter VII of the UN Charter, with the unanimous support of the Security Council, and the enthusiastic backing of all the Middle Eastern states, with the exception of Jordan. NATO's bombardment of former Yugoslavia in March 1999 eventually succeeded in forcing the Serbs out of Kosovo. It was again led by the US but this time without Security Council approval, and in the face of considerable international criticism. In this chapter my purpose is to re-examine the political and intellectual background to the debate on humanitarian intervention that has waxed and waned since the end of the Cold War, before considering if there are any new lessons to be learned as a result of the Kosovo crisis.

The Gulf War was initially fought to reverse an aggression, not for humanitarian reasons. Indeed, many of those opposed to the war pointed out that Kuwait's human rights record left much to be desired. But Saddam Hussein's brutal suppression of the northern Kurdish and southern Shiite rebellions after the war led the Western powers to risk offending some of their erstwhile supporters by their decision to establish safe havens for the Kurds and Shiites.[1] Operation Desert Storm was able

* An earlier version of this chapter appeared as 'The Concept of Humanitarian Intervention Revisited' in Albrecht Schnabel and Ramesh Thakur (eds), *Kosovo and the Challenges of Humanitarian Intervention: Selective Indignation, Collective Action and International Citizenship*, (Tokyo: United Nations University Press, 2000). I am grateful to the publisher for allowing me to reproduce sections from this essay.

to secure wide support because, while it repulsed Iraq's aggression, it left Iraqi sovereignty and territorial integrity intact. On the other hand, China and some non-permanent members of the Security Council were reluctant to approve further intervention once the primary objective had been achieved.

By contrast, NATO justified its intervention in Yugoslavia as a humanitarian operation from the start. In the British Defence Secretary's words, it was fought 'to avert a humanitarian catastrophe by disrupting the violent attacks currently being carried out by the Yugoslav security forces against the Kosovo Albanians and to limit their ability to conduct such repression in the future.'[2] But, on closer inspection, the two episodes reveal more continuity than change. It is true that, in Kosovo, the UN was only involved at the close of the campaign, whereas in northern Iraq the West argued that its actions were covered by previous Security Council resolutions. But, in neither case were the Western powers prepared to seek a new Security Council Resolution, for fear – and in the latter case the certainty – of facing a veto.

In the period between the Gulf War and the Kosovo crisis, the UN was involved in an unprecedented number of conflicts – fourteen in Africa alone.[3] The majority were intra rather than interstate conflicts and UN intervention was driven by the need to provide humanitarian relief, alongside, and indeed as an essential ingredient of, more traditional peace-keeping and peace-making functions. Most of these operations were based on Chapter VI mandates. In other words, they depended on the consent of previously conflicting parties. In the minority of operations that were based on a Chapter VII mandate – those in Somalia, Bosnia, Rwanda, Haiti and Albania, where the intervening states were authorized to use force to achieve their humanitarian objectives – opinions differ widely on their success.[4] In Bosnia, the war was only ended after the US had seized the diplomatic initiative from the UN and the peace-keeping operation had been taken over by NATO. Moreover, the peace conference held in Dayton, Ohio, in November 1995 was facilitated by the United States and its allies turning a blind eye to Croatia's ethnic cleansing of the Krajina, an action that was hardly consistent with the humanitarian objectives for which the UN operation had been established.

After Dayton, there was little further debate about the rights and wrongs of humanitarian intervention, or indeed about its practicability. Western publics – it was said – were suffering from compassion fatigue. The debate was inevitably rekindled, however, by the NATO action against Yugoslavia over its treatment of the Kosovo Albanians, if only because of the uncomfortable fact that most of the refugees, whose return was NATO's major war aim, had been forced out of Kosovo after the beginning of the bombing campaign.[5] The humanitarian motives of the NATO powers are not in doubt (although they clearly had other powerful

267

motives as well). What remains in doubt is whether humanitarian intervention is consistent with the prevailing norms of international society? In order to answer this question it will be helpful to locate it within the theory of international relations from which it derives.

Humanitarian intervention in liberal international theory

The concept of humanitarian intervention occupies an ambiguous place in the theory and practice of international society. At first sight, this may seem strange because, in other areas of social life, for example, medicine or public health, advances in welfare could not have been achieved without human intervention. Extreme advocates of *laissez faire* may cling to the view that social and economic progress has depended on governments refraining from interference in the market, but even a cursory examination of the record will prove them wrong. Only in international relations does the concept of intervention retain its sinister reputation.

The reason is not mysterious. It flows from the fact that the modern international system has been constructed on the basis of the principle of sovereignty. This principle is not only the foundation of international law but of the diplomatic system. It is sometimes argued that economic globalization has made it obsolete – that the money that lubricates the contemporary world is no more respectful of international borders than the tsetse fly. But while transnational market integration may indeed have made it more difficult for national governments to exercise sovereign authority, it has done nothing to replace international borders with an alternative structure. It is only when a doctor embarks upon a treatment expressly against the will of the patient that intervention becomes problematic. In international society the states are the patients but there are no doctors. It is for this reason that the term intervention is normally confined to coercive action to make another government – or armed movement – do something it would not otherwise choose to do.

The states system, which developed from the mid-seventeenth century was a self-help system. It established a quasi-constitutional order that outlawed religious war but was otherwise highly permissive. The formula *cuius regio eius religio,* the ancestor clause of the modern non-interference principle, left sovereigns free to pursue their interests by whatever means they saw fit, up to and including war for reasons of state and territorial conquest. Moreover, as the natural law tradition gradually gave way to legal positivism, lawyers became more concerned with developing the concept of a fair fight – *ius in bello* – in war between European states than with the requirement that the war itself should be just – *ius ad bellum*. Non-intervention, it seemed, was consistent with a system of power politics.

Sovereignty can be exercised either by prescriptive right, or under representative arrangements designed to reflect 'the will of the people'. Since the French and American revolutions dynastic rule has increasingly given way to various forms of popular sovereignty. But, from one point of view, whether rule is exercised by prescription or on the basis of representation, makes little difference: either way sovereign powers are ultimately accountable to the people over whom they exercise their authority. In democratic countries they can be removed through the ballot box; in authoritarian states, if the rulers systematically oppress the bulk of the population – minorities are, unhappily, another matter – they will eventually face a popular insurrection. Internally, it is thus ultimately the ethic of accountability that justifies the self-help system.

Self-help at the international level is more problematic. This is because, until the end of the nineteenth century, once across the border, self-help was more often than not translated as 'help yourself'. Colonial expansion had not seriously troubled the European conscience because, in a mercantilist age, it was taken for granted that there would always be winners and losers. A zero-sum worldview might not be very edifying but that was the way it was assumed to be. Since, under dynasticism, people had at best very limited political and civil rights – and in many countries none at all – European governments did not have to fear charges of double standards.

All this changed in the nineteenth century. Western imperialism was now driven forward by the two leading European democracies: Britain and France. For a time, they justified their enclosure of the non-European world by theories, which sought to explain Western dominance by analogy to Darwin's theory of natural selection. But however convenient, social Darwinism was never convincing. Once the idea of equality before the law, and equal civil and political rights, had been entrenched at home, it was only a matter of time before the discriminatory treatment of colonial subjects would appear contradictory, not merely to the victims, whose knowledge of their situation was brought home to them by exposure to Western education and values, but to the imperialists themselves.

John Stuart Mill attempted a moral defence of imperial intervention – in relation to the British annexation of the independent princely state of Oudh – on the grounds that since Britain exercised absolute authority in the surrounding territory, it could not escape responsibility for the destitution into which the ruler had allowed his country to fall.[6] Although in domestic politics it is widely held that governments must be held accountable for their actions, Mill's argument has not often been used by those wishing to claim a right of humanitarian intervention. They have been mostly reluctant to follow his logic, presumably because of the difficulty of distinguishing between humanitarian, and less worthy, motives for intervention. Indeed, at the international level, non-intervention, like non-discrimination in economic affairs, is generally assumed to be an impeccably liberal principle.

With a Millian approach to the problem of humanitarian intervention blocked off, the question has been discussed, on the one hand, in terms of the duties of governments to uphold individual human rights, and, on the other, of the recognition that, there may be some violations of these rights that are so massive as to justify a breach of the principle of non-intervention under exceptional circumstances. Theoretically, these two positions are not mutually exclusive, but in practice those who stress the first tend to see international law as the primary instrument for developing international society along progressive lines, while those who accept that it is impossible – and indeed undesirable – for the law to cover all contingencies, regard the law as a pivotal but in the final analysis subordinate institution of international society. In short, the first group, work within a legalist paradigm, the second within a political one.

The failure of legalism between the two world wars led to a reassertion of the primacy of politics, and, through the Security Council, the reaffirmation of the special responsibility of the great powers for international order – it had also been recognized in the Council of the League of Nations. Paradoxically, it was these same powers that were responsible for promulgating two new international crimes – crimes against humanity and war crimes. It was also the great powers that, in 1948, secured the passage of the Genocide Convention, which sought to establish the prevention and punishment of genocide as a peremptory norm of international law. It could be argued, therefore, that the post-1945 international society was deliberately reconstructed to uphold the principle of state sovereignty, but also on occasion to allow it to be breached. However, before 1990 such breaches of the non-intervention rule as occurred – and there were many – were not justified on humanitarian grounds. In those cases where such a defence could most plausibly have been offered – in the Indian intervention on behalf of the Bengali separatists in East Pakistan, in Tanzania's deposition of the Ugandan dictator, Idi Amin, and in Vietnam's action against Pol Pot's genocidal regime in Cambodia – it was not. By 1989 the majority of governments had ratified the Universal Declaration of Human Rights and its two supporting covenants, but this did not prevent them from sheltering, with impunity, behind Articles 2.4 and 2.7 of the Charter.

Thus, after 1945, international society was reconstructed on the basis of an unequal compromise between power and law. The use of force, other than in self-defence, was to be sanctioned only on the authority of the Security Council and only then when the Council determined that a threat to international peace and security existed and that all alternative means of settlement had been exhausted. Under the Genocide Convention there was also provision for a reference to the Security Council, presumably in the expectation – although this interpretation was never tested – that it would rule that genocide could also justify action under Chapter VII. In other words, it was tacitly accepted that deciding when to trigger the collective security provisions of the Charter could not be determined solely by objective criteria, and without reference to the national interests of the major powers.

Humanitarian intervention in the 1990s

How far has this traditional thought and practice been modified by events since the end of the Cold War? The collapse of communism and the disintegration of the Soviet Union were followed by violent conflicts in many parts of the world, which provided the setting for an expanded UN security role. There are those who argue that none of these operations were either appropriate or successful.[7] Nonetheless, where they followed, rather than accompanied, the negotiation of a political settlement – as in Namibia, Cambodia, and Mozambique – UN forces were able to reinforce the work of humanitarian agencies and contribute to political stabilization. On the other hand, where the humanitarian catastrophe was the direct result of the absence of any such settlement – or at least one to which the parties were seriously committed – UN intervention probably had more negative than positive results.

The reluctance of the major powers to sanction new peacekeeping operations in the second half of the 1990s is only partly explained by budgetary constraints. More centrally, it is related to the discovery, in the Somali and Bosnian conflicts, that there was no Chapter six-and-a-half solution. Traditional peacekeeping required the consent of the parties and, particularly where the UN was engaged in active peace building as well, their confidence in its impartiality. Enforcement, on the other hand, requires partiality, at least at the point of intervention and until those responsible for the crisis have been restrained and persuaded to co-operate.

This observation only seems obvious with hindsight. It was perhaps unfortunate that the UN's new role in the security field should have been tested in two of the most intractable civil conflicts anywhere in the world. In former Yugoslavia, once the overarching federal structure had been removed, the populations of the successor republics refused to accept the legitimacy of their previously internal – but now international – borders. What were formally interstate wars had all the characteristics of a ferocious civil war, in which compromise fails in the face of the passionate and self-righteous believe of the belligerents in the justice of their respective causes.

The result was that, even under Chapter VII, to which the Security Council eventually resorted, it was impossible to fashion a mandate that would allow the UN to do more than soften the worst consequences of the competitive ethnic cleansing in which all sides engaged. The preferred American strategy, of air strikes against the Serbs, whom they identified as the main culprits, had the advantage of not confusing humanitarian relief with peace enforcement, but it left those countries with troops on the ground dangerously exposed to hostage taking by the Serb dominated Yugoslav army. The open disagreement amongst the Western powers about how to deal with the crisis also inevitably whittled away at the UN's authority.

If the confusion in former Yugoslavia arose from the fact that the overlapping wars were at once civil and international, in Somalia, the collapse of the state had much the same effect. In both countries social life was reduced to the level of a primitive and anarchic state of war. The international response to the Somali crisis was again framed within Chapter VII mandates. But, in this case, the prospects for the restoration of stability were even bleaker. In Bosnia, the rival Serb and Croat communities seemed determined to make their political and communal boundaries congruent, leaving the hapless Bosnian Muslims trapped in the middle, but territorial partition could at least provide a basis for a settlement. Inter-clan conflict in southern Somalia was less susceptible to mediation, because, in a still predominantly nomadic population, the competition for power was not primarily territorial.[8] When the UN finally withdrew from Somalia, it left the situation in the country fundamentally unaltered.

It is important not to exaggerate the extent of the UN's failure in the interventions of the early 1990s. In both Bosnia and Somalia, lives were saved. In Somalia, where in order to deliver humanitarian assistance, NGOs had to buy protection with money that was then used to purchase the weapons and supplies that fed the conflict, the worst aspects of this vicious circle were broken. The failure was political, not humanitarian: those targeted were not coerced into changing their objectives, with the result that the major powers came to fear being drawn into conflicts, in which their own interests were not seriously engaged, and from which there was no easy escape. In the US, the Clinton administration led the way by setting new conditions under which the US would be prepared to contribute to multi-lateral peacekeeping operations – not only would American troops only serve under US command, but they would only engage in operations where time limits could be set in advance and an exit strategy established at the outset.[9]

The realization that civil conflicts could not be resolved on the basis of humanitarian intervention had disastrous consequences in Rwanda.

When, in April 1994, the Hutu dominated government embarked upon a systematic genocide of ethnic Tutsi, the UN peacekeeping force was scaled down to a point where it could not hope to stem the killing. Moreover, the nineteen countries that had promised troops for a traditional peacekeeping operation to oversee the implementation of the Arusha Accords withdrew their offer once it was clear that the agreement was dead and that the conflict had been intensified.[10]

In these circumstances it was perhaps not surprising that the Security Council deliberately refrained from identifying the Rwandan crisis as genocide. To have called the slaughter by its proper name would have made it difficult to avoid intervention. But to do what? In this case the allocation of blame was relatively straightforward, but since the guilty government in Kigali could plausibly claim to represent around 85% of the population it was unclear on what basis a new order could be constructed so long as Rwandan society remained divided along ethnic lines. Operation Turquoise, the French-led operation that was eventually established under a Chapter VII mandate, may have helped to stop the slaughter. But France had been so identified with the regime that had initiated the genocide that its failure to separate ordinary refugees from their political and military leaders was - rightly or wrongly - widely regarded as being politically motivated.

The failure to take effective action to stop the Rwandan genocide coincided with the decision of the Security Council to authorize the use of force to restore to power the elected, but subsequently deposed, Haitian President. In taking this decision, the Council referred specifically to 'the significant further deterioration of the humanitarian situation in Haiti, in particular the continuing escalation by the illegal *de facto* regime of systematic violations of civil liberties'.[11] For the first time, force was authorized by the UN to change the government of a member state. In this sense, a precedent has been set, and the territorial interpretation of sovereignty as effective control was called into question. Yet, whether Haiti will *in fact* establish a precedent seems doubtful - it was the American interest in stemming the flood of Haitian refugees to the US, rather than humanitarianism, that finally drove the operation forward.[12]

The answer to the question posed at the beginning of this section thus seems clear. Humanitarian considerations have greater political salience than during the Cold War, but they are insufficient to compel the international community to act in the absence of more specific motives. After the Cold War, Western governments took the lead in promoting human rights and democratic values, but their willingness to intervene in the domestic affairs of states whose governments transgressed these norms, remained highly selective, particularly where their own interests were not directly involved. The constitutional order of international society had not been fundamentally modified.

JAMES MAYALL

Kosovo and the future of humanitarian intervention

At first sight, this conclusion seems to be reinforced by the international reaction to the Kosovo crisis. Not only was it impossible to act through the Security Council because of the opposition of Russia and China to NATO's campaign, but the intervention was motivated at least as much by the need to maintain the organization's credibility as by humanitarian objectives. Nonetheless, the scale of the operation and the way it was finally resolved inevitably reopened the question of the place of humanitarian intervention in international society and the current understanding of its core principle of sovereignty. In conclusion, let us reconsider these questions under two heads – the legality of humanitarian intervention and its feasibility.

The law of humanitarian intervention

The Kosovo crisis exposed the sharp conflict between those who view international society within a legalist paradigm and those who insist on the primacy of politics. This dispute is not about the importance of the rule of law to international society but about whether it is to be the servant or master of the state.

During the 1990s, the Security Council adopted a series of resolutions sanctioning the use of force in support of humanitarian objectives – in Iraq, Bosnia and Herzegovina, Somalia, Rwanda and Albania. However, as Catherine Guicherd has pointed out, 'the combined right of victims to assistance and the right of the Security Council to authorise humanitarian intervention with military means do not amount to a right of humanitarian intervention by states individually or collectively.'[13] The Security Council was able to pass these resolutions because its permanent members were mostly in agreement – and even when China disagreed, it refrained from backing its dissent with a veto – and because in each case the Council ruled that the situation constituted a threat to international peace and security. Neither of these conditions obtained in Kosovo.

Faced with this reality, international lawyers have adopted one of three positions. Some have stuck to the letter of the Charter, arguing that NATO action was illegal and that, regardless of the merits of the ethical argument in this particular case, 'if it is accepted that a state or group of states can unilaterally decide to intervene ... The door will have been opened to all sorts of subjective claims as to when interventions are justified and when they are not.'[14] Others have suggested that the Security Council itself should be reformed by 'increasing the representation of Asia, Africa and Latin America, and replacing the right of veto by a system of qualified majority voting'.[15] Such reforms would widen the political basis on which Security Council resolutions depend, and complicate the political bargaining that underlies them but they would not in themselves

274

subordinate politics to the law. Reaching a consensus would face similar practical difficulties as would redrafting the Charter to provide for explicit criteria for humanitarian intervention. Whether the end result would justify the requisite investment of time and effort is doubtful.

Finally, there are those who argue that the legal basis of NATO's action is based on the doctrine of representation, which has underpinned the states-system since 1945. Marc Weller argues plausibly that humanitarian action is justified 'where a government or effective authority actively exterminates its populace, or where it denies to it that which is necessary for its survival, or where it forcibly displaces it'.[16] In these circumstances, the government cannot conceivably claim to be the exclusive international representative of that very population. Weller attempts to set restrictive criteria that must be met before a legal dissociation of government and population can be triggered, and suggests that in Kosovo, the 12–3 defeat of the Russian draft resolution in the Security Council, provides evidence that they had been met.

Time will tell if international society is, in fact, evolving constitutionally along the lines suggested by this theory. In those cases where peace-keeping operations have been authorized since the NATO bombing campaign – in East Timor, Sierra Leone and putatively the Democratic Republic of the Congo – there has been a retreat of Chapter VI mandates. These are relatively uncontentious (although in East Timor the Chinese refused to co-operate until the Indonesian government withdrew its objections) and, since they depend on the consent of all parties, are in any case consistent with the traditional order of international society. From a political perspective, moreover, the disassociation theory faces two problems. The first is establishing the criteria, ahead of time, so they be seen to be more than *ex post facto* ratification of a successful plea for intervention. More seriously, even if a fundamental dissociation is accepted as a legitimate trigger, whether or not the theory takes hold will depend crucially on the practical outcome of specific interventions. The law will not stand up if these turn out to have perverse effects.

Feasibility

In one sense NATO's action in Kosovo avoided two related contradictions in which earlier interventions were mired. The first was between ends and means; the second between peacekeeping and enforcement. Throughout the early post Cold-War period, the Security Council exhibited a disturbing tendency to will the end but not the means. In Kosovo, NATO made it clear from the outset that it was prepared to commit whatever level of air power proved necessary to force President Milošević to withdraw Yugoslav forces from the province. Since this was the objective, the problem of impartiality did not arise.

At a deeper level, however, it is not clear that these contradictions have been overcome. Apart from the question of legality, most critics of the NATO operation commentated on the reluctance of the intervening states – above all the US – to commit land forces. Their determination to fight a risk-free clean war (at least from their own point of view) revealed a weak point in the democratic armoury. It has been, in large part, Western public opinion, orchestrated through the media and NGOs, that has demanded international action in response to humanitarian disasters around the world. At the same time, democratic politicians have been understandably wary of putting their own citizens at risk in conflicts that do not directly concern them.

It is arguable that Milošević would have been prepared to back down sooner had it been made clear to him at the outset, rather than two months into the operation, that NATO would, if necessary, deploy its superior force on land as well as in the air. That they did not do so can perhaps be explained by the difficulty in maintaining solidarity in an Alliance, some of whose members would have refused to take part in a land war. On the other hand, since military opinion did not favour an unsupported air war, NATO's political leaders must accept responsibility for the very high-level damage inflicted on Yugoslavia in pursuit of their goals.

Peace enforcement raises the question of ultimate as well as immediate responsibility. The protection of the victims of persecution and the relief of suffering can be viewed as ends in themselves at the point of intervention. Over the long run, however, it becomes necessary to reconstruct society in ways that will insure against a recurrence of the initial disaster. How is this to be done?

A model of a kind is available. In Cambodia – and to some extent during the transfer of power in Namibia – the UN assumed many of the functions of the civil administration. In both cases it also organized and oversaw the first democratic elections. Then, under the terms of the agreement, which had been drawn up prior to its involvement, the UN withdrew. Unfortunately, the model is not well adapted to situations in which the state itself has failed or where – as in Kosovo – the peace that has been enforced requires the dismantling of the previous authority on the grounds that it shares responsibility for the humanitarian disaster.

In the early 1990s, there was talk of reviving the concept of a UN Trusteeship, in order to provide an impartial, stable and accountable administration, in countries that would require an extended period of reconstruction. Intellectually appealing, this idea, nonetheless, failed to win any backers. The major powers were reluctant to enter into commitments that promised to be open ended and expensive, and were likely to be criticized for reintroducing imperialism by the back door.

Once the immediate situation has been addressed, however, it is

difficult to avoid the conclusion that the logic of humanitarian intervention is imperial. How else is a broken society to be rebuilt? In 1945, the
victorious Allies demanded unconditional surrender of the German and
Japanese governments, precisely because they believed that the only way
to avoid history repeating itself, was to reconstruct society comprehensively. In these cases, the vital interests of the Western powers were so
deeply involved in the outcome, that there was no temptation to seek a
quick fix and then withdraw. It may be that events will force them to do
much the same in Bosnia and Kosovo. However, in contrast to the Second
World War, which was understood to be a fight to the finish from the start,
so far in post-Cold War interventions, the international community has
involved itself on the understanding that its liability is strictly limited. It is
true that, by the summer of 2000, there was no sign that the UN
administrations in either Bosnia or Kosovo, or their NATO shields, could
be withdrawn without provoking a fresh crisis, but while these amounted
to trusteeships in all but name, it was no accident that no one was
prepared to admit publicly that the possibility of international disengage-
ment in the foreseeable future is remote.

In a world without empire, limited liability is probably unavoidable, but
in the context of postwar reconstruction, it has obvious disadvantages.
The overseas empires of the European powers were hardly established to
protect the human rights of colonial subjects; but they did inadvertently
create professional administrations, staffed by men and women who
spoke the languages and understood the culture of the societies they
ruled. When the UN is brought in to deal with a humanitarian crisis, it has
necessarily to employ people on short-term contracts, few of whom will
have equivalent expertise. In both Cambodia and Somalia, a lack of local
knowledge allowed ambitious leaders to exploit the UN for their own
purposes. It is not immediately obvious that the UN will be able to avoid
this problem in Kosovo, where an international civil administration has
been set up, backed by the NATO-led force of over 50,000.[17]

Two separate problems arise from attempts to establish disinterested
administration in countries that have been traumatized by civil conflict.
The first concerns the appropriate agency; the second the nature of its
mission. The rate at which humanitarian crises followed one another after
the Cold War, meant that the UN was unable to mobilize the necessary
resources, acting on its own. The concept of a 'coalition of the willing'
authorized by the UN, was fashioned at the time of the Gulf War and
quickly established itself as a standard response to humanitarian crises.
After the reverses in Somalia and Rwanda, however, the Western powers
were reluctant to involve themselves deeply in conflicts, far removed
from their own vital interests.

The practical problem was how to avoid being drawn into such
conflict, whenever they captured the world's headlines, and, however

briefly, succeeded in mobilizing public opinion. The action of the Economic Community of West African States (ECOWAS), in mounting a peacekeeping operation in Liberia, initially without the authorization of the Security Council, was seized on as a model for the future. Local powers, supported if necessary with training and technical assistance from the West, should assume primary responsibility for maintaining order and justice within their own region. It could be plausibly argued that if one of the major obstacles to have effective intervention, is the absence of knowledge about local conditions, this is more likely to be overcome on a regional level, where normal business and diplomacy create networks across international borders, than universally. Chapter VIII of the Charter had envisaged regional organizations acting in support of the world body. At the end of the century, it seems more likely that, in future, the order will be reversed.

An analysis of this kind can be invoked to justify NATO's selectivity in concentrating on Kosovo, and ignoring many other crises, where the criminal activities of the authorities and their oppression of the population is comparable. On this view, Serbian policies in Kosovo, as earlier in Bosnia, threaten the stability, welfare and values of European states, in a way that is not true of East Timor or Sierra Leone. It is true that the wrongs to be righted are universal, but only those in the immediate neighbourhood have both the interest and ability to right them.

There is some force in this argument. It is, after all, the immediate region that feels the first shock of a humanitarian disaster, in the form of refugee flows and the social and economic problems that they generate. The asylum system was not designed for the mass migrations that result from ethnic cleansing and inter-communal violence. It is reasonable, therefore, for the countries most immediately affected by a crisis to accept primary responsibility for orchestrating the international response to it.

Unfortunately, it is also the governments most willing to act that are most likely to have their own political agendas (and clients) in the target state. In the case of East Timor, where the UN ultimately mounted a reasonably effective peacekeeping operation, after initially and disaster-ously allowing the Indonesian military to retain control of security in the run-up to the UN administered referendum on independence, it was the Australians who took the lead. There was a certain ironic justice in their doing so. Australia was the only country to have recognized Indonesia's annexation of East Timor in 1974. At that time – in the context of the fall of Vietnam to the communists – they were primarily motivated by a desire to protect their economic interests in Indonesia and more generally with the stability of the region. This was again their primary motivation in 1999, although the circumstances were very different.

In this case a regional power's pursuit of its own interests may be judged to have been relatively benign, even though the UN initially faced difficulties because the Indonesian military, in particular, felt betrayed by their erstwhile allies. The situation in Liberia and Sierra Leone, however, was more ambiguous. For much of the time that ECOWAS was involved in Liberia, the ECOWAS Military Observer Group's (ECOMOG's) work was undermined by the fact that several of its member states were backing rival factions in the conflict. And when a peace deal was finally negotiated, it was on the basis of a power-sharing agreement between the major warlords, who had previously been accused of devastating the country. Local knowledge, on which ECOMOG could draw, was certainly a crucial element in the process that transformed Charles Taylor from a hunted warlord to an elected president.[18] By the same token, it clearly required a subordination of humanitarian to political and strategic considerations.

Similarly, in Sierra Leone, the UN demurred, but nonetheless acquiesced in the inclusion of a blanket amnesty in the 1998 Lomé Peace Agreement, and for the incorporation of the rebel leader in the government. The tactic failed and ferocious fighting broke out again in the early summer of 2000. Whether it had any chance of success is debatable, but for the agreement to have had a chance the international community would have had to commit sufficient resources to give the rebels an incentive to co-operate. In the end the British intervened in support of the UN, making it clear both that their intervention was temporary and that it was in support of the elected government. Whether this action can stabilize the country over the long run remains to be seen. But since the government enjoys little support beyond the confines of the capital city, Freetown, it is difficult to be much more optimistic about a government victory, in the name of democratization, than on one based on power-sharing with the Revolutionary United Front (RUF), a more than usually murderous movement of bandits. By opting for a UN-sponsored administration in Kosovo, the intention is presumably to avoid a similarly unattractive trade off. Whether this is feasible remains to be seen, but the omens are not favourable.

The reason is partly a consequence of the local culture, but more fundamentally of an unresolved conceptual problem to which region-alisation provides no answer. As William Hagen has argued, the analogy between Serbian ethnic cleansing and Nazi genocide against the Jews, is misleading: 'Balkan ethnic cleansing does not require mass extermination but rather mass removal, which can be hastened along by displays of murderous violence drawn from the repertory of revenge killings and blood feuds.'[19] This is not to explain the violent politics of former Yugoslavia in terms of ancient hatreds – it is merely to suggest that the task of any new administration will be greatly complicated by having to operate in an environment where 'the ethic of blood revenge, binding individual members of extended families', has been 'grafted onto ethnic nationalism'.[20]

Just how complicated the task will be, was evident from the tension that erupted in August 1999 between NATO and the United Nations High Commissioner for Refugees (UNHCR). The war had been waged by NATO to prevent the ethnic cleansing of Kosova Albanians, not to facilitate Albanian cleansing of the Serbian minority – hence the importance NATO commanders quite rightly attached to its forces being seen to be impartial. Nonetheless, they were powerless to prevent a spate of revenge killings, which predictably led to a rapid outward migration of the Serb minority. This was aided on the ground by UNHCR, which, in the face of individual atrocities, understandably felt that its humanitarian mission would allow it to do no less. It is difficult to see how in this case two rights could fail to add up to a wrong. From the perspective of humanitarian intervention, the danger is that NATO will heave created a land, for the KLA – a movement that is a mirror-image of its Serbian enemy – to inherit. The UN administration is making heroic efforts to resist this outcome, but in a land where there is no serious evidence of inter-community reconciliation, the odds remain heavily stacked against success.

Notes

1. See James Mayall, 'Non-Intervention, Self-Determination and the "New World Order"', *International Affairs*, vol. 67, no. 3 (July 1991), pp. 421–9.
2. Quoted in Paul Rogers, 'Lessons to Learn', *The World Today*, vol. 55, no. 8/9 (August/September 1999), pp. 4–6.
3. For the full list see Marack Goulding, 'The United Nations and Conflict in Africa since the Cold War', *African Affairs*, vol. 98. no. 391 (April 1999), Table 1, p. 158.
4. For a range of assessments see Mats Berdal, *Whither UN Peacekeeping*, Adelphi Paper 281 (London, Brasseys for IISS, 1993); Adam Roberts, *Humanitarian Action in War*, Adelphi Paper 305 (London, Brasseys for IISS, 1996); James Mayall (ed.) *The New Interventionism: UN experience in Cambodia, former Yugoslavia and Somalia*, (Cambridge: Cambridge University Press, 1996).
5. For a sober, but powerful, statement of the anti-triumphalist position see Mark Danner, 'Kosovo: The Meaning of Victory', *New York Review of Books*, 15 July 1999, pp. 53–4.
6. John Stuart Mill, 'A few words on non-intervention', *Dissertations and Discussions*, (London: 1987), pp. 153–78.
7. See, for example, Edward Luttwak, 'Give War a Chance', *Foreign Affairs*, vol. 78, no. 4 (July/August 1999), pp. 36–44.
8. Territory is vital to nomadic peoples but not in the sense of being ring-fenced as under the conventional interpretation of sovereignty. As a local saying has it, 'wherever the camel roams, that is Somalia.'
9. James Mayall (ed.) *The new Interventionism, op. cit.*, p. 118, footnote 34.
10. See, Mark Goulding, 'The United Nations and Conflict in Africa since the Cold War', *op. cit.* p. 163.

11. Security Council Resolution 940, 31 July 1994.
12. See, David Malone, *Decision Making in the United Nations Security Council: The Case of Haiti*, (Oxford: Clarendon Press, 1998).
13. Catherine Guicherd, 'International Law and the War in Kosovo', *Survival,* vol. 41, no. 2 (Summer 1999), pp. 19-34.
14. Michael Byers, 'Kosovo: An illegal Operation', *Counsel*, (August 1999), pp. 16-18.
15. Catherine Guicherd, 'International Law and the war in Kosovo', *op. cit.,* p. 25.
16. Marc Weller, 'Armed Samaritans', *Counsel,* August 1999, pp. 20-2.
17. Security Council Resolution 1244.
18. For two assessments of this process from different perspectives, see, Adekeye Adebajo, *Pax Nigeriana? ECOMOG in Liberia*, Unpublished DPhil thesis, University of Oxford, 1999, and Emannuel Kwesi Aning, *Security in the West African Sub-region: An Analysis of ECOWAS's policies in Liberia,* PhD, University of Copenhagen, 1999.
19. William Hagen, 'The Balkans' Lethal Nationalisms', *Foreign Affairs,* vol. 78, no. 4 (July/August 1999), pp. 52-64.
20. *ibid.*

Index

282

INDEX